Dialectic and Difference

Dialectic and Difference is the first systematic exploration of Roy Bhaskar's dialectical philosophy and its implications for ethics and justice.

That philosophy has three aims: a dialecticisation of original critical realism, a critical realist reworking of dialectic, and a metacritique of western philosophy. In the first, real absence or negativity links structured being to dialectical becoming in a dynamic world. The second draws on Marx to locate the critical impulse in Hegel's dialectic in a material, open and changing totality. The third, metacritique, identifies a central problem in western philosophy from the Greeks on, the failure to think real negativity as the essence of change ('ontological monovalence').

Bhaskar's ethics connect basic human ontology with universal principles of freedom and solidarity. He marries ('constellates') these with a grasp of how ethical principles are historically shaped. His account of freedom moves from the infant's 'primal scream' to the eudaimonic society, but thinks the limits to freedom under modern social conditions.

Western philosophy systematically denies the real negativity that drives Bhaskar's dialectic. Metacritique traces this to Parmenides, and Plato's account of non-being as difference. It enables a critique of the tradition as a whole and specifically of the poststructural radicalisation of difference, understood as an anti-Platonic move on Platonic terrain.

This text is essential reading for all serious students of social theory, philosophy and legal theory.

Alan Norrie has recently taken up a Chair in Law at the University of Warwick. He was previously Drapers' Professor of Law at Queen Mary and Westfield College and Edmund-Davies Professor of Criminal Law and Criminal Justice at King's College London. He has a longstanding interest in critical realist philosophy and is President of the International Association for Critical Realism. His last book, *Law and the Beautiful Soul*, won the SLSA Hart Book Prize for 2006.

Ontological Explorations

Dialectic and Difference

Dialectical critical realism and
the grounds of justice

Alan Norrie

LONDON AND NEW YORK

First published 2010
by Routledge
2 Park Square, Milton Park, Abingdon, Oxon OX14 4RN

Simultaneously published in the USA and Canada
by Routledge
270 Madison Ave, New York, NY 10016

Routledge is an imprint of the Taylor & Francis Group, an informa business

© 2010 Alan Norrie

Typeset in Times New Roman PS
by Keystroke, Tettenhall, Wolverhampton
Printed and bound in Great Britain
by CPI Anthony Rowe, Chippenham, Wiltshire

British Library Cataloguing in Publication Data
A catalogue record for this book is available from the British Library

Library of Congress Cataloging in Publication Data
Norrie, Alan W. (Alan William), 1953–
Dialectic and difference : dialectical critical realism and the grounds of
    justice / Alan Norrie.
p. cm.
Includes bibliographical references and index.
1. Dialectic.   2. Bhaskar, Roy, 1944–   3. Realism. I.   Title.
   B809.7.N68 2010
   149′.2—dc22   2009019671

ISBN10: 0–415–56035–7 (hbk)
ISBN10: 0–415–56036–5 (pbk)
ISBN10: 0–203–86593–6 (ebk)

ISBN13: 978–0–415–56035–1 (hbk)
ISBN13: 978–0–415–56036–8 (pbk)
ISBN13: 978–0–203–86593–4 (ebk)

To my father, Tom, with love and gratitude

Contents

In the same rivers ever different waters flow . . .
We step and do not step into the same rivers . . .

Heraclitus

All process involves a distinction between the potential and the actual, and the potential is the seat of the nisus in virtue of which it is forcing its way towards actuality. . . . It is widely recognised that a process of becoming is conceivable only if that which is yet unrealised is affecting the process as a goal towards which it is directed.

Collingwood

Wholes . . . have been made the objects of scientific study . . . and there is indeed no reason why we should not study such aspects as the regularities of structure . . . which can be found in certain things such as organisms, or electrical fields, or machines. Of things that possess such structures it may be said . . . that they are . . . 'more than the sum of their parts'.

Popper

. . . consistent naturalism or humanism is distinct from both idealism and materialism, and constitutes at the same time the unifying truth of both. . . .

Marx

My project is normative.

Bhaskar

Preface

I first encountered Roy Bhaskar's dialectical philosophy in early 1994. I was already familiar with his earlier work on 'original' critical realism, and had used it to ground a critical understanding of law and justice. His work on dialectics came at the right time, since I was then thinking through the consequences of seeing law as a contradictory and antinomial phenomenon, and I needed a deeper analysis of what this meant. At that time, critical thinking about law was poised between Marxism and poststructural philosophy, and, while I found attractive themes in the latter, I remained unconvinced by its lack of emphasis on the social and historical dimensions of law. Dialectical critical realism seemed to offer the possibility of theorising what Derrida, for example, saw as the aporetic quality of legal analysis, while offering a deeper and more satisfying analysis of the grounds of aporiai than poststructuralism provided. In this regard, Bhaskar's emphasis on the Hegel–Marx relationship, which poststructuralism sought to bypass, still seemed the more fruitful approach. The fruits of this early interest in, and engagement between, critical realism, Hegel, Marx and poststructuralism are seen in the structure of the present work.

A first reading of *Dialectic: the Pulse of Freedom* is not easy. I found the idea of the 'socio-historical thrownness' and contradictoriness of being helpful in coming to terms with my understanding of law and justice. I tended to cherry pick ideas that were helpful, and not worry too much that I did not grasp the whole. For anyone starting *Dialectic* today, and reading this book is not a substitute for so doing, I would recommend that they too simply jump in and see what they get from it. Nonetheless, I became frustrated by my inability to understand the book as a whole, and I felt mystified by certain aspects. In particular, I could not grasp how Bhaskar's ethics fitted together with the socio-historical grounding of dialectic. Nor did I fully appreciate the significance of the 'metacritique' of western philosophy, developed in its final chapter. I determined therefore to enter into a more systematic study, and this book is the outcome. Perhaps unsurprisingly, it is in those areas where I had the most difficulty that I found the greatest interest, and also where I feel I have been able to contribute most to developing Bhaskar's original ideas.

Dialectic (and its companion *Plato Etc.*) involves ideas whose time has come but slowly. It has attracted, indeed, a certain amount of hostility, often focused on matters of style, but which has deeper reasons. As I say in the first chapter, neither original critical realists, nor Kantians, Hegelians or Marxists, nor poststructuralists have, for different reasons, found it easy to appreciate *Dialectic*. This is in part because it *is* difficult, a 'process-in-product' I suggest in the first chapter, but also because of its substantive argument. My aim is to get around problems of presentation in order to show the power and coherence of the argument, to consider criticism of it, and to develop it in the areas of ethics, justice and metacritique.

With regard to ethics and justice, the book seeks to develop dialectical critical realism in two ways. First, as regards the issue of judgement, it seeks to bring out the 'constellational' relationship between the socially structured, historically emergent, nature of ethics and the real, universalising impulse that lies within them. In consequence, dialectical critical realism asserts the morally real ('alethic') nature of ethical life, but points to the limited quality of ethical experience under modern historical conditions. It sets up a complex relationship between the morally real, the morally ideal and the morally actual, where the ideal and the actual are limited extrusions of the real under modern conditions. In a realist sense, there is a fuller, 'eudaimonic', form of justice that is still 'to come'. At the same time, in considering existing critical ethical approaches, it insists that universalising or particularising strategies are incomplete without a *philosophical* grasp of ethics' intrinsic socio-historical dimension.

Also associated with ethics and justice, but having a broader significance, is the engagement with poststructuralist philosophy, stemming from Bhaskar's meta-critique of western philosophy. The argument develops Bhaskar's understanding of the 'two great problems' of Greek philosophy, the 'one and the other' in pre-Socratic thought and the 'one and the many' in Plato and Aristotle. Put simply, the earlier problematic is concerned with the nature of being and becoming and how things change, while the latter is concerned with the relationship between universals and particulars. From the time of Plato, the latter problematic dominates and is decisive for both the Greeks and western philosophy as a whole. This leads to a failure to think about questions of change with an appropriate emphasis on the 'natural necessity' (the structured depth, the real negativity, the propensity for change) in things. Drawing on post-Nietzschean ontology, poststructuralism participates in this failure, for, in affirming radical difference against the universal, it operates as an anti-Platonism on Platonic terrain, that of the 'one and the many'. It is yet another of those 'footnotes to Plato' in western philosophy, to use Whitehead's phrase – which Bhaskar himself adopts in the title of *Plato Etc.*

I would like to make two small additional points. Roy Bhaskar's work can be divided into three periods: works of 'original' critical realism, the dialectical works, and those associated with his later 'spiritual turn'. This raises difficult and important issues of interpretation. Should one read his work as a whole, or should one emphasise and analyse particular elements? I personally endorse the ideas of original critical realism in the developed and radicalised form given to them by dialectical critical realism, and I believe there to be good arguments for extending the philosophy from the dialectical to the spiritual turn. However, I have delib-erately held off considering the relationship between the last two here. I believe that a full and fair appraisal of dialectical critical realism should be based on reading the dialectical works in their own right and not in the light of subsequent developments. Accordingly, I treat Bhaskar's dialectics in terms of their relation to original critical realism, which they explicitly build on, but not in terms of the spiritual turn. It is true that Bhaskar himself develops theorems of the presence of the past in the present and the future (see below, Chapter 2), so it would be valid to consider the work of the three phases together, but only once the works of the individual periods have been properly understood in their own terms.

Finally, a technical point: in quoting from Bhaskar's works, I have changed those words that end in '-ize' to the alternative '-ise'. I have never been able to reconcile myself in my own writing to the North American and Oxford style, and rather than have the two styles compete with each other in the text, I have taken this liberty in quoting from Bhaskar's works.

The writing of this book was aided by a period of sabbatical leave in part made possible by an Arts and Humanities Research Council (UK) award (AH/D 5000362/1), which I am happy to acknowledge. In writing it, I have benefited from discussions with many colleagues and friends over a long period of time. Amongst these, I would like to mention first and foremost Roy Bhaskar, who has been a tower of intellectual strength, and has encouraged me to complete the work at times when I thought it might defeat me. I would also like to mention my colleagues in the Centre for Critical Realism, Margaret Archer, Bob Carter, Andrew Collier, Kathryn Dean, Nick Hostettler, Jonathan Joseph, Tony Lawson and Sean Vertigan, who provide a supportive context in which to knock about, but rarely to agree upon, critical realist ideas. I would more broadly like to thank colleagues and friends in and beyond the areas of law and social theory whose views I have benefited from, or whose ears I have bent, over the last few years: Brenna Bhandar, Bill Bowring, Davina Cooper, Kitty Cooper, Roger Cotterrell, Hans Despain, Robert Fine, Peter Fitzpatrick, Mervyn Hartwig, Christoph Kletzer, Nicola Lacey, Susan Marks, Stephen Norrie, Craig Reeves, Ron Tuck, Mary Vogel. I would also like to acknowledge the kindly and supportive approach taken by Alan Jarvis at Taylor and Francis to this and other critical realist projects over the last ten years. I thank Richard, Stephen and Sach, Jennifer and Olive, and, above all, Gwen, who has been unfailingly supportive over an extended period of writing, with the stresses it produced.

I dedicate this book to my father Tom: life is a long song.

1 Introduction

Natural necessity, being and becoming

The recent republication of Roy Bhaskar's works of the early 1990s, *Dialectic: The Pulse of Freedom* (1993, 2008b)[1] and *Plato Etc.* (1994, 2009), provides an appropriate occasion for reflection on what has become known as the dialectical turn in his thought, the philosophical system that he called dialectical critical realism. When these books were published, they seemed destined to have a major impact on critical philosophy, social theory and in the social sciences generally, but this has not happened. Overall, they have tended to be marginalised, and even in critical realist circles it is only a mild overstatement to describe dialectical critical realism as the 'forgotten turn' in Bhaskar's work. Bhaskar himself moved in works published in the late 1990s[2] to spiritual concerns, and the effect of this later turn, whether the reaction to it was positive or negative, was to overshadow the dialectical works. To use a Bhaskarian metaphor, these works were subject to a 'squeeze' between two standpoints, that of original critical realism, by which I mean the philosophy advanced by Bhaskar up to the period of his dialectical work, and the post-dialectical works informed by spiritual themes. Now, with a measure of distance between these three periods of intellectual output, it is time for a reappraisal of Bhaskar's dialectic.

The aim of this book is to consider the nature and assert the significance of the arguments at the heart of dialectical critical realism, for it seems to me that it represents a novel, radical, coherent and deep philosophical system of potentially far-reaching significance which should be better understood. One major advance in that regard has been made recently with the publication of Mervyn Hartwig's *Dictionary of Critical Realism* (Hartwig 2007), which outlines in detail the concepts in Bhaskar's dialectical system. What it does not do is attempt an accessible monographic encapsulation, exploration or development of *Dialectic*'s main themes. That is the purpose of the present work.

Three aims and four elements

In this introductory chapter, I begin by reflecting on the reception and perception of *Dialectic* since its publication. I then introduce its three aims, and sketch how it seeks to achieve them in a dialectical philosophy involving four main elements. This involves reflecting on Bhaskar's pre-dialectical philosophy of critical realism, for dialectical critical realism represents, as its first aim, a qualitative development of this initial work as well as, its second aim, a renovation of dialectical thinking on critical realist ground. I focus on original critical realism's development of an ontological sense of natural necessity in both the natural and the social worlds, to which dialecticisation adds an understanding of how negativity lies at necessity's core. I explain this in the two main sections of this chapter as the move from an account of natural necessity as *being* to an argument for the intrinsic relationship between *being* and *becoming* in dialectical critical realism. Becoming involves, as we shall see, a sense of negation. The third aim, the development of a 'metacritique' of the general trajectory of western philosophy, is then briefly sketched in the final section after the four main elements in Bhaskar's dialectic – non-identity, negativity, totality and ethical agency or practice – have been established.[3] My goal in this chapter, then, is to introduce the reader to the three overall aims and the four main elements of *Dialectic*. In doing so, I focus on the primary move in the dialecticisation of critical realism, from a theory of being to a theory of being in relation to becoming. Before getting to these matters, however, I want to say something about reading Bhaskar's dialectical work and the reception it has received.

Philosophical difficulty

In considering the reception of Bhaskar's dialectical work, I will contrast views expressed in the pre- and post-publication periods. The question of philosophical difficulty has to be faced with regard to this work, and I will suggest that, while *Dialectic* is not easy, this is in large part because Bhaskar's dialectic cuts across the grain of many philosophical assumptions. When Bhaskar published *Dialectic*, and its companion *Plato Etc.* one year later, it was to a fanfare of praise. Pre-publication reviews recognised the significance of the argument, and grasped its essence. Peter Manicas wrote that Bhaskar 'goes back to the beginning of the western philosophical quest and offers a brilliant refashioning of the dialectic'.[4] He described dialectical critical realism as 'systematic, ontologically sustained and self-consciously ethical and political', and 'able to give stunning readings of key chapters in the history of philosophy'. It was 'a unique book full of gems'. William Outhwaite also described the book as 'stunning', and offered a similar verdict. Bhaskar 'develops his own programme of critical realism into a radically new and original theory of dialectics and a critique of previous theories from the ancient Greeks to twentieth century neo-marxism'. Comparing *Dialectic* with Sartre's *Critique of Dialectical Reason* for its scope and ambition, Outhwaite went on to say that it is 'hard to think of any other contemporary philosopher with the powers to bring this off' and that *Dialectic* 'will be one of the major reference points of philosophical and social thinking in the nineties and beyond'.

To declare my own position, I share this assessment of Bhaskar's dialectical work. Summarising its import, *Dialectic* takes Bhaskar's original philosophy of critical realism and radically reworks it through a deep engagement with the dialectical tradition. In the process, he renews dialectical philosophy itself.

Dialectical critical realism is developed through a wide range of reference in western philosophy, tracing modern problems in philosophy and social theory to their roots in Greek philosophy (hence the title of *Plato Etc.*). It advances a novel critique of Hegel's dialectic on the basis of critical realist protocols and what Marx might have written on dialectic had he found the time. On this basis, it produces a philosophy that both can underlabour for social theory and social science and also, less noticed but a specific focus of this work, develops an understanding of difference, change and relationality, together with the power and the limits of aporetic ethics. These, I will argue, can take dialectical critical realism to a position where it can challenge poststructural philosophy and, through its metacritique of philosophy, trump it. *Dialectic* is a work with an enormous range of social theoretical relevance, tying problems of agency, structure and causation to the nature of change in a dynamic world, and to the relationship between human being and nature on the one hand and human being and history on the other. In the process, it thinks through the relationship between historical emergence, the nature of human being, and its emancipation. At its philosophical core lies a theory of absence, which Bhaskar combines with his pre-existing arguments from critical realism for the significance of ontology. This is the basis for a realist understanding of human *being* in society and in nature which, through the account of absence, is aligned to a theory of *becoming* and change in a spatio-temporal world. The alignment of being and becoming is achieved in a manner that displays both a uniqueness of individual philosophical voice and a boldness of intellectual vision, and these give Bhaskar a fair claim to stand, as Outhwaite suggests, in the first rank of western philosophers today.

Against the 'Niagara of neologisms'

This is, as it were, the good news. In the light of the pre-publication comments and my own view of the achievements of Bhaskar's dialectical turn, it is sobering to reflect on the reception these works have since had. Consider the comments of two theorists who endorse what I have called original critical realism on their engagement with its dialectical form. Andrew Sayer describes how 'like many other readers, including enthusiasts for critical realism, I was largely defeated by [dialectical critical realism's] Niagara of neologisms, most of them inadequately explained, even in the glossary' (2000: 170). Of the ethical dimension of dialectical critical realism, Sayer was left with the impression 'of pulling global salvation out of the critical realist hat' (ibid.). Similarly, Alex Callinicos, in a book that otherwise acknowledges his debt to Bhaskar, writes that he remains 'wholly unconvinced by Bhaskar's claim to have established the truth of many of his metaphysical doctrines', and that a book 'as suggestive and full of brilliant flashes of insight as *Dialectic*' nonetheless shows signs of Bhaskar's 'intellectual decline', which, linking *Dialectic* to Bhaskar's spiritual turn, 'has, alas, been fully realised with [his] espousal of New Age spiritualism' (Callinicos 2006: 158). No doubt there is merit in saying what one thinks, even to the point of bluntness, but in an academic work these are unusually harsh words. And words matter. Sayer is a critical realist of long standing, while Callinicos more recently recognises his debt. They are both eminent figures in the field from whom others will take their cue. Outhwaite and Manicas both wrote of the 'stunning' quality of Bhaskar's argument. Sayer and Callinicos appear only to have been stunned by it.

Dialectic is a difficult, sometimes a frustrating, book. While careful reading reveals how what initially seem impenetrable and disconnected passages are in fact coherently linked, it can be hard work. It develops its own concepts, Sayer's 'neologisms', though Bhaskar is hardly the first philosopher to do that. Readers also come to it from their own backgrounds and with their own interests, and *Dialectic* tends to swirl between topics, showing their interconnection, but not in a way that is easy for readers with different, often non-philosophical, backgrounds to follow. For example, *Dialectic* has much to say about social theory and social science, but much of what it says on topics in that domain is linked with issues of a more fundamentally philosophical kind. Any social scientist who looks to *Dialectic*, for example, to illuminate the relationship between structure and agency will end up moving from discussion of 'four-planar being', which makes relatively easy sense as an extension of the original terms, to the 'concrete universal', which requires some background in Hegelian philosophy. Any theorist interested in the idea of change may fairly readily see the relationship it has with absence, for every 'becoming' is also a 'begoing' – that is, a negation or a passing away – but how is that linked to Bhaskar's critique of the general denial of absence and what he calls, somewhat forbiddingly, 'ontological monovalence'[5] as the 'primordial failing of western philosophy' (DPF: 406)? The point is that they are closely linked, but, in a book that seeks to work at many different levels, it may be hard for readers from different backgrounds to see what the links are. *Dialectic* is a big book with a big argument at its core, and it is a book in which the argument is plotted and worked out as the book proceeds. It is, as Bhaskar might himself say, a 'product in process'. That makes it a hard book, in which it is possible to get the wrong end of the stick, or not to see how the arguments ultimately fit together, in the short term at least.

An illustrative problem

In that regard, my own experience may help.[6] I approached *Dialectic* from the point of view of understanding the relationship between ethics and history: what was the relationship between the ethical impulse to judge matters normatively, and the observation that all our judgements are historically conditioned? Does the latter undermine the former? One of my initial concerns about *Dialectic* was how it was possible for Bhaskar to argue for ethical propositions as real, primary, autonomous, normative elements in human life when such life was constituted, as he also argues, in a world which was socially structured and historically evolved, and into which human beings were 'thrown'. How could Bhaskar write of the autonomy of ethical propositions in such a conditioned context? My initial reaction to *Dialectic*'s ethics was not unlike Sayer's. There seemed a sense in which Bhaskar's ethics were 'with one bound' set free from history. Bhaskar's arguments for the dialectical universalisability of an ethics of freedom, trust and solidarity, leading to what he calls the eudaimonic society, seemed at odds with what he had said about the historicity of human being.

With Nick Hostettler (Hostettler and Norrie 2003), I wrote what I thought a well-argued and persuasive case for the broken-backed and contradictory nature of Bhaskar's dialectic as between its ethical and historical commitments. Now, however, I think our argument was wrong because it fails to grasp the relationship between Bhaskar's ethics and his account of totality, and his theorisation of totalising concepts such as the constellation, co-relationality, and the idea of the separation and connectedness of levels in a totality. I did not, in short, grasp the relationship between totality and ethical praxis in *Dialectic* (though in my defence, I do not think it very well developed there, and I shall seek to bring it out in Chapter 5). A brief reference to the overall structure of *Dialectic* may help explain my problem. It consists of four long chapters in which the first and second build a critique of Hegelian dialectic on the basis of Bhaskar's theory of absence and his alignment of dialectic with realist ontological commitments. The third chapter concerns ethics and the fourth sketches a metacritique of the western philosophical tradition on the basis of a challenge to ontological monovalence (the denial of absence) in the name of real, determinate non-being (negativity). In my first reading of the book, I thought the first two chapters were right, the third misconceived, and I was unsure of the nature or implications of the argument of the fourth.

Now my view is that the book presents a coherent argument as a whole, and that one key to grasping its coherence concerns the role Bhaskar's account of totality (the third term in his dialectic) plays in siting both his ethics and the fourth chapter's critique of ontological monovalence in the western philosophical tradition. Missing the overall coherence of the argument by not seeing the significance of totality for the ethics and metacritique had misled me. It was in part the experience of getting Bhaskar wrong that convinced me that an attempt to write about *Dialectic* in a more compact and structured way, exploring some of its implications, could make it available to the wider audience it deserves. In this book, I will ultimately seek to demonstrate this coherence by showing how the arguments concerning natural necessity, materialist diffraction and totality developed in the first four chapters link together with the constellated ethics of Chapter 5 and the ethical conclusions of the metacritique of Chapters 6 and 7 to produce an overall focus on what I call the 'grounds of justice' in Chapter 8.

Against the grain

Dialectic is, then, a hard book, and that is no doubt one reason why it has not had the reception it deserves. This is, however, only one reason. A second concerns how dialectical critical realism cuts across the grain of most critical social theory and philosophy. If *Dialectic* is hard – and Bhaskar has developed something of a reputation as a difficult writer – what is it that turns a hard book into one that is dismissed as downright impossible, or a difficult writer into a Difficult Writer? At one level, it may be the text, as I have acknowledged, but at another it is the commitment of the reader and whether he senses that there is something in the text worth pursuing. If that sense is triggered, then the hardness of the book or the difficulty of the writer become lesser problems, even reasons for admiration. The writer is saying something so deep that it can only be said in a way that is dense and hard to comprehend. She is difficult only because the things she is engaging with are themselves difficult; her difficulty is her achievement. On the other hand, where a reader does not have the patience for an argument, sees it as going nowhere, there comes a point where he is inclined to give up and reject the book as plain impossible. Of course, it may be that *Dialectic* is impossible, its 'Niagara of neologisms' impenetrable – and I am not making an argument for difficulty as a virtue in itself. It may also be the case that *Dialectic* reveals the beginnings of a 'sad decline', as Callinicos avers. But if so, how to account for the praise heaped on it by Manicas and Outhwaite? How to account, politely, for those like myself who agree with them?

There is in truth an underlying problem about 'hardness' and 'difficulty' that has nothing to do with Bhaskar. His only sin has really been to write some long sentences and invent some new concepts in the pursuit of his philosophical instinct, ambition and conviction. The underlying problem is that *Dialectic* opposes the assumptions that many potential readers bring to it. Dialectical critical realism merges critical realist ontology with the idea of dialectical negation. It introduces the novel concept of real determinate absence to ontology via a critique of Hegel that is leveraged on Marx. This is a demanding and unusual marriage of traditions. As a result, *Dialectic* questions the assumptions of different theoretical approaches that might otherwise be engaged by it. First, it challenges original critical realism on the nature of ontology, which had always seemed so solid a foundation but now has to be understood in terms of absence. It requires critical realists, should they wish to follow Bhaskar's thought, to take Hegel and the dialectical tradition seriously. Many would not have anticipated this when they read his earlier works. Second, it questions the assumptions of Kantians, neo-Kantians and Hegelians, who all, one way or another, endorse Kantian transcendental idealism (even if, in the Hegelian dialectical move, to 'sublate' it), and therefore do not see beyond the 'pre-critical' word 'realism' to the transcendental operation Bhaskar had himself performed in original critical realism. Bhaskar's ontology is a product of his transcendental realist critique of Kant, leading to the charge of 'ontological actualism' he levels at both Kant and Hegel. Third, dialectical critical realism also questions the taken-for-granted understanding of poststructuralists, postmodernists and social constructionists, for whom realism of any kind is akin to a category error, and for some of whom the very use of the word 'ontology' is a concession to identity and power.[7] Even, fourth, Marxists, with whom Bhaskar has substantial historical and intellectual affinity, have found *Dialectic* an unfriendly work in the light of its author's aspiration to write philosophy at a deeper level than Marx himself, and his criticisms (which are not always well made, in my view) of substantive theoretical positions adopted by Marx (see Creaven 2002; Joseph 2006).[8]

In short, for all its heralding in advance, and the small but growing number of its admirers, *Dialectic* was destined to be a book whose time would come but slowly. All the more reason, then, to seek to explain as clearly as possible what this distinctive, original, challenging, annoying book is about, and to seek to explain its relevance for thinking today. With these initial comments, let us turn to dialectical critical realism's first and second overall aims, starting with the first, the reworking of critical realism in the light of dialectical themes. This involves beginning with pre-dialectical critical realism to see the material on which Bhaskar would work to develop his dialectic.

Original critical realism: the necessity of being

In *Dialectic*, Bhaskar identifies, as I have mentioned, three main objectives. The first is dialectically enriching and deepening critical realism, the second developing a general theory of dialectic, and the third outlining a totalising critique (a 'metacritique') of western philosophy (DPF: 2). These three aims are linked. Critical realism should be dialecticised (first aim), and dialectics should be transformed through its engagement with critical realism (second aim). The result would be the possibility of a dialectical critique of the nature and limits of western philosophy (third aim). There was thus in the first two aims a double operation to create a philosophical system that would push both critical realism and dialectics to a third, qualitatively new position from which to view the tradition as a whole. In the following two sections, I pursue these aims, beginning with the original critical realist position that Bhaskar's dialectic works on and from.

The first aim of *Dialectic* is 'the dialectical enrichment and deepening of critical realism', with critical realism 'understood as consisting of transcendental realism as a general theory of science and critical naturalism as a special theory of social science' (DPF: 2).[9] The objective was to take the existing forms of critical realism, its 'transcendental realism' as a general theory of science, and its 'critical naturalism' as a special theory of social science, and submit them to a further development. At its core, this involved thinking, we shall see, about how negativity or non-being, in the form of 'determinate absence', should be worked into an understanding of being. Put simply, however, original critical realism is a philosophy of and for the natural and social sciences which stresses the crucial role that being (ontology) plays in our understanding of how knowledge (epistemology) is possible. Against much modern philosophy, which, after successive 'linguistic', 'constructivist' and 'discursive' turns, is centred on questions of epistemology, critical realism insists on the importance of ontology. It maintains the centrality of an understanding of being in the natural and social worlds that grounds, but does not guarantee, our efforts to understand the way things are.

In *Dialectic*, Bhaskar sometimes puts this most simply in terms of what he calls, borrowing from Freud, 'the reality principle', meaning that there is a natural necessity in things that grounds our knowledge of them. The Freudian choice of term is purposeful, for Bhaskar argues that any attempt to renounce ontology will return to haunt philosophy. I will focus for now, however, on the idea of natural necessity. Emphasising ontology, Bhaskar's critical realism develops an account of being in which reality is stratified, and knowledge involves processes of accounting for the events we observe in terms of the underlying structures and other mechanisms which generate them. It is that process of structured, causal generation, operative differentially in the natural and social worlds, that Bhaskar calls natural necessity.

Transcendental realism and natural necessity

To pursue the idea of natural necessity, original critical realism, accentuating the role of ontology in philosophy, argues for a depth realism, in which knowledge formation is located, on the one hand, in the social processes whereby it is produced, and on the other, in the engagement between knowing subjects and the world they address (Bhaskar 1975, 2008a). Depth realism stresses that knowledge may be 'not only of what appears, but of underlying structures which endure longer than . . . appearances, and generate them or make them possible' (Collier 1994: 6). Such knowledge may not just go beyond and explain, but also provide accounts that contradict what appearances seem to tell us of phenomena.[10] Knowledge combines, on its subjective side, what is experienced of the world with the theories people develop to explain their experiences. Their experience of phenomena and their construction of explanations pertaining to them are thus related to events that are objectively manifest in the world. Underlying such actual events, however, are the structural causes and generative mechanisms that render the actual and events present and observable. Critical realism posits three domains of being here: the empirical, the actual and the real. In the empirical domain, one can identify the experiences of knowing subjects; in the actual, one can identify events and their experience by subjects; and in the real, one can identify both experiences and events, and the underlying mechanisms that generate events and make them available to experience. It was the identification of the third domain of the real, the broadest level of being, that drove Bhaskar's original work in the philosophy of science. This was a specifically *ontological* discovery, of the natural necessity or real depth of being beyond what was available to experience.

On this basis, Bhaskar was able to marry an understanding of two things. First, in the 'transitive' dimension he recognised the social construction of knowledge, accommodating the original Kantian insight into the role of human subjects in producing knowledge, which is carried on in different terms by modern neo-Kantian forms of constructivism. Second, he related scientific knowledge formation in the transitive sphere to objects of knowledge in the 'intransitive' dimension (Bhaskar 1975, 2008a: ch. 1). The existence of being independently of knowledge grounds knowledge, accommodating positivist and empiricist understandings of the objective side of its production. In this way, transcendental realism acknowledges the truth in, but also the limits of, the competing traditions constituted by Humean empiricism and Kantian transcendental idealism. Bhaskar was thus able to explain how science could be seen as a human achievement, prone to error and open to partisan argument, and therefore to deflection from the pursuit of truth, yet at the same time grounded in real-world events and structures. These could provide, *pace* positivism, no guarantees for knowledge, but could anchor its truth potential and make it possible for there to be an element of 'judgemental rationality' between competing scientific theories. Science could be more than social or communal conversation, and the problem of incommensurability between knowledge claims could in principle be addressed.

Pressing the role of ontology thus, and endorsing natural necessity as causal generation in the domain of the real, led Bhaskar to diagnose as a fundamental problem of western philosophy the correlative pairing of what he called 'ontological actualism' and the 'epistemic fallacy' (Bhaskar 1975, 2008a). To begin with the latter, because it is the more visible, most philosophy has a limited understanding of ontology, and compensates for this by over-emphasising what can be achieved by epistemology. The epistemic fallacy is one such over-emphasis, involving the reduction of being to knowledge of it. In the absence of a grasp of real ontology, the philosophy of science, especially from the time of Descartes and Hume, had asked itself how we could be certain of the truth of knowledge. Through reliance on the nature of knowledge itself, philosophers sought cognitive or epistemic guarantees for truth in place of the ontological grounds on which claims to knowledge could rest. They substituted epistemological criteria guaranteeing knowledge for ontological criteria grounding it. The epistemic fallacy derived from Hume-influenced philosophy of science works off an inadequate, empirical realist ontology of actual events, in which the real is reduced to occurring events without a sense of the depth, the structures, and the mechanisms that generate them. Bhaskar's transcendental realism accordingly opposed both the empirical realism of a Hume, stressing the knowing subject's experience of a flat, atomistic, actualist ontology of events in constant conjunction, and the transcendental idealism of a Kant, deducing the necessity of a priori categories in the human mind to supplement the weakness in an ontology of actual events (ontological actualism).

Both Hume's and Kant's ontology rested at the level of actual events and, seeing no basis there for the truth in things, their natural necessity, the result was either scepticism about its possibility (Hume) or resort to an idealist compensation in the knowing subject (Kant). Both commit the epistemic fallacy because they look for the truth of knowledge in the nature of knowledge itself, with Hume's sceptical denial leading to Kant's idealist affirmation. Transcendental realism combined an element of Kantian philosophy in that its (transcendental) line of inquiry concerned what must be the case for scientific knowledge to be possible, but departed from it in terms of seeing the answer as lying in a (realist) depth ontology of how the world is. In that regard, its realism is in the line of Hume, but taking realism beyond the empirical and the actual and to the underlying domain of the real. The natural necessity in things, their real being or ontology, grounds knowledge processes that explicate it and them. So much for being in the realm of nature: what of social being?

Critical naturalism: natural necessity in the social sphere

Turning now from the general philosophy of transcendental realism to its specific application to social science (Bhaskar 1979, 1998a), Bhaskar sustains his ontological realism under the specific conditions produced by the subject matter of social science, human agency and society. If transcendental realism negotiated a path between empirical realism and transcendental idealism, Bhaskar's critical naturalist philosophy of social science also steers a middle course. Here the path lies between the kind of positivist naturalism that reduces human conduct to observable behaviour or social effects, and hermeneutics, which reduces the social to interpretive action. In hermeneutics, a line is drawn between the interpretive nature of, and meaning dependence in, social science and the causal naturalism of the natural sciences. Bhaskar's argument is in favour of the latter, while accepting the hermeneutic argument. It is that natural necessity operates in the social sciences just as in the natural sciences, but its form varies because of the different subject matter of the social sciences – that is, human beings and societies. Social science starts with the hermeneutic insight that action is meaning-dependent, but to say so is not to concede that the analysis of meaning is exhaustive of its subject matter. To the contrary, intentional human agency is inconceivable without society, and society is a necessary, structuring condition for its possibility. At the same time, however, society and social structures exist only by virtue of the intentional human agency that reproduces and transforms them. In this context, human mind and intentional agency are emergent properties of a certain kind of physiological matter to which they are irreducible (a doctrine Bhaskar names 'synchronic emergent powers materialism' – SEPM (Bhaskar 1979, 1998a: ch. 3)). Reasons are central to human agency and intentionality, as hermeneutics contends, but they act as the irreducible and necessary form that causes assume in the social world. Causes via reasons then link agency to social structures, which stand as objects of study in their own right, and this link of intentions to reasons, reasons to causes, and causes to structures (which operate only by virtue of intentional agency) provides the possibility of naturalism – that is, the specific kind of natural necessity available in the social world. The idea of social causation is thus inseparable from intentional agency, without which it would not exist, but this operates in a two-way theory of structure and agency that Bhaskar calls the 'transformational model of social activity' – the TMSA (Bhaskar 1979, 1998a: ch. 2).

This is a complex argument, and one that I have had to concentrate into a few lines, but the upshot is to argue that if a realist respect for natural necessity is a central feature of the world explored by the natural sciences, the same is true, *mutatis mutandis*, in the social sciences. Naturalism in the social sciences, however, involves the concept- and activity-dependency of the social, leading to the crucial mediation of causes by reasons by virtue of its object of study. In this understanding, the different domains of the empirical, the actual and the real all continue to exist, for social phenomena may exist as the actual events that are experienced by observers, in the form of the intentional activities of agents, but these have deeper grounds in the structures which they reflect and reproduce through their agency. Under the TMSA, causation still operates by virtue of the reasons people possess for their actions, yet crucially – for it shows the structural depth in social affairs – the reasons people give for their actions do not constitute the only grounds on which they act. Thus, people do not marry with the intention to reproduce the nuclear family, and they do not work in order to reproduce the capitalist economy, yet these results are both the unintended outcomes of their actions (reproducing structure) and the necessary condition of their acting (grounding and enabling their agency). In contrast to the hermeneutic perspective, actors' accounts of agency are limited by unacknowledged conditions and unintended consequences as well as unconscious motivations and tacit understanding and skills. Allowing for these differences, however, natural necessity in a depth ontology of structures, transmuted into actions by reasons operating as causes, exists as much in the social as in the natural world. It is the task of social, as of natural, science to observe, investigate and explain it. The ontological domain of the real thus represents the grounding for knowledge across the scientific board.

The necessity of being

To summarise these developments of transcendental realism and critical naturalism, what they have in common is an account of natural necessity in a complex and deep ontological domain, that of the real. Natural and social science may both be seen

> as a continuing and reiterated process of movement from manifest phenomena . . . to the identification of their generative causes, which now become the phenomena to be explained. The stratification of nature imposes a certain dynamic logic to scientific discovery, in which progressively deeper knowledge of natural necessity *a posteriori* is uncovered.
>
> (Bhaskar 1998b: xii)

In specifically social sciences, the stratification of society, operating via the specific nature of human beings as intentional agents (under the doctrine of SEPM), and of societies as both reproductive of and dependent on agents, acts and intentions (through the theory of TMSA), provides its own kind of natural necessity. Ontology, natural or social, is central to the working of the world and any account of knowledge, be it in a natural or a social science, within it. Critical realism's central commitment, emerging out of asking questions about how knowledge is possible, is to the idea of an ontology endorsing depth and natural necessity – to a theory, in short, of the ontological necessity of being. If that in brief is critical realism, what does its dialectical form add?

Dialectical critical realism: being and becoming

We are now at the point at which we can suggest what a dialectical development might do to critical realism. It will integrate an account of becoming with the existing critical realist understanding of being. But what kind of becoming does Bhaskar have in mind? To grasp his argument, it will be helpful to bring in the second main aim of *Dialectic*, the reworking of Hegel's philosophy in the light of a critical realist understanding of ontology. This involves 'the development of a general theory of dialectic – or better, a dialectic – of which the Hegelian one can be seen as an important, but limited and highly questionable, special case'

(DPF: 2). Such a dialectic would 'be capable of sustaining the development of a general metatheory for the social sciences',[11] which would make them capable of 'functioning as agencies of human self-emancipation' (ibid.). Once we have seen how Bhaskar wants to renovate Hegel's dialectic, we will see more clearly what he means by becoming.

Dialectics compared

For Bhaskar, Hegel is both the exemplar of dialectical thinking and a block upon it. He provides the model for a dialectical system of thought, but that model ultimately proves dialectic's undoing. Hegel's system has three elements: identity, negativity and totality. It starts with the identity in a concept or a thing, that which makes it itself, *this* thing in distinction from something else. It shows how criticism of that identity leads it to fall into contradiction, but then how the contradiction can be resolved and identity restored in a further move to a higher level in Hegel's thought system. Hegel thus starts with *identity*, submits it to a *negative* critique, and then shows how the results of this *negativity* can be addressed when viewed in the context of the whole, the rational *totality*. Identity, negativity and totality are thus the three terms of the Hegelian dialectic, and the drive is to secure identity against the results of negative critique by viewing them from the perspective of (rational) totality.

Bhaskar's dialectic in contrast has four terms, and these are non-identity, negativity, totality and praxis (or agency). Where his terms are the same as Hegel's (negativity, totality), his usage is, he says, radically different. However, the difference is throughout because the underlying assumptions of the two dialectics are so different. Bearing in mind what I have said about Bhaskar's realist ontological commitments, it should come as no surprise that the main difference between him and Hegel resides in his emphasis on ontology in comparison with Hegel's on epistemology, of a rationalist and idealist kind. In the *Philosophy of Right*, Hegel claims that '[w]hat is rational is actual and what is actual is rational' (1952: 10), revealing the importance of thought in constituting the real. Note that both his negative critique and his positive restoration of identity through reason (rational totality) are moves that engage with the world, what he calls 'the actual', but they do so on the terms of thought. They impose a rational order on it, seeing it as the repository of 'the Idea', and restoring identity by virtue of thought at the level of totality. Bhaskar in contrast starts not with thought identity, but, as its 'first moment' (abbreviated to 1M), with the sheer, real difference that exists in the world (what he calls *non-identity*). He then moves to what he calls a 'second edge' (2E) of real *negativity* and contradiction that things in the world disclose. He locates such negativity in the world at the 'third level' (3L) of a real, open, unfinished whole (his version of *totality*) and then stresses the importance of a 'fourth dimension' (4D), the capacity for practical human *agency* to change the world. Bhaskar's four-term dialectic is composed, then, of non-identity, negativity, totality and agency, as compared with Hegel's three: identity, negativity and totality.[12] The weight is firmly placed in Bhaskar on ontology rather than the fusion of epistemological (rational) and ontological elements that governs Hegel's dialectic.

Non-identity (being) and absence (becoming)

Let us look at this in a little detail, focusing here on the relationship between Bhaskar's first two terms, non-identity and negativity, for this is the move that gets becoming in dialectical critical realism going. The starting point of non-identity is given to dialectical critical realism by original critical realism, for what Bhaskar has in mind is just a world, both natural and social, in which things happen according to causes and the nature of entities, independently of our understanding of them. For this reason, when Bhaskar talks of non-identity as real or sheer difference, he does not mean this in something like the poststructuralist sense of difference. Poststructuralist talk of difference does involve, *pace* some of its progenitors, an ontological move (Derrida 1994, 1999; Norrie 2005b), but the poststructuralist account of difference is fundamentally reductionist (actualist) in its form. For Bhaskar, non-identity as real difference is linked to what we have called natural necessity, or to 'natural kinds' which are to be found in the world prior to our attempts to understand them. More expansively, non-identity is also associated with the 'necessary stratification and differentiation of the world', with 'causal powers and generative mechanisms' (DPF: 392). It is that sense of real differentiation in the world of things that Bhaskar means by non-identity, not a generic, necessarily abstract, sense of difference as in poststructuralism. Non-identity is a way of talking about the real difference entailed by critical realist ontology and it provides the starting point, or first moment (1M), of dialectical critical realism. It is the moment of ontology and being bequeathed to it by critical realism, which gives a contrast to the Hegelian starting point of thought identity in the concept and the thing.

With regard to original critical realism, however, what is new in dialectical critical realism is supplied by its second moment (or 'edge' – 2E), the idea of negativity. Once again, Bhaskar does not have in mind here an abstract or metaphysical sense of nothingness, nor simply an operation in knowledge of negating a concept or argument (though that may be a part of it). What he means is the idea of real, determinate absence that exists in things, as part of what we have called their natural necessity. There is a helpful anticipatory passage in Bhaskar's pre-dialectical work, which sketches what he means by negativity and offers a promissory note for what was to come in his dialectic. It introduces the idea of absence, meaning negativity, clearly and simply. First, it asserts the ontological reality and causal significance of absence in the working of natural necessity:

> An entity may be absent from its spatio-temporal . . . region either because it is in some other region . . . or because it does not exist at all . . . either because it is finite and has perished . . . or because it never did exist . . . (whether it will or may come to exist or not). And the absence of such an entity . . . may

precisely, *qua* absence, have causal effects on objects in the relevant space-time region, and as such satisfy the causal criterion for ascribing reality to things. . . . Think of the missing collar-stud that makes the after dinner speaker late, the monsoon which doesn't come which makes the crops perish, the inconsolable loss of the bereaved one.

(Bhaskar 1991: 126)

Second, the passage asserts the philosophical need to think of both positive and negative qualities in reality. Accordingly, it nominates the doctrine in philosophy that refuses to recognise absence as 'ontological monovalence', for it allows only one kind of ontological value:

We are too apt to miss the importance of the negative in a purely positive account of reality. The tacit assumption is that the negative can always be analysed away in purely positive terms. This is the doctrine of what I shall call ontological monovalence. But it is pure dogma. The world, including the natural world, contains absences, omissions, liabilities, just as much as presences, commissions and powers.

(ibid.)

Thus far, the argument may be accepted, but it has yet to engage our interest in dialectics. Bhaskar then proceeds to develop a crucial link between absence as ontologically real and *absence as real negation*, in the sense of a quality that works on and in presence, brings out the world's dynamic and processual quality, and establishes *change* as integral to it. Note also that he relates the failure to see these things and the resulting commitment to ontological monovalence to a longstanding and deep-seated mistake in western philosophy associated with the Greeks:

Not only is the negative underplayed – philosophy's real inheritance from Parmenides; it is also not analysed as *a process – of real negation, of subversive or transformative change*. This is Plato's legacy to philosophy – the analysis of negation and change in terms of the quite different category of difference.

(ibid., emphasis added)

Setting aside for the present the reference to Plato's finesse of real change or negation in terms of a notion of difference, it is the emphasised words in the passage that are the key. Natural necessity involves change, and change involves the passing away, the negation, of what is in favour of what has come to be in its place. This is the key point in introducing a whole series of concepts to critical realism which denote negativity and change:

We shall see how critical realism, hitherto focusing on the concepts of structure, differentiation and change, *has itself to be given a second level of analysis, taking in the processual categories of negation, contradiction, development, becoming, emergence, finitude* and a third level of analysis revolving around the categories of totality and reflexivity.

(ibid.; emphasis added)

In this passage from Bhaskar's pre-dialectical work, we only get to the third level in Bhaskar's dialectic, (3L) totality, and there is no mention of the fourth dimension (4D), agential ethical practice. We shall look briefly at them in the next section. That apart, this linking of absence through change and movement to natural necessity lies at the heart of dialectical critical realism. Its key development is to take the theory of the structured nature of being (natural necessity) and to think about how being changes in time and space, and how philosophically that change is to be understood. Essentially, Bhaskar analyses change in terms of a process of movement in which a thing becomes something else, and in that process ceases to be what it was. What it was is no more, has passed into non-being, and has been absented through the process of change. This inevitable, ontological, processual quality of being, linking it to non-being qua the negation in change, is what ties being to *becoming*. Becoming is the absenting of what was in favour of the emergence of what now is, for every becoming is also, in some part at least, a 'begoing', an absenting of what was there.

The core move in Bhaskar's dialecticisation of critical realism is thus the development of his realist account of ontology as natural necessity in terms of the relationship between being and not-being, and therefore being and becoming. Absence plays a huge part, either as a noun, 'absence', or as a verb, 'absenting', and it is present in a variety of modes. Most centrally, it is there in the various forms of negativity and negation that constitute the world's movement. The emphasis is on real absence or absenting, in the natural and social worlds, and present to human being in its being and all its practices. Absence is there in the overall *ontology* of change (the absenting of the old in the emergence of the new). It is there in the sub-branches of ontology such as the *epistemology* of learning processes and dialogue (the absenting of error), and in ethics as the dialectics of *agency*, as the absenting of constraints upon freedom. Real, determinate absence in its relationship to change in what exists makes the world go forward, gives it its processual quality. It emphasises that life must be understood as about both being and becoming (and 'begoing' – passing). Every process of becoming involves the determinate absenting of the old in favour of the determination of the new, and this is at the core of the *dialectical* sense of natural necessity that has come to constitute Bhaskar's newly developed theory of being.

The account of being and becoming of the two previous sections has drawn on the first two aims of *Dialectic*, the dialectical enhancement of critical realism and the reworking of Hegelian dialectic in critical realist terms. It has done so by sketching the first two terms in Bhaskar's dialectic, 1M non-identity and 2E negativity, emphasising the role that realist ontology plays in establishing a new basis for dialectic, and the role that dialectic plays in developing original critical realism. In the final section, I move to the third and final overall aim of *Dialectic*, the provision of a metacritique of western philosophy, and I also outline as a prelude to this the third and fourth elements, 3L totality and 4D ethical agency, in Bhaskar's dialectic.

Reworking dialectic: totality, ethics and metacritique

The reason for linking together the third main aim of *Dialectic*, the metacritique of western philosophy, with the third and fourth elements in Bhaskar's dialectic, totality and ethical agency, is that the idea of totality is central to the possibility of metacritique, as indeed it is also central to Bhaskar's understanding of ethical practice. Accordingly, talking of totality, ethics and metacritique together makes most sense. First, I will say a little on totality in its own right, and then something on ethics and the relationship between totality and ethics. Thereafter, I turn to metacritique and its relation to totality.[13]

Totality

After non-identity and negativity comes the third element, or level, of Bhaskar's dialectic, 3L totality. The term is shared with Hegel, but in Hegel the totality is rational and in principle complete and closed, for reason has ultimately worked its way through the world, making explicit the sense of a rational whole that was implicit in it. Once achieved, the work of dialectical philosophy is done, for the totality is present and complete. This is seen in Hegel's *Philosophy of Right*, where the modern state and its law represent the culmination of a rational, historical process of development, and more broadly in his idea that history has come to an end. For Bhaskar, the realist idea of natural necessity substitutes a real ontological basis for Hegel's rationally grounded deployment of the epistemic fallacy. Nonetheless, a realist understanding of natural necessity, operating in a structured social world under the TMSA, also points to a sense of totality. The whole produces and enables its parts, and this is so even if, as Bhaskar argues, the whole can operate only *through* its parts. Structures too do not exist individually, but rather in their relationship with other structures constituting the whole. This generates the idea at the level of totality of holistic causality, which involves a causal relationship between structures in a whole. Natural necessity thus leads to a conception of a structured totality and, in the light of the workings of real negativity (change, process, becoming) in the whole, presents a conception of a totality that is in motion. The critical realist totality is thus in a process of becoming, is incomplete, and assumes an open future. The future cannot be closed, *pace* Hegel, through the dialectical rationalist triumph of the Idea. It is open, in process of development, subject to substantial change and the qualitatively new. This is the main difference between a realist, emergent sense of open totality, and one that is idealistic, rationally contained and, ultimately, closed.

From it, Bhaskar develops a number of concepts relevant to this level of being. Among them is the idea of holistic causality, just described. Another I would like to mention is that of the constellation (or constellationality), because it is central both to Bhaskar's account of ethics and to his idea of metacritique. The idea of a constellation was developed in the dialectical tradition by Theodor Adorno (1973), following Walter Benjamin (see Coole 2000: 173–9), but Bhaskar's use is his own, rooted in his realist ontology.[14] It is the idea that different entities or layers of being may be constellationally embedded in each other to constitute a totality. In this relationship, the embedded terms retain their individual importance, while the relationship between them is also crucial. A constellation, involving the interlocking of distinct entities within a whole, provides a sense both of the autonomy of the parts and of their dependence on the broader relation. For example, epistemology, the theory of knowledge, requires to be distinguished from ontology, the study of being, as original critical realism holds, but knowing is at the same time a subset of being, and the study or theory of being (onto-*logy*) is already epistemically committed. So, there is a complex, co-embedded, constellational relationship between the terms, not a clear analytical distinction between epistemology and ontology.

I mention this idea of constellationality in the field of totality as an illustration of how a totalising concept works, but I do so also because it is central to the working of ethics, Bhaskar's fourth dialectical moment, to which I now turn.

Ethical agency

In the fourth ethical dimension (4D) in his dialectics, Bhaskar develops a complex scheme of ethical elements involving, in bare terms, what it means to be free, to trust, and to enter into relations of solidarity with others. He talks about principles of dialectical rationality which press human beings, through the necessary universalisation of their practical commitments, towards ethical positions. These lead them eventually to the idea of the eudaimonic society, the best of moral worlds in which a fully developed understanding of the freedom of each is achieved only through the freedom of all. Bhaskar describes a process of universalising our actions which leads from the first 'primal scream' of the infant, through the desire for freedom, from trust to solidarity, to the eudaimonic society. From this very brief description, one can see echoes of both Aristotle and Marx, and this is especially borne out in Bhaskar's account of eudaimonia as a place where the freedom of each depends on the freedom of all. A key association, however, is also with Jürgen Habermas, whose theory of the universalisability of speech acts forms a model for Bhaskar's more generalised account of universalising commitments. However, Bhaskar is no Habermasian, and the reason this is so relates to his account of the constellation at the level of totality, and the role it plays in his ethics.

Earlier in this Introduction, I described my initial discomfort at what I saw as the contradictory relationship Bhaskar seemed to have evolved between an abstract, ideal ethics and a structurally grounded, historically embedded conception of realist dialectics. How could they fit together? Is there not, as Sayer put it, a critical realist rabbit being pulled from a hat here? At one time, I thought with Sayer, and viewed Bhaskar's ethics as an illicit move given his attention to historical conditions in the first two chapters of *Dialectic*. The answer, I now think, is that Bhaskar's ethics must be seen as an example of constellational embedding at the level of totality, in which the historical structuring of ethics and the possibility of their principled dialectical rationalisation must *both* be kept in play, in their distinction and connection. Neither is reducible to the other, while each interrelates with the other. Human being, with its undeniable normative dimension, is the socially and historically developed achievement of a particular species existing on a particular world at a particular time. By virtue of our nature, evolved in society and in history, we are a species that possesses the possibility of extrapolating through a process of reason to the dialectical necessity of an ethically complete world. Yet this possibility coexists with the need to recognise that ethical values are socially developed and deeply implicated in structures of power that are historically emergent. Bhaskar is very clear about the importance of these in thinking the western totality. He calls them structured power, or power$_2$ relations, or, more graphically, 'generalised master–slave-type relations', and any discussion of ethics must consider the constellational relation between these and the possibilities of moral agency, without either affirming the autonomy of moral agency or reducing it to its historical context. The historical and the ethical are constellationally co-embedded in a totalising dialectic that enables them to be co-present. This generates an account of ethics in the world that identifies how ethical experience can be real and irreducible, and at the same time connected to and influenced by historical conditions. This particular way of configuring moral issues is understood by viewing ethical agency as real, and in its constellational relation to totality.

Metacritique

Finally, we arrive at the third main aim of *Dialectic*, which is to provide 'the elements of a totalising critique of western philosophy, in its various (including hitherto dialectical) forms' (DPF: 2), and this would include 'a micro sketch of certain nodal moments in the history of dialectical philosophy' (ibid.). This is a huge topic, and I seek to explain and develop it in the final two chapters of the book. For now, I will say a little about the idea of a totalising critique, what Bhaskar calls a metacritique, and the way it links philosophical critique constellationally to the idea of totality. Metacritique starts from the critique of a philosophical problem, and moves from there to the systematic identification of error in a philosophy. This leads back to its original source or sources in philosophy, and then, in a further move, links it to underlying relations and structures of power in society. It is in this further move that the relationship between philosophy, as a *sui generis* form of knowledge, and history as its external 'other', is engaged at the level of totality. More specifically, Bhaskar denotes this further move by dividing metacritique into metacritique$_1$ (the identification of systematic error) and metacritique$_2$ (the tracing out of its historical roots). The latter reflects the idea of structured power$_2$ relations discussed above and denotes that philosophy is to be understood constellationally *both* in terms of its specific modes of argument and its particular, often systematic, problems *and* as these problems are emergent from history as forged out of struggles and structures in the realm of 'generalised master–slave-type relations'.

That is the core idea of a meta-, or totalising, critique, and Bhaskar uses it to diagnose fundamental problems at the core of western philosophy. In abbreviated form, the argument, which concerns the denial of absence, in the doctrine of ontological monovalence, is as follows. Absence has been systematically underplayed in western philosophy, starting with the ancient Greeks, in a way that has affected the entire tradition. Starting with Parmenides and Plato, there was a concern among elites to deny the possibility of significant change in society, what Parmenides called 'generation' and 'perishing'. To avoid talk of such things and thereby to protect the status quo, Parmenides banned talk of not-being, and thus of change, in favour of a theory of the world as an undifferentiated positive whole, 'the One'. Plato rejected this doctrine, but he shared Parmenides' concern to avoid talk of non- or not-being, and he did this by arguing that one could talk of it in a limited way. Not-being did not signify the opposite of being – that is, real non-being – but indicated only the *difference* between two forms of being, as in 'a is different from b, i.e. a is *not* (the same as) b'. The negative is retained, but only in a comparative, differentiating sense.

For Bhaskar, this is a fateful move in philosophy, for two reasons. First, the ban on talk of not-being has remained largely in place, especially in so far as it concerns real, determinate non-being, which has been, as the ground of change, thereby hidden from philosophical view in the western tradition. This has led to a bias against change and process in philosophy. Second, the result of the denial of non-being has been the triumph of actualist understandings of being which have denied the existence of natural necessity in the world. These in turn have encouraged the epistemic fallacy as a governing problem in western philosophy, one that reaches from Plato and Aristotle down to the present through philosophers of the Enlightenment such as Descartes, Hume and Kant. The epistemic fallacy, the reduction of being to knowledge, which Bhaskar had originally diagnosed in critical realism in Hume and Kant, is now pushed back to the beginnings of the western tradition, and its centrality is shown to be based on another philosophically problematic doctrine. That other doctrine is ontological monovalence, and it concerns the denial of non-being as a crucial element in ontology. Thus, at the core of Bhaskar's third aim, a metacritique of western philosophy, is precisely that which he has argued for as the central element in his dialecticisation of critical realism: the importance of real negativity, absence and becoming. That which drives his dialectic is that which is missing from the western philosophical tradition as a whole.

The grounds of justice

On the basis of these arguments, we eventually arrive at a developed position on the possibility of ethics and the grounds of justice which draws together the arguments for natural necessity, materialist diffraction and totality from Chapters 1 to 4 with the ethics of Chapter 5 and the ethical conclusions of the metacritique of Chapters 6 and 7. From Chapter 5, we have the idea of the constelled nature of ethics in a social totality, where natural necessity provides both a drive towards a 'perfectionist' ethics involving a eudaimonistic conception of freedom and a containment of that drive by social and historical conditions. The result is that what Bhaskar will explain as the ethically real nature of human being becomes displaced under modern conditions into a series of more limited ethical relations between 'the ideal' and 'the actual'. From Chapters 6 and 7, we see how the denial of change leading to the denial of absence and of natural necessity leads to a focus in ethics on two problematic standpoints, those of 'the universal' and 'the particular'. These are taken up in modern critical ethics as the abstract universalism of Kantianism on the one hand and the (equally abstract) radical particularism of Nietzschean poststructuralism on the other. In both positions, a failure to think through the role of material social relations (natural necessity) on issues of justice limits their ethical stance. These limits in modern ethical and justice thinking are traced back to the Greeks and their denial of real determinate absence.

Conclusion

All the arguments I have outlined here concerning Bhaskar's dialectic and its effects will be developed more fully in what is to come, but it was important to establish an introductory foundation in terms of his starting point in original critical realism. From there I have described how arguments about absence both radicalise his account of being in favour of becoming, and provide a realist understanding of dialectic to place alongside other irrealist forms such as Hegel's. This two-way engagement between dialectic and critical realism is based on the argument for real non-being in the being of the world, and it provides the first two main aims of Bhaskar's *Dialectic*: the enhancement of critical realism and the renovation of dialectic. The third aim, his metacritique, arises out of the development of dialectical critical realism itself, especially to the level of totality, and it focuses, as does the book as a whole, on the consequences of absence, especially, in this area, the consequences of its denial for the western philosophical tradition as a whole.

In the following chapters, I will develop these arguments at length. In Chapter 2, we shall consider Bhaskar's account of absence, how he argues for it, and its relationship among other things to change. In Chapter 3, we shall examine Bhaskar's critique of Hegelian dialectic, leveraged, as it is, on the more concrete and less philosophical materialist dialectics of Marx. Having explored absence and the creation of a critical realist dialectical method, we shall then be in a position in Chapter 4 to consider Bhaskar's account of totality and its various forms. This will allow us, in Chapter 5, to examine Bhaskar's ethics and the connection with and distinction from Habermas. Moving to metacritique in Chapter 6, we shall explore Bhaskar's analysis of the fateful first false steps taken by philosophy from the time of Plato and Parmenides onwards. This analysis will then lead in Chapter 7 into a critical appraisal of poststructural philosophy and its debt to Nietzsche, for a Nietzschean ontology is seen to be complicit in the Parmenidean–Platonic structuring of philosophy to exclude real absence in favour of difference. I shall then be able to suggest that some of the ideas central to poststructuralist thought are part of an old and partial story, not a radical break from it. Finally, in

Chapter 8 we shall bring together the argument as a whole, moving from natural necessity, material diffraction and totality in the earlier chapters to the idea of a constellated ethics and the problems linked metacritically to the denial of absence (problems of the universal and the particular). These provide a sense of the possibility and limits of modern ethics and of the grounds of justice.

2   Accentuate the negative

In the first chapter, we noted the significance of absence for Bhaskar's dialectic, and my intention here is to explore it in some depth. I begin with a consideration of terms. In the dialectical tradition, 'absence' has not until now had the import Bhaskar gives it. Words such as 'negation' and 'negativity' by contrast lie at its heart. Bhaskar uses these terms too; indeed, the three main sections of *Dialectic* dealing with absence refer sequentially in their titles to negation, absence and negativity.[1] However, 'absence' is his term of choice, and in the first section I consider why this should be so, though I argue that Bhaskar's terminology is essentially open, and not too much should be made of his favouring absence.[2] In a second section, I shall then look at the role absence plays in dialectical critical realism, in creating its 'second edge' (2E). Here absence moves critical realism forward from its original interest in natural necessity and real non-identity (its first moment – 1M) to its emphasis on the spatio-temporal character, the becoming, of being. This can be described as a move from thinking about the entities or products of social life to thinking about the *process* of their production, from 'product' to 'process', from being to becoming. In a third section, I shall then move to consider the reasons for giving absence priority over the present or the positive. I shall suggest that what is of real importance is its significance *in relation to* presence, though I shall note that there is a sense in which absence is primary, a sense caught in Bhaskar's conception of 'the constellational', the term developed in his account of totality.[3] Fourth, I shall focus on its importance for thinking critically about the development of western philosophy from its earliest moments. In particular, Bhaskar's recognition of absence points up the corresponding denial that lies at the heart of the western philosophical tradition and that he terms 'ontological monovalence'. I shall deal with this last briefly in anticipation of what is to come in Chapters 6 and 7, though it is philosophically central to Bhaskar's critique of western philosophy.

Finally, I shall return to appraise more fully the case Bhaskar makes for absence, and argue that it is a strong one driven by an overall vision of the ways in which human being in western societies is marked by a sense of what is lacking – or, of course, absent. At its heart, Bhaskar's dialectic, I shall argue, involves a vision of a world in which dominant social and economic power suppresses human possibilities, and the resulting lack is then repressed in its philosophy. *Dialectic* is at once a reflection on the philosophical effects of such power relations and a pointer to how things could begin to be different. Absence is a concept that denotes both a geo-historical and a philosophical problem and, in so far as philosophical understanding changes anything, Bhaskar's account is a contribution to addressing (and absenting) it.

Absence: what's in a word?

At the core of *Dialectic* is the concept of absence. Introduced early in the book, in discussing 'negation',[4] it is the springboard for developing critical realism by providing a 'second edge' (2E) based on an understanding of 'absence' or 'negativity'.[5] 'Absence' is, however, the term given central place in dialectical critical realism, for dialectic involves, at its most complete, 'the *absenting* of constraints on the *absenting* of *absences*, or ills' (DPF: 396; emphasis added). This formula sometimes feels slightly strained; we are not used to speaking of absence in quite this way, and we do not usually think of *dialectic* in terms of this kind of language. We must therefore explore it further and see how to make best sense of it. One thing is certain, however, and that is that Bhaskar sets great store by the need to think absence. Very early in *Dialectic*, he writes that 'by the time we are through, I would like the reader to see the positive as a tiny, but important, ripple on the surface of a sea of negativity' (DPF: 5). Since 'negativity' and 'absence' are very close concepts, I think we could as easily talk here of 'the present as a tiny, but important, ripple on the surface of a sea of absence'. In grasping what Bhaskar means, we will have cause to question just what this claim entails.

Verb and noun: the ubiquity of absence and the openness of terms

Two preliminary points should be made. Note first that two uses of absence have already emerged. We first spoke of it as an active verb – 'absenting' – and now we are speaking of it as an abstract noun, 'absence'. This is because Bhaskar wants to deploy the concept of absence both in terms of *being* and (especially) non-being, and in terms of *doing* and (especially) undoing – or, better, negating. It is here that we pick up especially the idea of becoming and what passes away in processes of becoming.[6] He uses the word as both noun and verb. This observation, as well as indicating something of what is to come, makes a second point about Bhaskar's usage, and that is simply that he wants to be as open and broad in his use of terms as possible. In discussing negativity, Bhaskar writes that his 'base concept of non-being is absence, *the simplest and most elemental concept of all*' (DPF: 239), but he wants to systematise absence as fully as he can. One way of doing this is to show just how wide-ranging the language of absence is. Absence involves non-being, negativity and negation, but he invites us to think of the varied ways we talk about negation. To absent can involve any or all of the following: to deny, reject, contradict, oppose, exclude, marginalise, denigrate, erase, separate, split, sunder, cancel, annul, destroy, criticise and condemn (DPF: 8). It is also present in all these specifically dialectical concepts concerning negativity: the hiatus, the margin, the void, the hidden, the empty, the anterior, the exterior, the excluded, the omitted, the forgotten and the feared (DPF: 238). It invokes the following specifically philosophical references: 'to absent, to constrain, to condemn, to injure, to refine, to qualify . . . , to limit . . . , to cancel, to suspend, to undo, to erase, . . . to nihilate, to annihilate; and more technically to mediate, transform, contradict, marginalize, sunder and void' (ibid.). Ideas of absence, negation and negativity, when viewed in this light, are much more present in our practical and philosophical ways of thinking than we might otherwise think.

Bhaskar's ambition is not, however, to make lists. It is rather to bring home to us the centrality of a concept of absence to our philosophical (and other) usage. As regards the western philosophical tradition, one of Bhaskar's main arguments, grounding his concept of ontological monovalence, is that it has not developed an adequate conception of absence. That does not, however, mean it has not been implicated, despite itself, in the language of absence, and Bhaskar wants us to be aware of this. But what is the specific magic of 'absence'? As we have seen, it is for Bhaskar just the simplest term for speaking about non-being, but he is not always insistent on its use. He is also prepared to emphasise the importance of the concept of negativity, as in the following quotation, where it seems to subsume absence:

> Negativity is the motive of all dialectics. . . . It is the single most important category, more general than negation because it [includes] the absent without a present or positive; it connotes more directly the negating process whereas negation suggests merely the outcome or result. Negativity embraces the *dual* senses of the (evaluatively neutral) *absence* and the (pejorative) *ill*, united in dialectical critical realist explanatory critique, the aim of which is precisely to *absent ills*.
>
> (DPF: 238)

One sees here a variety of terms (negativity, negation, the absent, negating, absence, ill) with a core meaning, but where different words have different inflections. Can we distinguish the variety of meanings and see why absence should come out ahead?

The meaning of terms: absence, non-being, negativity

'Absence' or 'negativity', 'negation' or 'non-being': what's in a term? Absence has first of all the sense of ontology inscribed within it: it derives from the Latin 'to be' (*esse*) and 'away from' (*ab*) – 'away from being', or 'being away from'. I think it is the ontological element that makes it attractive to Bhaskar, for his term must denote what he calls 'real non-being' (DPF: 5). However, absence, in the sense of 'away from being', does not quite catch all that Bhaskar would like. Thus, in the case of an entity that does not exist and that was never a part of being, for example the early modern scientific 'discovery' of phlogiston, to describe it as 'absent' in the sense of 'away from being' slightly misses the point, for the 'away from' in absence could signify that it exists or has existed somewhere else. In that situation, it is clearer to state that this is real 'non-being' plain and simple, and Bhaskar settles for this (DPF: 39). So, it may be that non-being is broader than absence. But if this is so, and if every instance of real absence turns out to be a case of real non-being, why prioritise absence as the central category?

As an abstract noun, simple non-being may have it over absence, but one problem is that there is no verb that complements 'non-being' in the same way as 'to absent' or 'absenting' complements 'absence'. So if the aim is to talk of a mode both of being and of doing, then absence, with absenting as its associated verb, is the preferable term. Besides, I think much of the focus of what Bhaskar wants to say lies in the sense of absence as a form of real non-being that is 'away from' what exists, in the sense of being that has been or is not yet, that is latent or immanent, that has perished or is in process of generation. With regard to the nature of ontology, non-being does not capture the possibility of a related becoming, passing away or deferral that the 'ab' in 'absence' signifies. Absence denotes a relationship between something that is away from being and what is in being that is central to Bhaskar's dialectical usage. Non-being is more black and white and denotes no connection between what is not and what is.

If absence has it over non-being, what of negation or negativity? Again, there is overlap. Bhaskar's realist insistence on an ontology of 'real negation' has as its primary meaning 'real determinate absence or non-being' (DPF: 5).[7] As we have seen, however, Bhaskar sees 'negativity' as broader than 'negation' because it includes 'the absent without a present or positive' (DPF: 238). In that sense, negativity might also include a state 'altogether absent from being' (DPF: 39) – that is, the simple non-being that absence fails to cover. Is, then, negativity with the associated verb 'to negate' (and the related abstract noun 'negation') a better term than absence and its associated derivatives? Perhaps, but there is a point about Latin derivation here too. 'Absence', as we saw, stems from the idea of 'being', whereas 'negativity' stems from the verb *negare*, meaning 'to deny'. So, negativity stems from a word denoting an action 'what a being *does*' (i.e. denies), rather than from what a particular state of being *is*, and this is carried forward into our usage. It signifies 'doing' more than 'being'. 'Negativity' is something that attaches to, or describes a mood of, being rather than constituting a state of being in itself. Negativity is not so much the same as non-being as depicting one of its attributes. As an abstract noun, it retains something of its active doing quality, rather than the idea that something 'is not' in an existential sense, as both 'absence' and 'non-being' signify.

These semantic differences are not spelled out by Bhaskar in *Dialectic*, but I hope it has been worthwhile to explore them here because of the discomfort that some have experienced with Bhaskar's usage. This may simply be the force of habit among dialectical thinkers in particular, who naturally are drawn to terms like 'negativity' and 'negation'. It may also be linked to the discomfort some feel in simply giving 'what is not' such a pivotal role in philosophy. Since Bhaskar argues that absence has been significantly marginalised in the western tradition, we might expect this. It may otherwise simply be a slight clumsiness in some-times using absence as a verb, 'to absent'. 'Absenting absence' does not trip off the tongue quite as readily as Hegel's 'negating the negation'. Whatever, it seems to me that Bhaskar, as a theorist who prioritises ontology, has good reason to switch to absence if he is going to speak of real non-being in a sustained way. In terms of English linguistic usage, there may be no perfect term, but absence works, first, because of its direct link to (non-)being and ontology, and second, because of the availability of a related verb. As competitor-words, 'negativity' shares the latter advantage of a verb ('negate'/'negation') but not the former, the clear link to real ontology, to real non-being. While 'non-being' shares the former advantage, the direct link to ontology, it does not link to a verb, and thereby to doing, becoming, negating and passing.

Perhaps as important to recognise as these distinctions, however, is that there is close connection in Bhaskar's usage *between* these different terms, and he often uses, depending on the context, one or the other. He also defines one term in terms of another, as we have seen when he defines real negation as 'real determinate absence or non-being' (DPF: 5). Ultimately, it seems to me, there are good reasons for deploying 'absence', but it would be a mistake to get too hung up on semantics. The spirit of Bhaskar's *Dialectic* is generous and open in its use of concepts, and this should be borne in mind in thinking through the meaning of terms. In a book devoted to seeing dialectic as the 'great "loosener"' (DPF: 44) of analytical thought, it would be strange to attach too much significance to small distinctions between terms.

Absence as product and process: a basic tour

The discussion of terminology indicates the direction of Bhaskar's thought towards the real ontological implications of absence. If we now turn to, as it were, the substance of absence, we can go to the definition Bhaskar provides in the glossary to *Dialectic*, and look at its different elements. It should be said that the passage I am about to quote is condensed and therefore requires elaboration. After it, I will examine its different elements, focusing particularly on the 'fourfold polysemy' (or meaning) of absence discussed in the middle of the passage. This will then be taken up in the following section. Here is what Bhaskar says of absence:

> Understood to include non-existence anywhere anywhen. It is systematically bipolar, designating absenting (distanciating and/or transforming) process as well as simple absence in a more or less determinate level-/context-specific region of space-time; and in fact reveals a fourfold polysemy: product, process, process-in-product and product-in-process – which may be recursively embedded and systematically intermingled. It includes, but is far from exhausted by, the past and outside. It is the central category of dialectic, whether conceived as argument, change or the augmentation of (or aspiration to) freedom, which depend upon the identification and elimination of mistakes, states of affairs and constraints, or more generally ills – argued to be absences alike.
>
> (DPF: 393)

Though this may seem daunting, the first two points in this passage reflect what we have already said. Absence is 'understood to include non-existence anywhere anywhen'. This is the limit point of absence, where it turns into non-being per se, as we have discussed. It is, he continues, 'systematically bipolar, designating absenting (distanciating and/or transforming) process as well as simple absence in a more or less determinate level [or] context-specific region of space-time'. Here, Bhaskar points to the role of absence as noun and verb, as a form of (non-)being, and as present in processes of doing or becoming. The latter involves its role in processes of change, and here we speak of absenting as a verb. This much we have already seen.

Thereafter, there is an important passage where Bhaskar goes on to say, drawing upon the 'bipolarity' of absence and absenting, that absence has a fourfold meaning ('polysemy') involving the language of 'product' and 'process'. This involves both its existence as achieved states of non-being (what he calls absence as 'product'), and its active involvement as absenting in the becoming and passing of entities (absenting as 'process'). Absence can thus be, first, a state of being, a product in the world, and second, intrinsic to change, to processes of development of things in the world. Reflecting its relationship to both being and doing, absence can be seen as both 'product' and 'process', for the world consists of things produced and processes of their production. At the same time, pushing the argument forward, 'product' and 'process' can both be looked at in terms of their engagement with the other. In a dynamic world, product is always in process, and process is always linked to the development of and in product, so that one can talk of absence as the 'fourfold polysemy' of 'product, process, process-in-product and product-in-process', and in any real-world situations these relations will be 'recursively embedded and systematically intermingled'.[8] And, going a little further, Bhaskar goes on to argue that since absence as process and as product and in their interrelation are real elements of being in the world, they are intrinsically linked to basic world contours of time and space. Hence, absence as product and process is closely linked to 'the past and outside'. We shall develop this realist understanding of absence in the world in the next section, but for the moment we should take forward the idea of absence as product and process and as grounded in a spatio-temporal world.

Finally, before we move on, there is the concluding sentence of Bhaskar's definition of absence, which reflects the breadth of his ambition for the concept. He points to three different contexts in which absence, 'the central category of dialectic', may be deployed. It may be 'conceived as argument, change or the augmentation of (or aspiration to) freedom'. In these different contexts, it is central either to 'the identification and elimination of mistakes', or to the negation of 'states of affairs and constraints' through causal processes, or to abolishing 'more generally ills' in the pursuit of freedom. Note two things here. The first is that 'ills' are taken to be synonymous with 'absences', albeit with a less neutral, more morally evaluative, colouring. This is a first statement of Bhaskar's approach to ethics, about which I shall have more to say in Chapter 5. The second is that absence operates at three different levels. In *ontology* (the causal change in 'states of affairs'), it is what engenders change. In *epistemology* (the 'identification and elimination of mistakes'), it is central to the process of argument and, by extension, the development of knowledge. In *moral praxis* (the 'identification and elimination of . . . constraints, . . . ills'), it is the spur to freedom. These are three key areas in which the identification and understanding of absence are central to Bhaskar's philosophy. However, it is worth pointing out that while ontology, epistemology and praxis all have their specificities, and can be the subject of different inquiries, ultimately they all come together: ontological change requires practical agency, which entails moral and epistemological knowledge that informs it. At a higher level, being, agency and knowledge are all indeed forms of ontology, and they are all redolent with absence and absenting. Put another way around, the pursuit of a world with an enhanced sense of freedom requires praxis, understanding and the bringing about of change. In this process, the absenting of absences, as well as the absenting of those structural constraints that keep absences in place, lies at the core. As both noun and verb, at the core of product and process, as involving states of being and forms of doing or becoming, absence is central. Let us now, however, take up the idea of absence as product and process in more depth.

From product to process: critical realism's 'second edge'

We have seen that absence has a role to play in the three areas of ontology, epistemology and moral praxis, and in this section I am going to focus on the first of these. It is here that the most general effects of absence are felt in Bhaskar's thinking, for it is central to his aim of moving the philosophy of critical realism onto dialectical ground. So doing, we will develop the account of being and becoming from Chapter 1, and that of product and process just outlined. Let me begin, however, by recalling how dialectic works in dialectical critical realism, according to the four terms represented as the 1M to 4D (MELD) schema described in Chapter 1. This will help us see the overall aim of Bhaskar's argument.

Critical realism and negativity

It will be recalled from Chapter 1 that Bhaskar writes of the need to move critical realism forward from its 'first moment' (1M) to a 'second edge' (2E), and then on to a 'third level' (3L) and a 'fourth dimension' (4D). Dialectical critical realism has four main terms, as opposed to the three in Hegel's dialectic. These are non-identity, negativity, totality and praxis (corresponding to Hegel's three of identity, negativity, totality),[9] and each of these terms corresponds to one of the four elements in the 'MELD' schema. Thus, 1M is the initial critical realist ground of non-identity, meaning irreducible, real difference in the world and our categories. This is then radicalised by the 2E account of negativity, related to the idea of totality at 3L, and submitted to the importance of praxis at 4D. It is the move to 2E that most directly implicates absence, for that move is constituted by introducing negativity into critical realism. Absence is the underlying concept that unifies the second edge that dialectical thinking adds to critical realism.

If we now focus in on the transition from 1M non-identity to 2E negativity, at 1M we encounter concepts familiar from pre-existing critical realist philosophy. These emphasise the sheer otherness of being within realist ontology, and therefore the basic alterity or non-identity in being. Critical realism argues for the real ontology, which is the natural necessity, of being in the world, and the possibility of knowledge as real reference to it. Critical realist categories derive from a basic transcendental deduction of what the world must be like for reference to occur. The real differences between epistemology and ontology, structure and agency, mind and matter, a cause and what is caused, change and the potential for the emergence of the new are all grounded in real non-identity or alterity in the world. In *Dialectic*, Bhaskar refers to original 1M as 'characterised by non-identity relations' and 'unified by the concept of alterity', and as emphasising the following:

> existential intransitivity, referential detachment, the reality principle and ontology which it necessitates. More concretely, it fastens on to the transcendentally necessary stratification and differentiation of the world, entailing concepts of causal powers and generative mechanisms, alethic truth[10] and transfactuality, natural necessity and natural kinds.

(DPF: 392)

This is the robust realist scheme developed by critical realism in its initial phase, and already outlined in Chapter 1, but it is then enhanced at 2E by categories associated with absence. What does 2E negativity add? Its concepts span 'the gamut of categories of negativity, contradiction and critique', generating dialectics of 'process, transition, frontier and node, but also generally of opposition including reversal' (DPF: 392). This is the general, broad and multiform view of negativity we have already encountered in Bhaskar's thought. More specifically, 2E negativity does three things that we will focus on here. First, it 'emphasises the tri-unity of causality, space and time in tensed rhythmic spatialising process'; second, it thematises 'the presence of the past'; and third, more generally, it asserts the importance of 'existentially constitutive process' (ibid.). These three elements relate to our preliminary discussion of absence as product and process, and the linkage to the spatio-temporal. Let us take them separately.

Negativity, causality and the spatio-temporal

What does Bhaskar mean by the 'tri-unity of causality, space and time' and what is the salience of locating it in 'tensed rhythmic spatialising process'? The key issue is to see how absence links with causality, space and time in the context of the original critical realist account of natural necessity. A central issue for original critical realism was to provide an account of causation in the world, and Bhaskar now wants to argue that causation involves absenting as process. His premise is that any process of change can be analysed in terms of absenting what was previously in existence in favour of what has now come to be. Every becoming is always also a begoing, or passing away, a process of change. Equally significantly, since causation is closely linked to change, processes of causation are processes of absenting previously given states of being. This means that objects in a dynamic spatio-temporal world are identified as much by what they *were* as by what they now are. Processes of change and causation are central to our understanding of the world, and they are intimately linked to ideas of absence and absenting. Causation concerns change, and change concerns absenting or negating an existing state of affairs. It forms the link between past and present, and it does so by negating or absenting a past state of affairs. There is, then, a basic connection 'between causality and absence. All causal determination, and hence change, is transformative negation or absenting. All causes are in space-time and effects are negations' (DPF: 44). This passage draws together 1M critical realism and 2E negativity. The 1M premise is that being is subject to the reality of causality. The added 2E argument is that causation in the grid of space and time entails change, which involves transformative negation (absenting) of the past to render the present. Reversing the argument, it is also clear that absence and absenting are necessarily grounded in a dynamic spatio-temporal universe on realist premises. Thus, processes of absenting are directly linked, on one side, to causation and change and, on the other, to spatio-temporality, the medium in which causation and change occur.

Bhaskar therefore argues for what he calls 'the tri-unity of causality, space and time' centred on an analysis of change as absenting. On this basis, dialectical critical realism 'extends realism about existence and causality to spatio-temporality, and specifically to realism about tensed spatialising process' (DPF: 250), for space-time is a 'relational property of the meshwork of material beings' (DPF: 53) – that is, beings who are existentially involved in processes of change and becoming. Being in the world is necessarily grounded in space and time, and the emphasis on absence, linking change to the past, present and future, means that being is always a matter of change in the process of becoming. The emphasis on the relation between absence (what is not yet) and presence (what is) underlines the dynamic and material character of a changing world of causes and emergent outcomes. This is a world of 'process, transition, frontier and node' – in short, a world where causation means movement, change, negation and, in general, the absenting in becoming and passing away. That is not to say, however, that dialectical critical realism emphasises becoming at the cost of being. Recall that 2E negativity is a move coming out of 1M material realities. What it does, rather, is to insist on the significance of becoming in relation to being, of change in relation to structure, and of process in relation to product. It is the combination of these terms that signifies the dialecticisation of original critical realism, and leads to the 'fourfold polysemy' of process, product, process-in-product and product-in-process outlined in the previous section.

Here, also, the relevance of *tense* to process becomes important. Accounts of events as past, present or future cannot be understood just in terms of a descriptive comparison of points in time. It is not enough to say that one event took place earlier than, simultaneous with or later than another event (DPF: 210, 251). Past, present and future signify real differences within tensed states, and therefore the irreducibility of space-time and the reality of tense. How are these states defined?

What is past entails that which is already existentially determined or determinate, whether known or not; what is present is the moment of happening or becoming; and what is future is the 'shaped possibility of happening (and of coming to be determined)' (DPF: 252). These states of being must be treated in a complex way, for past, present and future necessarily intermingle, but, at bottom, the reality of tense to process exerts itself. Its truth is seen in what Bhaskar refers to as the irreversibility of time and the impossibility of 'backwards causation' (DPF: 251). Antecedence, and therefore temporality, is 'essential to causality as becoming' (ibid.), while the assumption of backwards causation 'is in fact plausible only on the deprocessualisation of causality' (DPF: 252) – that is, on the false assumption that causality is not embedded in space-time.

What emerges, then, is the tri-unity, the co-embeddedness, of space, time and causality as the material meshwork underpinning the necessary spatio-temporal processuality of being in the world. This grounds the irreversibility of tensed spatialising process, and, finally, the idea of specific 'rhythmics' as tensed spatialising processes of absenting, being, and becoming. Bhaskar explains rhythmics as part of 'the phenomena of *emergent spatio-temporalities* [where] a system of material things . . . establish[es] new "rhythmics", where a rhythmic is just the spatio-temporal efficacy of the process' (DPF: 53). In these terms, a rhythmic appears to be a specific form of process-in-product. In more concrete terms, we might think of specific rhythmics as, for example, the time of a revolution, when process and product seem as one and the process takes on a life of its own, or as the *longue durée* of medieval history, where process appears to be, but is not, absent. It is a specific application of the tri-unity of space, time and causality, lending itself to concrete inquiry as to how processes of change seem in different times to speed up or slow down. Philosophically, the idea of a rhythmic ties causal powers to specific spatio-temporalities, so that 'we could say causality is transformative negation in processual (rhythmic) determination' (DPF: 52). Causality is real, tied to the spatio-temporal and tensed process, and based on the negation or absenting of determinate non-being in a dynamic and rhythmic world. Causality in critical realist terms is a 1M category, but it has a formal and static quality at that level. Bringing out the 2E negativity that lies at the core of every causal process broadens our vision by tying causation and change to space and time. It does this by inserting absence as processual, change-directed absenting at the heart of causality in a caused world. It affirms in consequence our understanding of being as always in process of becoming, of the process at the core of the product.

Development and application: existential constitution and entity relationism

These 2E theorems about the spatio-temporal reality of causality and change, about the importance of tense and the rhythmic quality of geo-history, and about the processual becoming of being have their effect on Bhaskar's philosophy as a whole. In particular, they constitute the basis for the linked ideas of 'the presence of the past' in the present and the future, and more generally that of 'existentially constitutive process'. If we begin with existential constitution, Bhaskar's point is that any entity contains within it, as part of its being, the process that constituted it. Since process is spatio-temporal 'becoming and begoing' (DPF: 54), we are existentially constituted by what is now apparently absent because past. He offers a promissory note for the doubtful:

> In the meantime, for those who doubt the propriety of such a close linkage (and emphasis on spatio-temporal process), just ponder the extent to which emergent social things (people, institutions, traditions) not only presuppose (that is to say, are dependent on) but also are existentially constituted by (as a crucial part of their essence) or merely contain . . . their geo-histories (and, qua empowered, possibilities for their spatialised futures). . . . Constitutive geo-history displayed in contemporary rhythmics or in the processual exercise of accumulated causal powers and liabilities is only one of several ways in which [to] consider the phenomena of the presence of the past (and outside). But just ponder the extent to which although we may live for the future, we live, quite literally, in the past.
>
> (ibid.)

Further, the phenomenon of emergent spatio-temporalities situates 'the possibilities of overlapping, intersecting, condensing, elongated, divergent, convergent and even contradictory rhythmics (causal processes) and, by extension, space-time measures (overthrowing, inter alia, the idea of a unitary set of exclusion relations)' (ibid.). As examples, he suggests 'the amazing and putatively contradictory juxtaposition or condensation of differentially sedimented rhythmics one can find in a city like Los Angeles or New Delhi, where temples, mosques, traditions, religious rites, weddings, inter-caste conflict, electric cables, motor cars, television sets, rickshaws, scavengers and disposable cans coalesce in a locale' (DPF: 55). In these examples, Bhaskar is trying to show how absence, by dynamising critical realist categories, can help us grasp the nature of change under modern conditions. Ideas of material structure, for example, from 1M critical realism remain crucial, but they are aided by a sense of the geo-historical fluidity that 2E thinking based on becoming and passing away brings. Structured being and spatio-temporal becoming, product-in-process and process-in-product are the combinations dialectical critical realism works with.

Existential constitution also takes us into the related theme of 'entity relationism', a conception we will consider further in Chapter 4 in thinking about totality.[11] If a thing is constituted spatio-temporally, it is constituted by its past, but also by those contexts, relations and structures that are part of, but 'outside', it. Geo-history constitutes us in both temporal and spatial terms, for we are all creatures in time and place. The basic idea is of intrinsic connection between an entity and its 'outside', or the co-constitution of entities by the past and the outside, leading to their essential relationality. If a thing is constituted by what lies outside it or in its past, then it is intrinsically related to both. This idea allows a further illustration of existential constitution, this time from my own work on law and responsibility. In brief, Bhaskar's emphasis on the relationality of seemingly separate entities is helpful in thinking beyond the received categories in law and morality concerning the identity of individuals and their responsibility for their acts. Put simply, law works on the basis of concepts that assert individual responsibility as the means and rationale for doing justice. But how do some people come to be those, for example, who commit crimes, and how does this relate to the pasts or the outsides (the environments) that have formed them? Lawyers and philosophers working with law often deploy essentially Kantian modes of thought which permit them to separate off questions of the past and the outside in favour of an isolated vision of the individual, whereas a Bhaskarian emphasis on the co-constitution of agency by present action and the causal effects of the past and the outside suggests another, more critical, problematisation of what responsibility entails. From this point of view, one can profitably see how questions of individual and social responsibility, and then (individual) legal and social justice, are dialectically entwined. Further, one can suggest that the many seemingly 'internal' problems of law are related to the suppression of this 'external' environment. One can achieve a dialectical understanding of how what is 'inside' relates to the denial of the past and the outside by the refusal of a relational analysis (Norrie 2000; 2005a: pt 2). The underlying point is that what we are, our being, must at the same time be related to how we come to be what we are, our becoming, and the tri-unity of causality, time (the effects of our past) and space (the effects of our context) as the meshwork of our material being signposts the relationship between what we are and the processes of our constitution.

The presence of the past

To return to Bhaskar, his examples of the specific structured rhythmic of the modern city anticipate a later section of *Dialectic* where he elaborates on the presence of the past. It assumes four basic forms, one of which has just been elaborated as the 'existential constitution' of beings by their history. Alongside existential constitution, there exists 'co-presence', which involves the coincidence of 'differentially distanciated space-times, established by disjoint, and possibly contradictory, rhythmics' (DPF: 140). An illustration would be the way in which 'rhythmically differentially sedimented structures' become imposed on a single episode, for example where the scion of an aristocratic family is the figurehead for a bourgeois, liberal democratic system, as in the Queen's opening of Parliament in the United Kingdom. The past, Bhaskar writes, 'may be encrusted, embedded in a landscape, say, or as an active part of the present' (DPF: 140). Every time I walk my dog across our local golf course, I encounter the remains of ridge and furrow earthworks from a previous form of agricultural production, privatised by enclosure then brought into the modern public sphere by philanthropic bequest. A third form is what Bhaskar calls 'lagged or delayed efficacy', meaning the way in which the past, not dead but dormant, becomes triggered in the present. Bhaskar suggests that the obvious paradigm here is psychoanalytic explanation, where the present symptom may be related to a suppressed but re-emergent past state. We could also take Marx's famous comment in 'The 18th Brumaire of Louis Bonaparte' on the delayed efficacy of the revolutionary struggle after it had been thought to be defeated: 'Well grubbed, old mole!' (Marx and Engels 1968a: 169). A fourth form relates to the specific experience of agency and its relationship to what has preceded it, to what we could call with a different than usual inflection 'living in the past'. Social structure and human agency presuppose each other, but agency is always constellationally contained in structure so that the agent always treads 'on pre-trodden ground'. She lives in an already pre-constituted world, so that she lives (and acts) 'in the past' *in order to* live and act in the present and for the future.

Finally, it is worth mentioning what Bhaskar has to say about living in the future as well as living in the past. The paradigm of futural action is 'shaped possibility of becoming' (DPF: 142), which rests as much on the past as the future. The past shapes the present and therefore shapes, without determining, possible futures, so that we must see 'there is a sense in which we, and entities generally, may be said to contain possible futures within us, and these may be vital to our being' (DPF: 143). But these possible futures 'are so qua product-in-process, that is as possibilities existentially constituted by their geo-histories' (ibid.). Therefore, there is a sense 'in which the most interesting case of the present as a future is mediated by, or even *dependent* upon the presence of the past' (ibid.). More generally, the future is always prefigured in human action, always present to us, since intentional agency is necessarily oriented to the future, which is 'the intentional object of every act' (DPF: 144).

These accounts of the interrelated reality of absence with the tri-unity of space, time and causality, together with the irreducibility of spatio-temporality, leading to existential constitution, entity relationism and the presence of the past in both the present and the future are all founded on an insistence that we think in terms of the role of absence in processes of change and causation, of the constellational dynamic of being and becoming. It is absence as becoming that links human being to its past and its outside, because to be in process of change is to be linked in the present to the past, and, in a structured material world, to the contexts that fashion us and which we in turn fashion. They rest upon a fourfold account of absence, as we have seen, as product (absence in a thing), process (absenting), product-in-process and process-in-product. All of this relates to a sense of the importance of absence in shaping presence, showing how a (2E) sense of a dynamic and changing processual world affects a (1M) *structured* environment. It is the various ways in which being and becoming can be understood as the different facets of ontology that lie at the core of Bhaskar's argument.

The primacy of absence

Such is the basic argument, but is it appropriate to place so much weight on absence? It might be accepted that becoming involves the passing away or absenting of a state of being, but it might be suggested that it is the positive emergence of the new that is of real interest. Why not speak simply of the emergence of things as new positivities in the world? Why emphasise negativity or absence in a thing over the positivity and presence it possesses? If we do, how far should the emphasis go, and what is the relationship between the absent and the present, or the negative and the positive? The idea that we see the positive as a tiny ripple on the surface of a sea of negativity, albeit an important one (DPF: 5), suggests that the stick is bent very firmly in favour of absence, but is this justified? In this section, I consider these questions by focusing more precisely on Bhaskar's argument for the primacy of absence, and by analysing four different points he makes in absence's favour. He sets these out as follows:

> (1) that we can refer to non-being, (2) that non-being exists, and that (3) not only must it be conceded that non-being has ontological priority over being within zero-level being, (4) but, further, non-being has ontological *priority* over being. In short, negativity wins.
>
> (DPF: 39)

Looking at these claims, the first two are not especially problematic from a realist perspective. The first argument (1) is a simple epistemological one, that non-being can be referred to, and this is conjoined with (2), its ontological counterpart. Both (1) and (2) are entailed by critical realism, for, epistemologically, concepts must refer to something beyond themselves if realism is to be satisfied. Similarly, ontologically, that which is referred to must also exist. These are relatively straightforward arguments, satisfied, for example, by noting that it often makes sense to say that the absence of a thing is relevant to a causal explanation, and that such an explanation would be incomplete without referring to what is not there.[12] Claims (3) and (4) are more problematic. Bhaskar wants to argue (3) that within an overall sense of being – that is, one that includes both what exists and what is absent ('zero-level being') – non-being has priority over being. And he wants to argue (4) that there is a *further* ontological sense, a deeper one, in which non-being has ultimate priority. How does Bhaskar argue for these claims? In the main, it seems to me that he argues more for (3) than for (4), so let us begin with (3) and then turn to (4). To anticipate my conclusion, I shall argue that the arguments for (3) are compelling, and they are the ones Bhaskar needs to make in order to defend the centrality he gives to absence. Ultimately, they rely on the idea of 'constellationality' that he develops in his account of totality. The argument for (4) makes intuitive philosophical sense, but it seems to be of limited relevance, relating as it does to the world only in a 'counterfactual' way.

Absence and presence: mutual entailment or priority of absence?

The initial arguments for (3) are in essence along the lines of claims that one cannot grasp the nature of any entity without seeing what it is not, as well as what it is. Whether these make an argument for the *priority* of non-being over being, rather than for the lesser claim of mutual entailment, is doubtful, but let us follow the argument. Bhaskar begins with two arguments about the role of absence in the identification of an entity. Identification of a thing is a human act, and absents a previous state of non-identification, indicating that absenting is central to a basic human cognitive process. At first sight, this seems a strange way of putting things, because identifying something is most naturally expressed as a positive act, but I think the point is right: that the positive and the negative coexist in any act of identification. Identification, in positively identifying, absents a previous stage of non-identification. It changes the world in both positive and negative terms, but note that this suggests a relationship of mutual entailment, not one of priority, between the terms.

Similarly, moving from the act of identification to the object identified, Bhaskar makes a parallel argument. This is that we can only grasp objects in thought by reflecting on what they are not, as well as on what they are. The specificity of objects depends upon their existence in a material space-time grid, and such a grid is composed of both absences and presences. The 'shape' of an object in the world is governed by its present coordinates, and these define both its 'inside' and its 'outside', the object and its ground, what it is and is not. Objects in a spatio-temporal world are shaped as much by what they *are not* and, emphasising their temporality, what they *were* (i.e. are not now) as by what they now are. A third argument is that we can talk about the role of absence (non-being) in relation to change. Here, Bhaskar argues that any causal determination, and hence change, is an example of transformative negation or absenting – that is, it absents what was previously there, in the formation of what now exists. Change produces something new, positive and present, but it also absents a previously existing state of affairs which is relegated to the past, the old, the absent, the no longer there. Change transforms by negating what an entity was; it involves its transformative negation.

These three arguments all concern the role of absence – in the (epistemological) act of identification, in the (ontological) constitution of objects and in the (practical) causal changing of such objects. We have already encountered the last two in the previous section. They all seem to me to be true, but limited in what they establish, and one-sided in the way they are put. Taking one-sidedness first, identification of an object *does* negate a previous state of non-identification. The spatio-temporal coordination of an object *does* depend on what it is (and was) not. Every process of causal changing *is* an absenting of a previous state of affairs. But at the same time, every act of identification is just that, a positive act. And every object depends as much on what it is as on what it is or was not. Similarly, every act of transformative negation (causal changing) is also the creation of something new and present. In other words, while it makes sense to bring out the negative in these situations, it does not make sense to exclude the positive at the same time. This points to what I see as the limited nature of these arguments: they do not establish priority of the negative, only the mutual entailment of negative and positive. Bhaskar in fact seems to accept this. He acknowledges that though we can only know the positive through the negative, 'the converse is equally the case' (DPF: 47). He states that the 'identification of positive existents depends upon a changing (and therefore at least ontologically bivalent) world' (DPF: 45). I agree, but the establishing of ontological bivalence (a world with both presence and absence) is not the same as establishing the *priority* of the negative over the positive. Rather, it argues for the importance of the relation of mutual entailment between positivity and negativity. Priority of one over the other would need something more, and Bhaskar has not yet supplied it.

In a later discussion of negativity,[13] Bhaskar returns to this issue with an argument that does go further, and it involves the concept of 'constellationality'. There he writes initially of the 'mutual dependency of the positive and the negative' in terms that confirm mutual entailment rather than priority, and he also accentuates the role the positive plays vis-à-vis the negative. Any 'determinate transformative negation' (i.e. real absenting) depends on positive social and natural material resources and structures in order to produce a particular outcome. The fruits of the negative work their way out through and in relation to the positive. This accentuation of the positive as a counterbalance to the previous insistence on the negative is instructive as to Bhaskar's overall view, but he still argues for the priority of the negative, in two ways. First, he suggests that processual transformation is overall a process of negation (the negation of a negation); and second, more importantly, he proposes that 'the positive is radically *constituted* by the negative qua formative process and [by] the presence of the absent in the guise of the past and outside' (DPF: 241). From this point of view, the 'apparent duality [of being and non-being] is dependent upon a negatively charged asymmetry' (ibid.), which works in favour of absence. There is a 'negative residue or trace structure, an absent in a present, never co-identical with itself' (ibid.) that is always at work behind and within the positive. The positive is, in short, always beholden to the negative in a way that gives the latter priority. Being, we might say, is always in debt for its present and future shape to processes of change and becoming (absenting), which act on what it is not, or not yet (what is presently absent).

The argument is that whatever a present or positive may be, it is always embedded in what it is not. There is a negative charge, residue or trace structure that occupies a position in relation to the positive and that fundamentally conditions, shapes or affects what the positive is, and will become. The positive remains irreducible to the negative, but is nonetheless intrinsically reliant on it. The asymmetry of positive and negative seems at first glance to favour the positive, because that is what we immediately see. However, the contingency and transience, the incessant movement, in the positive indicate that it is always in debt to what it at any one time lacks. What you see is *not* what you get, for processes of becoming, which transform and negate, reflect what is lacking in things. Processes of becoming respond to what is absent by absenting them. They *absent absences*, hence the overall sense of a negative process of negating a negation. Product and process are irreducible and co-entailing, but absence is present in both. It is present in process since becoming is always also begoing, and in product because the dynamic of 'production' (the development of product-in-process) is one that is inflected by what is lacking. A process of becoming, as R. G. Collingwood put it, 'is conceivable only if that which is yet unrealised is affecting the process as a goal towards which it is directed' (1945: 83). Being or product in a dynamic material world can only respond to what is absent in it, so that absence retains a certain priority.

In this regard, the negative can be said to contain the positive in the figure of what Bhaskar calls 'the constellational', the dialectical concept associated with totality we have already mentioned, and return to in Chapter 4. In it, one term is said to be contained within another, while retaining its significance and distinction. For example, as between being (ontology) and thought (epistemology), there is a constellational identity in which thought retains its vital import in human life, but must be recognised both as contained within the englobing term of being and as its emergent and distinct element. Thought is constellationally *overreached* by being (DPF: 115), while retaining its distinction from it.[14] As with thought and being, so with presence and absence. 'What is' exists within the broader realm of what is lacking, 'what is not'. It emerges in response to what is absent, changes and works its way out in relation to it. It is therefore overreached by it, and absence has priority over presence within an overall, 'zero-sum' sense of being. By this, Bhaskar means a sense of being as the totalised whole of being and non-being in their constellational relation. The priority of absence stems from the fact that in a dynamic world, there is always more to come than what presently exists, and, given that what is presently absent shapes what is to come, this gives it priority. What is present to us may look compelling, but its presence as well as its future is powerfully shaped by what it lacks. Absence always exercises its hidden power through shaping what is, and making it move on, become what it is not. It is observed in absenting process (becoming), but also in existing product (being), and this conditions, shapes or determines how absenting occurs. This gives us the dialectical realist formula of the absenting of absence and gives absence its asymmetric priority over presence.

Counterfactual priority?

Up to this point, we have been seeking to establish point (3) of the four points Bhaskar makes on the priority of absence. This allows us to accept the mutual entailment of presence and absence, and to see the latter as having an overall influence in their relationship. Presence is constellationally contained within absence. There was, however, a deeper sense (point 4) of a *general* ontological priority for absence which has not yet been broached. Bhaskar's argument is as follows. A world without voids (absences) would be one in which nothing could move or occur: absences are transcendentally necessary features of an intelligible material object world. A 'packed' world without absence is therefore impossible, but there is, in contrast, no a priori reason to exclude the opposite, a world that is a total void. Negativity is constitutively essential to positivity, but not vice versa. 'Non-being is a condition of possibility of being. . . . But there is no logical incoherence in totally not-being' (DPF: 46). In contrast, in 'a totally compacted space, i.e. a space without spaces, material objects . . . could not move, so that the Cartesian–Newtonian paradigm of action' (DPF: 239) would be fatally flawed. Whereas voids 'are necessary for motion, and motion necessary for causality and hence change over time' (ibid.), neither motion nor substance is conceptually necessary for voids. We can make sense of a world with nothing positive in it, a total void, but we cannot make sense of one with things in it that do not also contain voids. Not only would such a world defeat the Cartesian–Newtonian paradigm, it would also, shifting contexts, make human communication impossible. Thus, a sentence without absences, pauses or spaces would be unintelligible, so that 'absence is a condition of any intelligibility at all' (DPF: 240), whereas a world without sentences or intelligibility – a world without humans as we know them – can be imagined.

In part, Bhaskar's argument for the out and out priority of absence does no more than re-establish the import of absence for presence, their mutual entailment, but it also argues for logical precedence. We can imagine 'the void', but we cannot imagine its converse, a purely positive world, so that in the last analysis negativity must prove the state that has ontological priority and 'wins'. The argument has, I think, an intuitive plausibility, but the question then is what to do with it. As Bhaskar says, his argument is 'counterfactual', so that '[w]ithin the world as we know it, non-being is at least on a par with being' (DPF: 47). We could agree with the thought experiment on the priority of absence, but why make it if we must always return to a world in which positivity exists on a par with absence? Perhaps it reinforces the general sense of the significance of absence, but the argument for the irreducible relationality of negativity and positivity, with the constellational overreach of the negative, where absence also wins, seems to me more important and to be sufficient to achieve what Bhaskar needs. As he himself says, 'All of this could be summed up by saying that in dialectical critical realism *the negative constellationally overreaches the positive*' (DPF: 242). In terms of points (3) and (4) in his initial arguments, it seems to me that this makes (3) the important one: to establish the *this-worldly* primacy of absence, and Bhaskar makes a good case for it. What is needed is a sense of the incessant play of absence, negativity, non-being on the structure of present and positive being in a dynamic material world, where the absent will continue to shape the present through absenting process.

A final example from Bhaskar's own philosophical practice may illustrate the point. The third main aim of *Dialectic*, it will be recalled from Chapter 1, was to submit the western philosophical tradition to a metacritique, and this was to be based upon its historic failure to understand absence, leading to a general failure to resolve its problems.[15] Western philosophy is, in consequence, deeply contradictory and unstable. It is, then, because absence is 'the missing metacategory par excellence' that dialectical critical realism must, according to Bhaskar, investigate the '*systematic intermingling* of categories, concepts, critiques and figures rather than a unilinear procession' (DPF: 184) in western philosophy. Note what this means: it is the messy, diffused reality of what philosophy says and does not say, based on the absence of a valid concept of absence, that is worth metacritical investigation – not absence per se. In Bhaskar's own practice, it is the determinate philosophical reality, and the interplay between positive (what it says) and negative (does not say) elements within it, that is important. The determinate, emergent reality that is modern philosophy is driven for Bhaskar by a dynamic that has at its core an absence – absence itself. As he says in connection with Hegel:

> Hegel was fond of saying that the essence of dialectic was seeing the positive in the negative. . . . For us, it is more correct to say that it is to see *the negative in the positive*, the absent in the present, the ground in the figure, the periphery in the centre, the content obscured by the form, the living masked by the dead.
>
> (DPF: 241)

This seems to me to be the core relevance of absence for Bhaskar's dialectic. It is based on a constellational relation between absence and presence in which mutual entailment is to the fore. Yet, as I have also argued, absence has a certain primacy, for it is absence, the absence of absence in western philosophy, that shapes the development of philosophy. The philosophically counterfactual argument as to the primacy of absence perhaps serves to affirm this relationship, but it is the relationship between absence and presence that remains crucial. Bhaskar is not, as he says, 'primarily concerned with nothing or nothingness, but with *real determinate non-being*' (DPF: 239), and this term already discloses a relation between what is (the determinate) and what is not (non-being). For Bhaskar, negativity definitely wins, but not as an abstract, other-worldly, metaphysical form of being.[16]

This illustration from Bhaskar's own philosophical practice in his metacritique neatly moves us to the final section of this chapter, in which I outline the concept at the heart of that critique, the philosophical denial of absence that he calls ontological monovalence. Before getting there, however, I wish briefly to consider some objections to Bhaskar's argument offered by Alex Callinicos.

Criticisms of Bhaskar's account

Callinicos has written that Bhaskar's claims for absence lack sufficient argument and presage his 'later lapse into spiritualism' (2006: 196). In a debate between the two in 2002, Callinicos asks 'what kind of philosophical argument does [Bhaskar give] for the ontological priority of absence over presence?' (Bhaskar and Callinicos 2003: 94). He suggests that 'unless I've missed something', the closest Bhaskar comes to defending his position is in just three sentences:

> the identification of a positive existent is a human act. So it involves the absenting of a pre-existent state of affairs, be it only a state of existential doubt. This may be taken as a transcendental deduction of the category of absence, and a transcendental refutation and immanent critique of ontological monovalence.
>
> (DPF: 44)

Callinicos did in fact miss quite a lot. He missed the language of philosophers and of everyday life, which is redolent with forms of absence, the crucial analysis of causation in terms of negation, absenting, becoming and begoing, and the constitution of things by what they are not. He missed the four different claims Bhaskar makes for absence which we discussed above. One might also ask what precisely is wrong substantively with the three sentences Callinicos quotes as a way of establishing the reality (though not the priority) of absence, apart from the fact that he does it in three sentences. In part, Callinicos's concern may hinge upon what is meant by a transcendental argument, which I consider in a moment.

A further concern Callinicos has is that speaking of absence as Bhaskar does opens the door to illicit spiritualism. The 'priority of negation or absence or not-being . . . is established by an appeal to the role of human agency in absent*ing* things', and this gives human beings an illicit, spiritual role in relation to the world 'since the thesis is meant to apply to the physical as well as the social world' (Callinicos 2006: 196). Since *Dialectic* has to do with 'physics, cosmology and so forth, there is something problematic about making an essential ontological category depend upon freedom, because freedom is a property of agents', and once 'we define absence, . . . as a fundamental ontological category, in terms of freedom, we're making human agency in some sense paradigmatic of reality itself' (Bhaskar and Callinicos 2003: 95). This argument illicitly conflates critical realist dialectics in the natural and social worlds. In this book, I concentrate on what I take to be the main focus of *Dialectic*, its role in the social world, but it is true that many of the arguments Bhaskar deploys would be relevant *mutatis mutandis* (but there is the rub) in the natural world too. It cannot be forgotten that at the core of critical realism is an insistence that the natural and social worlds must be treated in terms of what they have in common *and* what makes them different (see Chapter 1). In the social world, of course, human agency must be at the core of critical realist concerns, both original and dialectical. Causal processes that entail absenting occur in both the natural and the social worlds, but in the latter (and in humans' interactions with nature), human agency as causal and absentive is central. This, of course, is not the case in the natural world taken by itself, so that human agency as absenting *is* central to Bhaskar's *Dialectic*, but only in its proper place.

An underlying problem in this is the role of transcendental argument, as Callinicos sees it, in *Dialectic*. For him, Bhaskar's use of such argument seeks a degree of ontological certitude in the manner of Kant's transcendental idealism (Bhaskar and Callinicos 2003: 93), whereas all that Bhaskar can in truth provide is an understanding of ontology based on accounts of scientific practice which are open to 'rival interpretations' (Callinicos 2006: 159). It would therefore 'seem better to strip away the transcendental superstructure that obscures what is interesting and original in Bhaskar's work and offer it simply as a philosophical presentation of the world as revealed to us by the sciences' (ibid.), which could be wrong. In this spirit, the validity of talking about ontology is that, following Quine, all theories make ontological commitments (Callinicos 2006: 160). All this, however, is precisely Bhaskar's point, and indicates the nub of his transcendental realist argument. Scientific theories, and, importantly, human practices more generally, cannot escape ontology. In his response to Callinicos, Bhaskar made the point that a transcendental realist argument did no more than start with what its opponents were prepared to grant as a matter of fact or importance about the world, and then ask what could be deduced from it (Bhaskar and Callinicos 2003: 98–9). There is no 'transcendental superstructure' to Bhaskar's philosophy, only arguments about what the world must be like for a variety of things to be possible in it. Transcendental arguments in this regard share many similarities with other modes of argument such as immanent or dialectical critique, and indeed explanations in science themselves. All such arguments say, 'we have a certain phenomenon or a position which someone is holding, let's see what must be the case for that phenomenon or position to be possible' (Bhaskar and Callinicos 2003: 97).[17]

Ontological monovalence and metacritique

The preceding sections have outlined Bhaskar's use of absence in his dialectical philosophy as the basic 2E dialectical operation he performs on original 1M critical realism's account of being as natural necessity. Bhaskar has always been a philosopher of and for the natural and (especially in his dialectical philosophy) social sciences, and the illustrations of the second section show how the dialectical philosophy connects with the latter. However, Bhaskar is also a philosopher concerned with the nature of western philosophy as a whole, and he is also a philosopher of ethics, and his argument in his dialectical work is that it is possible to create a philosophical system based on absence that can reach into these areas too. In this section, we look at Bhaskar's account of ontological monovalence, the argument that absence has been excluded from the western philosophical tradition, generating many of its problems. The aim is to prepare the ground for discussion in later chapters, for Bhaskar's account of ontological monovalence and his metacritique of western philosophy is taken up in Chapters 6 and 7, but I also want to make clear the link between absence and Bhaskar's metacritique. Whereas up to now we have seen how absence should become a part of philosophy in order to ground a sense of becoming in the being of the world, in the metacritique we examine the stasis that accompanies a failure to comprehend absence, and the reasons, themselves based upon absence, why an account of absence should be absent. Here, we are looking, first, at the denial of real absence in the western philosophical tradition through a doctrine of ontological monovalence, which is the orthodox negative counterpoint to Bhaskar's innovative affirmation of its significance. Linked to this, however, is Bhaskar's metacritique in a sense of the geo-historical conditions that sustain ontological monovalence.

What is ontological monovalence?

In the first chapter, we noted *en passant* that Bhaskar associates absence with a key problem in western philosophy going back to the Greeks, Parmenides and Plato that he calls 'ontological monovalence'. This is defined as 'a purely positive account of reality' (DPF: 400), by which Bhaskar means an account in which absence has been denied. Pressing on the significance of absence therefore provides a 'critical cutting edge' aimed at 'the Parmenidean doctrine of ontological monovalence, the Platonic analysis of negation and change in terms of difference and the Kantian analysis of negative into positive predicates' (DPF: 392). In the light of critical realism's ontological commitments, absence is real and determinate, as we have seen. It really exists in the world, but western philosophy has typically little to say about it. In so far as it deals with it at all, it takes its cue from the pre-Socratic Parmenides, who issued a stern command:

> Never will this prevail, that what is not is –
> bar your thought from this road of inquiry.
>
> (Barnes 1987: 82)

Behind this was a conservative desire to protect the status quo from fundamental change, for if not-being existed, it implied change in things, their rise and fall. Denying not-being established the essential unchangeability of being:

> One story, one road, now
> is left: that it is. And on this there are signs
> aplenty that, being, it is ungenerated and indestructible. . . .
> Thus generation is quenched and perishing unheard of. . . .
> generation and destruction have been banished far away. . . .
>
> (Barnes 1987: 82–3)

Now, in Bhaskar's analysis, Parmenides set in train a way of thinking about absence that was fateful for western philosophy. Crucial here was Plato, who responded to this prohibition on talk of not-being by its sideways acceptance and accommodation. He suggested that not-being could exist, but only because it could be analysed in terms of difference – that is, in terms of different forms of positive being that were not the same as each other.[18] Among the moderns, Kant avoids absence by arguing that a negative predication of an object can be recast in positive terms. Bhaskar's response to this is to argue that recasting the negative as a positive may miss its true sense, which reflects a reality not caught in the positive restatement: 'Pierre's absence from the café doesn't *mean* the same as his presence at home' (DPF: 7). Of course, Plato's and Kant's are not the last words on absence. More recently, and more promisingly for Bhaskar, Sartre distinguishes a sense of negativity in the world (*négatité*), which he finds interesting. This differs from an abstract metaphysical conception of nothing or nothingness such as Heidegger's, which Bhaskar would reject, but Sartre ties *négatité* to human consciousness and experience.[19] For Bhaskar, that would be only one form of determinate negativity, and does not capture its broader significance, as ontological absence in the world. Generally, negativity is associated with the dialectical tradition, but this has been linked, after Hegel, to operations of reason, logic and mind. This ultimately includes phenomenological approaches such as Sartre's, so that a full ontological sense of real determinate absence is lacking there too.

If these classical and modern approaches fail to ground an understanding of real absence, they participate either actively or by default in a doctrine of onto-logical monovalence – that is, they accept that reality is composed of one kind of 'thing', the present or the positive, that which is and which lacks real absence. Not only is this wrong in itself, it also acts to deny or sequester the possibility of real change, for it obscures the true nature of cause and effect as processual and absenting. It obscures those things that a grasp of absence enables, in particular an understanding of real causality and change in the world. A purely positive account of reality cannot ultimately consider how the world might change in fundamental ways, because it cannot grasp that radical futures containing what is absent in the present or the past might emerge into being in the future. It therefore legitimates the way things are. The spirit of Parmenides lives on, for his bar on thinking not-being, with its explicit rejection of generation and perishing, remains tacitly or actively in place. In short, Bhaskar argues that a purely positive account of reality is '[f]atally flawed by the transcendental deduction of the necessity for real negation or absence' (DPF: 401), and it acts 'ideologically to screen the epistemological and ontological contingency of being and to sequester existential questions generally'. The result is that it 'dogmatic-ally reinforce[s the] positivisation of knowledge, and eternalisation of the status quo' (ibid.). Against ontological monovalence, Bhaskar argues for 'ontological bivalence – or better, polyvalence' (DPF: 400–1) – that is, a sense of the world constructed out of the absent as well as the present, together with potentially other modes of being which possess different kinds of valency, or no valency at all.[20]

From this brief account, we can see two things. First, that ontological mono-valence is in Bhaskar's view deeply embedded as a failing in western philosophy. Second, there is the implication that this is linked to a dynamic of thinking *and power*, for the doctrine of ontological monovalence has a conservative effect on our understanding of the possibility of change. Let us briefly explore these two claims a little further.

Ontological monovalence in western philosophy

As regards the first claim, the substance of the argument is better left to Chapter 6, but it is worthwhile simply to sketch its outline. Broadly, Bhaskar wants to take the original 1M critical realism from Chapter 1 and to extend its critique of philosophy in two ways. First, he wants to argue that problems of modern philosophy, which were also his focus in his earlier work, need to be set in a longer timescale than he previously allowed. Original critical realism had as its target ontological actualism, the epistemic fallacy and the denial of natural necessity in the philosophies of the Enlightenment, the line of argument that included Descartes, Locke, Leibniz, Hume and Kant. Dialectical critical realism now sees the initial problems as lying further back in the western tradition, with Parmenides, Plato and Aristotle. The 'squeeze' on natural necessity begins with the ancients at what Bhaskar now calls the 'Platonic–Aristotelian fault-line'. This sees Aristotle as already caught in 'a vice' between Plato and Hume, and the moderns as simply giving a new turn to an old problematic: the denial of natural necessity.[21]

Second, Bhaskar wants to argue for a deeper philosophical problem within the tradition than those already identified within original critical realism. Whereas previously he identified ontological actualism and the epistemic fallacy as bars on the grasp of natural necessity, dialectical critical realism sees these errors as undergirded by the denial of absence, in the doctrine of ontological monovalence. In my view of his argument, it is this which, starting with the ancients, encourages ontological actualism and the compensatory epistemic fallacy to obscure natural necessity. The denial of ontological absence leads to the actualist denial of ontological depth and stratification and, with them, the other associated problems that structure western philosophy. Bhaskar now argues that there are 'two mutually reinforcing category mistakes' (DPF: 357) that inform its development: ontological actualism and the epistemic fallacy on the one hand and ontological monovalence on the other. What is the relationship between them? Does the one give rise to the other, or vice versa? How are they connected? As I have said, I think Bhaskar's argument is that ontological monovalence prefigures the other problems by encouraging ontological actualism. As we shall see, however, he is not entirely clear on this matter. One aim in Chapter 6 will therefore be to consider how the discovery of ontological monovalence integrates with original critical realism's 1M critique of western philosophy's ontological actualism and the epistemic fallacy.

Philosophy and power relations: metacritique

Taking now the second tack in Bhaskar's critique of ontological monovalence, the relationship to power, critical realism thinks of philosophical critique in two ways. First, there are the philosophical methods of immanent and transcendental critique which start from where a theory is, and develop a further position or thought in relation to it. Second, it develops an explanatory critique of the grounds that may create and sustain the error in thought that immanent and transcendental critique have uncovered. Both types of critique seek to move thinking on to a further position in relation to the original material; they do not involve simple modification in the initial account. For this reason, they can both be described as forms of 'metacritique'. Sometimes Bhaskar writes simply of metacritique, but he uses the term more precisely to distinguish metacritique$_1$ from metacritique$_2$. In a philosophical critique, a point of inconsistency or absence is identified, and this is taken up in a metacritique$_1$, which identifies a ground or reason underlying an absence or inconsistency and seeks to correct it. In a metacritique$_2$, the absence is additionally explained in terms of some more general problem to be found in the world associated with the theoretical problem. The latter aligns metacritique with investigation of the connection between modes of thinking and more general modes of being in a particular socio-historical environment. With regard to the specific problem of ontological monovalence in the western philosophical tradition, Bhaskar discovers this by metacritique$_1$ of that tradition,[22] and then raises the question as to what a metacritique$_2$ of the problem should look like.

Here, Bhaskar introduces to his analysis an understanding of the impact of historical power structures on western philosophy, and, through them, another important level at which we have to identify absence and its importance to philosophy. What underlies and grounds ontological monovalence within the philosophical tradition is that tradition's embeddedness in structured power relations, what Bhaskar calls 'power$_2$ relations' or, in a more metaphorical usage, 'generalised master–slave-type relations'. The idea of power$_2$ relations draws upon a contrast with power$_1$, which is the capacity intrinsic to the concept of action to effect change. It indicates in general the power in action which is 'the capacity to get one's way', whereas power$_2$ involves getting one's way 'against either the overt wishes and/or the real interests of others in virtue of structures of exploitation, domination, subjugation and control' (DPF: 402) – that is, in virtue of 'generalised master–slave-type relations'. We shall return to precisely why Bhaskar should use the latter terminology,[23] but for the meantime it is only important to see how he draws together the existence of *geo-historical* absence, in the shape of social relations of denial and exploitation in western societies, with absence *within its philosophical tradition*. When Plato and Parmenides denied the negative in western thinking, they did so out of a ruler's concern to rule, and to deny the possibility of fundamental change, the generation of the new and the destruction of the old. A purely positive account of philosophy in which 'what you see is what you get' safeguards against change and in so doing reflects 'a class-divided and sundered society' (DPF: 356). The denial of real absence, metacritically$_1$ identified as a problem in philosophy, is metacritically$_2$ related to the material ground of generalised master–slave or power$_2$ relations.[24]

In conclusion, the metacritical identification of absence with both philosophical critique (what is lacking in philosophy) and structured power relations (what is lacking in a world that can generate such a philosophy) reveals that an account of philosophy should be written at two levels. There is first the level of the problems it sets itself but fails to overcome (metacritique$_1$), and second the level of the relationship between philosophical argument and social relations (metacritique$_2$). Because absence is present in both geo-history and philosophy, it is the key to drawing these two levels together. In a world where power$_2$ seeks to maintain the status quo, with all the negativity and absence this entails, philosophy has become a means of denial that this is the case. Absence in the world is linked to its denial in philosophy. A key aspect of the philosophical understanding of that world that must therefore be overcome (absented) is the denial (absence) of absence in the development of being. To deny absence through the philosophy of ontological monovalence is to deny the philosophical understanding of the possibility of real change in a power$_2$-dominated world. To affirm absence through a theory of ontological bi- or polyvalence is a way of addressing repetitive problems of modern philosophy, but also of identifying the underlying reasons and grounds for their existence, and, to that extent, moving to absent them.

Conclusion

In Chapter 1, we saw that Bhaskar identified three main aims of, and four principal elements in, dialectical critical realism. The three main aims were the dialecticisation of critical realism, the renovation of dialectics on critical realist ground, and the development of a general metacritique of western philosophy based on the achievement of the first and the second aims. Of these three aims, it is the first and the third that have been developed in this chapter. The second, the critical realist innovation of dialectic, will be considered in the next.

As for dialectical critical realism's four principal elements, these were (1M) non-identity, (2E) negativity, (3L) totality and (4D) ethical agency. In this chapter, it was (2E) negativity that played the main part, operating as the means to bring absence to bear on the existing understanding of natural necessity supported by original (1M) critical realism. In consequence, the aim of this chapter was to analyse the idea of absence and its near-synonyms, and then to develop the analysis by thinking of how absence operates both as a mode of (non-)being, absence as noun, and as a mode of activity associated with being, absenting as verb. Thus, we get the idea of a relationship between being and becoming, or one between being as 'product' and becoming as 'process'. From there we moved to think about how these were not separate elements. Being involves becoming, for product is always in process, and becoming is always attached to being, for process is always in relation to product.

In examining the relationship between being and becoming, we can now see that it will include being-in-becoming and becoming-in-being to reflect the 'fourfold polysemy' of product and process discussed at the end of the first main section. Just as product and process shadow being and becoming, so do product-in-process and process-in-product have their counterparts. In this light, we can appreciate that our initial foray into being and becoming in Chapter 1 was more limited than it should be. 2E negativity certainly brings the idea of processual becoming as absenting and change to bear on 1M being as natural necessity, as developed in original critical realism. But 2E negativity is not just processual becoming as absenting to counterpose to being. It is also present in being, as the determinate non-being which, in a dynamic material world, shapes and gives direction to the evolution of being. Negativity is always already present in being as becoming-in-being or process-in-product, as that which gives it its possible future trajectory. What being lacks shapes what being is and the ensuing dynamic of what it will become, so that being is always about both absence in the sense of the non-being within it, and absenting, in the sense of the becoming that ensues.

The idea of a 2E negative edge brought to bear on original 1M critical realism was introduced at the end of this chapter's first main section, and explored in depth in the second. There the tri-unity of causality, space and time emphasised the significance of becoming, process and change to being as the existential core of natural necessity. In a dynamic material world, the core of natural necessity is causality, and causality is intrinsically spatio-temporal, so that the 'material meshwork' of being is always linked to absence in process of becoming. Our rootedness in material time and space, and therefore our geo-historical nature, means that tense is real and it generates differential rhythmics of process-in-product as the medium of life. We are always constituted within spatio-temporal contours, generating a sense of our intrinsic relatedness to the past and also (what appears to be) 'the outside'. We are what we are because of those things that we are not (the causal context 'outside' us), and because of what we were (the past). We are at any given time product-in-process, while living our lives exemplifies process-in-product, just as we are being that is becoming, and exemplify the spatio-temporal becoming that is in our being.

The claim that absence is crucial to presence, or the negative to the positive, was examined in some depth in the third main section of the chapter. There, we took up the idea that absence as not-being is within presence, so that negativity is not the simple becoming suggested in Chapter 1. Here we saw that the idea of determinate non-being already indicates a relationship of mutual entailment between being and not-being, for the idea of determinacy suggests those points where absence and presence meet in an entity. It is this contact between the positive and the negative that gives us the *determinacy* both of non-being and of positive being alike. Determinate non-being *implies* mutual entailment. Yet, at the same time, I agree with Bhaskar's prioritisation of non-being in that it is the absence in being in a dynamic world that constitutes the lack that points to the possibility of change. It does not, I think, determine change – that would be too strong a claim – but it does indicate the absence or lack to which determinate change is oriented. This is the 'negatively charged asymmetry', the 'negative residue or trace structure, an absent in a present' (DPF: 241), as Bhaskar describes the priority of absence. Such a priority of absence does not, however, in my view get us quite as far as seeing 'the positive as a tiny, but important, ripple on the surface of a sea of negativity' (DPF: 5).

Finally, the development of 2E negativity represents a crucial starting point for our understanding of Bhaskar's third main aim in *Dialectic*, the development of a fundamental critique of the trajectory of western philosophy. If real absence or non-being should be seen as central to the nature of being, then the western philosophical tradition is marked by a specific and corresponding absence: absence itself. Bhaskar calls this denial of absence 'ontological monovalence', a one-valued ontology recognising only what is, and not what is not. The failure to grasp the import of absence is fateful for western philosophy, generating its primary problem fields and unresolved dilemmas. But this is not simply a problem in a mode of thought. It is also itself related to an outside, to spatio-temporal, or geo-historical, practice, and, anticipating ideas from Chapter 4 on the nature of social totality, it is one that is associated with the history of the west and its underlying power$_2$, or generalised master–slave-type, relations. The absence of absence is a problem in philosophy diagnosed by metacritical$_1$ philosophical analysis, but also a problem in western society identified by metacritical$_2$ analysis of philosophy's link to power$_2$ relations. This links the denial of absence in thought to a world where the absence of a full sense of freedom (described below in Chapter 5) endures down the millennia. This is not a coincidence.

In a way, this last point can be used to unify Bhaskar's analysis of absence, for it is the idea of philosophy as operating in a geo-historical context that fundamentally lacks emancipation that leads to the denial of absence. A world where the absence of human emancipatory possibilities must be legitimated is precisely the kind of world where philosophy, with its power$_2$ commitments from the time of the Greeks, must play its part. The absence at the heart of western societies, which drives them forward through successive forms of master–slave-type relations, is precisely the thing that philosophy finds the hardest to comprehend. Indeed, it is precisely the thing, absence, in its very concept, that philosophy has sought to suppress. Parmenides and Plato knew what they were doing when they barred talk of non-being for its link to 'generation and perishing', and then finessed its significance through an account of absence as difference. Bhaskar's reinstatement of absence is thus a metacritical$_1$ step in the direction of addressing specific problems within philosophy, and also, by identifying the metacritical$_2$ link between philosophy and western geo-history, a means of addressing the broader historical condition.

3   Diffracting dialectic

Of Bhaskar's three main aims in *Dialectic*, we now turn to the second, the recasting of dialectic on the ground of critical realism. If the first aim was 'the dialectical enrichment and deepening of critical realism', and the third is 'the outline of the elements of a totalising critique of western philosophy, in its various (including hitherto dialectical) forms', the second is 'the development of a general theory of dialectic . . . of which the Hegelian one can be seen as an important, but limited and highly questionable, special case' (DPF: 2). In this chapter, I focus primarily on the second of these objectives, for it is on this that the development of what Bhaskar calls a materialistically diffracted dialectic depends. This involves a process that releases dialectic from its 'Hegelian moorings' (Hartwig 2007: 141), and is a question both of form and of method. As regards form, diffraction is associated in science with the breakdown of light in contact with an object, or in a prism. In the process, what initially appears a unitary phenomenon is fractured into different shapes and patterns or is fragmented into a range of different elements. This fragmentation and fracturing is also, however, an opening up, as we see a spectrum of shades or light patterns within an original unitary form. In the process, in addition, we come to understand how the field of light exists *in relation to* the original unitary form. Fragmentation and fracturing, difference, variety, and the relationship between what is broken and what is one – these are all elements that are caught in Bhaskar's account of the diffraction of dialectic. It indicates above all that the programmed, rationally 'linear', unifying quality of Hegel's dialectic is to be opened up to a more plural, differentiated vision in which the disjoint, multifariously contradictory nature of modernity is no longer unified by the work of dialectical reason. In the process, it is rendered more available for investigation precisely by stressing its actual fragmented and fractured character.

As regards method, Bhaskar's approach involves the *materialist* diffraction of dialectic, indicating a break with the idealism that governs not only Hegel's thought, but also that of his Greek predecessors in the dialectical tradition, Parmenides and Plato.[1] To these, Bhaskar opposes a materialist method that draws on the original 1M critical realist account of a depth ontology involving structures described in Chapter 1, and he links this to an account of Marx's critique of Hegel and the 'substantive' materialism of his analysis of contradiction. Diffracting dialectic thereby becomes a way of advancing dialectical critical realism by taking sides in, and commenting on, the relationship between Marx and Hegel.

Realism and materialism have always been closely linked in critical realism, for, in an ontology emphasising structural depth, critical realism constitutes the method of inquiry, while materiality in the natural and social worlds constitutes the object of study. The relationship between them is however developed in dialectical critical realism, since 2E negativity is introduced into the picture. As we saw in Chapter 2, what lies at the core of natural necessity in a dynamic world is the tri-unity of causality in space and time as the 'material meshwork' in which becoming and process are understood alongside being and product. The logical extension of this dialectical understanding of being and becoming in the material world is the understanding of dialectic in a materialist way, and hence, linking this to the identification of the fractured nature of modern reality, we arrive at the idea of its materialist diffraction. Broadly, the emphasis in the materialist diffracting approach is to encourage an understanding of the material world as the place in which dialectics have their process, ground and play, rather than seeing dialectic as the means, in the idealist tradition, of controlling and unifying that ground.

The chapter has four main sections, the first two of which are devoted to engagement with Hegel, the second two with Marx and critical realist ontology. For reading purposes, this conveniently divides it into two halves. In the first section, I examine Bhaskar's analysis of Hegel's dialectic in both general and specific terms – that is, both as an idealist dialectical philosophy, and as a specific form of reasoning with three different moments. In the second, I consider Bhaskar's initial immanent critique of Hegelian dialectic, which identifies its limits. Thereafter, in a third section, I look at Bhaskar's realist conception of contradiction in comparison to Hegel's in the light of materialist and critical realist themes. Contradiction becomes a richer, more complex, enduring and worldly phenomenon in this account. In the fourth section, I then examine the fuller idea of diffracting dialectic that immanent critique of Hegel and the account of contradiction lead on to. I begin, however, with Hegel, for if a modern critical philosopher is to locate his thought in the dialectical tradition, he must engage with the greatest and most challenging of modern dialecticians.

Hegel's dialectic

In the Preface to *Dialectic*, Bhaskar writes of the four terms of dialectical critical realism in comparison to the three of Hegelian dialectic:

> The terms of the critical realist dialectic are non-identity, negativity, totality and transformative praxis or agency, in comparison with the Hegelian trio of identity, negativity and totality. However, my accounts of negativity and of totality are radically different from Hegel's.
>
> (DPF: xiii)

We have already met the four terms of dialectical critical realism in the first two chapters as the movement from its first moment (1M – non-identity, alterity) to a second edge (2E – negativity), leading in turn to a third level (3L – totality) and a fourth dimension (4D – praxis). The last two are considered in Chapters 4 and 5. In this chapter, we consider Bhaskar's argument for a novel dialectic, initially conceived in relation to an account of determinate non-being (in Chapter 2), and now emergent from critical engagement with Hegel's three-term account. When Bhaskar refers to Hegel's dialectic in these terms, he has in mind the account in Hegel's *Logic* of the movement from the understanding (the sphere of identity) to that of negative dialectical critique (negativity), and then onwards to positive, speculative reason (totality). This yields a three-element movement in terms of Understanding (identity)–negative Dialectical critique (negativity)–positive speculative Reason (totality), or U-D-R movement for short,[2] and we will consider this threefold movement in this section. Thereafter, in the second section of the chapter, we will examine Bhaskar's immanent critique of Hegelian dialectic.

It will be helpful first to consider what Hegel and Bhaskar have in common. Both are clear that their philosophy should be situated within a tradition of dialectical thinking that is as old as western philosophy itself. 'Among the ancients,' Hegel wrote, 'Plato is termed the inventor of Dialectic'; while in modern times it was 'Kant who resuscitated the name of Dialectic, and restored it to its post of honour' (1975: 117). The title of *Plato Etc.* makes it clear that Bhaskar sees things similarly. It is clear that if the dialectical tradition spans two and a half thousand years, and takes in such different thinkers as Plato and Kant, then this is a tradition that is not just longstanding, but one that must be broadly grasped. For Bhaskar, the richness of dialectic is seen in the 'spread of connotations' with which it is historically associated. This includes 'argument and conflict, disputation, struggle and split, dialogue and exchange, but also probative progress, enlightenment, demystification and the critique of illusion' (DPF: 17). To this must be added the small matter of materialist diffraction, the subject of this chapter. Throughout *Dialectic*, Bhaskar reminds us that his own thinking, like Hegel's, must be located in this broad, living and, *pace* Hegel, open tradition.

As for Hegel, Bhaskar identifies 'two principal inflections of the dialectic' (DPF: 15) in his thought. First, it involves a broad, logical *process of reason*, and here there are both 'process' and 'reason' elements to take into account. Second, more narrowly, it is the *actual mechanics of that process*, a 'method, practice or experience of determinate negation' (ibid.). It is in this second, more detailed aspect that we meet the Understanding–negative Dialectical critique–speculative Reason (identity/negativity/totality) progression in Hegel, but its precise character depends on the broader sense of a process of reason, and this Hegel derives from the Greeks. Let us look at these broad and narrow elements separately, beginning with dialectic as process of reason.

Dialectic as process of reason

If Hegel's account of dialectic in general involves a process of reason, this gives rise to questions concerning both process *and* reason. I start with the latter. In the Greek world, one primary source of dialectic (which means 'the art of discussing') is Socratic dialogue, which is oriented, in its own conception of itself,[3] to the reasoned and disinterested pursuit of truth. Plato develops this in that he, as Hegel put it, 'employs the dialectical method to show the finitude of all hard and fast terms of understanding' (Hegel 1975: 117). This involves a sense, originally from Heraclitus, and passing through the Sophists, of the flux inherent in all phenomena. In Plato's metaphysics, however, it is dialectic that mediates and controls flux and finitude by permitting rational access to a relationship between phenomena in flux and the ideal Forms that inform them. There is an ongoing relation between the phenomenal present, in a state of constant change, and the eternal, accessed by reason, which is universal and unchanging. Thus, in the *Parmenides*, Hegel says, Plato 'deduces the many from the one, and shows nevertheless that the many cannot but define itself as the one' (1975: 117). But if Plato is among the ancients 'termed the inventor of Dialectic' (ibid.), Hegel also acknowledges the role of the earlier Eleatic philosopher Parmenides in initiating 'the proper history of philosophy' by first identifying 'knowledge by thought'. With him, 'for the first time we find pure thought seized and made an object to itself' (1975: 126), an idea that Plato was to take up in his theory of the Forms. Thus, from the beginning, dialectic was instantiated in western philosophy in a particular way. It was associated with establishing universal foundations *in thought*, the Forms or Ideas, and, through such rational foundation, the supremacy of mind in relation to world. As Bhaskar puts it, in this 'inaugural moment of the western philosophical tradition, fundamentalism, classical rationalist criteria for knowledge and dialectic were indissolubly linked' (DPF: 16). It is the foundational warranty of being by knowledge that, finding its expression in a dialectical connection between the Forms and the flux, starts the dialectical tradition off. It is this that links Plato and the ancients to Hegel and the form modern dialectics would assume in his philosophy.

After Plato, dialectic went into decline in the thought of Aristotle, for whom it was only a discursive preliminary to syllogistic reasoning (DPF: 16). It was then retained in the practice of medieval disputation before being revived ('restored . . . to its post of honour' (Hegel 1975: 117)) by Kant for modern philosophy. Bhaskar suggests that Kant took over Aristotle's sense that dialectic involved relying on premises that were inadequate for knowledge, as well as the contrast between analytics and dialectics that informs his philosophy. For Kant, dialectic was a pathology of reason, representing the state of contradiction or antinomy into which reason falls when it is not properly connected to experience. What was required was a grasp of the significance of human subjectivity in developing the categories which make experience intelligible. Kant's move to transcendental subjectivity combined, in Bhaskar's terms, 'rationalist demands on knowledge with empiricist criteria for being' (DPF: 17), but it did so at a price. It left the 'thing-in-itself', the real ontological object of knowledge, unknowable. The result was an unstable pact between transcendental idealism and empirical realism, and this led to a series of splits, contradictions and antinomies in Kant's philosophy:

> For Kant this was enlightenment, but it entrained a systematically sundered world and a whole series of splits, between knowledge and thought, knowledge

and faith, phenomena and noumena, the transcendental and the empirical, theory and (practical) reason, duty and inclination, this world and the next (splits which were also interiorised within each term separately), as well as those expressly articulated in the antinomies.

(DPF: 17)

For Hegel, these splits and rifts in Kantian philosophy were at once reflective of the nature of modern living in general, and the product of an incomplete understanding of how dialectic operates in philosophy. Renovating the latter would be a way of reconciling the former. Hegel sought to bring together two things. First, there were Greek ideas of dialectic and the predominance of mind and reason over phenomena. Second, there was recognition of the nature of modernity and its attendant conflicts, especially as these related to questions of subjective freedom in an objective world. It was the sense of a world confronted with seemingly unavoidable conflict that Hegel sought to rationalise and resolve in his philosophy, bringing a Platonic reliance on ideal reason to bear on modern splits and contradictions. Hegelian idealism would unite a Parmenidean–Platonic emphasis on reason as a means to unify and control recalcitrant being with recognition of the fragmented and conflicted nature of modernity.

Dialectic as process of reason

As we approach Hegel's rational solution to Kantian antinomy, however, we need to recognise the second strand in Greek dialectical philosophy. I said above that dialectical thinking involves a *process* of reason, and that it was necessary to consider the process aspect in itself alongside the role of reason. Here, Bhaskar contrasts the two main trends in Greek philosophy. One is associated with the Eleatic school, including Parmenides, who specifically emphasised the role of thought, the other with the earlier Ionian school, which emphasised more the significance of process and change. The *processual* development of reason is seen in the way in which dialectic involves either ascending movement to a higher reality (for example, in Plato, to the Forms), or a descending movement from such a reality to its manifestation in the phenomena of the world. For Hegel, putting these together gives rise to processes of reason that result in an active, quasi-logical pattern of taking thought as independent from the world, actualising it in the world, and redeeming it as reason in a progressive, moving, state of ideal-actual completion. We then get processual depictions of reality involving 'a quasi-spatio-temporal pattern of original unity, loss or division and return or reunification' (DPF: 17). In this way, an Ionian–Eleatic marriage of process and reason gives rise to Hegelian dialectic in which the ideal or absolute is actualised by first alienating itself from the world, then rediscovering itself in it, and restoring its original unity in a more complex and developed form. Thought moves up and down, from the rational and universal to the particular and vice versa, in processes of ascending and descending dialectics that constitute the moving paths of reason in the world.

From these elements of process and reason, Hegel composes his dialectic, and Bhaskar identifies three key themes that run through it: *spiritual monism*, *realised idealism* and *immanent teleology*. As regards spiritual monism, Hegel's aim was to find a way in philosophy of returning to the ethical 'expressive unity' that Greek society had seemingly enjoyed, and that Kant's philosophy denied to modernity (Taylor 1975). There was a need to restore wholeness to life in a way that nonetheless accepted the gains of modernity in terms of individuality and diversity. Hegel's spiritual monism – that is, his sense of an immanent ideal oneness – would thus involve and be moderated by plurality through a conception of unity-in-diversity, while at bottom expressing monism, the unity in the diversity. As regards the second theme, realised idealism, the way to achieve such a unity was through the development of a complete and self-consistent idealism, in which, in the ascending phase of his dialectic, unity would be achieved as the work of mind:

> For Hegel the problem of elaborating a non-reductionist and subjective monism gradually became tantamount to the problem . . . of developing a complete and self-consistent idealism. Such an idealism would, in fusing the finite in the infinite, retain no dualistic or non-rational residues, thereby finally realising and vindicating the primordial Parmenidean postulate of the identity of being and thought *in* thought, underpinned by a progressivist view of history.
>
> (DPF: 18)

As regards the third element, immanent teleology, this was the result of a corresponding descending phase of the dialectic, whereby the ideal, the fruit of mind and reason, would be shown to be immanent in the world, as the infinite within the finite:

> in the Hegelian *Geistodyssey* . . . , the principle of idealism, the speculative understanding of reality as (absolute) spirit, is unfolded in the shape of an immanent teleology which shows . . . how the world exists . . . as a rational totality *precisely* so that (infinite) spirit can come to philosophical self-consciousness. . . .
>
> (ibid.)

These are the broad, rationalist, idealist dimensions that structure Hegelian dialectic as process of reason, relating it to the Greek concerns initiated by Parmenides and Plato. With them in mind, let us now turn to the narrower sense of dialectic, as a threefold movement of identity, negative critique, and totality through speculative reason.

Hegel's three-term dialectic: identity, negativity, totality

If we focus on dialectic as the dynamo at the heart of this reasoning process, we encounter Hegel's three-part dialectic, with the move from identity to negativity, and thence from negativity to totality. The three specific moments in the reasoning process identified by Hegel in his *Logic* are described as those of Understanding (pertaining to the establishment of identity), of Dialectic (as negative, critical reason) and of speculative, or positive, Reason (leading to a conception of rational totality), giving the movement that Bhaskar describes as from U to D to R. Let us follow Hegel's account.

To begin with, it should be noted that dialectic has a double meaning for Hegel in the U-D-R process. First, it is the overall movement through all three stages; and second, it is used to designate the middle stage of the movement, a moment of 'dialectic proper', which is that of negative critical reason (or 'determinate negation'). Hegel writes, describing the three terms of the overall movement, that logic 'has three sides: (α) the Abstract side, or that of understanding; (β) the Dialectical, or that of negative reason; (γ) the Speculative, or that of positive reason' (1975: 113). In this narrow formulation, the middle term, dialectic 'proper', is one element in the movement of thought. At the same time, however, Hegel writes of dialectic as involving all three elements, as taking thought forward from the Understanding by virtue of negative reason, and then onward again through positive speculation. The negative is 'at the same time the positive' so that 'the [negative] dialectical stage has the features characterising . . . logical truth, the speculative form, or form of positive reason' (1975: 119) within it. Thus, in a broader sense, dialectic involves both negative-critical and positive reason and, since negative reason is also inherent in the limits of Understanding, dialectical logic becomes the whole three-term process.

Taking the three terms individually, Understanding involves thinking which 'sticks to fixity of characters and their distinctness from one another', establishing a set of 'limited abstract' entities, and 'having a subsistence and being of its own' (Hegel 1975: 113). In this realm, which is vital to every field of science, knowledge 'begins by apprehending existing objects in their specific differences', by 'stereotyp[ing] each in its isolation' (1975: 114). Importantly, thought here is 'acting in its analytic capacity, where its canon is identity, a simple reference of each attribute to itself' (ibid.), and its main requirement 'is that every thought shall be grasped in its full precision, and nothing allowed to remain vague and indefinite' (1975: 115). This is the realm of analytical *identity*, where a thing is itself and not something else, and the object of thinking is to identify the precise lineaments of things. Hence, the Understanding is a realm of subjective identification and of objective identity; it is a realm of what Bhaskar comes to call subject/object identity thinking.[4]

In contrast to the Understanding's realm of precise definition, separation and distinctiveness, finitude and self-identity, there stands the second moment, of negative Dialectical critique, where 'finite characterisations or formulae supersede themselves, and pass into their opposites' (ibid.). Dialectic in this sense is the inherent tendency of things not to be tied down to one single definition, but to contain different and ultimately oppositional aspects such that their finitude or identity is ultimately undermined from within. The limitations of the finite 'do not merely come from without', for there is an 'indwelling tendency' by which the 'one-sidedness and limitation of the predicates of understanding is seen in its true light, and shown to be the negation of them' (1975: 116). In making this point, Hegel points to our experience of the world:

> Everything that surrounds us may be viewed as an instance of Dialectic. We are aware that everything finite, instead of being stable and ultimate, is rather changeable and transient; and this is exactly what we mean by that Dialectic of the finite, by which the finite, as implicitly other than what it is, is forced beyond its own immediate or natural being to turn suddenly into its opposite.
>
> (1975: 118)

Where finitude and change in the object goes, so too does thought. Our concepts come to confront their limits and contradictions as thought at the level of the Understanding breaks down. This leads to the third and final stage, of positive or speculative Reason, where reason 'apprehends the unity of terms (propositions) in their opposition' and thereby picks out what is 'affirmative . . . in their disintegration and in their transition' (1975: 119). Here positive reason repairs contradiction by showing how one-sided thinking, betrayed by the oppositions it engenders, presses to a wider perspective and a deeper reason. Speculative thought 'expressly rises above such oppositions . . . which the understanding cannot get over, and absorbing them in itself, evinces its own concrete and all-embracing nature' (1975: 120).

From this, we can see how Bhaskar identifies the Hegelian dialectic as a threefold movement from Understanding to negative Dialectical critique, and then to positive, speculative (dialectical) Reason. We can also appreciate why the underlying terms of the movement are identity, negativity and totality. We have seen that Understanding is the location of identity, and that identity is negated. However, the fact that a concept involves contradiction or self-negation does not cancel it. Where a determinate thing is negated, this gives rise to further determinations, which will in turn be negated by the rational restoration at the higher level (the 'negation of the negation'). Hegel says, following Spinoza, that the 'foundation of all determinateness is negation' (1975: 135), but he also inverts the maxim since, as Bhaskar notes, 'negation always leads to a new, richer determination' (DPF: 20), and this is the transformation of an entity by negation. At the core of Hegel's method is, then, a process of *determinate* negation, which is also one of *transformative* negation (ibid.), and since what is transformed is also retained in its sublation, every transformative negation is also, Bhaskar says, a *preservative determinate* negation (DPF: 23). In principle, nothing is lost as the process of negation becomes one of creating and enriching a totality of thoughts, experiences and objects. Hence, identity and negativity lead to totality, the three terms of the Hegelian dialectic.

These, then, are Bhaskar's initial views on Hegel's dialectical philosophy. He has set them generally in the context of the dialectical tradition, and more specifically within the logic of a three-part process that has as its dynamo the negative critique of identity and the resolution of ensuing problems in a rational totality. That process can ascend from the particular to the universal, or descend from the universal to the particular, but, whichever, it leads to a sense of how things come together in an idealised, dialectically reasoned whole. Hegel 'grasps concepts and forms of life in their systematic interconnections, not just their determinate differences, and considers each development as a product of a previous less developed phase, whose necessary truth or fulfilment it, in some sense and measure, is' (DPF: 22). As with the ancients, thinking is in command even if, importantly, it takes place in relation to specific objective forms in the world. This is his *realised* idealism, discussed above. Dialectical critical realism must therefore consider how it will deal with the relationship between thinking and the real vis-à-vis the philosophical idealism at the heart of Hegelian dialectic. It will consider how a materialist understanding of natural necessity and causality can be brought to bear on dialectics, and what an ensuing materialist account of dialectic will do to Hegel's terms. But first, Bhaskar will consider Hegel's dialectic critically, in its own terms, for the absences that indicate the need to diffract dialectic.

Hegel's immanent critique: towards diffraction

To pursue an immanent critique of Hegel is properly to hold him to account, for it is to submit him to the same kind of negative dialectical critique as he submits others. At the same time, every negative limit that is exposed points beyond itself, towards a higher form of understanding. Eventually, Bhaskar will argue that materialist diffraction of dialectic is just such a higher form. For the moment, however, he prepares the ground by showing how Hegel's dialectic is in its own terms undialectical, in the sense of being dialectically limited and incomplete (DPF: 23–28). Bhaskar's immanent critique pursues two paths: first, whether Hegel's dialectic is true to reason; and second, whether it is true to reality.

True to thought

A philosophical system based on realised idealism (constructing an idealised reality) is prone to difficulties along the two lines it brings together. On the one hand, there is a question about its ability to sustain itself as a mode of thought; on the other, there is a question about its ability to reflect in thought the world in which thought participates. For Bhaskar, Hegelian dialectic is found wanting along both lines. It fails to be true both to itself as thought process and to the world it seeks to realise through thought.

As regards being true to itself as process of thinking, Hegel's philosophy must be true to its core idea of sublation. That is the idea that any determinate negation that cancels a proposition or state of being must also preserve it in the ensuing transcendence (*Aufhebung*). The limit in a concept or an entity identified by negative Dialectical critique is repaired by the subsequent move to a higher level in a way that retains, in dialectical brackets as it were, the original negating problem or conflict. Yet in this process of negation, Bhaskar argues, the one thing that is *not* preserved is the negativity that is supposed otherwise to drive the system forward. The Hegelian totality is in the end complete and closed, for speculative philosophy achieves an end state, realised idealism, which it configures as rational social history. In the process, negativity is returned into positivity within the overall totality. Further, if negativity is not maintained, neither too is error, partiality or one-sidedness. The drive of speculative reason secures the truth that lurks within error, transforming our view of what a moment earlier had appeared to be error. In the process, error ceases to be error. Hegel might, Bhaskar suggests, want to say that the erroneous is retained as a partial aspect of the truth, but ultimately either an error is cancelled or it is not. Either an *Aufhebung* negates an error (negates a negation) in order to move to a higher level, or it does not, in which case it does not genuinely move to the higher level. If it negates the error, then the error is not retained *as error* but as something else: a position which, viewed from the higher level, has been corrected. Thus, Hegel is untrue to his sublatory method, for some things – absence, negativity and error – are not preserved in the process of moving from negative Dialectical critique to positive speculative Reason. Negativity becomes transformed in the new, more complete whole that the higher-level sublation brings into being.

This objection to the non-preservative sublation of error and negativity may seem *recherché*, but it links to an underlying problem. As negativity is lost, so positivity and identity are restored in the greater totality by reason. Those concepts and objects of the Understanding which were negated at the lower level are shown to have been necessary all the time at the higher. The three-moment process returns us to the contradictory fruits of the Understanding, now reconciled by their existence in an overall totality. This permits an analytic reinstatement of identity once the work of speculative reason has been carried out. What was previously seen as a negation at the lower level is now itself negated at the higher, so that the positive comes back into play.[5] Bhaskar articulates this criticism as follows:

> The driving force (in principle) of Hegelian dialectic is the transition, paradigmatically of the elements (e) and (-e), from positive contraries . . . violating the principle of non-contradiction . . . into negative sub-contraries . . . retained . . . in a cumulative memory store, as the dialectical reader's consciousness or the path of history moves on to a new level of speculative reason. At this stage they are now retrospectively redescribed as moments of a transcending totality. *Contradiction has cancelled itself. And they are now, in what we could call Hegel's analytic reinstatement, restored to their positive self-identity.* No longer contradictory, they now illustrate what [can be called] 'dialectical connection'.
>
> (DPF: 62; emphasis added)

In short, Hegel does not maintain a genuine sense of dialectical contradiction, but at best a sense of dialectical *connection*[6] which is buttressed by dialectical logic, in the context of a progressivist view of history. This can happen precisely because, in Bhaskar's terms, negativity is cancelled in his system, with the knock-on effect that positivity is restored. The positivity of identity, in the realm of

Understanding, gives way to contradiction in the negative Dialectical critique, but there is then a more complex analytic reinstatement through the working of positive speculative Reason.

This then leads to a further consequence. Hegel has identified the important role played by negative Dialectical critique, both in theory and in objects in the world, and he has also identified the most basic form of critique, immanent critique. But his philosophical idealism means that he always resolves the problems he identifies *in theory*, so that the practices and objects in the world that he critiques always remain in place. He emphasises thought's speculative resolution of contradiction in a fuller, more rational understanding of the world, but this means that the actual world, with its existing contradictions, *becomes* the rational world. The result is that where there are real contradictions in the world, Hegel has no way to resolve them, and they return as unresolved contradictions in his philosophy. The result is therefore not rational resolution but the maintenance of conflicted heteronomy and the consequent 're-appearance of a Kant-like rift', indeed a series of such rifts, in his philosophy (DPF: 27). Because he resolves real-world problems in thought, Hegel falls back into a position that ultimately replicates the dualisms Kant had identified as the lot of modernity. A still existing gap between philosophy and reality reduces his philosophy to contradiction so that it, the expression of the universal, cannot in the end be true to itself in a contradictory world. In consequence, the universal breaks down. This is a problem for Hegel's thought, and hence his ability to remain true to thinking. Its inevitable corollary, however, is an inability to be true to the world it represents, as we shall now see.

True to the world

That dialectics should be true to the world is a central requirement for a dialectical critical realist, but the same is also true for Hegel, for his realised idealism entails idealising *reality*. There is a double relationship in which, to repeat the quotation, '[w]hat is rational is actual and what is actual is rational' (Hegel 1952: 10).[7] Thought must seek to be true not only to itself, but also to the world of which it is a part. As regards the ability of Hegelian dialectic to reflect in thought the world in which it participates, Bhaskar's criticism concerns the incompleteness of Hegel's accounts of totality and negation, and also, more generally, his dialectical method. These lead to Bhaskar's argument for a more complete dialectical critical realist account of dialectics. I begin, however, with Bhaskar's critique of Hegel's resort to the category of the 'demi-actual'.

Bhaskar's claim that Hegel's dialectic necessitates a category of the demi-actual stems from his formula that 'the actual is rational'. This works only for those things that the rational is prepared to embrace. Objects that are otherwise perfectly worthy of study may fall outside Hegel's rational method either because they are not deemed to be of sufficient interest, or because they do not fit into the overall rationalising narrative Hegel wants to give. Reason may be deaf to entities which in consequence come to occupy a strange half-existence in the Hegelian world as 'the intransigent class of demi-actual and demi-present surds, irrational existents such as Krug's pen'[8] (DPF: 274) or 'the number of species of parrot' (DPF: 73). The general deductive practice of designating entities as either significant for reason or not becomes particularly important with those demi-actuals of an urgent political or social character which Hegel sees as necessary to mention, but cannot rationalise in his system. We will return to these shortly, but let us first consider Bhaskar's criticism of Hegel's account of totality.

As regards totality, Hegel insists that what is required is completion of the whole, which is then closed because it is complete. For him, an open totality is a disaster, for it is one where '[s]omething becomes an other', which 'likewise becomes an other, and so on *ad infinitum*', giving rise to a 'wrong or negative infinity' and an 'endless iteration' (Hegel 1975: 137). For Hegel, an incomplete (open) totality would, as Bhaskar puts it, 'conjure up the spectre of an infinite regress – it would be a "bad infinite"' (DPF: 24). In contrast, a 'good' totality for him safeguards against this scenario by being closed against repetition. Bhaskar's response is to argue that an open totality may, but does not have to, lead to infinite regress. It could lead instead to the emergence of genuine novelty and difference in an open future, a possibility Hegel must deny. But why, in the light of our experience and understanding of change, should we accept his denial?

In terms of historical understanding, we noted above that Hegel's dialectic is underpinned by a progressivist view of social development, so that in modernity, that development is completed. The closure of the Hegelian totality accordingly results in the thesis of the end of history. Closure and the analytic reinstatement discussed above are also linked, so that any possible future is thought in terms of a continuing present. There is a reaffirmation of positivity which gives rise, says Bhaskar, to 'the constellational identity of the future within the (Hegelian) present' (DPF: 24).[9] Because the world is complete and closed, there is no scope for a further stage in world history that would negate the present. What we see is what we get, but this vision is achieved at the price of philosophy being untrue to a world in which change is possible. The rational promise of closed totality and the ensuing bad infinite of an open future misrepresent how the world is.

In critical realist terms, it is Hegel's ontological actualism and lack of a sense of structural depth and real absence that exclude the possibility of open totality. We are aware of the openness that exists in the world, embodied in the possibility of genuine surprise, or of 'something new' happening. We know, of course, that reality can sometimes appear to be an 'endless iteration', though it is just at such times that we are most often surprised by change. In any case, any valid theory of totality must be able to situate *both* possibilities, repetition and real change. Bhaskar's account of open totality (building on his understanding of the possibility of differential spatio-temporal rhythmics in Chapter 2) can do so, but Hegel's cannot. This means that a dialectical theory endorsing 'the concept of an open totality must be more true (complete and adequate) than [one limited to] the concept of a closed totality, because it is more comprehensive, englobing and contains the latter as a special case' (DPF: 26). Totalities can be open or closed, and the latter is the limit and exception, not the rule. Thus, the more complete dialectical theory will be the one that allows for both possibilities.[10]

Just as a dialectical theory adequate to the world must be more inclusive with regard to the possibilities of totality, so it must be with negation and sublation. As we know, Hegel focuses on moments of negative Dialectical critique which provide a determinate negation and then lead to resolution at a higher level in the rational totality. However, in real-world contexts this account of determinate negation (together with the other forms mentioned previously) hardly covers the range of possibilities for negation in the world. Real negations, as well as being determinate, may also be indeterminate or underdeterminate in their form or outcome. In geo-historical contexts, their lineaments may be irreducibly 'fuzzy', and not present as the kind of clear contradiction that is entailed by determinate negation, or the opposing of two forms of determinate being to each other. Similarly, transformative negations may be, but often are not, of the preservative form that the theory of sublation requires. Indeed, in so far as every social form is dependent on finite (human) being, it must be the case that all real change involves elements of *non*-preservation. All space-time beings are ultimately non-preserved 'vanishing mediators', part of the world's inevitable ebb and flow. In any genuine change in the world

> it is clear that something has to be lost, even if it is only time. . . . On the other hand, it is equally obvious that processes occur in geo-history which are not, at least with respect to some determinate characteristic and within some determinate space-time band, negating but purely accretory, cumulative engrossments or developments.
>
> (DPF: 28)

Dialectics must be able to account for the different kinds of outcomes possible in an emergent world. Once we move to the real, spatio-temporal situation of outcomes of negation, a range of diverse results may be identified. Hegel's stock idealist answer is that we start with contradiction expressing negation and end with resolution, but outcomes must include non-resolutory results, non-reasonable resolutions, non-sublatory resolutions and non-reconciliatory sublations (DPF: 28).[11] If we look at dialectical processes of negation in the world, they rarely conform to one particular type. Bhaskar points to the multiform quality of real-world processes of negation and change, and does not see them as tied, as Hegel's idealism requires, to an *ex ante* thought pattern that has its model in rational resolution, ultimately in a logical form. This differential quality gives a clue to what a diffracted dialectic would look like: open and pluriform, yet structured and grounded, just like the world of which it is a part.

Finally, Bhaskar identifies questions for Hegel's dialectical method, and these too link to the idealism and the resulting non-inclusivity and non-representivity of his dialectics. At the core of Hegel's method is the sense that the conceptual development he depicts is 'autogenetic' – that is, driven by an immanent logic. If so, the most appropriate transitions that should occur are those that are 'teleonomic' in form – that is, where the problem or limit is genuinely implicit within the concept or object, so that the drive is *ex ante* and the solution 'pushes out' from within. An alternative form is where there is a 'teleological' pull exerted by the observer who identifies from without an inadequacy that requires to be repaired. Only the former kind of determinate negation fully satisfies the requirements of the Hegelian system, so that one could distinguish between 'good' and 'bad' radical negations within it (DPF: 24). Similarly, there is a tension between the linear and logical form of Hegel's dialectics and their representation of phenomena. While the requirement of linearity is imposed on Hegel by his desire to produce a rational dialectical narrative, his dialectics in truth 'job around all over the place' (DPF: 25). Linearity of logic or thought, a dictate of reason, is imposed from outside on a world that may disclose very different, non-linear patterns. This too gives a clue to diffraction of dialectic, which will affirm that this is indeed the nature of worldly dialectics. Thus, the failure to open dialectics up to the multiform possibilities of the 'external' world, registered earlier in relation to negation and totality, is also seen in the formal limits Hegel imposes upon his own system. Being untrue to the world eventually rebounds back on his ability to be true to the requirements of thought, for these are two sides of the same coin.

Bhaskar on Hegel

Thus far, we have outlined the general and particular elements in Hegel's dialectical method, and followed Bhaskar's immanent critique of problems with that method. From these problems, we get a sense of the rigid character of Hegelian dialectics, their inability to sustain themselves as forms of thought, and to reflect adequately on the world of which they are a part. In claiming, however, that Hegel idealises reality, thereby apparently resolving social conflicts in thought while they remain in place in the world, is Bhaskar fair to Hegel? While what he says may be true of some of Hegel's thought, for example the early *Phenomenology of Spirit*, where matters are resolved by the synthesis of subjective consciousness and objective spirit, and the dialectic does seem to 'job around', this is not the case with other works where objective worldly development predicates the development of spirit as much as vice versa. In the *Philosophy of Right*, for example, there are real historical reference points which match the process of development in thought so that the dialectics of thinking and the geo-historical is two-way, not one-sided, in these works. Up to a point, this is correct, and it is acknowledged as such by Bhaskar, who recognises the objective, worldly side to Hegelian dialectics. That is why there are two sides to Bhaskar's critique: Hegel needs to make his philosophy true both to itself *and* to the world. As regards modernity, as we noted, Hegel's aim is to fashion philosophy in a way that reflects the modern experience of pluralism and unity in a unity-in-diversity. Even if at bottom it remains idealist and monistic, his thought must embody and express modern realities, implying an active two-way process in which the real ('the actual') must be respected.

Nonetheless, Hegel's development of the objective side to his philosophy is severely restricted at those points where it confronts contradictions in modern social reality. At such points, contradictions in reality remain unresolved in his thought, giving rise to the realm of the 'demi-actual'. His thought in turn is undermined by the contradictions that confront it. The *Philosophy of Right*, for example, is an attempt to think in a dialectically rational way about the development of modern liberal forms of freedom, property, justice, civil society and the state. In so far as philosophical idealism is involved in rationalising such institutions, thinking and reality often intertwine quite comfortably, indeed elegantly. However, when it comes to the problems of liberal society, Hegel has more difficulty. In his treatment of the problem of poverty, for example, he notes how pauperism undermines the liberal conception of justice. He does not, then, simply ignore poverty and its effects, but nor does he have the philosophical means to deal with it in his system. Pauperism, he notes, leads to 'a loss of the sense of right and wrong' (Hegel 1952: 150) and accordingly 'takes the form of a wrong done to one class by another' (1952: 277). This is an honest and realistic appraisal of the impact of poverty on a sense of justice, but these observations undercut the entire development of the first part of the *Philosophy of Right*, which establish a universal sense of right and wrong. They lead to a contradiction in his philosophy as to whether modern society produces institutions based on individual justice or class wrongs. This split in thought reflects a contradiction in society. It is overcome neither in thought, where it is left to lie at the margin as demi-actuality, nor, of course, in reality itself. The contradiction ultimately drags Hegel's thought down to its level, when he argues that reaction to poverty and justice should be met with increased repression. He suggests that it is legitimate to increase punishment where society is internally weak, justifying 'the penalty of death to a theft of a few pence or a turnip' (1952: 140), and he backs the police to 'diminish the danger of upheavals arising from clashing interests [until the] tension should be eased through the working of a necessity of which they themselves know nothing' (1952: 150).[12] But what precisely *is* the necessity in civil society in the light of the contradiction he has, quite candidly, identified, but failed to reconcile in his philosophy?

It is also important to note that, in focusing on Bhaskar's immanent critique of Hegel in preparation for his account of diffraction of dialectic, I have omitted much in *Dialectic* that provides a more nuanced analysis. Bhaskar is more inclined to draw on Hegel in his representation of how, at the level of epistemology, dialectic works as learning process. This may be thought to be the natural home of Hegelian dialectic, and where its limits are accordingly less obvious (DPF: 33–7). Moreover, Bhaskar is alert to the different directions that are to be found in Hegel, in terms both of his actual writings and of the different possibilities his philosophy presents. Calling him a 'deeply ambiguous figure' (DPF: 64), Bhaskar identifies two Hegels, Marks I and II, where the former is the 'first practitioner of a new sociogeo-historicist mode of thought and expressly interested in change' (ibid.), while the latter is the 'last great metaphysician who (almost) succeeds in realising the traditional goals of philosophy [while becoming] increasingly fearful of change' (ibid.). It is the latter who has come under fire in Bhaskar's immanent critique, though Bhaskar notes that even the mature metaphysician presented 'brilliant diagnoses of real, including non-logical, dialectical contradictions [such as those] of civil society' – which, as we have noted, 'he never sublates' (ibid.).[13]

I can only give a brief indication of Bhaskar's more complex account of Hegel's philosophy, for it is time to move on with our exploration of diffracting the dialectic. Following his critique of Hegel, we begin to get a sense of what a diffracted dialectic, true both to the world and to theory, would look like. It would require, first, that negativity, and error generally, remain as real-world entities that cannot be finessed or lost through the cunning of reason. So long as error remains in the world, it must be thinkable within dialectics. Second, the sense of identity in things that concepts purvey remains valid, within limits. Conceptual identity *is* a feature of the world, but it must be grounded in non-identity and real change, and not taken at its face value, or falsely reconstituted in philosophy. It is the relationship between entities and their pasts and outsides that gives them their real-world dialectical fluidity. Where 'Kant-like rifts' exist in identity and in the things identity covers, these must be acknowledged as real elements, and not simplistically resolved through reason. Third, as dialectics open up to the world, we must be open to worldly phenomena and not permit an *ex ante* method to separate the rationally actual from the 'irrational' and the consequently demi-actual. It is not the privilege of philosophy to legislate this kind of gap. Fourth, we require a more open conception of totality, to include totalities that are themselves open and incomplete, for the future is not subject to a plan. The same is true, fifth, of negation and its effects, which must be regarded pluralistically, as generating determinate change, but also indeterminate and underdetermined real-world effects. Equally, sixth, we must be open in our conception of the different possibilities of resolution, non-resolution and irresolution that pertain to real-world contradictions. Seventh, if Hegel's dialectics 'job around', that tells us something about the kind of diffracted dialectics we need but Hegel's linearity does not supply. The world requires a dialectics more able to reflect its messiness, its perturbation and change, and its unfinished character, not one that cleans everything up and provides it with a linear ordering. Textual linearity is no substitute for the ongoing play of contextual disorder that natural necessity and the material meshwork of causality, space and time in an open future bring. In this way, the immanent critique of Hegel's method pushes us towards the idea of a diffracted – that is, an open and multiform – dialectic. What we now need to add, under the direction of critical realist categories, is the idea of its specifically *material* character. A crucial staging post en route to this conception is Bhaskar's analysis of contradiction, and we now turn from the critique of idealist dialectic to the elucidation of a materialist method that can underpin the idea of diffraction.

Materialist diffraction: contradictions

If Bhaskar is to relocate dialectic on the terrain of critical realism, the analysis of contradiction is an obvious target. It is central to the idea of negativity (for contradiction is a form of negation), and negativity and contradiction are central both to Hegelian and Bhaskarian dialectic. In Hegel, negativity is central to negative Dialectical critique as the middle element in the U-D-R movement, and in Bhaskar it constitutes the second edge (2E) in the MELD schema. Thus, if negativity lies at the core of both dialectics and the idea of contradiction, and if Bhaskar's dialectic offers radically different terms to Hegel's even where they use the same words,[14] we should expect the idea of contradiction to represent a major point of engagement between the two philosophers. Further, if Bhaskar couches his approach to dialectic in terms of its *materialist* diffraction, then we should see this in operation in his analysis of contradiction.

I approach this here by discussing, first, Bhaskar's discussion of what it means to be a materialist, where he draws on Marx's critique of Hegel and the materialism that informed Marx's own analysis. I then examine how Bhaskar links this to Marx's materialist view of contradiction and consider Bhaskar's analysis of the idea of dialectical contradiction. Having considered the idea of a materialist usage of contradiction, I then proceed to develop the sense in which such a view entails the idea that contradiction should be diffracted.

Marx's materialism

Marx's materialism develops through the course of his writings, and is present in his early critique of Hegel on the state and civil society (Marx 1975). His critique is addressed to Hegel's philosophy of a thought identity between subject and object – that is, his view that being and thought are brought together in thought. Using Bhaskar's terms, Marx finds in Hegel the realised idealism and analytic reinstatement referred to in the previous section. In it, what is lost is the idea of a materially structured world that generates the forms of the actually existing order, and the contradictions immanent in it. What Hegel specifically lacks is an understanding of how those forms suggest an ideal and misleading representation of 'a real world capable of being differentially, changeably and better described, classified and explained' (DPF: 90). Instead, Hegel follows the ideal misrepresentation and produces an ideological image of the present as the inevitable and eternal representation of the ideal: 'an ideologically saturated mediation of social (including epistemic) reality, viz. *Das Bestehende* and its existing power$_2$ (master–slave), discursive and legitimating relations' (ibid.). In philosophical terms, these social relations 'are the real conditions of possibility of positivistic experience and speculative philosophy alike' (ibid.). With his analysis of the commodity form under capitalism, Marx pursues this understanding of the relationship between thought and being, but the basic grasp of that relationship is already formed in the early work. By the time of *Capital*, Marx's materialism had made him 'a scientific realist committed to the view that explanatory structures, or . . . essential relations, are (a) distinct from, (b) often, and even normally, out of phase with . . . and (c) perhaps in opposition to the phenomena . . . they generate' (DPF: 345). This is the basis for Marx's materialism and scientific realism, though, Bhaskar adds, he 'never satisfactorily theorised his scientific . . . realism' (ibid.) as he did his specific, material object of study. Nonetheless, from Marx Bhaskar develops a line of thinking that links modern social forms not to their ideal representation in a universalising dialectic but rather to their material generation in social processes.

Marx's materialism is, however, broadly based. It operates at a number of different levels, emphasising 'causal, not conceptual, necessity', and limiting teleology to its proper place in human affairs – that is, to 'the intrinsic aspect of human agency, which presupposes intentional causality' (DPF: 95). Beyond intended actions, the world lacks teleology either in its structures or in any compelling sense of linearity such as Hegelian reason would confer. Key to Marx's development as the creator of 'a concrete science of human geo-history' are materialist 'conceptions of ontological depth, structural change, intra-active . . . and open totality and transformative agency' (DPF: 96).[15] Here Bhaskar aligns Marx's materialism with critical realist categories. Hegel in contrast fails 'to sustain the objectivity of nature and being generally, as radically other to thought, as independently real and as neither teleologically dependent upon, causally necessitated by, nor conceptually reducible to alienations of spirit, thought or any kind of mind' (DPF: 92).

For Bhaskar, Marx's materialism has three forms. It is *epistemological* in its implicit understanding (again, in critical realist terms) of 'the existential intransitivity and transfactual efficacy of the objects of scientific thought' (DPF: 91). Against Hegelian affirmation of ultimate subject/object identity and a world composed of surface, actualist forms, Marx bases himself upon 'alterity and difference, structure and transfactuality, absence and change, reflexivity and open totality, transformative agency and metacritique' (ibid.). His materialism renders him a critical realist before the fact, for his concrete and theoretical analyses assume the kind of understanding developed by critical realism in both its pre-dialectical and its dialectical phases. More generally, Marx is an *ontological* materialist in his recognition of the emergence of mind from matter and of the social from the biological. There is also his understanding of 'universals as properties of particular things' (DPF: 93), and his insistence that knowledge is irreducibly a posteriori of an empirically ascertained and ontologically deep, structured world. Linked to this, there is his substantive understanding of social processes as giving rise to ideas and practices. Extractable from Marx is an overall (again, proto-critical realist) commitment to the 'empirically controlled investigation of the causal relations within and between (geo-) historically emergent, developing humanity and intransitively real, but modifiable nature' (DPF: 94). Finally, the most distinctive Marxian materialism is *practical*. This asserts the constitutive role of human agency in reproducing and transforming society, and his conception is akin to the transformational model of social activity developed by Bhaskar in his pre-dialectical work.[16] Putting these three forms of materialism together, Bhaskar will say that historical materialism 'presupposes epistemological, is rooted in ontological, but consists in a substantive elaboration of practical materialism' (ibid.).

These comments on Marx's materialism constitute an alternative intellectual standpoint to Hegel that is both substantively materialist and methodologically realist from which to engage with the idea of contradiction, and to think through materialist diffraction. Before getting there, however, we need to focus in on the idea of contradiction itself.

Contradiction in Kant, Hegel and Marx

The question of contradiction takes us briefly to Kant, then to Hegel, and on to Marx. As we saw, Hegel credited Kant with restoring Dialectic 'to its post of honour' (Hegel 1975: 117) in modern times, but he was nonetheless highly critical of the way he did so. For Hegel, Kant's problem was that 'contradiction does not affect the object in its own proper essence, but attaches only to the Reason which seeks to comprehend it' (1975: 77). In Kant, the 'blemish of contradiction, it seems, could not be allowed to mar the essence of the world' so that 'thought or Reason, and not the world, is the seat of contradiction' (ibid.). Contradictions, however, are not just the preserve of Reason, but 'appear in all objects of every kind, in all conceptions, notions, and Ideas' so that 'to know objects in this property of theirs' (i.e. as contradictory) is vital to philosophy. The 'true and positive meaning of the antinomies is this: that every actual thing invokes a coexistence of opposed elements . . . a concrete unity of opposed determinations' (1975: 78).

On its face, this is a realist objection to Kant, for contradictions reside in things as well as in thought of them, but the problem with Hegel is that his realism does not go very far. While acknowledging 'the blemish of contradiction' in the world, he does not let it stay there. Contradiction in objects is vital for philosophical theory, it is true, but it is vital in order to illuminate the 'Dialectical influence of logic' (ibid.), and, as such, that influence takes us back to the speculative re-appropriation of worldly realities by thought. Hegel acknowledges the oppositional ways of the world, but only in order to re-appropriate them through and for Reason. So doing, his realised idealism achieves the analytic reinstatement discussed in the previous section, and this leads him, says Bhaskar, to describe 'the contradictions of the sundered world at the dawn of the age of modernity (which Kant prefigures) in a non-contradictory and reconciliatory way' (DPF: 63).

Against this Hegelian approach to the identification and resolution of contradictions in thought stands Marx, but Bhaskar suggests that Marx uses the idea of contradiction in no fewer than five ways. First, Marx speaks of *logical inconsistencies* in discourse, which are related to the idea of simple logical contradiction. These may or may not be related to the other kinds of contradiction that Marx identifies. Second, there are what Bhaskar labels *non-dialectical oppositions*, the example given being the contradiction between supply and demand, where these are understood as relatively independent 'external' forces operating against each other. This is the territory of simple, external contradictions, which Kant termed *Realrepugnanz* (DPF: 70). So far, there is nothing particularly Marxian in what has been identified, but this changes with the third kind of contradiction, which is a *structural dialectical contradiction* intrinsic to a particular social relation. Such a contradiction would include that between wage labour and capital or between the use and exchange value of commodities within capitalism (ibid.). The effect of such contradictions is to provide the conditions of possibility of a fourth kind of contradiction, *geo-historically specific dialectical contradictions* (ibid.). These emerge in consequence of structural contradiction and lead to crises, change or transformation in particular societies under particular conditions.

Finally, at a deeper level there exist contradictions that relate structural oppositions to existential contradictions for human beings at the core of their being. Bhaskar calls this kind of contradiction an original *generative separation*,[17] which may have a variety of implications for basic human relations. Under capitalism, it involves no fewer than five splits for humankind. These begin with a 'split or alienation of the immediate producers from the means and materials of their production' (DPF: 70). This has the effect of generating an alienation of human beings from their labour and, resulting from this, further alienations of such beings 'from the planes of their material transactions with nature, their social interactions with each other, the network of social relations in which they produce, and ultimately themselves' (DPF: 70–1).[18] There is a fivefold generative separation under capitalism, which involves contradiction for human being at the most fundamental level.

This fivefold separation is something we shall develop in Chapter 4,[19] but the main point here is to identify, through Marx, a materialist and realist way of dealing with contradiction. Such an approach looks for real contradictions in the spatio-temporal, caused world and finds them at three different levels: as structural contradictions affecting the general organisation of society; as specific geo-historical, persistent and episodically effective oppositions; and as deep existential conflicts affecting humankind in its core being. These are real contradictions of a structural, conjunctural and existential kind, identified in the analysis of the material conditions in which human beings live. But they raise rather than resolve questions concerning our understanding of contradictions. If these *are* the substantive, material contradictions for human beings, what exactly is a materialist contradiction in philosophical terms, and what, especially, is one that is dialectical?

What is a materialist dialectical contradiction?

To answer this question, Bhaskar begins by distinguishing 'internal' and 'external' contradictions.[20] The latter are pervasive in the form of constraints in both nature and society, and are just a consequence of living in a world of irreducible difference and non-identity, of finite 'determinate spatio-temporal being' (DPF: 57). This is the realm of Kantian *Realrepugnanz*, mentioned earlier, and is not of especial interest to dialectical analysis. Where there is determinate and different being, it will come into conflict and contradiction with other such being. Internal contradictions, on the other hand, are of interest. They are the product of the possibility of emergent entities, of totalities, and in general of 'internally related grounded ensembles' (ibid.). An external contradiction 'specifies a situation which permits the satisfaction of one end or more generally result only at the expense of another: that is, a bind or constraint' (DPF: 56). An internal contradiction is the same, but the bind or constraint comes from within rather than without. It involves

> a double-bind or self-constraint. . . . In this case a system, agent or structure, S, is blocked from performing with one system, rule or principle, R, because it is performing with another, R′; or, a course of action, T, generates a

countervailing, inhibiting, undermining, overriding or otherwise opposed course of action, T'. R' and T' are radically negating of R and T respectively.

(ibid.)

Dialectical contradictions are a form of internal contradiction, but their internal quality is better understood by first examining the broader set of dialectical *connections* of which they are a part. Such connections are 'between entities or aspects of a totality such that they are in principle distinct but inseparable, in the sense that they are synchronically or conjuncturally internally related, i.e. both (some, all) or one existentially presuppose the other(s)' (DPF: 58). Bhaskar writes that here we are 'in the domain of . . . *intra-* rather than *inter-*action', which may involve existential constitution of a thing by something else, or its permeation by or containment within it, or just an intrinsic connection. These terms take us back to Chapter 2, where, it will be recalled, existential constitution illustrated the effects of 'the past' and 'the outside' on a social life understood as rooted in the material meshwork of space, time and causality. So, when Bhaskar talks of dialectical connection as involving internal or intra-relations, he has in mind the connections in material beings in a dynamic world. He is thinking very much in spatio-temporal terms, and he accordingly explains that a connection may be 'absolute, epochal, structurally periodic, conjunctural or momentary' (ibid.). Where things existentially presuppose other things, this is also linked to the process (becoming) and product (being) analysis discussed in Chapter 2. Existential presupposition 'may hold between absences and absentings as well as positive instances and processes,' and 'causal connections and existential dependencies may be transfactual or actual' (ibid.) – that is, they may exist between a structural element and an actual existent, or between actual existents. Dialectical connection in a materialist understanding is pervasive in a spatio-temporal, caused world.

Turning from connections to dialectical *contradictions* adds to the sense of intrinsic, existential connection the additional feature that the elements in an entity

are also opposed, in the sense that (at least) one of their aspects negates (at least) one of the other's, or their common ground or the whole . . . , so that they are tendentially mutually exclusive, and potentially or actually tendentially transformative.

(ibid.)

Thus, a dialectical contradiction is a form of internal contradiction where a thing, idea or practice discloses an internal, or intra-, relationship with something else. The two entities appear to be, but are not, distinct. They are dialectically connected *and*, within that connection, there also inheres contradiction. The simpler mutual entailment of dialectical connection is replaced by the mutual exclusivity *within* mutual entailment of dialectical contradiction. The double bind is constitutive of the entity, thought or practice in question, and the intra-connection/contradiction is, to reiterate, fundamentally spatio-temporal in its terms on a materialist analysis. Here we are in the realm of contradiction within 'entity relationism' and existential constitution.

It is now possible to align Bhaskar's philosophical account of material dialectical contradictions with Marx's analysis of the different forms that material contradictions take under modern social conditions. For example, where Marx talks of a structural dialectical contradiction between labour and capital, Bhaskar will represent this as a mutually entailed ('dialectically connected') and tendentially mutually exclusive ('dialectically contradictory'), materially structured ('product-in-process'), historically emergent ('process-in-product'), social ('ontological') relation. Where Marx might write of the working through of a specific, conjunctural, geo-historical contradiction in practice, as he did, for example, in 'The Eighteenth Brumaire of Louis Bonaparte', all the above elements would be present plus the vivid specificities of time, place, conditions and personalities that make the essay so readable. For Bhaskar, this would be a fine example of the depiction of 'process-in-product-in-process', subject to the specifics of space and time ('spatio-temporal rhythmic'), and answering to the structural ('transfactual') dialectical connection and contradiction that results in Marx's 'Well grubbed, old mole!'

Of course, Bhaskar's philosophical language lacks the immediacy, colour and practical relevance of these more concrete analyses, but comprehension must occur at different levels, and we are interested in what it means to talk of material dialectical contradictions. The question that still remains concerns the import of seeing such contradictions as 'diffracted' in the Bhaskarian approach.

Diffracting dialectic: logical and dialectical contradictions

In the Introduction to this chapter, I suggested that the idea of diffraction involves both a process of breaking down and differentiating what may otherwise appear a unitary phenomenon, and a process of opening it up to broader scrutiny and understanding in a more holistic way. The relationship between logical and material dialectical contradictions in Hegel and Marx illustrates these different elements. For Hegel, logical contradiction is (ultimately) the unifying, dynamic force in dialectic, that which gives it its 'teleonomic push' and reconciles the rational and the real. However, his insistence on the grasp of the real in thought leads to an essential, illicit fusion of two different things: dialectical logic and real-world contradictions. On a materialist and realist approach, a separation is maintained between a logical contradiction and its dialectical grounds of existence, though the separation also involves a connection. For Marx (and Bhaskar), logical contradictions are important, but as signs of something else. They cannot be 'cured' by sublatory reason, for reason is not in the driving seat. What must be grasped is the link between contradictions in thought and their underlying structural grounds. In exploring the real, material ground of a logical contradiction, Marx expands the field of contradictions to include material contradictions that may or may not give rise to specifically logical ones. The latter may be dialectical – that is, expressing an internal contradiction – but they represent only one kind of dialectical contradiction in a much broader field.

Opening up the field of dialectics thus allows us to see that it is possible to describe dialectical contradictions without oneself committing logical ones.

Dialectical contradictions of the type described by Marx may be 'straightforwardly [and] consistently described and scientifically explained' (DPF: 71), and the logical contradictions that may ensue from living with dialectical contradictions may be equally described and explained. For example, Marx had resort in his critique of the commodity form to the ways in which reality was mystified in the value, wage and legal forms. The resulting logical contradictions in how people spoke about these matters, and the underlying material contradictions that gave rise to them, could be consistently described, explained and related to each other. Considering the commodity form and the mystifications to which it gives rise, 'the notion of a real *inverted*, or otherwise mystifying, conception of a real object, perhaps the result of the ensemble or ground containing the very phenomena mystified, may be readily [understood]' (ibid.).

What Bhaskar is pointing to here is the relationship between a (logical) contradiction in belief, or as a belief is expressed in action, and the underlying ground that generates it. In this regard, he draws a crucial distinction between Marx and Hegel. The latter operates with the idea of contradictions embodying *the identity of opposites*, which the rationalist dialectical method reveals and resolves. The former works with the idea of a *grounded unity of opposites* that the materialist dialectical method explores and seeks to understand. For Marx, as a practical as well as a philosophical materialist, resolution of a contradiction is also possible, but this involves something additional: a change not just in thought, but of states of affairs in the world through practical engagement. Marx's concern is with dialectical explanation and practical transformation as opposed to Hegel's 'transfigurative redescription of, and reconciliation to, *Das Bestehende* (the actually existing state of affairs)' (DPF: 61) through the rational resolution of contradiction. In all cases, Marx looks to structural and geo-historically specific contradictions and their relation to underlying generative separations in specific societies as the basis for explaining the logical contradictions emphasised by Hegel.

What we get from this in terms of (materialist) diffraction is a sense of the variety of kinds of contradiction, the relationship between them at different levels, and the way in which these different phenomena and levels constitute a related whole. Like the fragmented spectrum of coloured light that is produced by directing a unitary beam at a prism, we open up the possibilities for contradiction and their relations to each other under a materialist viewpoint. Dialectical contradictions represent a field of play rather than the engine of a unitary intellectual process. Nor can understanding of diffraction be a prioristic, for how the field is constituted will vary according to structure and conjuncture, relation and context. One should think of contradictions of different kinds operating at different levels, and in complex interaction with each other. Contradictions in the world may be more or less antagonistic in their form, depending on whether the antagonism is 'partial or latent or rhythmically dislocated, [or is] manifest to a greater or lesser extent in conflict' (DPF: 59). Conflict in turn 'can be covert or overt, transfactual or actual, as well as being conducted in a variety of different modes' (ibid.). From such a starting point, a complex depth realist picture of contradiction and conflict as either real or actual, or (structurally) real but (actually) absent or present, is possible. The spectrum of possibilities remains broad on a materially diffracted dialectic. Nevertheless, however the real contours of contradiction emerge in the geo-historically specific material meshwork of society, it is never a question of *reducing* logical contradiction to its grounds of being. Logical contradictions remain a *sui generis* part of the world, possessing their own materiality. They must be engaged with in their own terms while relating them to their underlying grounds of existence. In a realist framework, this is a crucial requirement for social scientific work, for human meaning, as we noted in Chapter 1, always mediates structural relations. That (1M) original critical realist argument is necessarily carried forward into the 2E dialectical form with which we are engaged here.

Diffracting dialectic: immanent, ideology and explanatory critique

It is important also to note that materially diffracting dialectic develops the forms of critique available to social science. As we have seen, the key critical move in Hegel is to immanent, or negative, dialectical critique (D in the U-D-R movement). Analytically, this move involves two things. First, there is the articulation of the concept of the Understanding discussed or isolated at D, which may be termed D_1. Second, there is diagnosis of the lack or contradiction subsequently identified in it, which can be called D_2. These two moments at D (D_1 and D_2) then serve as the transition point to drive the dialectic forward through speculative reason (R). After Marx, Bhaskar suggests, there is also a third moment, D_3, to be considered. This is reflection on the inconsistency between D_1 and D_2, and those materially grounded conditions that sustain its existence and persistence and prevent, often enough, its resolution.

For Hegel, logical contradiction indicates a failure of reason, so all that is required is a rational sublation of D_1 and D_2 at R. Why diffract the dialectical process to identify D_3 and dwell on the discrepancy between D_1 and D_2? In 'differentiated and non-idealist' (DPF: 29) dialectical contexts, dialectics are particularly concerned with exploring how D_2 contradictions endure as materially achieved ideology. The dialectical method of immanent critique at D_2 becomes in consequence ideology critique at D_3 (ibid.). With Marx and Bhaskar, ideology critique, the D_3 identification of the grounds of contradictions, is distinguished from the internal understanding (at D_1), or logical critique (at D_2), of any particular D_1–D_2 contradiction. For Bhaskar, ideology critique becomes linked with the critical realist practice of depth-explanatory critique – that is, the identification of the underlying generative mechanisms or structures that represent the grounds for ideas. This becomes possible just because materialist dialectic involves the *grounded* unity of opposites, for that grounding generates the place of ideology and for depth-explanatory critique opened up at D_3. It also, in consequence, bars the door to a simple further step of rational resolution. Identification of the D_3 material grounds of logical critique takes us away from idealist thinking and into the relevant social totality where dialectic operates.

Diffracting dialectic: constellating dialectical and analytical thought

Finally, there is the relationship between dialectical and analytical thought under an account of materialist diffraction. For Hegel, analytic thought operates at the level of the Understanding and is exposed to dialectical critique at the second moment, D, in the U-D-R development. For Bhaskar, the material grounding of the moment of dialectical critique (D_3) generates a different relationship between analytics and dialectics. This involves the idea of a 'constellation' between thinking and being to explain the relation.

The argument is as follows. If we consider any thought or action that embodies analytically a logical contradiction ('A/not A'), the result will be inconsistency, incoherence or indeterminacy in thought or act. The actor will either do contradictory things or be blocked by the contradiction and not know how to act. The conflict cannot, however, lead to a simple absence of thought or action, for even suspending one's thought or not acting will be a response to the situation by omission. Thought or action is unavoidable, and both are determined by more than simple logical consistency. To think otherwise is to fall into the Hegelian trap of logicising being, more generally in critical realist terms, to commit a form of the epistemic fallacy. The things people think and the reasons why they act in a material, spatio-temporal world are the product of thinking *in that world*, not just of thinking per se, so that determinacy in thought or action is the product of the contextualised 'thrownness' of thinking in a geo-historic context.

Now, 'thinking in the world', as we might call it, is an example of Bhaskar's figure of the constellation, what he calls the 'constellational identity of the intrinsic [here, thinking] within the extrinsic [in its geo-historical context] or, loosely, the rational within the causal' (DPF: 58).[21] There is a constellational, embedded relation between thinking and context, or, putting it differently, between the analytical and the dialectical, understood in a realist, materialist way.[22] Logical contradictions, as we noted, are not just contradictions in our thought or as our thoughts are embodied in action. When they exist, 'they are real constituents of the *Lebenswelt*' (DPF: 58), and they abide. As enduring social entities or grounds, they may be consistently described and explained, and they may or may not be overcome in practice. If analytical thinking, the sphere of clear distinctions that Hegel describes as the Understanding, is the sphere in which logical contradictions are detected, then dialectical thinking is not just their immanent critique and ensuing rational resolution. It is, rather, that form of thinking which starts in immanent critique (D_2 above) and is then traced to its underlying grounds (D_3 above), where it becomes the englobing, contextualising, *constellated* understanding that deepens our grasp of the nature of analytical claims. This includes a sense of their truth or necessity, but also the limits of that truth in and to particular contexts. A dialectical critique will ask of any analytical claim: what does it state, misstate or not state by virtue of the context that contains and conditions it? However it works, it does so because of the constellational relation it enjoys in relation to analytical modes of reasoning.

Such an approach allows Bhaskar to say that '[d]ialectical critical realism will situate, [and] not just negate, "logic"' (DPF: 67). This is important for an understanding of modern western, especially Anglo-American, philosophy with its emphasis on the analytical virtues. Against it, Bhaskar argues that such philosophy discards history in favour of a logic-driven analysis of concepts. In so doing, it becomes 'the normally unconscious and characteristically aporetic normalization of past, and denegation of present and future, change' (DPF: 64). Analytical philosophy takes our present concepts, which reflect a process of (dialectical) historical development, to be the 'natural' concepts for philosophy to discuss. Lacking a sense of the (dialectical) relationship between (analytical) concepts and (constellating) history, it cannot see beyond the current state of the world and the concepts it has produced. A constellational embedding of the analytical within the dialectical opens up this relation, pointing to the limits of the analytical without ever suggesting that analytical concepts lack theoretical or practical import. If it is a function of analytical thinking that it denies or is blind to dialectics, dialectics, the deeper form of thought, responds by diagnosing the analytic's intrinsic limits, constellationally locating it in a context, and moving beyond it.[23]

Materialist diffraction in practice

From both Bhaskar's immanent critique of Hegel and his discussion of Marx and contradictions, we see how a substantively materialist and methodologically realist approach to dialectic opens up the different possibilities that exist within it. At the beginning of this chapter, I linked diffraction to fragmentation and differentiation, and also to the opening up of phenomena in themselves and in their relation to each other. The effect of Hegelian idealism in contrast is to produce a spiritual monism which, despite its emphasis on unity-in-diversity to reflect modern pluralism, is nonetheless an effort to create a dialectic that is linear and centrist in form. Diffraction involves breaking dialectic up into its differentiated and plural worldly forms, discovering it where and as it is in reality. With it, it becomes possible to

> consider ontological and epistemological dialectics and their relations apart from one another, so potentially turning up very different dialectical structures. More generally the critique of a monistic dialectic which is centrist, expressivist, actualized and closed broadens the diffraction into a multiplicity of topological modes, including systematically intermingled and embedded ones.
>
> (DPF: 92)

Once we loosen the grip of idealist dialectic, we are able to look for dialectics where we find them, in their real-world habitats and, in terms of their form, in their natural, irreducible complexity. We can view them in terms of the patterns they disclose, rather than in terms of an overall shaping and ordering that artificially pulls them together and presents them in a linear fashion. Dialectics can, metaphorically, begin to speak for themselves, and they do so in all fields of human knowledge and activity. They work in and out of the contexts of which they are a part. Indeed, in a differentiated world 'it may be wrong to talk as if "dialectic" specified a unitary phenomenon' as opposed to 'a number of different topics and configurations' (DPF: 96). Generally, breaking into the Hegelian monistic circuit 'permits us to call upon . . . a galaxy of topologies, choreographies and genealogies' (ibid.). These are all a part of dialectic on this more open, extended account. Diffracting dialectic extends dialectical relations into a variety of regions and a range of modes. Dialectics are reflected throughout the different zones of social and natural being, in the knowledge, ethics, practices and natural and social relations that constitute human being in the world. They relate accordingly 'to patterns or processes or relations in philosophy, science or the world; [to] being, thought or their relation; [to] nature or society, theory or practice' (DPF: 96). In these different areas, dialectic 'may be structured, synchronic, location-ally periodised or geo-historically dynamic, diachronic, processually spatio-temporalised, tensed or tenseless, generic or subject-specific, abstract or concrete, universal, mediated or singularised' (ibid.). In all this, however, the other side of a materially diffracted dialectic is the relations *between* things, existing either at the same or at different levels to each other. Diffracted dialectics are also about connections, especially in an ontologically deep, structured material world, and one of the aims in grasping the differentiation of dialectic is so as to be able to see more clearly how different things are connected.

We could perhaps stop here with what amounts to a general invitation to think in a dialectically diffracted manner across the range of fields that constitute human life, and to explore the topic of dialectics in the further areas of totality, ethics and the critique of philosophy that are pursued below. Three examples, however, may help to illuminate the general position, one from social dialectics, which operates as an illustration of what has been said, the other two in philosophy, which can serve as reflections on diffraction. The final example, on 'diffracting Marx', permits a brief reflection on the controversy over Bhaskar's broader, substantive views on Marx.

Diffracting social dialectics

For Bhaskar, social dialectic

> may focus on the condensation of rhythmics, of structurally sedimented institutions, the network of social relations between positioned practices, the mutability (or stasis) of inter-subjective inter-/intra-actions, the nature of their material transactions with nature or the kinetics of the intra-subjective sphere, the communicative, moral or power$_2$ relationality of the social fabric. It may be totalising or compartmentalising; . . . directional and/or chaotic . . . , uniformal, differentiated or pluralistic, centrifying or localising, grounded or not.
>
> (DPF: 97)

In considering what Bhaskar has in mind here, one is reminded of the differential social rhythmics juxtaposed in a modern city such as Los Angeles or New Delhi, discussed in Chapter 2.[24] These illustrate diffracted dialectics among 'the phenomena of emergent spatio-temporalities' and 'the possibilities of over-lapping, intersecting, condensing, elongated, divergent, convergent and even contradictory rhythmics' (DPF: 54). One can think precisely of the 'condensation of rhythmics' in such places, and how these produce a range of dialectics involving 'structurally sedimented institutions', complex and conflicting 'networks of relations', vivid kinds of change and equally astonishing forms of stasis, increasingly difficult transactions with nature, and the widest range of psychic conflicts and transformations for people. All these represent the contexts in which communication occurs, moral demands are made and felt, and structured power relations are lived. The result may be to open up groups to each other, or to close them off, and interactive dynamics may be progressive or regressive, with chaos as a backstop. With their interrelated trajectories and varying outcomes, these are the stuff of dialectical analysis. Yet in their diffracted plurality, it is crucial to retain a sense of the relation between the parts and the whole, so that change rests on stasis, sedimented institutions sponsor new networks of relations, new networks place further strain on transactions with nature, and psychic conflicts and transformations mediate all these things. Similarly, one must also identify the structural grounds operating at different levels, for example of economic 'globalisation', which underpin and shape all the other elements, and always in multiple further sets of dialectical relations.

To some this may still appear too sketchy, but Bhaskar's aim is not to provide the substantive social analysis that would clothe his terms. His role as a philosopher is to identify and underlabour for the application of concepts in specific scientific inquiries, not to carry those inquiries out. It seems to me, however, that there is a real openness and breadth to his thinking which permits us to think through the diffuse and diverse nature of an often fast-changing social reality without at the same time simply surrendering to its difference. On change, think of his emphasis on becoming and process-in-product, discussed in Chapter 2. On fragmentation, diffracted materialistic dialectic in this flexible, open, plural form is also attractive. Its openness to difference permits reflection on the conflict between Marxist and postmodern accounts of society. This allows one to acknowledge much of the truth that postmodernists identify in the failure of 'grand narratives', or of too rigid and therefore reductionist ways of grasping social phenomena. A materially diffracted dialectic is open to the intrinsic complexity and differentiation of phenomena, but, against postmodernism, and with Marxism, it has an advantage. Difference is not acclaimed at the cost of losing sight of the structured whole in which the array of phenomena can be grasped. One of the values of a materially diffracted dialectic is that it is able to comprehend fragmentation and the ephemeral in modern life while stressing continuities, and that some things, structures, traditions, institutions, continue to endure. The pace of change and the durability of things must in every case be discussed a posteriori, in the light of the evidence, and a materially diffracted dialectic is open to all possibilities. It is concerned with things that last, as well as things that come and go in an instant, with 'elongated dialectics and dialectics of balance, but also . . . the evanescent trace or the shooting star' (DPF:

202). As a result, materialist diffraction gives support to those who would argue that a non-reductionist, pluriform understanding of dialectics resides at the core of Marxian historical materialism (Creaven 2002: 95–9).

Diffracting philosophical dialectics

Here, I am thinking of the diffracted dialectic in dialectical philosophy itself. As we have seen, this can be analysed in terms of the critical historical and philosophical limits to be found in individual dialectical philosophers such as Plato or Hegel. This may involve a sense of engagement in favour of either the preservative or non-preservative sublation of previous philosophers. If sublation is wholly or partially non-preservative, there is a determinate negation that leaves the past behind. Since philosophy is generally understood by Bhaskar as 'only a moment in a practical ensemble or totality', so that 'any dialectic in philosophy [will] be jagged and non-linear' (DPF: 92) as it is pulled about by social forces, the diffracted dialectic of dialectical philosophy is likely to display a fractured and fragmented quality. However, this would not be the whole story, for dialectics diffracted, we have said, may exhibit both continuity and development and rupture and contradiction. Philosophical dialectics for a dialectical philosopher like Bhaskar must have a double quality, for his own work must be located within the dialectical tradition that he himself critiques and seeks to recast. Hence, he must both tell the critical story of the failure of existing dialectical philosophy, and also identify the achievements of previous dialectical philosophers in the tradition of which he is a part. Since we have spent so much time on the former in this chapter, it is appropriate to say a little about the latter.

Bhaskar's account works its way from Plato and Parmenides, as we have seen, to Kant, Hegel and Marx, primarily by way of negative critique of their limits. Yet there is a progressive dimension to the epistemological learning dialectic of which he is himself a part. Going back to the Greeks, the dialectical tradition starts with Heraclitus, who provides the initial formulation of *dialectical contradictions* involving 'internally related, mutually exclusive forces of non-independent origins' (DPF: 100). From Socrates, there come *dialectical arguments*, which are marked by the idea that truth can be disclosed through discussion. From Plato comes the idea of *dialectical reason*, which involves the relationship between the passing entities of the world and the infinite truths embodied in the Platonic Forms. From Aristotle, there come *dialectical propaedeutics*, which in his thought involve the preparation of the ground for scientific reason, and broadly derive from Socratic argument. For Bhaskar, Aristotle sets

> the boundary conditions for that continual circulation in and out of the sphere of formal reasoning, in which meanings and (e.g. truth) values remain fixed and determinate (or stable in their indeterminacy), characteristic of all (meaningful) discourse in science and ordinary life alike.
>
> (DPF: 101)

Moving on from the Greeks, in both Plotinus and Schiller there is the idea of a specific type of *dialectical process* involving 'an original undifferentiated unity, geo-historical diremption or diaspora and an eventual return to a non-alienated but differentiated self or unity-in-diversity' (DPF: 101–2). From Hegel, there is the idea of *dialectical intelligibility*, which for him 'depends upon the teleologically generated presentation, comment on (i.e. immanent critique of) and preservative supersession of conceptual and socio-cultural forms' (DPF: 102), albeit that these operate under the method of realised idealism. From Marx, *dialectical praxis* involves 'the unity of theory and praxis . . . in practice (not, as Hegel, in theory) in the non-preservative transformative negation of oppressive social forms, most notably, in Marx's case, the capitalist mode of production' (ibid.). Such praxis, it should be added, sets out from a materialist understanding of diffracted dialectic. Then, from Kant, Hegel and Marx together, we get the idea of *dialectical freedom*. This is dependent upon 'the achievement of absolute reason in dialectical praxis' and 'encompasses the absenting of constraints, including ills generally, which comprise lack of freedoms' (ibid.). This last Bhaskar links especially to his own ethics, which we shall consider in Chapter 5.

When heretofore existing dialectical philosophy is examined under the gaze of diffracted dialectic, a double story must be told. It is the story of philosophy in the constellated shadow of power relations, and of philosophy as a halting, yet developing, engagement with the world and what it means, historically and existentially, to be human. This double story leads to a vision of dialectical philosophy as implicated and challenging, as structured by and critically engaged with the world, as a mode of thought between power and freedom from it. The same, however, is true of modern philosophies that may not be regarded generally as dialectical, but which reveal commonality and alignment with the dialectical tradition. Here, Bhaskar singles out two philosophers, Habermas and Derrida, with whom a dialectical engagement is immanent. Habermas is himself a dialectical philosopher who resumes the 'original sense of dialectic as dialogue' (DPF: 96), and who is also connected to the Kantian ambition for dialectical freedom (see Chapter 5). Derrida's deconstruction, on the other hand, which is usually regarded as anti-dialectical, not least by Derrideans, becomes an alternative choreography *within dialectic*, and both the Habermasian and Derridean orientations to dialectic are linked by Bhaskar to those like himself 'pursuing the materialist line of negation as essentially involved [with] discursively moralised power$_2$ relations' (ibid.). The specific arguments for this diffracted dialectical reading of apparently non-dialectical philosophy, especially in its poststructuralist mode, await us in Chapters 6 and 7. My aim here has been to identify the other, affirmative, side of the process of a diffracted philosophical dialectics.

Diffracting Marx

The comments above concerning the grounding of diffracted plurality together with the general thrust of his argument against Hegel point to a strong connection between basic themes in Marx and Bhaskar's dialectical critical realism. This has not, however, meant that *Dialectic* has been well received by Marxists. In this brief section, I wish to explore one such reaction, by Sean Creaven, who argues that Bhaskar misunderstands both his own relationship to Marx and Marx himself (see also Joseph 2006). From this discussion, we can arrive at a sense in which it is necessary to see Marx's own thought as diffracted.

On the Bhaskar–Marx relation, Creaven suggests that while dialectical critical realism offers 'important insights for Marxism, it neither outflanks nor transcends Marxian dialectic, but is rather dependent on it, and often in unacknowledged ways' (2002: 78). More strongly, he argues that 'Marxian dialectic is foundational to [dialectical critical realism], not vice versa' (2002: 115). This suggestion of a turf war is not very helpful. I hope enough has been said to indicate that Bhaskar does indeed draw on Marx in order to elaborate his idea of a diffracted dialectic, and openly so. It should also be clear that his aim is not to 'outflank' or 'transcend' Marx, but rather to offer a philosophical comprehension of what it was that Marx, and any other ontologically committed realist practitioner of the social or human sciences, is trying to do. For Bhaskar, Marx's work must be comprehended at three levels: in terms of, first, his critique of political economy; second, the broader 'research programme and transformational practice of geo-historical materialism' (DPF: 351); and third, the philosophical theorisation of his scientific realism (DPF: 345). Whereas the first of these was highly developed by Marx, the second was not, and the third was 'never satisfactorily theorised' at all (ibid.). As a philosophical underlabourer for the social and human sciences, it is at the third level that Bhaskar's dialectics make their contribution. They help realise

> Marx's unconsummated desire 'to make accessible to the ordinary human intelligence' – though it will take more than two or three printers' sheets – 'what is *rational* in the method which Hegel discovered and at the same time mystified', as well as to clarify the exact relation between Marx's own dialectic and Hegel's one.[25]
>
> (DPF: 1)

Like Bhaskar, Creaven acknowledges that Marx remained an applied dialectician who 'did not find the time to submit his own dialectical method to systematic analysis' (2002: 107), or theorise his relationship to Hegel. There is work to be done at this level, and Bhaskar has sought to do it, but it does not mean that he has sought to 'outflank' Marx. Though Bhaskar's aim may be to 'transcend' in the sense of to 'sublate' him, by developing the more abstract level that his thought requires, this is plainly a sublation of the preservative kind.[26]

Where Creaven has a more legitimate ground for concern, however, is in regard to Bhaskar's comments on Marx's substantive theory and how undeveloped philosophical assumptions at the third level of his system feed into errors at the second level of his geo-historic materialism. These in turn provide, for Bhaskar, a basis in Marx's own thought for many of the gross, politically inhuman acts carried out in the name of Marxism in the twentieth century. In passages that are compacted, Bhaskar writes, for example, that it is not evident that Marx can be acquitted of a variety of charges including 'class/power$_2$ one-dimensionality; presentational linearity; proleptic endism,[27] mediated through the residues of a technologically derived functionalism; Prometheanistically displaced triumphalism; [an] unfolding evolutionism; and . . . a [reductive] programmatic practical-expressivism' (DPF: 93). There is no space to pursue these different, elliptical claims, but nor is there really much purpose in doing so. Creaven objects to this line of analysis on the basis that it must rely on disparate comments from different Marx texts since Marx never developed, as Bhaskar agrees, an overall viewpoint (Creaven 2002: 95–9, 123–9). He is right to do so, for, as Bhaskar acknowledges, 'corresponding to each charge' he makes against Marx, 'one can find contrary evidence in his oeuvre' (DPF: 93). It is precisely the incompleteness of Marx's work, Bhaskar's own premise, that makes the cherry-picking of quotations so problematic. A similar problem is to be seen in Bhaskar's claim that Marx is the original source of 'the sins of his successors', for example in the former Soviet Union, where

> the voluntaristic attempt to build socialism in one country, on the basis of a supposedly omniscient commandist party state . . . , leading to the sinking of the USSR into an undifferentiated expressive unity . . . can be given Marxian credentials, however much Marx would have loathed the outcome.
>
> (DPF: 350)

Again, it is not so much the substantive characterisation that is at issue as the validity in deriving it. As Bhaskar acknowledges, he is arguing here 'to some extent, with the benefit of hindsight' (ibid.), and also selectively, since many different currents of thought, equally indebted to Marx, fought over the direction that the Soviet Union should take. Methodologically, the argument is also at risk of overstating the importance of ideas in historical contexts, which materialist diffraction would oppose. In terms of the idea of the constellation of the internal (thinking) and the external (geo-history), Bhaskar should argue for the greater significance of the latter, for ideas must be materially contextualised. The long and the short of it is that, if Bhaskar is right to claim that Marx's philosophical understanding of his project remained unachieved, one cannot give fragments of his thought the status of an achieved philosophy for which he can be called theoretically to account.

Conclusion

If the first aim of *Dialectic* is the dialecticisation of critical realism, one might describe its second aim, the recasting of dialectic on critical realist grounds, as the 'critical realisation of dialectic'. That, at any rate, has been the focus of this chapter. In it, we have considered the idea of materialist diffraction as a question of *form*, in which the linear and ultimately monistic dialectics of Hegel are given over to fragmentation, fracturing, difference and variety, and within this process the relation between the fragmented and fractured parts is also stressed. When we look at the diffraction of contradiction in the materialist vision, or more generally the fractured nature of the modern world, we are also concerned as to how things exist in relation to each other. In that regard, we have also focused on materialist diffraction as a question of *method* – that is, an assertion of the substantively materialist and philosophically realist understanding that underpins diffraction, in the way that Hegel's idealist reliance on thinking and mind ultimately sustain monism and linearity in his philosophy. To argue for materialist diffraction has led to a focus on Hegelian dialectic and its critique, and in this chapter we have followed the route of establishing the nature of that dialectic, identifying Bhaskar's immanent critique of it, and then examining how, on the basis of aligning himself with Marx, Bhaskar then produces a diffracted account of contradiction and a more extended sense of the possibilities of diffraction under modern social conditions.

How does this leave the relationship between Hegel, Marx and Bhaskar? If Bhaskar's immanent critique of Hegel knocks at the door of a critical realist appropriation of dialectic, it is through Marx that the door is opened. In the preface to *Dialectic*, Bhaskar writes that the book is the site of an encounter between 'a dialectically developed critical realism and Hegelian and Hegelian-inspired dialectic' (DPF: xiii). While this maintains, develops and enriches critical realism, it entails 'a non-preservative sublation of Hegelian dialectic' (ibid.). This may seem a contradiction in terms, since 'sublation', being the English translation for the German *Aufhebung*, means both to cancel an existing problem and to maintain its terms in any ensuing resolution; any sublation is, by definition, preservative. There is, however, a famous precedent for such ambivalence to Hegel, in Marx, for whom it was also necessary to acknowledge something of abiding import in Hegel, while radically shifting the terms of debate. In Marx, this was presented in the form of a metaphor:

> The mystification which dialectic suffers in Hegel's hands by no means prevents him from being the first to present its general form of working in a comprehensive and conscious manner. With him it is standing on its head. It must be turned right side up again, if you would discover the rational kernel within the mystical shell.
>
> (Marx 1954: 29)

Since Bhaskar's philosophically materialist diffraction of dialectic draws upon Marx's critique of Hegel, one of the consequences of following Bhaskar's argument is to present a dialectical critical realist interpretation of what Marx meant by this metaphor. But what of 'non-preservative' sublation? It should first be noted that sublations involve the 'determinate transformative negation'[28] of an existing state of affairs, and, as such, 'may be totally, essentially or partially preservative' (DPF: 12). It seems to me that while many elements of the Hegelian dialectic are not preserved in Bhaskar's dialectic, other ideas, core to the general idea of dialectic, are. In order to think this through, we need to compare the two dialectics of Hegel and Bhaskar in the three- and fourfold movements they develop. It will be recalled that Hegel's three terms of the Understanding–Dialectic–Reason (U-D-R) in his *Logic* represent moments of *identity*, *negativity* and *totality*.

Bhaskar's four terms in comparison are those of (1M) non-identity, (2E) negativity, (3L) totality and (4D) practice, and he argues that where his terms are the same as Hegel's – that is, negativity and totality – they are in fact substantially different. Whereas Hegel's starting point is identity in the concept and the object proposed by the Understanding, Bhaskar's starting point is sheer, real-world, ontological difference, *non-identity* in the world, in our thinking of that world, and indeed in the very act of thinking itself. The absence implicit in being as non-identity, that is, the determinate non-being that constitutes it, together with its dynamic becoming, are the driving force for thinking *negativity* at the second edge.

How does Bhaskarian negativity differ from Hegel's? Mainly in that it stresses real determinate absence in the world, which lies at the core of being and identity, and is the driving force for change given the spatio-temporal causality of all being (its natural necessity). In Hegel's *Logic*, in contrast, nothingness creates the transition between being and becoming, but in order to start the evolution of the categories and rationalise the existence of the middle step of negative Dialectic in the U-D-R triad. This gives it an essentially cognitive, thinking and questioning, role. While Hegel insists that change is in objects of the world as well as in our thoughts of those objects, his emphasis on the identification of contradictions in cognition and logic and their resolution in reason draws negativity away from the world, and into thought. With Bhaskar, the emphasis on the natural necessity of being that sustains dialectical connection and contradiction, and that is animated by real determinate absence, retains first and foremost the sense of negativity in the world, working outside, and of course also within, philosophical thought and action. In the (constellational) relationship between thinking and the world, it is a question of where the weight is placed.

As regards the third level of *totality*, one difference in the Hegelian and Bhaskarian terms was discussed above. A Hegelian totality is a bad totality if it is open, because it is the essence of the drive to rational totality that it should close and complete itself. For dialectical critical realism, real totalities are typically open, while a closed totality would be an exceptional, limit case. It is also clear that themes such as the spatio-temporality of worldly development point in the direction of continuing change and a conception of open totality. We shall develop the analysis of totality in Chapter 4. Finally, as regards *practice*, this is something we have not considered in this chapter, but we shall do so in Chapter 5. In broad terms, Bhaskar's argument is that such a category is rendered essentially otiose in the Hegelian dialectic, for in a rationally complete world, all action is essentially given in advance within the forms of the world. For Bhaskar, to the contrary, the reality of agency is given in the material constitution of human beings who, operating in an unfinished world, are capable of acting on and changing it. While they have no choice but to act (or omit to act), they do have choice in their actions, and this leads to the possibility of real change, alongside that of simply reproducing existing social relations and structures.

This is a fairly categorical list of differences between Hegel and Bhaskar. What, then, is maintained of Hegelian dialectic? In general terms, it seems to me that the kind of systematising intent evident in the U-D-R movement remains in place in

Bhaskar's 1M–4D development. The latter can be seen as an attempt, through the assertion of realist and materialist protocols, to reconfigure the process of thinking in relation to the world so that the dialectical critical realist system first builds out and away from, and then returns to ground, the Hegelian system as a special and limit case within itself. Bhaskar does not, for example, deny the possibility of a closed totality, but includes it as one possible state of being alongside that of open totality, arguing that the more inclusive system of dialectics is the one that recognises the real possibility that *both* could exist. Bhaskarian totality sees in Hegelian totality a lesser and incomplete, because idealist and rationalist, model of itself. To that extent, Bhaskar draws on what Marx describes as Hegel's achievement in presenting dialectic's 'general form of working' (Marx 1954: 29), albeit in a mystifying – that is, non-materialist and irrealist – form. Similarly, Hegel, Marx and Bhaskar share a sense of dialectic as involving a form of motion (the ancient Greek emphasis on process) of a generally dynamic and historical world. With Hegel, however, reason is aligned a prioristically with a progressivist view of history as the dynamo of development. With Marx and Bhaskar, movement comes from natural necessity, the material grounds discovered a posteriori and the contradictions they embody, alongside responding human agency (from the TMSA – see Chapter 1), in a dynamic that may be progressive or regressive, or exhibit elements of both, and that is, above all, open.

More specifically, the question can be answered by thinking about what 'the rational kernel within the mystical shell' (ibid.) is for Marx in the Hegelian dialectic. In Bhaskar's reading of Marx, reason is replaced as the generalising, resolutory element in Hegel with Marx's identification of the material as the underlying, generally non-resolutory, dialectical ground, and this provides the sense that untying dialectic from reason could 'liberate' it, yielding a 'genuinely multi-dimensional and dynamic logic' (DPF: 63) on the basis of the myriad forms operating geo-temporally in the actually existing world. Diffracted dialectic and materialist contradiction retain crucial elements of existing dialectical thought, however, including those of intrinsic connection and contradiction, and these suggest the basis for Marx's inversion metaphor. Bhaskar suggests that Marx's debt to Hegel 'turns largely . . . on the notion of the dialectical explanation of contradictory forces in terms of a structured common ground' (DPF: 87). The substitution of a real, differentiated, material 'structured common ground' for Hegel's rational identity of opposites opens up the possibility of a very different, richer conception of dialectic, while retaining a core debt to Hegel. In Bhaskar's terms that debt operates in the overlap between the negative dialectical moment (D) in Hegel and the moment of real determinate negation at 2E in his own scheme. Despite their crucial differences, Bhaskar, Marx and Hegel are all dialecticians in a tradition, and the nub of the matter is internal connection and contradiction, and the movement in thought and things these enable. In sum, Bhaskar's realism builds on Marx by showing how the material can be comprehended in a philosophical system that in one part builds on, in another part transcends, in a third part negates Hegelian dialectic. What is specifically retained is a sense of negation and movement in dialectical connection and contradiction, albeit this is rethought on a materialist, realist terrain. With this goes the importance of thinking thought and being in process. I therefore argue that Bhaskar's is a partially preservative sublation of Hegel.

As for Marx, what he lacks, according to Bhaskar, is not a sound theoretical practice, but the underlying philosophy that would ground it. That philosophy would be, as we have seen, consistent with critical realism, indeed critical realist *avant la lettre*. For example, Marx's analysis of the 'real inverted, or otherwise mystifying, conception of a real object' such as the commodity 'may be readily accommodated within a critical realist stratified, non-monovalent, totalising ontology' (DPF: 71). Such an ontology was indeed the kind to which Marx was committed in his mature work, though he never fully developed it there. Marx may indeed be read as a critical realist, his theory being consistent with the idea of '(transfactually) extended structural depth, in the mode of ontological stratification' (DPF: 63). Hegel in comparison only 'achieves . . . the co-presence of absence and presence within an (actualist) extended temporal stretch in the mode of succession in time' (ibid.). Bhaskar accordingly underlabours for Marx, and any other social or human science that takes its ontological commitments seriously, while Marx provides much of the theoretical leverage for materialist diffraction to occur.

Finally, I want to bring out the link between materially diffracted dialectic and the (3L) move to totality pursued in the next chapter. That move is already implicit in the idea of materialist diffraction, for we have noted that diffraction involves fragmenting and fracturing, but also opening dialectic up to connections between what is differentiated and its relation to the whole. To think of the broad ambit of dialectic is also to think about how diffracted elements hang together, whether it be in the form of a constellation (an explicitly totalising concept to be explored in the next chapter), the link between (analytical) thought and historical (dialectical) being, or, at a more concrete level, the connections between the first/third world city (Los Angeles, New Delhi) and processes of economic globalisation. Diffracted dialectic is also about the sets of relations and therefore the wholes within which 'things fall apart'. It implies, in other words, totality.[29] In the previous two chapters, I have introduced, first, a dialecticised critical realism, which generates a holistic sense of natural necessity as being and becoming in a dynamic spatio-temporally caused world (in Chapter 2), and second, a 'critically realised' dialectic, which establishes a materially diffracted dialectic. Putting both together, we have an understanding of the world as the place of a dialectically dynamised and diffracted natural necessity, which requires now to be understood from the point of view of the (3L) level of totality.

4   Opening totality

We have now considered how Bhaskar launches his dialecticisation of critical realism and his 'critical realisation' of dialectics. In terms of the MELD schema, these are essentially 2E moves based on negativity. Dialecticising critical realism by integrating absence and being, and 'critically realising' dialectic to produce a materialist conception of diffraction, both concern real determinate non-being in the world. In the process, however, both moves point beyond negativity to a third level of analysis, that of totality. Thus, to think of the spatio-temporal causality of human being (Chapter 2) is to think of the presence of the past in the present and the future, and of the relationship between identity and its outside. Similarly, to think of materialist diffraction of dialectic is to think (Chapter 3) of how fragmentation and fracturing are ultimately the relata of a structured, contradictory whole. Both involve thinking holistically about human being and social life. A conception of totality is thus implicit in the causal linking of seemingly discrete entities in a world where dialectical negativity prevails. 2E negativity in its various forms entails 3L totality, so, in terms of the MELD schema, we move from 1M perduring non-identity to 2E real negativity, and on to 3L open totality (this chapter), before moving (in the next) to 4D agency.

Totality, then, is the place where different things are seen in their connection, and are viewed as a whole. Among its categories are some we have already encountered and some that are new. It includes ideas of internal relationality and intra-activity, for it is here that we encounter most fully the idea 'of the existential constitution . . . of one entity or category by another' (DPF: 380), and the 'essentiality of contradiction to change' (ibid.). Such ideas point towards an understanding of the whole, and are best seen from that vantage point. From here, we also 'begin to appreciate dialectic as that great loosener which breaks down exclusive dichotomies – between present and past, process and product, one being and another' (ibid.). It allows us to bring out more fully the import of thinking identity in constellational, rhythmic and, we shall see, dispositional terms, in a way that asserts the 'co-incidence of identity and difference and identity and change' (ibid.). It allows us to see that neither analytical logic, nor discursivity more generally, though indispensable to life and knowledge, 'constitutes . . . [or] determines ontology', though both are essential and contained in it (ibid.). Here too is the realm of what Bhaskar calls concrete universality, which links universals, particulars and individuals (in a specifically Bhaskarian way), of holistic causality, and conceptions of mediation and reflexivity essential to grasping the whole. At this level, we also understand the 'Tina syndrome', a totalising conception of how knowledge works, which is in turn embedded in a geo-historical and ethical understanding of the whole. These are all ideas we explore in this chapter.

While things are viewed as they 'come together' in the realm of totality, this requires two provisos. The first is that if the inherent impulse in totality is to connect, this already implies differentiation between things that are connected. It is as important to be able to disconnect, distinguish and divide, for differentiation, 'as all good dialecticians have understood', is a 'necessary condition of totality' (DPF: 270). Dialectic is in fact 'the art of thinking the coincidence of distinctions and connections' (DPF: 180), the understanding of how distinct things are connected. Dialectic accordingly requires a conceptual vocabulary that can handle the idea of distinction-in-connection. Conceptions, for example, of holistic causality, constellationality, mediation and reflexivity seek to describe how things retain their difference in connection. Second, dialectical critical realism participates, as we have seen, in the tradition of dialectical thought, but its roots in critical realism provide its own orientation. It underlabours for the concrete sciences, and aligns its understanding of method, specifically materialist diffraction, to them. It accordingly views the world and its philosophy as fragmented and fractured, and refuses to resolve geo-historical contradictions in thought.

Accordingly, the general dialectical impulse to see things coming together in totality is tempered by the understanding that this may also be the realm where things are split and liable to fall apart. Contradictions are understood as they exist and endure in the world, and have their effects on thought. Where material contradictions persist at different levels, things may be *systematically* out of kilter. It is accordingly from the point of view of the whole that we see how forms of disconnection within connection, of detotalisation within totality, of split or fragmentation within the whole, operate. These include forms of what in psychoanalytic terms may be called repression and compromise, as well as forms of projective identification with that which detotalises. Diffracted dialectic means an open, diffracted totality where detotalising tendencies in the whole are multiform, and crucial to our understanding of the world, and its philosophy. To think totality always involves thinking of distinction, difference and change alongside connection and relations to the whole, and, under conditions of material diffraction, it also means that connection must itself be diffracted to include splits, fractures, contradictions and disconnections.

This chapter has four sections, the first two of which will deal with Bhaskar's general account of totality, and then the third and fourth its specific application. (For reading purposes, it therefore splits down the middle.) In the first section, we shall explore Bhaskar's account of totality, its open and partial character, the role of sub-totalities and differentiation in it, and the holistic understanding of causality it generates. In the second, we shall examine those dialectical figures that link differentia to totality, including ideas of levels, mediation, constellationality, duality, reflexivity and meta-reflexivity. I mentioned the figure of the constellation previously,[1] and we will now examine it in more depth. Thereafter, in the two final sections we shall turn to examine two specific forms of totality, concerning the character of philosophy and the nature of personal identity. In the third section, we shall examine the western philosophical tradition from the point of view of totality, and especially as it concerns its split and fractured character. This involves its disconnected or detotalised nature from the point of view of the whole. We shall focus on the idea of a 'Tina syndrome' and its link to alienation, concepts that concern philosophy but have implications beyond it. Finally, in a fourth section, we shall consider Bhaskar's account of the nature of personal identity in the form of the concrete universal, a figure he borrows from Hegel but renovates in critical realist style. At this point, we shall 'retotalise', drawing together the ethical implications of alienation and the figure of the concrete universal to set the scene for the following chapter, on ethics.

Totality and totalities

Here we shall discuss Bhaskar's idea of totality and consider some possible difficulties. This is a crucial dialectical figure that is prefigured in Hegel, but given a different sense in Bhaskar. For Bhaskar, we are in the realm of open totality, and he also distinguishes totality from partial totality and sub-totality – hence the pluralisation in the subtitle. After considering why we should think in terms of totality, we look at Bhaskar's account of totalities as open, partial and differentiated, and as including sub-totalities. We also see how he accommodates difference within the whole, and how causality operates in a totality.

Vindicating totality

Let us begin with two basic questions. First, why should we think in terms of totality at all? A general answer can be drawn from what we have seen so far. The idea of totality is necessitated by the nature of the natural and social worlds. If we think of spatio-temporal causality as central to human life, then human beings are caught in a structured flow of being and becoming in which the totality of past, present and future relations is implicated. If we think of dialectics as diffracted, we need to think of the grounds of diffraction, and how the whole is to be understood. Added to these general points, Bhaskar gives some examples from everyday life to illustrate why a sense of totality is central to being. To think of a language, a sentence, a text, a book or even a word is to think of entities where one has to grasp something as a whole as well as in its individual parts. A book is internally composed of meaning structures that reach from the totality of the language in which it is composed to the structures of individual words and sentences that make it up, and to the broader meanings and references that hold it together. It is at the same time an 'inside' and 'outside', both self-contained and located in its context. Any book, or system of knowledge production that uses books (or their ancient or modern analogues), involves thinking in terms of totality. What is true of books is true of communication in general: individual acts of communication make sense only within broader systems of meaning, speech, writing, and so on. Meaning is a social phenomenon, and sociality involves a sense of the whole, of totality. Totality is everywhere, and therefore needs to be grasped in philosophy. The following passage starts with the idea of a text, and generalises the point:

> [A text] is an internally related totality [and so] are the elements of a language, or the ebb and flow of a conversation, the sequential 'habitus' of a routine, the systemic interdependencies of the global monetary system, a play, a sculpture, or an experimental project oriented to the demediation of nature. Or consider simply a musical tune, melody, beat or rhythm. Or reflect on the semantic structure of a sentence, bound in a complex of paradigmatic and syntagmatic relations (and metaphoric and metonymic presuppositions). Or on its physical structure – for instance, the location of the spaces and punctuation marks within it. Not to treat such entities as totalities is to violate norms of descriptive and hermeneutic adequacy.
>
> (DPF: 123)

Second, what is involved in thinking about totality? Let us take the idea of a book as composed of an 'inside', the meaning in the text, and an 'outside', the sense it derives from its geo-historical and cultural context. Grasping the totality of a book involves breaking with 'our ordinary notions of identity, causality, space and time' (DPF: 125) and seeing things as 'existentially constituted, and permeated, by their relations with others' (ibid.). Thinking totality means thinking about the intra-relations between things, and Bhaskar identifies three different kinds of connectedness. First, there is 'existential constitution', in which 'one element or aspect (moment, determination, relation, etc.) . . . is essential and intrinsic to . . . another' (DPF: 123). Moving away from the book example, think, perhaps, of parenting love for a young child's emotional development. Second, there is 'intra-permeation', where one element is present within, but not essential to the nature of, the other. Think of the relationship between an adult son or daughter and an elderly parent. Third, there is 'intra-connection', where 'one element . . . is causally efficacious on an element internally related to it' (ibid.). Think of how a long-absent parent may still trigger reactions in their adult offspring. To think in any of these ways is to see 'our ordinary notion of identity as an abstraction' from those things that are an 'external' part of it – that is, its 'existentially constitutive processes of formation' (DPF: 125). In general, this involves thinking of an entity's geo-history, and how the external and the processual become part of its make-up, its 'existentially constitutive inter-activity (internal relatedness)' (ibid.).

Similarly, if we move from thinking about identity to causation, this involves, from a holistic viewpoint, 'the causality of a upon b affected by the causality of c upon d' (ibid.). In this context, we see how 'emergent totalities generate emergent spatio-temporalities', in the sense of complex, emergent geo-historical situations with their particular rhythmics. Further, thinking of totality in a materially diffracted world – that is, in a context of multiple, overlapping partial totalities –

any situation viewed holistically is constituted by a variety of spatio-temporalities. This returns us to themes of co-constitution already developed in our discussion of absence in Chapter 2, and in particular the presence of the past and the outside. Thinking holistically is central to our understanding of how historical processes operate. Thus, whether we think of identity or causality, totality involves recognising the ways in which parts are constituted within broader wholes at the same time as they constitute those wholes. Applying such thought to causation itself, we begin to talk about holistic causality, of which more below. In general, however, when we think of totality, we think of how things hang together, and how the parts are intra-connected in, and co-constituted by, the whole.

Totality, partial totalities, sub-totalities

If totality is central to our understanding of identity or causality, what form does it take? Bhaskar argues that we should think in terms of open and partial totalities rather than of totality itself. He distinguishes three different ideas of totality. The first is a comparatively simple conception of totality in which the whole is achieved and complete. This conception includes both the 'Parmenidean One' (to be discussed in Chapter 6), the idea of a complete, undifferentiated whole, and the more complexly idealist Hegelian rational totality, already discussed in Chapter 3. Bhaskar sees the latter, despite its modernist pluralism, as a narrow, limit case within an open and diffracted world, for it still claims the possibility of closure. The second is the idea of sub-totalities, which are the site of 'discontinuities, hiatuses, spaces, binds, barriers, boundaries and blocks between totalities' (DPF: 126),[2] and the third is that of partial totalities. It is the second and third that lie at the core of Bhaskar's thinking. Sub-totality is the term he uses to denote the splitting, fracturing and broken nature of the whole under conditions of material diffraction. Partial totality is the broader term. It is less morally committed, and includes sub-totality. It indicates both the necessity of thinking totality, and the impossibility of thinking its completeness in an open, diffracted world. In such a world, change and the emergence of the new is always possible, so the totality is incomplete. This means that while we need to think in terms of totality, there is a sense in which we cannot, and the idea of partial totality fills the resulting gap:

> the only plausible concept of a totality is that of a partial totality, rife with external as well as internal, and (not the same thing) accidental as well as necessary connections, replete with gaps, discontinuities, voids as well as pockets of thoroughgoing (sub-) totality.
>
> (DPF: 270–1)

There is a general reason in an open, emergent, diffracted world to conceive of totality as open, incomplete and partial. Such a view draws our focus down a level to the partial wholes that make up the only possible sense of 'the whole' where the future is open. In 'the social world we are almost always concerned with partial totalities', which inter- and intra-act, and are plural and open-ended in their form.

The world is primarily composed of 'compartmentalised sub-systems within systems, wholes with holes, themselves possible wholes (with holes, boundaries, frontiers and other limits)' (DPF: 85). A classic illustration is 'that of those emergent totalities called persons' (ibid.) with all the conflicts and intra-permeations they contain, on which more in the final section below. Partial totalities operate in conditions of social stratification and 'intra-position' to each other. They are open to 'constitutive geo-histories, emergent rhythmics, multiple binds, reflexivity, openness and transformative agency' (DPF: 126). In the following passage, Bhaskar describes his diffracted, partial and pluralistic conception of totality:

> Dialectical critical realism sees totalities within totalities (but studded with blocks, partitions and distance) recursively. But they are by no means all, or normally, of the Hegelian, pervasively internally relational, let alone centrist, expressivist and teleological kind. Rather they are punctuated by alterities, shot through with spaces, criss-crossed by traces and connected by all manner of negative, external and contingent as well as positive, internal and necessary determinations and relationships, the exact form of which it is up to science to fathom.
>
> (DPF: 55–6)

This intrinsic complexity in totality, its inter- and intra-relationality, arises from materialist diffraction of the dialectic, which, as we saw in Chapter 3, opens dialectic up to all sorts of differentiation. It decentres totality and exposes it to the multiform connections and contradictions of the world. A plurality of partial and overlapping totalities is 'shot through by all manner, angle, level and kind of determination', so that 'the theoretical possibilities increase exponentially' (DPF: 126). This approach to totality approximates what Hegel, but not Bhaskar, would call the 'bad infinite'. For Hegel, this is the idea that the world is subject to an endless reiteration of its problems, and never to their resolution. He, of course, resists this vision, though his attempt at rational containment involves 'arbitrary devices of constellational closure and generally unilinear presentation' (ibid.). For Bhaskar, by contrast, a bad infinite would be the specific material product of a particular world order, one characterised by problems of sub-totality – that is, contradiction, split, alienation, and the like. In such a world, a complete or closed whole would be impossible. Closed totality can only be the dream of a particular idealist method. In any case, more generally, where the future is open, so too is the whole, so that totality can never be complete in a world that is unfinished. Within a conception of open totality, the focus shifts to the materialist diffraction of partial and plural totalities, where the bad infinite may reside in sub-totalities as a form of geo-historical natural necessity. There are therefore both general reasons, pertaining to the openness of the world, and specific reasons relating to the world as we know it, why the idea of a closed totality cannot be the model to be followed, and a sense of open and partial totality should prevail.[3]

Problems of plurality and differentiation

Bhaskar's aim is to claim a conception of totality that is compatible with the material diffraction of dialectic, and that contrasts with Hegel's closed, thought-based, linear model. In moving to an open, plural and partial conception of totality, does he confront his own difficulties? Two perhaps suggest themselves. First, in depicting a world of plural, intermingled, partial totalities, does he develop a sense of totality so pluralistic as to perform no useful function in his theory? If the plural possibilities for totality are so great as to be exponential, does Bhaskar approach his own version of bad infinity: a pluralism without explanatory potential? His answer is the realist one that the idea of an exponential range of possibilities veering off towards infinity misses the real, grounded nature of human being in geo-history, and the actual totalities it contains. Change cannot be known a priori, but it can be understood a posteriori, in terms of pre-existing structures and states of affairs, and social and natural potentials. The world thus imposes its own 'reality principle' on the available possibilities. The exponential does not in practice materialise because of 'the finite, limited and conditioned character of real partial totalities' (DPF: 126). Knowledge of such totalities is possible only after an 'a posteriori subject-specific inquiry that a totality, such as a mode of production, can be described, or the real definition of an object such as a crystal be furnished' (ibid.). For all the variance these may reveal, their real characteristics ground the possible futures that are available, even allowing for their multiform intermingling. We are in the realm of finite, structured plurality, not infinite, plural structure. Just as materialist diffraction of dialectic involves differentiation and fragmentation in relation to grounding elements, so too must a pluralised and open conception of totality be referred to its real grounds of being. Nevertheless, such thinking encourages a sense of totality that is sufficiently flexible to be aware of the real fluidity that lies at the core of social life:

> thinking of totalities as intra-actively changing embedded ensembles, constituted by their geo-histories (and/or their traces) and their contexts, in open potentially disjointed process . . . and in *structured open systemic flux*, enables us to appreciate both the flickering, chameleon-like appearance of social being and the reason why narratives must be continually rewritten and social landscapes remapped.
>
> (ibid.; emphasis added)

Taking the emphasised phrase at the core of this statement, it is the grasp of the world as both 'structured' *and* in 'open systemic flux' that is the promise of a materially diffracted dialectic and its related conception of open and partial totalities.

A second problem is one of definition, explanation and judgement. If, as we have just seen, 'narratives must be continually rewritten and social landscapes remapped' in an evolving world, where does truth lie? We now lack the steer of Hegelian reason and see that thinking totality involves breaking with ordinary notions of identity, so that things are 'existentially constituted, and permeated, by their relations with others' (DPF: 125). How, then, do we deal with problems of identity and individuation, concerning the explanation, definition and scope of things, and how they should be articulated in knowledge? Bhaskar's argument is that 'in the domain of totality' it is necessary to argue for 'spatio-temporal, social and moral (real) relationism', and 'to conceptualise entity relationism' (DPF: 123). He acknowledges that this raises questions of definition, explanation and judgement: 'When is a thing no longer a thing but something else? When has the nature, and so the explanation for the behaviour, of a (relative) continuant changed?' (DPF: 125). Bhaskar's answer is that in general such questions are resolved 'only by reference to the explanatory power of the theory which a particular *découpage* permits' (DPF: 55). At first sight, this seems like a rather non-realist account of distinction, for it links questions of definition to questions of theory construction, which inevitably are linked to a theory's own explanatory purposes. Does this not illicitly subjectivise the whole process of thinking about entities in totalities?

Bhaskar argues that it does not, again on account of 'what I will call the "reality principle" (invoking its Freudian ancestry) [which] imposes its own stratification on science and lay life' (DPF: 55). It is the relationship between theory and the world it seeks to explain in its structured depth, real relations and natural necessity that maintains a realist 'discipline' on the process of distinguishing and relating. Distinction and connection is not a matter of 'anything goes', but of understanding phenomena in their real structured relationality and connection, and the 'explanatory power of the theory' is a realist one, related to its capacity to explicate how natural necessity works in the world.

Holistic causality

Thus far, we have considered the dialectical critical realist understanding of totalities, how a realist conception safeguards against over-pluralisation of a conception of open and partial totality, and against over-subjectivisation of questions of definition in a relational context. If these are problems of an excessive pluralisation, the opposite problem would be that of reductionism by insisting too strongly on the grounded or structured underpinnings of plural phenomena. Here, Bhaskar needs a conception of causality that can theorise the relationship between the parts and the whole, which can conceive of causality in totality. Accordingly, he develops an account of holistic causality, which he links to existing forms of causality in critical realism to provide a fourfold view. First, there is the view of causality that critical realism develops from its original conception of a depth ontology of structures, generative mechanisms and antecedent causes which operate transfactually to produce effects in the natural and social worlds. Second, drawn from the idea of a naturalistic social science is the conception of agents' reasons as causes that are necessary for action to reproduce or transform the world. Third, in Chapter 2 we saw that causality was given a new significance in terms of its intrinsic link through absence to the idea of spatio-temporal determination (the tri-unity of causality, space and time). Adding to these the fourth idea of holistic causality gives a fourfold analysis of causation to include 'the transfactual efficacy of the generative mechanisms of a structure, the rhythmic (spatio-temporal) exercise of their causal powers, possibly multiply mediated by holistic causality, and, in the human sphere, dependent upon intentional human agency, codetermining a conjuncture' (DPF: 395). We should pause to note that what we have here is a 1M–4D account in which each moment in the Bhaskarian dialectic reflects a different element in causation. At 1M, there is transfactual efficacy; at 2E, spatio-temporal causality; at 3L, holistic causality; and at 4D, the causal power of agency.[4] We should also register that, as with absence, Bhaskar notes the various forms that causation can take, ranging from the 'rather bold' idea of determination through a 'milder' range of forms which include 'conditioning, limiting, selecting, shaping, blocking, influencing' (DPF: 126–7). Causation may operate to 'stimulate, release, nurture, enable, sustain, entrain, displace, condense, coalesce, bind, in addition to the poietic "generate" or "produce"' (ibid.). What does holistic causality add? If we take determination as the generic causal term, then specifically holistic causality operates where, first, a totality in its form or structure causally determines its elements, and, second, the elements in their form or structure causally co-determine each other and so causally determine or co-determine the whole (DPF: 127). Holistic causality operates between the whole and its parts in a co-constitutive manner.

Of holistic causality, a number of points can be made. The first is that, in a world where a focus on finite and limited partial totalities constitutes the aim of scientific investigation, holistic causality cannot be ethically 'expressive or centred in the way that Hegel's totality is' (DPF: 124). Bhaskar's vision of holistic causality is therefore 'quite consistent with a gamut of species of domination' (DPF: 127), but the larger point relates to how such domination is identified. This cannot be achieved a prioristically, only a posteriori as a consequence of social scientific investigation of a social formation – that is, in accordance with the 'reality principle'. Second, pursuing the anti-Hegelian line, what Bhaskar has in mind is a sense of totalities shaped by their co-position in the world, rather than according to any pre-existing vision. Thus, totalities may be 'asymmetrically weighted', and it is an open, and presumably changing, question to be resolved by inquiry as to what degree the different elements enjoy autonomy or dominance in the whole. Different elements may possess structurally or conjuncturally greater or lesser degrees of determining power. Recalling also that we deal with partial totalities, any totality may be grounded in, or otherwise linked to, another totality of which it is a part, or to which it is related.

Third, there is the question of how the structured co-position of partial totalities shapes holistic causality. As structured entities, they 'may contain or be contained by dialectically contradictory (and more or less antagonistic) or, on the other hand, mutually reinforcing or supporting . . . relationships' (DPF: 127). Such relationships 'may depend upon dual, multiple, joint or contextual action' (ibid.), and super- or intra-structures may be emergent from within the totality. Any specific totality is also spatio-temporally emergent out of a specific geo-historical context (the broader confluence of totalities in nature, history and society) and is in open process with regard to what lies within and outside it. Accordingly, any totality is inherently mobile, with its form, elements, effects and configurations subject to continuous change. Such changes are themselves the effect of holistic causality in action, and they occur within the overall context of determinate negation:

> These changes or determinations must be understood as transformative negations or absentings, rhythmically exercised, holistically explained and subject to or mediated by intentional causal agency in the social world. . . . '[Causal] determination' [involves] transfactual efficacy, transformative negation, tensed (spatialising) process, holistic causality and intentional absenting or agency.
>
> (ibid.)

This passage confirms the fourfold nature of causality in dialectical critical realism – as (1M) transfactual efficacy, (2E) spatio-temporal process, (3L) holistic causality and (4D) intentional agency. It also reminds us of the key role 2E absence and absenting play in causal process while also asserting the ultimate role of 4D causal agency in reproducing or transforming the world. These comments have described the basic nature and operation of totalities in Bhaskar's system. In the next section, we shall examine some of the mechanisms and forms that permit them to work.

Before moving on, however, it is worth considering Bertell Ollman's view that Bhaskar's account of totality lacks a sense of how partial totalities are internally related in an overall sense of the whole (Ollman 2003: 177). Against this, one should note Bhaskar's account of holistic causality and the general way in which partial totalities are related within an open, unfinished sense of totality. More generally, Ollman argues that Bhaskar does not have a philosophy of internal relations, but rather one that contains examples of both internal and external relations, which leads him to a 'nuanced version of the philosophy of external relations' (ibid.). Bhaskar's dialectical work, Ollman continues, may be moving in the direction of internal relations, but this is against the grain of his overall position. In this chapter, I argue that Bhaskar's dialectical philosophy emphasises the importance of internal relations throughout. His philosophy itself, as we are seeing, illustrates how one position immanently entails another as we move through the MELD schema. But more than this, Bhaskar's account of totality focuses, as with his account of contradictions in Chapter 3, on internal relations in a realist framework in which internal connections are established by a posteriori, rather than a priori, determination. This is an account that foregrounds the internal, not a nuancing of an external position.

Ollman's own position, based on Marx's philosophical method, has much in common with Bhaskar's, but he overstates the claim for the universality of internal relations. He writes that 'since the relations that "constitute" any social thing are said to include its ties to "natural" as well as to other social things, it would appear that everything in reality is internally related' (ibid.). But where, for example, an earthquake precipitates a social revolution because the efforts of the state to deal with its effects are inadequate, is the impact of the earthquake 'internal' or 'external' to the social relations in place? There may be a deep philosophical sense in which we could say that everything, in an emergent material world, is interconnected, but without understanding the sense in which an earthquake is external to the internal logic of social relations, we would so overplay the nature of internal relations as to lose our grasp on their real salience. In a structured, emergent world, internal relations are central – and they are central to Bhaskar's dialectic – but we need to retain a sense of the role of what we call chance, as well as, as we shall see, of the powers of agency and the possibility of the qualitatively new, and all these too are incompatible with a wholesale, a prioristic account of internal relationality.

Dialectical figures in totality

In thinking about totality, we have to consider those concepts that establish its architecture. If totalities function by virtue of holistic causality, what internal forms do they take? We have seen that totality is the place where different things come together, and this gives us a starting point in terms of how real difference (what Bhaskar here calls *heterology*) is related to the whole. An initial means of structuring difference is in terms of the way it operates at different *levels* in the whole. This in turn generates the need for a concept that can explain how such levels work together and through each other (*mediation*). Thereafter, a crucial structural figure for understanding the relation between distinct entities in totality is the *constellation*, and linked to it is the idea of the *dual* and what Bhaskar calls *hiatus-in-duality*. I conclude this section by considering how one specific dual, that between structure and agency, generates additional forms for thinking totality, such as ideas of *reflexivity*, the *perspectival switch* and the *meta-reflexive situation*. These are germane to the operation of one specific partial totality, the human agent.

Starting with difference (heterology)

In one sense, the least interesting thing to say about totality is that it involves the whole. Totalities are important because of the relations they entail between the whole and its parts. For that reason, Bhaskar begins his account of totalising figures not with a discussion of totality but with an examination of the various forms of 'otherness' that exist in a world understood holistically. These he refers to under the generic term of 'heterology'. Something is heterologous where it has a relationship of difference with another entity, or contains elements of difference in itself. It is most obviously contrasted with 'homology', where things have an affinity to each other, but heterology, like absence or cause, has different inflections. Bhaskar links it with 'alterity', which is the real difference between language and its object, or the sheer irreducible existential otherness of the world.[5] This idea of course is particularly important for a critical realist dialectics, for it takes us back to the starting point in 1M critical realism. Significantly, he also links it with 'heteronomy', where something is 'not true for and/or to itself', and where the contrast is with 'autonomy', where it is, as well as with 'alterology', which he also uses to mean 'untrue-to-self-or-situation' (DPF: 105).

'Heteronomy' and 'alterology' pick up senses of difference where a thing exists in an imperfect relationship to itself – that is, where its difference involves a disconnection between what it is and what it could be. They denote positions of subtotality in a partial totality. They are ethically charged and important for Bhaskar's discussion of detotalisation, as we shall see in the following section, where heteronomy is linked to alienation. In any case, the different terms suggest a family resemblance of meanings, and what they all have in common is a sense of real otherness or difference. Difference may be simply out there in the (1M) world ('sheer alterity'), or it may be inherent in any dialectical framework as the moment of negativity or becoming in (2E) dialectics. It must exist in all but the most irreducibly monistic conceptions of (3L) totality, for example the Parmenidean One. It is relevant to the (4D) ethical ways humans lead their lives (for example in Kant's vision of the moral ills of heteronomy, or the young Hegel's or young Marx's view of alienation, or the mature Marx's view that the freedom of each is a condition for the freedom of all). These uses of a terminology of heterology, difference and distinction are picked up in Bhaskar's account as he explores how things 'hang together' in a dialectical account of totality. What is most important to see at this point, however, is that totality, a figure of the whole, begins with difference if it is to reflect on the world it represents, or if it is to be of scientific interest.

Levels

How is difference organised in the whole? A first step is to recognise how a totality can be made up of distinct, yet interconnected, levels, with each enjoying both a *sui generis* importance and being linked to other levels in the whole. Two rather different examples of thinking deploying levels may be given. The first, going back to Chapter 3, is socio-historical. It is of Marx identifying the way in which contradictions in a social whole can operate structurally, conjuncturally (with geo-historic specificity) and existentially, for humanity itself.[6] These constitute three different levels, with the last-mentioned being the deepest, though notions of depth and surface must be handled with care. Thus, while the 'generative separation' Marx identifies under capitalism involves split and alienation at the deepest level of human being, it is at the level of structure and its contradictions that such separations are in fact generated. Similarly, the geo-historically conjunctural looks like the surface level in comparison to structural depth, but it is the level at which real change through human agency may ultimately take place, and therefore it has a certain primacy. The three levels are real, different and interconnected, indeed intra-connected, but metaphors have their limits, and simple models of depth and surface may not reflect the reality. Nonetheless, talk of how a phenomenon may be organised, or have different implications, at different levels is a helpful way of understanding the nature of things as a whole. In general parlance, it makes good sense to discuss a complex phenomenon by saying that 'at one level it is x, while at another level it is y'.

Levels generally connote ontological stratification and may involve thinking 'vertically', in terms of structural depth, or 'horizontally', in terms of the lateral causal effects of structures or systems on each other. They are important in the understanding of the social and the historical world, as the example from Marx indicates. The idea of levels is in any case already present generally in 1M critical realist ideas of ontological depth, and the realist relation between a thing and the different, emergent levels of being that constitute it (e.g. the chemical, the biological, the mental, the social that co-constitute human being). It is present in Bhaskar's original account of 'synchronic emergent powers materialism', whereby mind emerges from matter. Thus, the argument for co-acting levels in a totality which Bhaskar articulates here renders a sense of totality that was implicit in original critical realism explicit.

A second, very different example of thinking at different levels is specifically philosophical. It concerns a certain kind of problem or paradox, known in modern philosophy as the self-referential paradox. Such problems, of which there are many, occupied twentieth-century philosophers, but can be traced back to Plato and his 'self-predicative paradoxes' whereby a thing is explained in terms of itself (see generally DPF: ch. 4.2). They involve either an essentialism or vicious regress, which is avoided for Bhaskar by explaining things in terms of their properties at the different levels of real structure or totality, which constitute the entity in question (DPF: 236). An example here is the 'heap paradox', whereby we can never tell how many grains of sand piled together constitute a heap, or when the removal or addition of one grain makes the difference. Such a problem, Bhaskar argues, occurs only because we fail to understand that the reality of a heap occupies a different level to that of individual grains of sand. The problem, which is 'still taken very seriously by contemporary philosophers' (Audi 1999: 865), arises only 'because we insist in characterising totalities in the same way' – that is, at the same level – 'as their units, elements or parts' (DPF: 319).[7]

Mediation

If we start with the idea of *difference* working at distinct *levels* in a totality, how is the necessary connection or intra-relation between levels understood? Holistic causality indicates one aspect, but another, intrinsic mode is provided by the concept of mediation. This indicates how things are linked together, and one entity has its effects *through* another. Mediation is important to both an idealist and a realist dialectic, but in different ways. In Hegel, mediation is the means by which every moment is linked via the process of dialectical reason to every other moment. The progression of reason is always mediated by the moment, and each mediating moment is both determinative and an intermediary in the movement of reason. Mediation connotes both indirectness, in that reason passes through and by means of the distinctive moment, and, in Hegelian dialectic, it is involved in hierarchy, in that mediation takes one up and down dialectically rational progressions to and from the Idea to create totality.

In the dialectical critical realist totality, mediation occurs where and as it is found in the world, with emphasis placed upon the material connections that underlie distinctions or moments and which have their effects causally within spatio-temporal contexts. Entities are both determinative and mediating of underlying structures or relations. They are effective in their own right – that is, in their difference or alterity – but also as intermediaries channelling indirectly structural or holistically causal forces. Generally, 'if A achieves, secures or eventuates in C (either in whole or in part) via or by means of B, then B may be said to mediate their relation' (DPF: 114), and geo-historical process generally mediates relations 'in the tensed tri-unity of causality, space and time' (ibid.). Hegelian indirectness, but not hierarchy, is maintained in the critical realist account of mediation, and this is observable in real world processes.

Mediation can also assume specific concrete forms such as 'the media', with their own processual, rhythmic qualities as in, for example, the stretching of space and time in the 'global village', the 'mediatisation' of modern social relations, for example by 24-hour news gathering, or 'postmodernist virtualisation or hyperrealisation effects' (DPF: 113). Such media processes, while possessing their own *sui generis* existence, are themselves thoroughly connected, for example to processes of commodification, which, at different levels, they mediate. Generally, the past mediates the present and future, structure mediates agency (and vice versa), rhythmics mediate causality, and, to take another particular example, philosophy is mediated by 'the deep analogical grammars of lapsed science and contemporary society' (ibid.). (Note the 'internal' and 'external' elements in this account of mediation in philosophy, something to which we shall return in the next section.) Mediation is thus a crucial concept in terms of exploring the relationality that links identities and causal processes. It is central in a number of keys to the idea of entity relationism within an account of totality, reflecting generally how human agency and thought, or social phenomena more generally, emerge in a mediating context of historical structure and holistic causality, and how phenomena which may be studied in their own right connect with processes, structures and relations that seem at first sight to be separate.

Constellationality

We have moved from *differentia* to the different *levels* of their existence, and then to the connection between them permitted by *mediation*. If mediation involves intra-connection between things that maintain their distinction, we now need to understand that idea in the context of the whole. Why are we not just left with differentiated categories and their connections at different levels? Answers already given indicate the structuring of plurality and the possibility of holistic causality, but we need a figure that can express the holistic connection between things. This is provided by the idea of the constellation, and later that of the dual which can be located within it. We have already witnessed examples of constellationality in the two previous chapters. In Chapter 2, we discussed the relation between being and absence (being as constellationally embedded within absence in an overall ('zero-level') conception of being). We also considered in Chapter 3 the relation between being and thought (thought as constellationally contained within being), and between analytical and dialectical forms of thinking (where the former is constellationally embedded in the latter). The constellation is a 'figure of containment in an over-reaching term . . . , from which the over-reached term may be diachronically or synchronically emergent' (DPF: 395).[8]

Like mediation, constellationality can be referred to in both materialist-realist and idealist contexts.[9] For Hegel, the constellation is a figure of closure, for constellationality is ultimately a matter of the rational containment of phenomena, and of a resulting *identity* of the universal and the particular. For Bhaskar, by virtue of the real nature of entities, individual things enjoy relations of constellational *unity* rather than *identity*, of a looser *connection* rather than *containment* (in a narrow, controlling sense). The reductionism that constellational identity entails is not generally an option in a critical realist totality. It is constellational containment, identity and hence closure in Hegel that gives rise to the 'intransigent class of demi-actual and demi-present surds, irrational existents such as Krug's pen' (DPF: 274) commented on earlier.[10] For Bhaskar, to the contrary, the constellation is a connecting figure that sustains the possibility of mediation (the moment of difference in connection) of the constellationally embedded terms. For example, thought is constellationally contained, in the sense of embedded, in being. It is an emergent property of, and is over-reached by, being, yet retains its importance both in its own right and in the co-constitution of human being (DPF: 115). Constellational relatedness thus exists between epistemology and ontology, where epistemology is a form of ontology, emergent from it and co-acting with it. Similarly, 'one can write of the constellational unity of dialectical and analytical reason' since they are 'bound together as essential and interdependent aspects of the transitive dialectical process of science' (ibid.). Equally, one could formulate the relationship between reasons and causes or mind and matter in such terms.

Constellationality involves an overall co-relation, emergent from its parts and containing them, which depends on the real relation of the individual terms, together with the relative autonomy between them, making mediation possible. Mutual intra-action and co-mediation in a constellational state, rather than subsumption of one term within another, are stressed. Constellationality, it should be noted, is central to understanding questions of agency, identity and ethics. As regards agency, the original TMSA points to a constellational relation in which agency is embedded in structure, yet structure is dependent on agency for its reproduction or transformation. Hence the constellational relationship is layered in terms of understanding agency within structure, working towards the significance of agency for structure. As regards a person's identity, this is subject to change in a structured, social world of which the person is a part. Bhaskar sees this as a relation of constellational unity between the self and what is other to it. Personal identities (as an 'inside') are forged out of history (as an 'outside'), so that who we are can be understood in terms of an embedded constellational relation between identity and change over time. Here, we have to think historically or diachronically of 'the constellational unity of identity (qua continuity of spatio-temporal personality) and change . . . in conceptualising the self as the dispositional identity of the embodied agent and her changing causal powers' (DPF: 183), and synchronically, of how 'a thing both is and is not itself'. Here we have 'the constellational unity of identity (qua sameness of subject) and difference', a figure that expresses 'the widespread phenomena of constitutive intra-relationality'. Finally, one can also talk here of the relationship between the 'political' and the 'ethical' in constellational terms – that is, of a 'constellational unity . . . of the ethical and . . . the political within the political' (DPF: 279), something we will consider further in Chapter 5. These, we shall see, are important arguments for Bhaskar, for they allow us to hold onto a sense of what one can call the structuring of subjectivity without losing a sense of subjectivity working within structure. The concepts of mediation (difference as effective within connection) and the constellation (the relational holding together of linked differentiae) permit this. Constellationality is a crucial complement to mediation, for if the latter reflects on effects by indirection, the former reflects on the holistic relation that holds different things, with their co-mediating effects, together. They are developed immediately below and will become important in our discussion of retotalisation in the final section of this chapter.

Duality, hiatus-in-duality and perspectival switch

I have spent some time on constellationality because it involves an important and original realist use of a term already familiar in the dialectical tradition. Linked to it is the figure of the dual, which also sustains the independence of linked terms, while insisting on their interdependence (DPF: 115). Duals in fact may be seen as the core elements out of which constellational relations are built. I will spend less time on this but use it to introduce some further dialectical terms, the exotic sounding 'hiatus-in-duality' and the idea of 'perspectival shift'. These terms are particularly related to the nature of human agency as it operates in the structure/agency dual.

One way of approaching the idea of the dual would be to compare it with dialectical critical realism's focus (Chapter 3) on antinomies in modern philosophy. These constitute one-sided appropriations of questions concerning thought or being under, Bhaskar claims, conditions of historically generated structured power ('generalised master–slave-type') relations. Philosophy wrenches one side of what is in effect a dual out of its overall context and falsely hypostatises it with regard to the other side. Many of the problems of antinomialism or false dichotomisation to be found in modern philosophy can be better understood in terms of a constellational relation between duals which preserve but link the terms in opposition, and show how both sides intra-act. The dialectical alternative to false dichotomisation is to see the opposed terms' constellational unity – that is, how they function together as a dual. Such ideas fit comfortably into a landscape of constellations, for a constellation is a way of thinking the relation of embedding or co-presence between terms that would otherwise appear as simply oppositional. Indeed, duals may be seen as the core elements in constellational relations 'as in the duality of practical and theoretical reason within the constellational coherence of theory and practice within practice' (DPF: 246).[11] Duals may be exemplified by 'the duality of absence and presence in spatio-temporal mediation, of theory

or practice in absolute reason, or of structure and agency in social practice'
(DPF: 115).

With this background, let us pursue the relationship between structure and
agency specifically as a dual, and the other dialectical forms to which it gives rise.
It is already plain that structure and agency cannot be artificially separated:
structure cannot exist without agency to maintain and/or transform it, and agency
presupposes a context that makes it other than merely random. More than this,
agency qua social practice is the activity that takes structure into account and either
reproduces it or seeks to renovate it. Agency is necessarily structure oriented,
mediated, shaped and engaged. To say this is not to fuse the terms or reduce one
to the other, but to identify, in mediational and constellational terms, their
intraconnection alongside their distinction. Can one, then, develop further the
sense of difference in connection? To do so, Bhaskar argues for what he calls the
'hiatus', or 'hiatus-in-the-duality', a conception that suggests a gap, or moment of
discontinuity. This is important because it leads one to see how, within a duality
of terms, separability and inseparability may coexist and reductionism be
safeguarded against.

In general, the hiatus is a theoretical term identified in order to think a real
relation of separation in connection. However, it may also be helpful in concrete
social contexts, where either structure or agency may seem not to operate. We have
seen how processes or forms of mediation may become concretised as media, with
their own rhythmics and other sui generis qualities. There are situations too where
the hiatus may become actual and manifest. For example, in the opposite situations
of the revolutionary moment, where agency enjoys a sense of its own autonomy,
and that of social stasis, where the dead hand of structure seems to suffocate any
attempt at agency, the hiatus seems to emerge concretely, in its own right, as a
suspension of duality.[12] In both situations, it would be wrong to think that reality
could be reduced to the operation of one term, yet for a period the hiatus as
suspension assumes actual form. Eventually, it is pushed back into the (theoretical)
background, as either structure reimposes itself on the revolution, or the new bursts
out in the situation of structural stasis, often when least expected. Here we are
dealing with concrete historical experiences, but they reveal a key aspect of the
dialectical understanding of the structure/agency dual and the separateness/
connection it entails. Hiatus-in-duality is always present, always protecting the
relative autonomy of both structure and agency in their duality. Where the duality
becomes dislocated in this way, and one of the terms appears to go absent, it leaps
into focus as a moment of hiatus in history per se. Yet, theoretically, one must
remember that we are dealing with a hiatus *in duality*, and therefore insist on the
(temporarily) absent term, be it structure in the revolutionary moment or agency
in the time of stasis.

Linked to the idea of hiatus is that of 'perspectival switch', which, in the duality
of structure and agency, indicates the need to account for a social result in terms
of both historical and structural grounds and the perceptions and meanings of
actors. It involves the switch between two different perspectives with regard to one
outcome. Perspectival switch is philosophically grounded in 1M critical realism's

insistence that natural necessity in the social world is concept, meaning and agency dependent. It is impossible to think of the effects of social structures on outcomes without perceiving how they are mediated by the actions, perceptions and meaning investments of agents, while structures always have their effects on agency. Perspectival switch is rendered valid and necessary by virtue of the need to see things from both sides in a dual or constellated relation, operating at, and as, the point of hiatus in duality.

Meta-reflexivity

Finally, pursuing the significance of the structure/agency dual, we move from the perspectival switch in the hiatus to the possibilities for agency provided by the idea of 'reflexivity' and the 'meta-reflexive' situation. These figures indicate the possibility and importance of maintaining the nature and significance of agency for change. Reflexivity involves perspectival switch, for it

> is the inwardised form of totality. . . . In its most basic form it specifies the capacity of an agent or an institution to monitor and account for its activity. It is thus intimately connected to the phenomena of the historicity of social spatialised processual change and the futuricity of praxis . . . [and] to the possibility of a meta-reflexive situation.
>
> (DPF: 272–3)

Reflexivity is the agent's ability through perspectival switch to reflect upon her situation, to step in and out of it, and to relate her experience to her broader understanding of the world. Bhaskar's idea of the meta-reflexive totalising situation emerges out of a brief encounter with Derrida and Habermas, whom he sees as 'antinomialists', and tacitly complicit dialectical antagonists, each tugging on one side of an antinomy resoluble in terms of duality. Deconstruction attacks the logocentricity of the text, but wishes to be read and to communicate; it therefore assumes against itself that a measure of communication is possible. Habermasians argue for the possibility of undistorted communication, but they ignore the myriad ways in which distortion is intrinsic to (as opposed to potentially influential on) communication. Between the two sides, we therefore have a 'stalemate in which both sides accuse the other of self-referential paradox' (DPF: 147). The way out of the stalemate is through 'the concept of a meta-reflexively totalising situation – another dialectical perspectival switch in the key of constellationality' (DPF: 273).

What Bhaskar has in mind here is the ability of a constellationally formulated dual of agency and structure to credit both the powers of agency (or subjectivity) and the effects of structure (or objectivity). Deconstructive semiotics (Derrida) and reconstructive hermeneutics (Habermas) represent one-sided, complicit antagonists in their support for either agency, subjectivity and reason (Habermas), or the objectivising of subjectivity through discourse or the text (Derrida). An appropriately distanciated, yet conjoined, constellation-based dual of the agent and her structural context, including the possibilities of hiatus and perspectival switch, permits one to understand how an overall reflexivity of agency in its context is possible. Bhaskar illustrates the point with the example of an agent engaged in a scientific research project:

> Consider an agent N's participation in, say, an experimental programme. . . . [S]he engages in a distanciated and self-reflexively monitoring participation in a particular aspect of it. Suppose she has to test, as a member of the research team, a particle's spin. She is focusing on untying a knot in a cord. She is competently doing so. She is aware of the role of her task in the context of the overall programme and in the context of the hierarchy and plurality of projects with their own rhythmics in her life. She could recall last night's TV, she is aware that she has an unconscious, that the sign has a trace structure, of the metaphoricity of language use, the very language she is using now, that she is subject, in a multiplicity of dimensions, to the inertial drag of the past and its delayed causal efficacy. She knows that she will die as so much cosmic dust at the same time as she is untying the knot and attending to the matter at hand; just as she knows about, and perhaps is skilfully employing, the metaphoricity of language while chatting to a colleague about last night's TV. She knows all this in a meta-reflexively totalising (reflection on her praxis and) situation of her life. She is a stratified agent engaged in transformative practice, including intersubjective communication . . . , who, in virtue of being a stratified self, no more has to forget her Nietzsche in untying a knot than lose her capacity to speak French in saying 'yes please'.
>
> (DPF: 148)

To avoid the reductionism of both discourse-based understandings of objectivising structure (the loss of subjectivity) on the one hand, and communicative accounts of subjective agency (the loss of sedimenting structure) on the other, a theoretical account of the duality of such terms in their constellational unity, co-presence and embeddedness is required. Such a view, related to ideas of perspectivality and hiatus, permits one the middle ground of reflexivity and, with it, the further possibility of the meta-reflexive totalising situation. Note, however, that this is not a God's-eye view, but a realistically grounded, constellational unity of the subjective-in-the-objective for the sake of the subjective. It is subject to correction and revision both because it may prove to be wrong and because it operates in an open, emergent totality where things, and therefore their assessment, change. Meta-reflexivity is important for conceptions of ethical agency, as we shall see in the next chapter. For the moment, it is necessary to move from an understanding of how things hold together within totality to how, under particular conditions, they may be in danger of falling apart.

Detotalisation: philosophy and its (historical) discontents

We have now developed our account of totality in dialectical critical realist terms and the figures that structure it. In the remainder of this chapter, I focus on two issues that have been referred to or implicated in what has been said thus far. The first is the idea of sub-totality, which involves, as we saw, the idea of 'discontinuities, hiatuses, spaces, binds, barriers, boundaries and blocks between totalities' (DPF: 126). Here we are in the realm of detotalisation within totality, and I want to investigate this in relation to two of Bhaskar's concepts, the idea of the 'Tina syndrome' and that of alienation, briefly raised earlier in relation to autonomy and heteronomy. Both are grouped under the general theme of 'philosophy and its discontents' in this section, though we shall see that an underlying concern is ethical. The second issue, to be discussed in the final section of the chapter, is that of the 'concrete universal', in Bhaskar's usage of the term. This is an Hegelian term originally, but Bhaskar develops it in contradistinction to Hegel, and in the light of the structure/agency dual at the core of the transformational model of social action (the TMSA) in original critical realism. Here the relevant concepts to discuss are those of 'four-planar being' and the 'social cube'. I develop this under the theme of 'retotalisation' to indicate how, in a detotalised world, Bhaskar makes space for ethically retotalising agency. For now, we turn to detotalisation and the Tina syndrome. My argument will be that the detotalisation of philosophy tracked by the Tina syndrome is linked to the historical experience of heteronomy (alienation) and, through that, the existence of 'generalised master –slave-type relations'.

False necessity: Tina formations

As we have seen, dialectical critical realism is interested in the ways traditional philosophical dichotomies are underpinned by, and implicated in, power structures, summarised as generalised master–slave-type or power$_2$ relations.[13] Such relations sustain limited visions of the nature of philosophy and its forms and, indeed, of the world of which they are a part. Dichotomies, antinomies and falsely one-sided understandings are signs of such limits. Philosophy, and the sciences more generally (in so far as they reflect philosophical misunderstandings), are subject to these detotalisations which reflect and help maintain a power$_2$ structured world. Detotalisation is defined by Bhaskar as a split, meaning a dichotomy, a fission or split-off, a fragmentation, which appears as a projected exteriorisation of an internal relation between things that is illicitly denied (DPF: 396). Detotalisation, though it occurs within totality, is nonetheless implicitly against it, in that it works against the connections and relations which link things together. It detracts from wholeness, hence it involves a 'sub-totality'. Underlying such splits are fractures in the world itself, and in this section we consider two dialectical motifs that express this relationship between splits in philosophy and fractures in the world. The first of these is the Tina syndrome, which indicates how detotalising elements are managed in the structure of philosophy and other forms of knowledge, while the second, alienation, considers how an underlying generative mechanism, generalised as master-slave-type relations, can engender detotalisation in the world and thought. I begin with the Tina syndrome.

The term draws ironically on Margaret Thatcher's phrase of the 1980s urging the necessity – 'there is no alternative' – of a monetarist solution to the problems of the British economy. Bhaskar's point is that such a necessity is not really necessary, for other choices, radical or conventional, are available. If the necessity is accepted, however, it entails a series of consequences that also become necessities in their own right. The case of Thatcherism as a theoretico-practical dual is perhaps worth exploring. The Tina necessity of monetarism was buttressed on one side by a legitimising ideological claim to defend individual freedom, and on the other by a form of 'law and order' politics that brought Britain, in parts of the country and for a period, close to a police state. Thus, the original Tina statement necessitated as its consequence further 'Tina defence mechanisms' (a legitimating ideology of freedom and a legal–political–material practice of repression) which connected with the primary necessity (a 'Tina connection') to provide a discursive and practical defensive shield. In the process, the original (false) necessity was sustained only by legitimating ideas that contradicted the practices accompanying them (individual freedom in a proto-police state). This generates the idea of a 'Tina compromise formation' as a set of ideas and/or practices which are brought together to guard the vulnerability in the initial false necessity, and which themselves assume their own falsely necessitarian, contradictory guise. You cannot expect to close down an industry based in tight-knit communities with a strong culture and values without attracting serious opposition, so it becomes a further necessity to deploy violent, extra-legal policing to contain it, in the name of freedom.

The example indicates something of Bhaskar's idea of a Tina syndrome. Underlying it is a sense of the 'reality principle' that informs a critical realist understanding of the world. To embark on a theoretico-practical project in the name of a false necessity commits one to a tangled web of contrivances that somehow hold the project together without resolving a basic problem. Things may work for a while, but reality has a habit of biting back. In a Tina formation, the Freudian ancestry of the reality principle (as, indeed, of the 'compromise formation' (DPF: 11)) is brought out. Here is Bhaskar's own, more philosophical, account of the workings of Tina necessity, resulting in the Tina syndrome:

> But what happens . . . if a transcendental or dialectical [i.e. real – A.N.] necessity, established (let us suppose) by sound argumentation, is contravened? To contravene such a necessity, in some theory or practice, is, insofar as the necessity pertains to the world in which we must act, to contravene an axiological (or practical) necessity too. . . . Theories and practices which violate such necessities, if they are to survive and be applicable to the world in which we . . . act: (a) require some defence mechanism, safety net or security system, which may well, in systematically related ensembles, (b) necessitate supporting or reinforcing connections, in the shape of duals,

complements and the like elsewhere; and (c) need to assume the cloak of some conjugated compromise formation in a world where axiological necessities press about them. Such mechanisms, connections and formations are Tina ones and the whole complex comprises the 'Tina syndrome'.

(DPF: 116)

It should be clear from this passage that Tinas operate at various levels in the world, and are by no means confined to the socio-political domain whence their name derives. Bhaskar's own interest is in how they relate to western philosophy.

Philosophy and the Tina syndrome

The Tina syndrome is important for Bhaskar, for his general view is that the history of western philosophy from Plato onwards represents a series of Tina compromise formations, and he thinks that specific episodes in philosophy can be seen as exercises in Tina thinking. Taking general history first, what is lacking throughout western philosophy, he argues, is a proper understanding of the polyvalent (to include absence) quality of ontology, and the import of natural necessity for being in the world.[14] In place of a sufficiently realist ontology, an emphasis on the role of knowledge over being (the epistemic fallacy) and a corresponding flat, actualist and monovalent, ontology are established. The coexistence in epistemology of the epistemic fallacy with an actualist (no depth), monovalent (no absence) ontology represents a bar on the philosophical understanding of both knowledge and being that moves from Plato and Aristotle to Descartes and Hume, then on to Kant and Hegel and up to the present. The failure to comprehend absence and natural necessity leaves even the greatest thinkers to argue in one-sided terms, and they accordingly tend to come in pairs. One will argue one side, a second the other, in a false dichotomisation invoking a dialectic of complicit philosophical antagonists, as exemplified in the previous section.

Pursuing the Bhaskarian line, a proper basis for understanding knowledge and being would emphasise that knowledge is both socially produced and engaged with the world, and that the world is structured and deep. It contains its own necessity, which includes absence, and this is the real ground of being, permitting an understanding of change. This constitutes the 'transcendental or dialectical necessity' referred to in the quotation above, which philosophy cannot properly grasp. These central aspects of knowledge and being are forced from the picture by ontological monovalence, the epistemic fallacy and the resulting 'primal squeeze' they place on the understanding of knowledge and being. Together, the epistemic fallacy, ontological monovalence and primal squeeze constitute the 'Unholy Trinity'[15] of irrealism. They are central to western philosophy from its inception, especially in Parmenides and Plato, but their consequences cascade down the philosophical generations. The irrealist trinity accordingly remains central to all subsequent philosophy and, in terms of the Tina syndrome, has to be (a) Tina defended, (b) Tina buttressed and (c) otherwise Tina accommodated as it wends its way through history. The forms and arguments constituting the Tina elements vary over time and context, but the underlying problematic remains in place, generating defensive moves in a variety of Tina compromise formations.

Turning to specific philosophical episodes to illustrate this, we could briefly mention the discussion in this chapter of Derrida and Habermas as complicit dialectical antagonists who evade in significant ways either the transcendental necessity of subjectivity in an objective world (Derrida) or the intrinsic effects of objectivity on the subject (Habermas). For Bhaskar, the aim would be to show how both protagonists would defend, buttress and manage the one-sided insights that animate their conflicting philosophies. (At the same time, he would find elements in both philosophies with which to make common cause, for a one-sided argument will have some right on its side.) I shall return to Derrida in a moment. One extended illustration of philosophy as Tina compromise formation, however, is to be found in Bhaskar's treatment of Hegel. His overall argument is that Hegel's marriage of objective idealism and ontological actualism represents 'another instance of a Tina formation in the tacit duplicity of dialectical antagonists' (DPF: 117). Objective idealism, we have seen, involves a form of the epistemic fallacy through the role it gives to reason embodying itself in the world, and it predicates in consequence an actualist, empiricist vision of ontology. It is the combination of epistemic (rational) control over an ontological realm understood in actualist terms that ensures the closure of history, and the creation of the demi-actual in reality. The latter represents a Tina anomaly in Hegel's argument, requiring defence and control. Bhaskar pursues this analysis more specifically in his interpretation of the different philosophical forms that Hegel discusses in the early sections of the *Phenomenology* related to the master–slave dialectic, the Stoic, the Sceptic and the Unhappy Consciousness. All three represent irrealist orientations to reality: scepticism is its denial or denegation, stoicism an indifference to it, and the Unhappy Consciousness is a flight from it into asceticism or other-worldliness. Hegel is able to handle these different denials of reality, which are also implicit in his own project, only by what is in effect a hugely elaborate Tina formation, the *Phenomenology*, where the epistemic fallacy, represented by reason, leads the Stoic and his unhappy friends onto the sunlit uplands of Spirit.

More, however, than simply seeing these attitudes as central to the Hegelian Tina problematic, Bhaskar wants to present them as profoundly linked to the development of modern philosophy more broadly, especially in so far as it is grounded, as so much is, in the Humean brand of scepticism. Such, indeed, is the dominance of sceptical attitudes to reality within philosophy that Bhaskar describes it as 'a veritable citadel of the Unhappy Consciousness' (DPF: 406). There is also a sense here of the restless, shifting forms of philosophy, from stoicism to scepticism, to efforts to combat them, and back again, as it wrestles with problems it cannot overcome because it misunderstands ontology. This effort may include philosophies that are, on the face of it, critical of the tradition. For example, Derrida's deconstruction offers concepts that provide a negative, critical engagement with philosophy, but does so from a position that is itself prey to the tradition's structural weaknesses. Despite its critical stance, it can be placed in the line of Hegelian Tina thinking, for it was 'stoic indifference to reality' that 'gave rise to a post-structuralist collapse to scepticism, in which Derrida can write "there is nothing outside the text" and probably neither mean, definitely not believe and certainly not act on it' (DPF: 213).[16] This is the Tina syndrome in operation, a mode of thinking involving internally contradictory, unserious, compromising and defensive qualities, where the appearance of resolution gives way before problems that can only be expressed and reconfigured:

> Metacritically, . . . the denegation or violation of . . . necessity must deploy itself as an auto-subversive, radically negating, internally split, axiologically inconsistent Tina compromise formation, necessarily presupposing what it (explicitly or implicitly) denies. . . . Tina formations are internally contradictory, more or less systemic, efficacious, syntonic (and . . . regressive) ensembles, . . . displaying duplicity, equivocation, extreme plasticity and pliability and rational indeterminacy (facilitating their ideological and manipulative use). Moreover, they generate a characteristic range of paradoxes and effects.
>
> (DPF: 117)

Tina means trouble. If that is what Tinas are, I now want to pursue their underlying grounds and how they come about. I begin by comparing the Tina syndrome with some alternative critical foundations, before proceeding to identify the link Bhaskar draws between the Tina, alienation and generalised master–slave relations.

Tinas in critical thought

The Tina is Bhaskar's version of Hegel's 'bad infinite', albeit in a different context, for this is a realm of repetition as false necessity. In this regard, Tina thinking, as I have said, is of significance beyond philosophy's shores. In different terms, it has been remarked upon by a range of modern thinkers that includes Freud, Marx and, taking him more positively, Derrida. It will be recalled that Bhaskar's borrowing of the term 'the reality principle' is with reference to Freud, and so is his account of 'compromise formation' (DPF: 11). We also saw in Chapter 2 how Bhaskar's thematisation of the presence of the past invokes both Freud's and Marx's thinking on the 'return of the repressed'.[17] Tina repressions return in new ways, encouraging sustained and systematic efforts at repression. Bhaskar aligns his concept of Tina formation with Marx's account of ideology.[18] Why not, then, stick with the term 'ideology', or perhaps something like Althusser's idea of an 'ideological problematic' (Althusser 2005)? These terms involve an emphasis on the structured, historical dimension to thought, which Bhaskar would himself endorse, but he seeks something different with the idea of the Tina syndrome. It is a way of thinking about the internal nature and patterning of ideology as thinking moves and negotiates the world. Tina analysis involves the intrinsic in thinking, where the concept of ideology as structure of thought reflects more on its extrinsic dimension. The Tina involves a perspectival shift to the position of thinking itself in a theoretico-practical dual, itself embedded in the dual of thought and its context, wherein thinking operates in terms it believes to be its own, though they are not, or not entirely so. Tina analysis assumes an explicitly internal standpoint, albeit it links it, as we shall see, to the externals of alienation and structured power relations.

As for Derrida, his concepts of 'supplementarity' and '*différance*' relate to the surplus of meaning required to fulfil a concept while pushing beyond, and thereby undermining, it. Deconstructive concepts have something in common with dialectical thinking. Derrida may be regarded, indeed, as involved in metacritical or dialectical comment, in the making of a 'dialectical remark', on the hierarchies of traditional philosophy (DPF: 118). There is common ground between deconstruction as a form of negative dialectical comment and any critical dialectics. However, there is an ontological limit to deconstruction. Bhaskar finds that Derrida's models are 'too closely tied to the practice of hierarchical inversion, chiasmus and erasure' and that the 'more general concept of a Tina formation is required for the analysis of the effects of the violation of any axiological [i.e. real – A.N.] necessity' (ibid.). He adds, reflecting upon the difference between the realist Tina formation and irrealist deconstruction, that the way a Tina formation manifests itself 'on any particular occasion, in a multiply determined, contradictory, agentive and internally and externally related world, will be both contingent and variable' (ibid.). A too programmatic, a prioristic injunction to invert or erase, to deconstruct in the manner of Derrida, is insufficiently attuned to how the problems of philosophy are embedded in an ontologically real, geo-historical world with its changing forms. On the 'reality principle', it is natural necessity in the world that yields those forms in their historical specificity which supplementarity or *différance* exposes, but deconstruction lacks a sufficient interest in material and spatio-temporal specificity. Analysis of Tina formations on the terrain of a materially diffracted dialectical totality yields a posteriori connections to spatio-temporal historicity, not generic, a prioristic injunctions to invert and deconstruct.

Philosophy, alienation and the master–slave dialectic

If the Tina syndrome represents the intrinsic aspect of an historical process that on its extrinsic side is ideology, and involves efforts to defend detotalisation, what underlies it? Detotalisation may take many forms, but at root Bhaskar finds an ethical connection to the idea of alienation, and here, perhaps, his designation of philosophy as a citadel of the Unhappy Consciousness indicates the path. Issues of detotalisation are to the fore in alienation, which involves split and contradiction where there ought to be wholeness or connectedness. In relation to the detotalisation that informs modernity, the underlying problem is the 'splits, inconsistencies, divisions such as those of class, gender, ethnicity, etc. and alienation – the estrangement of part or whole of one's essence from one's self – generally' (DPF: 360). Split and alienation go together so that the 'real problem of alienation' acts 'as an index of the detotalisations and other effects of the contradictions and splits in the world of late/postmodernity' (DPF: 316). Alienation ties in with the discussion at the beginning of this chapter of heterology and heteronomy, meaning lack of autonomy. As with Tinas, it operates at a variety of levels in the social totality. It means

> being something other than, (having been) separated, split, torn or estranged from oneself, or what is essential and intrinsic to one's nature or identity. What is intrinsic to oneself need not be internal to, in the sense of physically inside, one – as in the case of a person's kindness . . . ; and what is still essentially one's own at one level (e.g. one's humanity) may be alienated at another (e.g. by being subjugated to gross indignity). To be alienated is to lose part of one's autonomy.
>
> (DPF: 114)

Bhaskar relates alienation to two accounts of the nature of modernity, those of the young Hegel and Marx. In Hegel, alienation is seen in the early theological writings in the figure of the Beautiful Soul, and its inability to find a place in its community, leading to a situation of Unhappy Consciousness (DPF: 167).[19] Linking this with our discussion of the Unhappy Consciousness in matters of epistemology and ontology, Bhaskar's ambition is for a vision in which problems in western philosophy are mediated by fundamental ethical questions about the nature of human being in western societies. To be an Unhappy Consciousness in philosophy today is to participate in and to express a deeper alienation experienced in modernity. There can be no ultimate separation between questions of how we know the world and questions of how we live in the world. Detotalisation in epistemology is part and parcel of a world in which alienation is engrained. Moving from the young Hegel to the work of his early maturity, Bhaskar finds a change in Hegel. Now alienation is embodied in the figures of the *Phenomenology* that we discussed above, the Stoic, the Sceptic and the Unhappy Consciousness:

> Thus to stoicism, corresponds indifference, and to scepticism the denial (or rather denegation – rejection in theory, acceptance in practice) of . . . relations [of domination, exploitation, subjugation and control]. And one can align the unhappy consciousness [in philosophy] . . . to two phases, namely (i) the introjective internalisation of the master's viewpoint or aspirations or ideology and/or (ii) the projective duplication of what the slave, lacking the imaginary world of religion (Kantian 'rational faith'), finds in fantasy, film or soap in a surrogate compensatory existence.
>
> (DPF: 154)

Here, basic philosophical standpoints are linked to more concrete, ideological, alienated ways of accommodating oneself to the status quo. Modern scepticism, for example, has its real basis in private property, for, as Alexandre Kojeve remarks, 'only those who need not sell their labour power can afford to be sceptics' (DPF: 331).[20] Bhaskar draws on 'certain general attitudes, from the sections immediately following Hegel's master–slave dialectic', stoicism, scepticism and the Unhappy Consciousness, which are 'conventionally associated with geo-historical periods', but he wants to portray them as contemporary, alienated orientations to power. Hegel, of course, sought to overcome the alienation associated with them in philosophy, whereas for Bhaskar these are enduring real-world mindsets expressed philosophically.

Turning to Marx, alienation lies at the core of what Bhaskar calls an original 'generative separation'[21] under modern conditions. This is the basic fivefold split that begins with the alienation of the immediate producers from their labour, its product and the means of its production. This core form spawns alienation across the four planes of human being. These will be discussed in the next section as 'four-planar social being', but in essence they involve alienation in material transactions with nature, in social interactions between people, in the networks of social relations, and finally alienation from oneself. Now, as with Hegel, this view of alienation is linked to the idea of master–slave relations, in Marx's case as 'wage slavery'. This relates to 'a characteristic feature of the capitalist mode of production: the exploitative relation intrinsic to the wage-labour/capital contract . . . hidden at the level of inter-personal transactions by fetishism' (ibid.). Bhaskar's aim, then, is to pull together two references to master–slave relations: Hegel's account of philosophical consciousness in the master–slave dialectic, and Marx's analysis of modern capitalism as involving wage slavery. From Marx, Bhaskar finds a structural explication of the nature of alienation in modern society. From Hegel, he finds a set of philosophical standpoints that he (Bhaskar) associates with forms of alienation in modern philosophy. Putting them together gives a designation of modern philosophy in terms of its link to structured, 'generalised master–slave-type (power$_2$) relations' (ibid.). The terminology ties philosophy to the structured generation of alienation and elucidates the underlying relation to the philosophical repetition that occurs in the Tina syndrome. In the process, it provides Bhaskar with his own critical realist version of the master–slave dialectic.

Does Bhaskar, however, go too far in talking of the 'generalised' nature of these power relations? The amalgamation of Marxian and Hegelian preoccupations is a way of talking about philosophy and alienation under modern conditions. Can this be 'generalised', presumably to include thinking about philosophy across historical periods, including ancient forms (e.g. Greek slavery)? There is in fact a good reason for generalisation. What these different kinds of slavery have in common is that they generate forms of heteronomy for human beings, which are then recapitulated *mutatis mutandis* in philosophy. Problems of scepticism and stoicism are of course not just modern. They go back to the classical origins of philosophy, where one also finds, it will be recalled, the foundational denial of natural necessity and absence in Parmenides and Plato. Bhaskar's argument is that issues of alienation lie at the core of western philosophy from its inception because it is articulated in the context of (different kinds of) structured power relations. Notwithstanding historical difference, however, there remains an underlying unity – and this is Bhaskar's point – that ties together the most basic moves in the western philosophical tradition. For some, this may appear as an illicit collapsing of important distinctions (Creaven 2002; Joseph 2006), but what Bhaskar wants to establish is a sense of how the western philosophical tradition *as a whole* can be understood as continuously committed to forms of alienation. At one level, historical specificity is crucial, but so too, at another level, is what unites the tradition across the epochs. If it can be rightly said that all philosophy consists of a series of footnotes to Plato (and we shall pursue this argument in depth in Chapter 6), we need to take seriously the commonality within philosophy across time. Bhaskar's generalisation of different forms of exploitation as master–slave-type relations is helpful in thinking continuity across different power structures in a way that historically specific arguments, correct at the appropriate level, miss.[22]

Bhaskar draws the links closely between western societies and western philosophy, using his own version of the master–slave dialectic as a way of thinking about the evolution of historical forms of exploitation, and how those are recapitulated in one common philosophical tradition. Putting together detotalisation, alienation and Tina compromise formations, one might say that Tinas are philosophical (and other) responses to the effects of alienation, and the detotalisations alienation brings. While totality is a way of thinking how things are held together, we also need to think about how a specific geo-historical totality engenders disconnection. In that context, we must include an understanding of the detotalisations, the sub-totalities, that are maintained in it. Of course, these go much further than philosophy itself. Nonetheless, philosophy is a site of detotalisation, and an important one. Addressing totality thus involves a double move, of seeing what it means to talk of the whole, through the notion of partial totalities, and of the whole as the site of fundamental splits, as sub-totalities. But if we have pursued the idea of detotalisation and sub-totality, we also have to think about whether it is possible for philosophy to conceive of humankind as responding to it. If detotalisation is prevalent, is retotalisation possible?

Retotalisation: the concrete universal

I now complete this chapter with an account of individual human being in the shape of 'those emergent totalities called persons' (DPF: 85). Here, I focus on Bhaskar's remodelling of Hegel's 'concrete universal' and his nomination of what he calls the 'concrete singular' alongside his expanded account of the structure/agency dual in terms of 'four-planar being'. Having explained this development, I will then conclude the section by linking the discussion to the problem of detotalisation by alienation and the possibility of retotalising human being through agency and ethics.

The concrete universal

For Hegel,[23] universality, particularity (specificity) and individuality (singularity) are moments in the development of the Idea. Universality develops into the particular or the specific, and then in a further stage into an individuality or singularity that unites the universal and the particular. 'Universals are embedded in particulars and individuals,' Michael Inwood (1992: 304) writes, and the 'individual that results is as much universal as individual' (ibid.). In Hegel's conception, however, the universal dominates. The particular (the specific) and the individual (the singular), while necessary, are dependent and secondary. For Hegel, 'Individuals derive their status from the universality involved in them', so that while he recognises the particular differences between individuals, 'he subordinates them to what men have in common' (ibid.), and with regard to the highest faculty, reason, they do not essentially differ. Universality requires particularity and individuality in order to become a concrete universal, but the universal remains pre-eminent. As Hegel says in the *Philosophy of Right*, 'the rational is the high road where everyone travels, where no one is conspicuous' (1952: 230).

For Bhaskar, Hegel's universal dominates the particular and the individual. Since Bhaskar insists on the concrete spatio-temporality of being in the world, any account of universality that ignores this will fall short. In submitting the world to the rule of reason, Hegel is committed to a subject–object identity theory which fails to grasp that the (social) world works according to a processuality that includes the effects of the human mind, but is not reducible to them. Without material diffraction, the dialectic remains in the grip of the positive speculative moment, reason as the universal. Bhaskar wants to introduce a counterweight by proposing a concrete universal in which the universal and the individual are mediated by a particular that is processual and spatio-temporal. Concrete universality has to be seen in the context of stratification, spatio-temporal processualisation, totality and mediatedness, and in the light of the effects of negativity. All these elements give to the individual as a universal a sense of the real singularity that exists in the world, for in this processing of individuality, individuals are inseparable from the effects of real change and difference. This is a radical geo-historical treatment of the concrete universal which shifts the emphasis to the concrete singular and its spatio-temporal dispositional identity. It adds a fourth element to the concrete universal alongside universality, particularity and singularity, so that, instead of an Hegelian triad, we get a Bhaskarian 'four', or 'quadruplicity':

> [O]nce the idea of process, conceived as the mode of spatio-temporalising structural effects, is combined with the Hegelian emphasis on specificity or particularity (which may itself be more or less structurally sedimented and/or spatio-temporally localised), in addition to the moments of universality and singularity, then it is clear that the [concrete universal] must reveal itself as a quadruplicity.
>
> (DPF: 129)

Further, since in his account of totality the future is open and subject to multiple determination in a structured plurality of partial totalities, the universal in its concreteness is subject to a multiplicity of determinations, and therefore becomes an open, 'multiple quadruplicity'. This is the 'minimum formula necessary for the concrete universal' (ibid.) under the terms of the materialist diffraction of dialectic and the opening of totality.

Four-planar being

What does it mean to theorise the concrete universal in these terms, and, in particular, how do they relate to ideas of identity and agency to be found in critical realism? Here we revert to the TMSA from original critical realism and its development as 'four-planar being'. Bhaskar also refers to this as the 'social tetrapolity', and relates both to the idea of the 'social cube'.[24] The four planes of being are those of (1) material transactions with nature; (2) inter- and intra-subjective (interpersonal) relations between differently situated agents; (3) social relations at the non-reducible level of structures, institutions and forms; and (4) the (internal) stratification of the personality. The original TMSA by contrast has a rather abstract and simplified feel in its division of the 'social parts' into two, structure and agency and their inter-relation, so the novelty of the four-planar conception is that it expands the elements necessary to speak holistically about human being in both the natural and social worlds. Further, Bhaskar draws upon Margaret Archer's work (1995) to argue for the significance of space-time to four-planarity so that human being involves a 'multiplicity of (potentially disjoint) rhythmics, conceived as tensed socio-spatialising process . . . as a cubic flow, differentiated into analytically discrete moments, . . . as rhythmically processual and phasic to the core' (DPF: 160). In this overall vision, the individual planes of being should be seen 'as subject to multiple and conflicting determinations and mediations and as displaying to a greater or lesser extent (more or less contradictory) intra-relationality and totality; more generally, as embodying all the moments of the concrete universal' (ibid.). Stating this, Bhaskar draws together two languages, those of critical realism and its (now developed) four-planar version of the TMSA, and of dialectical theory with its (now materially diffracted) concrete universal. This works through the stipulation that the social cube (four-planar being) reflect all those moments which constitute concrete universality, producing a strong emphasis on the concrete singular as the real point of mediation of the four different planes of being.

To what vision of concrete singularity does this give rise? Bhaskar illustrates the very different rhythmics that may engage an individual at different levels of her being. First, there is her life narrative, her biography. Second, there is her stratified internal personality taking the form of 'the lagged causal efficacy of her unconscious, her unwritten biography' (DPF: 163). Both elements go towards plane (4), the stratification of her personality. Third, 'there is her life cycle as an organism (a human being) and specifically as a woman' (ibid.), which relates to plane (1), her material transactions with nature. Fourth, there is her daily praxis, which engages in various very different social practices, each with their own rhythmics, and taking her down various 'space-time routes through the cities, dwellings, worksites, landscapes in which she lives' (ibid.). This engages her (plane 2) in interpersonal relations with differently situated agents, and (plane 3) with structures, institutions and forms. Fifth, these latter represent more generally the crucial background of differentially sedimented structures, institutions and social relations which co-constitute her. Sixth, there is the 'development of specifically civilised geo-history in the context of human geo-history, inserted in the rhythmics of species, genera and kinds, located in a geo-physical development of a solar system, embedded in the entropy of an expanding universe' (DPF: 164). Of this deepest level, pertaining especially to planes (1) and (3), she is a small but significant part. Of course, it is necessary to grasp that all four planes are inter- and intra-connected with numerous feedback effects along the way.

Recalling agency

This is a radically contextualised view of human being in which the 'emergent totalities known as persons' are located in their concrete universality as concrete singulars at the point of mediation provided by the four planes of human being.[25] The sense is of the 'thrown' character of human individuality in a world in which diffraction means differentiation and fracturing. Where the world contains sub-totality, individual personality must internalise detotalisation as well as provide the ground of individual difference. The question then arises as to what the implications of this vision are for our understanding of human agency, and the ethics attendant to it. Our main discussion of the latter awaits the next chapter, but some points can be made here, especially concerning agency. First, in considering the possibility of agency, the thrown quality of four-planar being must be read alongside our discussion of duality, constellationality and mediatedness in the agency/structure relation in the second section of this chapter. These ideas are maintained in the shift to four-planar being. They stress the irreducibility of agency to structure (and vice versa), so a multiply thrown subject remains a subject and agent possessing powers, emergent for human being, to think and act, to do so for reasons, and to be a cause in the world. By a perspectival switch to the standpoint of the agent, we can similarly see that, even for a thrown subject, all actions possess the fullest range of active qualities, as cognitive, affective, conative, expressive and performative, and therefore express her identity. The result accordingly is not a loss of agency or identity by virtue of our radical diffraction as persons, but rather a changing 'dispositional identity of the subject with her changing causal powers' (DPF: 165). This holds onto the sense that selfhood in a four-planar, or concretely universal-singular, conception changes over time and is at the same time irreducible and real. Identity endures as it mediates the different aspects of four-planarity across time and place. From this conception of identity and agency, it is clear that selfhood is possible and capable of the reflexivity and meta-reflexivity discussed earlier. This is true with regard to contemplation not only of the world that makes it, but also of its capacity to reflect on its own developing dispositional identity over time.

In considering the self, it is always essential to recognize how identity is affected by difference, change and absence, including the effects of detotalisation and alienation. It is dependent on 'the degree of centrification, fragmentation or alienation of the subject', and on the 'open systemic, multiply and conflictually determined nature of . . . our internal pluriverses' (DPF: 167). There are forces that constitute persons, and these may operate beyond the powers of individuals to affect, but they are nonetheless capable of seeking to understand and to act on or against them. Accordingly, two things are always ongoing: change with regard to the self's internal pluriverse, and the possibility of its reflexively and meta-reflexively totalised monitoring. Such a double possibility stems from the duality of agency and structure, and the linked chain of dualities which includes reasons and causes, theory and practice, mind and matter, and, ultimately, knowledge and being, located as appropriate in their different constellational settings. In each dual, the first term remains irreducible to the second, and grounds the possibility of meta-reflexively totalising, this-worldly, thought and action in the concrete here and now.

This version of the concrete universal as concrete singular also has significant implications for how we think ethically about human being. The concrete singular as an individual 'consists in a core species-being, [and] particular mediations and rhythmics, uniquely individuating her or him as in effect a natural kind sui generis' (DPF: 395). The core universality in this, which is only ever analytically separate from the concrete singularity in which it is embedded, is nonetheless the ground for a basic equity among differently situated individuals (DPF: 178). At the same time, the concrete singularity of each, with its particular needs, places, differences and views, represents 'the key to the realm of freedom, including the abolition of human heterology' (DPF: 131). Accordingly,

> our totality ethically prioritises the individual – the concrete singularity of each is the *condition* for the concrete singularity of all – while recognising the determining role played by material circumstances (including, of course, ideas), particularly in the form of structurally sedimented institutions inter-locked with discursively moralised oppressive power$_2$ relations.
>
> (DPF: 273)

The concrete universal-singular is the place of (1M) real material difference, and (2E) negativity as an individual is thrown in space-time. It is characterised by (3L) wholeness as a partial totality, which includes the detotalising effects of sub-totality, and is capable of (4D) ethical agency, as we will see. If sub-totality qua detotalisation can be acted against, concrete singularity remains as the criterion for an ultimate ethical wholeness, albeit in a world that continues to be open, changing and incomplete. Thus, it has to be borne in mind that the 'moral evolution of the species is to be regarded as unfinished' (DPF: 398), for totality remains open to the evolution of the new and the different. Moreover, as a partial totality in its own right, and at its own level, this is also true of and for each concrete universal/singular human agent. Each individual remains as a concrete singular open to the future and in process of development. In this context, the possibility of meta-reflexively totalising understanding as the basis for ethical action remains both possible and ongoingly necessary to the future development of individuals and the world. This is all the more so in an open world where the future contains unanticipated developments.

Conclusion

Bhaskar's account of totality builds upon the foundations provided by first-level critical realism and the second edge of absence to develop a materially diffracted third level in which Hegelian rationalism and universalism are displaced by an awareness of how the spatio-temporal world shapes dialectic and the resulting totality. Totality in things is prevalent in the social (and natural) worlds, and it is plural, partial and open. Alongside and within partial totalities, we need to recognise detotalising tendencies which are reflected in the idea of sub-totalities, while the plurality of partial totalities is held together by the concept of holistic causality. Among the dialectical architecture of totality, we find a variety of ways in which difference is maintained in the whole. The relatively simple idea of levels leads to the idea of mediation, but the whole is theorised in line with mediation's sense of distinction in connectedness by the constellation and, at the core of the constellation, the dual. These figures theorise the relationship between intrinsically connected yet different, *sui generis* elements, and their value can be seen in their ability to maintain a range of dualistic connections that would otherwise be overlooked or misunderstood: agency and structure, reasons and causes, theory and practice, mind and matter, knowledge and being. Around the agency/structure dual in particular, we examined the further conceptual developments involving hiatus-in-duality, perspectival switch and the meta-reflexive totalising situation. These ideas become important once, having considered the detotalisation of life under alienating conditions, we look for a way in which human beings may reclaim their world through retotalisation.

Moving to detotalisation, sub-totalities and alienation, we examined the idea of the Tina syndrome as a means of considering how ideas work under the shadow of false necessities brought about by power. We saw how specific episodes in philosophy, and the tradition as a whole, could be brought under this analysis. One episode in particular, Hegel's depiction of various philosophical attitudes emerging from his master–slave dialectic, became our focus as we considered how Stoicisim and Scepticism pervade modern philosophy, especially via Hume, making it a 'veritable citadel of the Unhappy Consciousness' (DPF: 406). These philosophical forms effectively lead to the denial of ontology qua natural necessity and real absence, and act as philosophical means of replicating the conditions of alienation to which people are subject. Involving Marx alongside Hegel, this alienation is a product of 'generalised master–slave-type relations' so that there is a connecting line of analysis between the deepest problems of western philosophy, alienation and human heteronomy in the ancient and modern worlds, and the existence of different kinds of structured power relations. This is Bhaskar's version of the master–slave dialectic in action.

This leads to a sense of the modern world in which humankind is subject to alienation and power$_2$ relations, and the question arises, how may we comprehend the possibilities for change? This returns us to the question of structure and agency, which has now been developed to include the four different planes of human being alongside a materialised and diffracted conception of Hegel's concrete universal as the concrete singular. These arguments stretch our conception of the structure/ agency dual and its constellational relations, but they do not deny the essential truth of agency, maintained from 1M critical realism through a series of duals that enable us to uphold the place of agency with regard to structure, alongside that of reasons with regard to causes, mind with regard to matter, theory with regard to practice, and knowledge with regard to being. All these terms maintain their importance, mediating the constellational relations of which they are a part, and upholding the emergent power of human agency and the possibility of the meta-reflexive totalising situation.

At the same time as agency is maintained in the concrete universal and four-planar being, so too are certain important ethical values developed. These include the core species-being caught in the universal aspect of the concrete universal-singular, and the understanding that the radically differentiated nature of concrete universality as concrete singularity provides us with a standpoint from which to think the ultimate goals of ethics. If that standpoint remains necessarily open and incomplete, it nonetheless provides us with an ethical basis from which to take aim at detotalisation and alienation in concrete singularity as it exists in the here and now. Thinking through this issue, however, is a matter for the next chapter, where we shall focus fully on ethics and the nature of human being.

5 Constellating ethics

We are now in a position to complete the four-part dialectic of dialectical critical realism, represented as the MELD schema. We began with 1M original critical realism and an ontology of real, determinate non-identity, into which we inserted a second-edge (2E) understanding of negativity as absence, and of the importance of being as becoming. Negativity as the basis for the spatio-temporalisation of being and its irreducible contextualisation then pointed to a move to a third-level (3L) sense of the whole or (open, partial) totality, and now we turn to 4D, the importance of agency as ethical practice. This is the move that completes Bhaskar's dialectical journey, and it returns us to the early (1M) insistence on agency as a human power enduring in and through social structure. Now, however, that power has to be thought in the context of 2E spatio-temporality and contextualisation and 3L totality, as a result of which it now presents itself as four-planar being generating the concrete universal as a concrete singular, and located in an understanding of levels, constellationality, duality, hiatus, perspective switch and meta-reflexivity as the dialectical architecture in the realm of totality.

The chapter has three main sections. In the next, I outline some basic starting points for Bhaskar's morally realist, alethic conception of ethics before, in the following section, fleshing out its three main themes. These are based around meta-ethical dialectics of knowledge and emancipation, truth, judgement and solidarity, and desire and freedom. Together these produce a dialectical rationality or universalisability that is the basis for thinking about ethics today. Thereafter, in a third section, I broach the relationship between ethics and history in a section that looks at the relationship between the realistically grounded development of an ethics of dialectical universalisability and the realist and materialist approach that grounds Bhaskar's dialectic. These are held together, I suggest, by the idea of a constellational relationship between ethics and the spatio-temporal and geo-historical development of human being, or between what Bhaskar calls (making a perspectival switch) the 'intrinsic' (ethically centred) and the 'extrinsic' (historico-material) dimensions of human experience. In looking at Bhaskar's dialectics in this way, we will see how he delivers a vision of ethics as an exercise in concrete utopianism for a world in need of change. He accounts for modern ethics in terms of what I will call a dialectic of the ideal (how the ethically best world is reflected in the ethical present) and the actual (the forms of ethics available under modern conditions). In this dialectic, both ideal and actual have their place, and neither, in a constellational relationship, is reducible to the other. In the course of the analysis, we will consider the criticism that Bhaskar's ethics are marred by abstraction and formalism (see, for example, Creaven 2002: 119–21).

Ethical starting points

I begin by taking a passage from Bhaskar that introduces in programmatic terms the various elements in his argument for a dialectical critical realist ethics. I aim to provide an initial core statement (though not a complete one) that we may have in mind as we proceed. It introduces ideas of desire and freedom, which I then link to an orienting comment on the relationship between Bhaskar and Habermas. From this starting point, I examine the role of (2E) absence and the concept of 'alethia' in Bhaskar's ethics, before outlining the moral realism and ethical naturalism that structure his philosophy.

From desire to freedom

The passage I focus on begins as follows:

> Ethical dialectics will take us, via ethical naturalism and moral realism, from the primal scream induced by the absent parent(s) through (to use slightly archaic language) the education imposed on desire by the reality principle or axiological necessity, in a dialectic of truth and freedom, mediated by wisdom to universal human emancipation in a society in which the free flourishing of each is the condition of the free flourishing of all.
>
> (DPF: 98)

This statement covers a lot of ground in one sentence. It identifies the main ethical forms Bhaskar relies upon in his account: ethical naturalism and moral realism. Ethical naturalism will be familiar to those who have read Bhaskar's pre-dialectical work, and both it and moral realism, which is an extension of the idea of ontological realism into the moral realm via the concept of 'alethia', will be explained in due course. Let us, however, set them aside for the moment and focus on the substance of the argument. Here, the statement identifies the core idea that desire grounds the existential experience of human being as at once governed by necessity, and in search of freedom. When pushed to their limits, the conflicting demands of this experience push the individual to an idea of human freedom and emancipation as the utmost possible satisfaction of desire, and therefore, in so far as this is possible for material beings, liberation from necessity. This is given a universal quality by the realisation that the freedom of each is dependent on the freedom of all. As we will see, this is not all of Bhaskar's argument, for a role has to be found for judgement, trust and solidarity (see the next section), not to mention the overall 3L constellation of ethics (see the third section), but it gives a preliminary taste of how things proceed according to principles of dialectical universalisation.

What we have is a process of dialectical logic or rationality in which thinking consistently from one's concrete reality as a needy being to the ultimate satisfaction of one's ends entrains the thought of a eudaimonic world for all. This thought is, to a limited degree, and variably according to the contingencies of place and period,[1] ingredient in our evolution as human (social and natural) beings. At the same time, achievement of such a world is not just a matter of thought but, according to the duality of theory and practice, is dependent on our agency, and the struggles in which we must participate. Thus, the process of dialectical logic, of reasoning from what we are to what we could be, pushes us forward as agents in a dialectic. This proceeds from our first desire to be free from material need to an eventual desire by extension for freedom of a most complete form.

The passage begun above continues by describing dialectical logic in five different terms, as follows:

> Absolute reason or dialectical rationality, alethia, theory/practice consistency and dialectical universalisability impose a tendential directionality to this rhythmic absenting of constraints on wellbeing and possibilities.
>
> (ibid.)

Again, we will come back to terminology, but the important point is that these ideas sustain a sense of the reason and universalisability that lie within ethical thinking. They are linked, however, in this passage to agency, in the form of processes of absenting those things that get in the way of freedom. This leads to a stress on the importance of a radical ethical agency to bring freedom about, expressed in the following complex sentence:

> [Moral development] is contingent upon a transformed transformative total-ising transformist praxis (which will revolve in large part around hermeneutic hegemonic/counter-hegemonic struggles in the context of discursively moralised power$_2$ relations), itself dependent upon the rationality of agents and the contingency of accidents in a contradiction-riven but open systemic world [as to] whether freedom or rational autonomy of action will be.
>
> (ibid.)

The idea of 'transformed transformative totalising transformist praxis' is daunting. A shorter way of describing what Bhaskar has in mind, avoiding the allure of alliteration, is that of 'totalising depth praxis'. Recalling the possibility of 'meta-reflexively totalising' theory from Chapter 4, this is praxis (on the 'other side' of the theory–practice dual), and it is at once radically negatory and positive. It pursues the absenting of absences, and, in consequence of its totalising and depth orientation, the absenting of constraints which sustain absences. What is at stake is a conflict between the most basic elements and drives in human nature and the ability of human beings to find ways to sustain these in a world that denies them. Note here the reference to power$_2$ relations and, recalling our discussion of philosophy under master–slave-type conditions in the previous chapter, the way those 'discursively moralise' the status quo. Bhaskar conceives human nature complexly as human being-in-society-in-nature, but as entailing primary existential qualities such as desire, and, as we shall see, sociality and trust. These give rise to a tendency for humanity to seek a world adequate to itself, which, though it may be denied or suppressed, continues to press its image through the succeeding generations, for, the passage concludes, '[w]hat is certain is that, so long as humanity survives, there will always be a conatus for freedom to become' (ibid.). It is this desire to, and for, freedom that gets the principles of dialectical rationality going, and drives dialectic forward.

This is key, but it is not all, for the equally important idea that principles of dialectical rationality must be constellated in open totality awaits us in the final section of the chapter. We may, however, pause to note that it is this idea of a conatus to freedom that gives *Dialectic: The Pulse of Freedom* its sub-title. As Bhaskar notes at the end of his discussion of ethics, dialectic is best conceived as an

> inner urge that flows universally from the logic of elemental absence (lack, need, want or desire). It manifests itself wherever power$_2$ relations hold sway. It is the heartbeat of a positively generalized concept of freedom as flourishing and as autonomy and as reason. It is irrepressible.
>
> (DPF: 298, cf. 385)

Thus, dialectical logic, embedded in human, natural-social being is the starting point for ethics in Bhaskar's project. It relies, as we have seen, on absenting and a sense of the 'alethic' in philosophical doctrines which are described as morally realist and ethically naturalist. Before we move to consider what these terms mean, it may be helpful to compare Bhaskar's account of dialectical rationality with another account with which it has something in common, that of Habermas.

Bhaskar and Habermas

In a 1980 essay, Bhaskar wrote of the debt he owed to Jürgen Habermas, even though they came to 'rather different conclusions' (Bhaskar 1989: 202). What was of value in Habermas was a 'transcendental argument from language as a universal medium of discourse' leading to 'a materialistically mediated conatus to consensus' (Bhaskar 1989: 189), but only, Bhaskar added, if it were set in an appropriate critical realist perspective. The similarity between the two thinkers in terms of 'transcendental argument' and what has been sketched above of a universalising dialectic (of desire to freedom in Bhaskar's case) should be clear, but two differences must be noted. First, in Bhaskar it is not just discourse or speech acts that are universalised, but other dimensions of human interaction. Bhaskar is not against universalising linguistic practice, but he thinks the universalising strategy should be extended radically:

> if there is a sense in which the ideal community, founded on principles of truth, freedom and justice, is already present as a prefiguration in every speech

interaction, might one not be tempted to suppose that equality, liberty and fraternity are present in every transaction or material exchange; or that respect and mutual recognition are contained in the most casual reciprocated glance? It is an error to suppose that ethics must have a linguistic foundation; just as it is an error to suppose that it is autonomous from science or history.

(Bhaskar 1986: 210; 1989: 114)

The message in this earlier work, borne out by what was to come in *Dialectic*, is that human being in its various existential aspects generates ethical impulses of a universal kind, and that these relate to the freedom of all under conditions that permit such freedom to exist. So there is a generalisation of Habermas's discourse ethics (1984, 1987) to dialectics of knowledge and emancipation, truth, judgement and solidarity, and desire and freedom, but there is also, second, a crucial qualification. The universalising argument must also be placed in an overall critical realist framework, and this would recognise that ethics are not autonomous from the materiality of history. Habermas's philosophy is irrealist in its neo-Kantian synthesis of hermeneutics and an 'essentially unreconstructed empirical realism', as well as in its consensual theory of truth (Outhwaite 1994: 40–1), so that he 'still scathingly attacks ontology . . . while the rationality of his whole project points to the need to thematise it as a social science which . . . should be explicitly realist' (DPF: 375). Without realist ontology, it should be noted, his system becomes antinomial and anti-naturalist as the 'extra-communicative or extra-discursive constraints on communicative interaction' are hermetically sealed off from action. Thus marginalised, they nonetheless reappear in the split between system and lifeworld, 'in the guise of the colonisation of the lifeworld by the reified systems of economy and polity coordinated by . . . money and power' (Bhaskar 1989: 189). Bhaskar's aim against such antinomialism is to explain how dialectical critical realist ontology maintains a relation between (expanded) processes of dialectical rationality and spatio-temporal processes of social and historical development without falling into a split vision. In the third section, this aim will take us to the figure of the constellation within the theory of totality, but it is helpful to flag it up here, in the context of the relationship with Habermas. Broadly, in what follows it will be seen that there is a certain resemblance between the two philosophers in terms of their universalisation strategies. However, where Habermas's reliance on the ideal speech situation leads him to a formalistic, procedural, essentially Kantian view of morality (albeit on a 'postmetaphysical' basis) (see, for example, Habermas 1990: 120–2), Bhaskar's universalisation on the basis of a range of real ontological claims leads him to include a Kantian moment of freedom alongside a substantive ethics of human flourishing, which he then co-articulates with a constellated, structural and historical, account of their emergence.

Absence

Returning now to the passage from *Dialectic* on which we have focused, we might ask how the transcendental argument described there as the basis for praxis is put into action. To answer that, we pick up the role of absence or negation from Chapter 2 and transpose it to the specifically ethical realm. Here, Bhaskar extends the concept of absence as a noun to include conceptions of 'ill' and 'constraint' in the ethical domain. We know from the earlier chapter that absence is closely tied to causation, and that it can be deployed both as a noun to describe a particular state of non-being and as an action verb (to absent). The noun usage is now expanded more substantively to see absence as an ill, as the absence of a healthy or right state, to which it can be concretely referenced in a particular situation. In so far as the ill holds back the person or state of affairs of which it is a part, it is a constraint on development in a positive direction. Ethical praxis can be seen as the absenting of such an ill or absence – Bhaskar's (realist) equivalent of Hegel's 'negation of the negation'. For Bhaskar,

> [t]he cardinal points turn on appreciating that absence exists, causes effect absentings (changes – that is to say, changes *are* absentings), ills can always be seen as absences, which act as constraints, and that (empowered) praxis can always be seen as potentially absenting (causally efficacious) agency, which can remove remediable ills.
>
> (DPF: 207)

Later, Bhaskar expands the discussion further by pointing out that absences qua ills and constraints may be related to structures of power, becoming 'constraints$_2$,' which are related to social inequalities and exploitation in power$_2$ relations, and that these also constitute moral ills. For people caught up in them, recalling the discussion of detotalisation and alienation in the previous chapter, they represent morally wrong or untrue ways of being; they represent moral untruths. In so far as these depend upon ideological misrepresentations, this also must be taken into account:

> Conceptually, the most important thing to appreciate at the outset is that any ill . . . can be looked upon, or dialectically transposed, as an absence, and any absence can be viewed as a constraint. Such constraints include constraints$_2$ and inequities. Such ills may be seen as moral untruths. Thus we have the metatheorem: ills → absences → constraints (including inequities) → (moral) falsehoods → (and, if categorially absurd, I shall write them as 'ideologically'[2] so).
>
> (DPF: 259–60)

The reference to 'moral untruths' takes us to the conception of morality with which Bhaskar works. Key here is the idea of moral realism, which gives rise to what Bhaskar calls an 'alethic theory of moral truth'. Let us look at moral realism and alethia separately, beginning with alethia.

Alethia

By alethic truth, Bhaskar refers to a conception of truth that he sees as immanent in critical realism, because of its emphasis on the intransitive dimension in ontology. Alethia, the anglicised version of *aletheia*, meaning truth (Hartwig 2007: 24), implies that things have their own truth regardless of the propositional terms in which we know them. It is the 'truth of, or real reason(s) for, or dialectical ground of, things, as distinct from propositions, possible in virtue of the ontological stratification of the world' (DPF: 394).[3] Broadly, it signifies the kind of truth available by virtue of an understanding of the world in terms of realist ontology. In ethics, it represents the real grounds of ethical action and thought, and therefore the possibility of moral realism. Bhaskar equates alethic truth with natural necessity in things which he calls the 'reality principle', discussed in the previous chapter. In ethics, alethic truth is the 'directionality imposed on the education of desire by the reality principle', which will lead 'not to an end state, but to an objective process of universal human self-realisation, eudaimonia or flourishing(-in-nature)' (DPF: 176). More broadly, he links it with the idea of absenting ills in pursuit of freedom as the truth of, and the good for, human being.[4] A simple statement is as follows: 'In the moral realm, alethic truth, the good, is freedom, depending on the absenting of constraints on absenting ills' (DPF: 212). This in turn ties in with the idea of a dialectical logic immanent in human being to give 'the definition of dialectic as absenting absentive agency, or as the axiology of freedom' (DPF: 176), and the claim that 'absenting constraints on absenting absences is the alethia of dialectic' (DPF: 177).

Further, indicating the ontic truth co-present in a world constituted by conditions of detotalisation, heteronomy and alienation, he writes that alethic truth 'is dialectical reason and ground in theory *and the absence of heterology*; it is true to, for, in and of itself' (DPF: 219; emphasis added). This links alethia to the discussion of the previous chapter. In a world where alienation is present, the grounds of alethia developed from natural necessity, dialectical rationality, and the possibility of absenting agency diagnose and point beyond the untrue within. In the domain of ethics, alethia is the true as the morally good, which is 'freedom, in the sense of universal human emancipation' (DPF: 220). Or, as Bhaskar puts it in *Plato Etc.*, linking alethia with concrete universality as singularity, 'moral truth or alethia is universal concretely singularised autonomy' (PE, 144).

Moral realism

Alethia is thus the moral truth in and for human being and is the basis for Bhaskar's moral realism. Moral realism involves the idea that 'morality is an objective real property' (DPF: 259), existing in the spatio-temporal world of which humankind is a part. Some care, however, needs to be taken in understanding the different facets of this claim, and this is seen in the different ways Bhaskar states it in *Dialectic* and *Plato Etc.* In *Dialectic*, it seems to me, it is not stated fully. Bhaskar writes there that moral realism must be seen from two standpoints. From the subjective point of view, it is involved in the transitive dimension of social life because it involves the first person, 'action-guiding character of moral claims and judgements' (ibid.) and relates to 'a set of intra-subjective, inter-subjective, social and social-natural relations' (ibid.). That is right: if there is a moral truth in and for human being, it must, according to time and place, be more or less available to guide actions. Second, from an objective point of view, it concerns 'the intransitive morality of an always already moralised (or a-moralised) world' (ibid.). That too is right: if moral realism is true, it must in some way coexist with actually existing, however inadequate, moral standpoints. But it is not the whole story. Bhaskar goes on to say that this distinction between the transitive and intransitive dimensions allows his moral realism to be critical, and to sustain the irreducibility of ethics to descriptive sociology. What seems lacking here, however, is precisely the assertion of a moral realist ethical standpoint per se that guides action, and stands against 'actually existing morality'. Neither a transitive, social-relational, action-guiding first-person ethics nor an intransitive account of an already moralised (amoralised or demoralised) world necessarily have much to say about the objective, alethic basis of ethics. Both, however, depend on its existence – the one for guidance, the other in order to mark it as, precisely (and only), 'actually existing'.

Plato Etc. formulates the matter better to bring out the objective quality of a moral realist ethics per se *alongside* actually existing moralities in the intransitive dimension and first-person action-guiding considerations in the transitive dimension:

> Moral realism entails that the objects of morality . . . are real and in this sense intransitive. *There is thus a potential distinction between moral reality* (and at the ontological, including alethic level, moral truth), . . . *and actually existing morality*. . . . At the same time, morality signifies an action-guiding relationship [and] lies on the transitive-relational side of the transitive/intransitive divide.
>
> (PE: 108; emphasis added)

This is surely right. Moral realism invokes a world in which people live their lives as first-person agents through moral categories in the transitive dimension. Yet these same categories can, by virtue of a perspectival switch (see the previous chapter), be described, redescribed and subjected to critique as real objects in the intransitive dimension, separately from the perceptions of individuals working with them. Ethics are ontological and alethic in their nature and have an intransitive object,[5] yet they are action guiding and agent linked at the same time. The possibility of redescription and critique, however, entails a deeper moral sense in the intransitive dimension, which the alethic, objective morality of moral realism grounds. In the intransitive dimension, it is likely, in a world governed by power$_2$ relations, that gaps will exist between what is morally true and what is understood as true in actually existing moralities. Ethics as they actually exist, on a moral realist basis, will necessarily generate a conflict in the intransitive dimension of moral experience between what is, and what is held to be, morally true. This is in turn picked up as a conflicting sense of what ethical obligation entails in the transitive dimension for thinking and acting moral agents.

In sum, it is an ontological sense of alethic truth-in-the-world for humans-in-society-in-nature that lies at the core of Bhaskar's moral realist ethics. When we seek to express moral truths in and about the world for humans-in-society-in-nature, we in principle seek to access moral truths about that world. It is 'in virtue of its basic world-reporting meaning (its descriptive "this is how things are in the world" component) that truth-talk satisfies a transcendental-axiological need, acting as a steering mechanism for language-users to find their way about the world' (DPF: 214). The Habermasian language (albeit against Habermas's own usage) is not accidental, but Bhaskar retains a broader sense of how moral truths are derived and to be understood. In so far as humans wish to find their way ethically in the world, it is not just language but also the general nature of that world and their place within it as desiring, acting, socialising creatures – in short, the 'reality principle' – that will guide them to the alethic truth of ethics.

Finally, we should note here that truth talk about the (moral) world has four different elements. It is, first, 'normative-fiduciary', meaning that it is communicative in the sense of saying 'trust me – act on it'. Second, it is 'adequating', meaning it provides an epistemic sense of what is 'warrantedly assertable' – that is, what may reasonably be said about the world. Third, it is 'referential-expressive', meaning that it links what is asserted epistemically in the transitive to the intransitive dimension of knowledge. Fourth, it is alethic, in that it accesses 'the truth of or reason for things and phenomena, not propositions, as genuinely ontological, and in this sense as objective in the intransitive dimension' (DPF: 217). These four elements Bhaskar calls the 'truth tetrapolity'.[6]

Ethical naturalism: from facts to values?

If Bhaskar wishes to ground action as the absenting of absence in claims about alethic truth and moral realism, this raises questions about how we come *to know* what is morally true. It is here that his doctrine of ethical naturalism, brought forward from his pre-dialectical work, plays its part, in the following way. If we say that morality is an objective real property of human being in the world, how do we come to know it? More concretely, how would we come to know that an actually existing morality is the constitutive morality of a particular historical society, and in consequence is morally false, or of limited necessity? How, more broadly, would we move from knowing things about how the world works to conclusions of a moral kind? Bhaskar's ethical naturalism seeks to answer such questions. It holds that we can know and examine moral standpoints, and relate their content to the world of which they are a part. More importantly, in examining how the world is, we can draw conclusions of a critical, moral kind from our knowledge. It thus 'implies that moral propositions can be known; and, in particular, social-scientifically vindicated' (DPF: 259). The claim is that we can move from knowledge about the world to knowledge of moral truth contained in it. Accordingly, contrary to the 'naturalistic fallacy', there is 'no unbridgeable gulf between fact and value, or theory and practice' (ibid.). For Bhaskar, the transition from 'is' to 'ought', or from fact to value, lies at the core of his argument. It 'presages the transitions between and dialectics of theory and practice, form and content, centre to periphery, figure to ground, desire to freedom' (ibid.), and it leads on to the radical agency contained in what he calls the 'sensitised solidarity of . . . totalising depth praxis and the dialectics of de-alienation and emancipation' (ibid.).

How, then, is the transition between facts and values achieved? Bhaskar's argument concerns the nature of social scientific knowledge and its potential for liberation, and it has four elements. It is, first, that social science simply is not, and cannot be, evaluatively neutral. Second, he argues that this is seen in the idea that social science can act as an explanatory critique and as a critical form of rationality. Third, he contends that it can operate as a form of emancipatory axiology.[7] Fourth, he suggests that it can be seen as a form of dialectic. Let us look at these arguments in turn.

As for the first, there are two reasons, one more straightforward than the other, why social science cannot be evaluatively neutral. First, Bhaskar argues that it is 'pretty obvious that social scientific discourse is in fact evaluative, as is the principal reason for it, the value-saturated character of what social scientific discourse is about' (DPF: 261). Our understanding of the world, we might say, is 'always already moralised' so that 'the point is to remoralise it' (PE: 151). On this argument, social science is already steeped in normativity, so that the facts it constructs are never just facts, but are always value-implicated. There can never be a fact–value gap because the way it is formulated involves a false premise. This indicates that Bhaskar's approach does not involve a straight resolution of the fact–value gap, but rather a sense that its terms are falsely constituted, or hypostatised. In terms of the materially diffracted dialectics developed in Chapter 3, the distinction between facts and values would appear to be just the kind of split, antinomy or false dichotomy that exists in theory and the world by virtue of the kind of world it is. Rather than accept a false starting point, resolution should involve deeper consideration of the grounds which predicate it, and the terms in which it is to be understood.

Staying with this argument, Bhaskar suggests that there is a more interesting way of taking it. This is to establish not that social science is value impregnated, but that it is value-implicational in the way that it works, even if we assume it starts from factual premises. Here, the argument is that the subject matter of social science is made up not only of social objects but also, as we saw in Chapter 1, of beliefs about them, and that such beliefs can be shown by inquiry to be false. Further, social science can explain *why* the falsity comes to exist, in terms for example of an ideology critique revealing the interests that false knowledge serves. Falsity of beliefs and the conditions that ground it are, however, viewed negatively from the point of view of an inquiry that is itself committed to truth. Accordingly, 'one can move without further ado to a negative evaluation of [what has been explained in these terms] and a positive evaluation of any action rationally designed to absent it' (DPF: 262). Such evaluation is implicit in the development of social scientific knowledge by virtue of its own truth-seeking goals.

There is, however, an important qualification to this 'move without further ado', which needs to be explored. Such a standpoint must be expressed 'subject to a *ceteris paribus* clause,[8] in virtue of the openness of the social world and the multiplicity of determinations therein' (DPF: 261–2). This means that there may be special reasons not to pursue the action that will remove the conditions of falsity. Generally, Bhaskar suggests that the tendency will be to support their removal, but there may be countervailing reasons why not to. The problem then is, what would stop the *ceteris paribus* clause from broadening out and overthrowing the tendency against absenting the false? What stops the exception from becoming the rule? Bhaskar's answer is that, by virtue of the truth-seeking function of knowledge, there is a presumption in favour of the tendency and against falsehood. To invoke the *ceteris paribus* clause places an onus on the person so doing to explain why she rejects efforts at liberation from falsehoods, or the grounds that support or generate them. A lie may indeed be 'noble', but where truth is the default position, it would be necessary to justify it.

These are Bhaskar's two basic arguments for moving from fact to value. The first seems to me to be sufficient in itself: human beings-in-society-in-nature just are normatively endowed.[9] The second argument may, indeed, be an extended version of the first, though it does pick out the specific normative commitment in the pursuit of knowledge, and it also identifies as a significant limit condition the *ceteris paribus* clause. On both, the basic world-reporting character of knowledge in a normative world, and the necessity for humans to engage in it, lie at the heart of the derivation of 'values' from 'facts'. People's ontological 'thrownness' in a world where knowledge and its reporting constitute one aspect of the 'reality principle' means that knowledge and the conclusions it produces are inherently normative. Note, however, that though the world may disclose its truth to investigation, this entails hard work for science, and it may fail. Further, falsity may be embedded in the world, and remain so until praxis and struggle change it. There can therefore be what Bhaskar calls an 'alethic truth of falsity' (DPF: 262) concerning how people live, for example under structures that alienate them, and the beliefs those structures engender. Knowledge can disclose such falsity and is by that fact alone already implicated in its removal.

These arguments, which I have treated at some length, constitute the basis for Bhaskar's first claim, that social scientific knowledge cannot be evaluatively neutral. The other claims can be dealt with more quickly. The second is that a social science explanatory critique (identifying an error and explaining the grounds which engender it) involves a critical rationality. The claim here is that 'to criticise a belief is implicitly to criticise any action based on or informed by it' (DPF: 262). An explanatory critique, simply by virtue of identification of error and what error is based on, is already a form of critical rationality acting through knowledge formation against the things it reveals. Knowing is already a form of doing. Further, as the third point, social science can be in itself an emancipatory axiology in that social scientific understanding not only addresses critically how the world is, but also, if only by negative implication, proposes ways in which it could be better. At the very least, it invokes the thought that 'things could be other than they are'. It proposes minimally the thought that an error could be negated. Note also that in so doing, social science acts on those actual, substantive aspects of the world with which it is engaged. In its *form*, it seeks to enlighten and understand, but it does not do so in the abstract. It is always engaged with the specific and the 'contentful'. It therefore reveals the need, *ceteris paribus*, not for change in general, but for change with regard to any specific object of study. It thereby provides a *content* to set alongside the formal claim that critical rationality can uncover falsities in the world. Hence Bhaskar's claim that the move from 'fact' to 'value' is also a move from form to content. It is important to understand this, we shall see, when it comes to considering the claim that Bhaskar's position is essentially abstract and formal.

Social science can, in sum, help provide the 'content of the explanatory critical theory complex' (DPF: 403), which would be required to change (an aspect of) the world. In the terms of the previous chapter, its content is constituted by its understanding of the nature of four-planar being (and hence concrete universality) in a particular setting (and hence concrete singularity). Here, we come to the fourth possibility for social science, that it constitutes part of a dialectic of knowledge and practice that leads to change. To think that things could be other and better than they are in terms of the identification of grounded falsehoods already posits a sense that alternatives should be possible. In a 'contentful' context, this gives rise to specific ideas of what better possibilities might be. Bhaskar describes such ideas

> as an exercise in concrete utopianism, postulating an *alternative* to the actually existing state of affairs, incorporating unacknowledged and even hitherto unimagined possibilities for the satisfaction of wanted needs and wanted possibilities for development, grounded in . . . the context of a different social order.
>
> (DPF: 263)

Thus, we end with a relationship between social science, understanding, discovery and the possibility of concrete utopian projection. In the context of a philosophy that moves from theory to practice (for people cannot avoid the need to think and act, and even to omit is to act), this posits the dialectical praxis to 'absent . . . constraints on absenting absences or ills . . . ; that is, [to participate in] dialectic or the axiology of freedom'. In this setting, social science helps enable, through its analysis of four-planar being in the context of the normative commitments implied by knowledge,

> an orientation to the criterion of concrete singularity – truly the key to the realm of freedom – of each and all, and of each as a condition of all, by absolute reason, autonomy and the absence of heterology, that is, each agent is true of, to, in and for herself and every other.
>
> (DPF: 264)

To jump ahead, this is the point in emancipatory axiology where social science joins with totalising depth praxis to constitute what Bhaskar will call the 'ethical tetrapolity'. But to understand that, we need to explore in depth his exposition of an ethics based on dialectical rationality. Let us end this section, however, by summarising what has been said. The building blocks of Bhaskar's ethics are an understanding of negation or absenting which occurs in a world where it is possible to work with the moral (alethic) truth of what human being is. This engenders a moral realism concerning human being in the world, or human nature-in-society-in-nature, and we can access such truths through an evaluatively committed or implicated naturalistic social science. The latter comments explicitly on the nature of four-planar being and may posit concretely utopian alternatives as a means to participate critically and dialectically in processes of change. It becomes part of a potential movement informed by the dialectical rationality available to human beings as thinking, communicating, acting, feeling creatures, and it is to a fuller explanation of such rationality we now turn.

Dialectical rationality: from 'primal scream' to eudaimonia

Thus far, we have seen how knowledge is implicated in processes of dialectical rationality in two ways. First, it is the bridge between ethical naturalism and moral realism through processes of knowledge formation that are normatively committed. Second, the importance of knowledge, or of discursive practices more generally, is that they presuppose the possibility of truth in speech acts. It is here that Bhaskar aligns himself with Habermas, but it will be recalled that he wishes to extend the Habermasian argument. If truth, freedom and justice are prefigured in speech acts, then equality, liberty and fraternity are present in 'every transaction and material exchange', but respect and recognition are also 'contained in the most casual reciprocal glance' (1986: 210). These are bold claims that require critical consideration, but we must first lay the argument out. In pushing the latency of ethics across the range of human being, Bhaskar's argument is that a focus on knowledge ignores in particular issues of solidarity central to many accounts of ethical commitment, for example those developed by Marxists and feminists. Also omitted is an adequate account of the core substantive content of ethics that would be supplied by, for example, a developed theory of freedom or equality. In this section, we examine how Bhaskar deals with the questions of solidarity and freedom central to his understanding of ethics. Both arise from basic existential components of human being, with solidarity linked to the giving of judgement between people, and freedom linked to our nature as desiring, acting beings. (We have already sampled the latter in the previous section.) In *Plato Etc.*, Bhaskar observes that we are 'at once desiring acting creatures and judging speaking beings' (PE: 141). While there is no ultimate separation between these two attributes,[10] 'we can derive the formal criteriology for the good society from either alone' (ibid.) – that is, from either the notion of action or that of judgement.[11] From the disposition to make judgements in personal relations comes a dialectic of judgement and solidarity, while from our constitution as desiring agents comes a dialectic of desire to freedom. In this section, we examine both routes, beginning with the former, and we also consider how they are connected.

Trust, solidarity and judgement

I begin with what Bhaskar calls the 'judgement form' and its implications. When we are asked for advice and make a judgement, judgement takes a form that involves four dimensions. It will be 'expressively veracious', 'imperatival-fiduciary', 'descriptive' and 'evidential'.[12] The first two concern the relationship between she who makes the judgement and he to whom it is made, while the latter two concern the trustworthiness of the judgement. Together, they imply a relationship of trust, grounded in the nature of the world, between two people. Importantly, each of these aspects of a truth judgement involves the capacity for it to be universalised; that a judgement can be universalised is a criterion for its truthfulness. Let us take these four qualities of the judgement form singly.

Consider a judgement you might make if consulted by another with regard to a practical decision they must take. Your opinion will be, first, 'expressively veracious' – that is, it will express a truth as to how you think they should act, with the universalising implication that this is what you and others would do in exactly the same situation. To fail to do so is to be guilty of performative contradiction or theory/practice inconsistency (DPF: 177). Second, it discloses 'imperatival-fiduciariness', meaning that this is what the person ought to do on the basis that the advice is given in good faith. If expressive veraciousness entails a statement that 'this is the best thing to do in the particular circumstances of the person involved', then imperatival-fiduciariness is the linked communicative aspect of saying 'trust me, do it'. What kind of imperative is presupposed here? If we were to put it in Kantian terms, it is neither categorical nor hypothetical. It is derived neither from the abstract, universalistic premises of the categorical imperative,[13] nor from the simple utilitarian or technologistic premises of the hypothetical imperative. It is addressed to the concrete singularity of the individual in their precise circumstances, as the best thing for them to do, 'in accordance with [their] wants, in a potential dialectic of wants, needs and interests' (DPF: 221). It is therefore an 'assertoric', subjectively oriented, imperative.[14] Third, the judgement would have to be descriptively accurate for it to be truthful, and this is universalisable in the sense that 'in exactly the same circumstances the situation would repeat itself' (DPF: 178). Fourth, the judgement has to be grounded evidentially in terms of its grasp of the overall situation in which the action is required. This aspect of the judgement is universalisable in that, in the same circumstances, the reasons for it would turn out to be the same. Both aspects are based on a grasp of the depth stratification and concrete singularity of being from which the situation of the enquirer emerges.

These are the four core elements of the judgement form, and they combine ideas of trust and solidarity with substantive answers to the question what it is best for a person to do. Note that while the first two terms concern the *form* of the relationship between the addresser and the addressee, the second two concern the *content* of the judgement. But the four are conjoined by the nature of the judgement which says 'trust *me*, this is, on the available evidence, the best thing for *you* to do'. There is a parallel here with the nature of substantive knowledge achieved by inquiry in ethical naturalism. Judgement represents a bridge from *form*, the in-principle trustworthiness of judgement giving, to *content*, the soundness of the substantive, concretely singularised judgement.

The judgement form can be seen to have four linked implications. First, it depicts a relationship of trust between two moral agents. One pictures two individuals, who contain a core universal humanity but who also embody the particular mediations and rhythmics specific to their concrete singularity. In their relationship, the judgement form brings the two together because the possible universalisation of all the elements 'functions as both a test for consistency/sincerity and a criterion for truth' (DPF: 178). The judgement form binds the giver and the receiver of advice in an ethical commitment to being truthful. Judgement combines truth and solidarity through placing oneself in the shoes of the other. In considering the other's concrete singularity, one acts in the time and for the purpose of judgement as if one were in that person's position. If the person addressed by the judgement suffers constraints, then the giver of judgement identifies with her and against the constraints through the judgement. This entails a relation based on truth and solidarity:

> [I]f the addressee is constrained in the satisfaction of her wanted needs, the addresser in his fiduciary judgement implies both his solidarity with her and his commitment to the content of the explanatory critical theory of her situation, including the alethia of her concrete singularity, involving, inter alia, a theory of human nature-(needs and interests)-in-society-in-nature.
>
> (DPF: 179)

Further, second, in the process of solidarising truthfully with another, one notes a developing dynamic, a dialectic by implication, latent in the giving of judgement. To give judgement honestly commits one to a general understanding of the position of the other, and by reflection this returns one to consideration of one's own situation and its relation to that of the other. Giving judgement leads into a process of developing awareness of the relationship between a self and another, and, through that, a development of self-awareness with regard to others. It involves a dialectic of self- and other-consciousness (DPF: 210) that moves beyond the particular case.

Third, the judgement form implies a relationship between theory and practice. In one sense, this is obviously the case, for any judgement is already an intervention and a practice, just as every practice is theorised. This is an example of a constellational dual, in the language of Chapter 4.[15] But Bhaskar wants to extend the commitment in the judgement form further than this. Thus far, it is limited to the involvement of thinking oneself into the position and the commitments of the other and no more. Where, however, the constraint is an absence that constitutes an ill, then identifying the ill from a position of identification with the person experiencing it implies in principle a commitment to absent the ill itself. Further, it implies in principle the commitment to abolish all like ills, and, by further extension, a universalising commitment to an end state without ills for this person, and all others so placed. It leads ultimately to commitments to identify universal ills, and from there to abolish them in practice. Single acts of judgement lead ultimately, by processes of dialectical entailment or rationality, from individual to general thinking in solidarity with others, and from such solidarity to praxis:

> As any social ill can be seen as a constraint on freedom, this entails that any expressively veracious moral utterance implies a commitment to universal human emancipation and a society in which the concrete singularity of each and all is realised. . . . [It also implies] a commitment to the totalising depth praxis and the research inquiry necessary to inform it, including practical help in the subject$_2$-addressee's self-emancipation from her current situation.
>
> (DPF: 179)

Finally, fourth, the ethical implications of the judgement form are resolutely 'perfectionist'[16] in their form. They move from the human capacity to give judgement in solidarity with another to the axiological commitment to act in solidarity in the absenting of ills with the other, and indeed with all others. From there, by extension, they lead to the creation of the place where all ills are absent, the eudaimonic society. Integrating the dialectic of self- and other-consciousness, such a society is sincerely universalisable only in terms such as those provided by Marx, who spoke of 'the free development of each [as] the condition of the free development of all' (Marx and Engels 1968: 53). In Bhaskar's more extensive language, this means a society

> grounded in the concrete singularity of each and every one (and the former as a condition for the latter), based on the core human equality derived from our shared species-being . . . , and oriented to the processes of human flourishing in the context of concern for future generations, other species and nature generally.
>
> (DPF: 179)

All this, then, is rationally derivable by processes of dialectical implication from the possibility of sincerity in the judgement form. This is a bold, indeed breathtaking, position that immediately raises a sceptical counter-argument of the kind that asks, 'is this *really* how judgement, or people, operate?' Two questions may be outlined at this point. The first is whether there is not a huge gap between 'the ideal' and 'the actual' in this account of ethics. Does every act of judgement really commit one in this way? Do we not often self-consciously limit our commitments? And what of the cynical, or even deceitful, advice giver? Bhaskar's response to these questions is the subject matter of the final section, where we consider the idea that ideal and actual ethical positions do indeed coexist in constellated co-relation with each other. To anticipate briefly, Bhaskar will acknowledge the gap between the ideal and the actual while maintaining that its existence does not amount to denial of the ideal. Rather, it leads to the question of how one understands their relation.

A second, related question may be dealt with here. It is raised by Andrew Collier (1998), who suggests there is something damagingly formalistic, even Kantian, in this account. How can an abstract elucidation of categories like trust and solidarity provide us with an ethical *content* to put together with the *formal* deduction implicit in the argument from dialectical universalisability? Recall, however, that the assertoric imperatival quality of the judgement form puts the addresser in touch with the actual position of the addressee, understood in four-planar and concretely singular terms. Despite the abstraction of Bhaskar's language, the judgement form is firmly rooted in the 'reality principle' discussed in Chapter 4, for judgement must be (we have seen) descriptively accurate and evidentially valid. Though he speaks of a 'formal criteriology' for ethics, this is not the kind of formalism that comes with Kant's categorical imperative or its modern neo-Kantian variants. The generalisations of the judgement form take us *into* worldly realities, not away from them, as occurs with, for example, the Rawlsian 'veil of ignorance'. Similarly, the extension of Habermasian philosophy from speech acts to sociality and desire does not lead to the kind of ethical foundationalism practised in the 'ideal speech situation'. In place of idealised speech abstracted as a formal frame to judge moral truth, there is 'a simple transfactual, concrete and singularised criterion of moral truth' (DPF: 179) – that is, an orientation to the concrete singularity of human being in its four-planar context. The advice, support or action associated with judgement are all, like the judgement itself, rooted in the particular situation of the addressee, where the ills to be abolished are concretely experienced and identified.

In this light, the nub of Collier's objection to Bhaskar's 'formal criteriology' can be addressed. In essence, Collier's concern is Hegel's against Kant: that ethics based on universalising strategies depend on a prior selection of ethical premises that are not formulated by the practice of universalisation, leading to an empty formalism. 'In order to make the universalisability principle look plausible, one has to presuppose that the description under which the act will be universalised is the relevant one' (Collier 1998: 697), but universalisation provides no genuine criteria of relevance. It is an empty signifier. At one level, Bhaskar's response is, as we have seen, that claims about judgement (and, as we shall see, freedom) are concretely grounded in what it means to be human. This is a basic ontological claim with which, at least as a matter of philosophical method, Collier is unlikely to disagree. At another level, there is still a concern about the description of what is to be universalised. Collier suggests, for example, that we 'consider the war crimes that have rationalised themselves as "defoliation" or "population adjust-ment"' (ibid.), his point being that, *described in these terms*, there is nothing necessarily wrong with what is done. The universalisation strategy is vacuous because it is dependent on description in one set of terms rather than another, and universalisation does not choose the terms. But the example shows why the criticism is not damaging to Bhaskar. His ethics are rooted not only in what is universalisable for human action, but also in knowledge that is generated by investigation of the world, and that is descriptively accurate and evidentially valid. The reason that we are able to designate acts of 'population adjustment' as war crimes is precisely that we are able to investigate and explain the phenomenon in question in terms of acts and events in a context and structure of social relations that make 'war crime' a more accurate assessment of what happened than 'population adjustment' (cf. PE: 110). Bhaskar's ethical naturalism, the truth tetrapolity and the judgement form, all grounded in the reality principle, work against the charge of ethical formalism. Universalisation is intrinsically linked to understanding of the world, and competing claims about description of that world are in principle resolvable. Judgement is concretely singularised and assertoric, and the judgement form is linked to the emancipatory role of social science in investigating the substantive world. Bhaskar's philosophy moves from form to content.

Finally, and summing up the overall argument, this linking of dialectical principles of rationality to the investigation and understanding of worldly phenomena, and of both to solidarity and ethical praxis for emancipation, gives rise to what Bhaskar calls the 'ethical tetrapolity', mentioned at the end of the previous section. Put fully, the move in the ethical tetrapolity is from the commitment in expressively veracious moral judgement to fiduciariness in communication. This involves solidarity, and leads to a totalising depth praxis, which involves forms of social (depth-explanatory) inquiry. These provide the substantive content on which both judgement and emancipatory praxis can draw. There is, then, a two-way relationship between (formal) trust and (substantive, contentful) knowledge on the one hand, and praxis and freedom on the other.[17] Trust and knowledge lead to praxis and advances in freedom, with checking back from praxis for further thought and revision of practical objectives. The ethical tetrapolity is expressed formally as follows:

[axiological commitment implicit in the expressively veracious moral judgement] → (1) fiduciariness → (2) content of the explanatory critical theory complex ↔ (3) totalising depth praxis of emancipatory axiology → (4) freedom qua universal human emancipation.

(DPF: 262)

This is the end point of Bhaskar's 'formal criteriology' of ethics, involving trust, knowledge, ethical practice and freedom (PE: 141). We are thus led via the judgement form and the ethical tetrapolity to the concept of freedom, but we have yet to consider this in depth. In turning to it now, we will see how Bhaskar builds an argument that starts with desire and moves through various grades of freedom to the eudaimonic society, providing the specific ethical content for the good life and society. We turn, then, from the dialectic of judgement and solidarity to that of desire and freedom.

Desire and freedom

In considering the terms 'desire' and 'freedom', Bhaskar eventually provides content to the idea of eudaimonia, which represents the morally real goal for human being. This is a state of fully achieved freedom at the end of a road that starts with humans as desiring, acting beings and the simple demand for freedom from immediate necessity their condition entails. It involves a 'dialectic of desire to freedom [which] is at once a dialectic of desire and a dialectic of freedom' (DPF: 279), and which Bhaskar also calls at different points the dialectic of agency (DPF: 285) and the dialectic of material interest (DPF: 210). Its goal is to bring out the nature of concrete singularity, and the overall 'goal of a society in which the free flourishing of each concretely singular agent is a condition of the free flourishing of all' (DPF: 280). It begins, however, with what is universally at the core of each concretely singular being. In setting out Bhaskar's argument, I will consider how he treats the dialectic of desire, agency and freedom, how he then brings together the two dialectics of desire and freedom and judgement and solidarity, and how he on this basis argues for a progression in forms of freedom leading to the idea of the eudaimonic society.

We examined the dialectic of desire and freedom at the beginning of the previous section, where we saw that desire grounds the human experience of being as at once governed by necessity and seeking liberation from it. Desire installs in the human hard drive a sense of freedom which, pursued to its logical conclusion, leads to its fullest possible development, which must be a freedom for all. Let us briefly recall that argument, but then focus in particular on what may seem a problematic move from the freedom of one to the freedom of all. Desire, the argument begins, is the quality of 'desiring acting creatures' (PE: 141), hence the dialectic of desire can also be nominated the dialectic of agency. Here is the description of it from *Plato Etc.*:

> It is informed desire, experienced as an absence or lack, that drives praxis on. Now it is analytic to the concept of desire that we seek to absent constraints on it, i.e. to be autonomous or self-determining in some relevant . . . respects. In seeking to satisfy my desire, I am logically committed to the satisfaction of all dialectically similar desires. (This . . . is implicit in action as such.) . . . In absenting a constraint I am thus committed to the removal of all (remediable) constraints as constraints, i.e. of constraints insofar as they are dialectically similar in being constraints; and thence to the realisation of [the] assertorically sensitised concretely singularised equality of autonomy.
>
> (PE: 142)

This covers much ground. The relationship between desires and absences (or ills, lacks and constraints) is easily grasped, for a desired object is one that is at present lacking, and absenting that lack is the satisfaction of the desire, and liberation from the necessity it imposes. Here we have the absenting of an absence. At the same time, the link between constrained desire and freedom can be grasped, for satisfaction of any desire expresses a person's freedom to gain what he or she lacks. Of course this depends on what we mean by freedom, but more on that later. The more difficult question concerns how seeking to 'satisfy my desire' commits me to satisfying 'all dialectically similar desires', and, in particular, that removing constraints on *my* desires commits me to removing all constraints on *others'* desires. There is a move from first- to third-person concerns here, but how does Bhaskar make it?

It could be argued that, from the logic of dialectical universalisability, all constraints on desire exhibit the same structure of being constraints. Therefore, to desire to absent one constraint is by extension to desire to absent all, including constraints on others, as well as those appertaining to oneself. But this seems over-generalised. Surely more would be required to get from my desire to absent absences *for me* to a general desire to absent constraints on others? It seems to me that Bhaskar does not rely on so over-generalised an argument. Desire sets the dialectic off towards eudaimonia, but it does not complete the journey alone. It fits rather into a broader picture of the nature of agency in a social world. It is 'set off by the absence or lack implicit in desire' (DPF: 285), but not completed by it. It is itself part of a broader dialectic that starts with absence and desire, but then moves on through the sociality implicit in assertoric judgement and the judgement form. It then links with immanent critique and depth explanatory knowledge through the doctrine of ethical naturalism, before arriving at universal human emancipation and the eudaimonic society via totalising depth praxis. In other words, absence and desire join with judgement and solidarity in the terms of the ethical tetrapolity described earlier to produce an overall account of the principles of dialectical rationality. The development in Bhaskar's ethics is thus, I suggest, cumulative, rather than discrete and differentiated (*pace* PE: 141). We can see this if we consider how his account is grounded in what he calls 'primary polyadisation' and 'referential detachment'.

Connecting desire and solidarity: primary polyadisation

Why should absence and desire and judgement and solidarity join together? My suggestion is that Bhaskar draws on both the individual-focused emphasis on desire to generate freedom and the other-focused emphasis on solidarity to generate judgement, but these are not two discrete lines of argument that must be artificially pulled together for eudaimonia. It should be said that it may not matter if they are discrete, provided both arguments are valid, but in any case they are intrinsically connected. To see this, let us return to desire and agency. The argument starts from desire, and its relation to experienced absences, which are unfulfilled needs, lacks, wants or desires. A key moment is the initial emergence of elemental desire evident in the situation of primary polyadisation, which is the splitting of the infant from the mother. There is a real, existential separation here, which grounds the 'reality principle' for each and every person. It provides each human being with their own point of what Bhaskar calls 'referential detachment' in and on the world. This is an inexorable moment of discovered individual desire, but it is at the same time a moment of trust and solidarity, for the discovery is of both individuated need *and* reliance on another to satisfy it. Both aspects emerge from primary polyadisation, and the referential detachment to which it gives rise. A few words on the latter will elucidate the argument.

Referential detachment begins life as a concept associated with the relationship between knowledge and being. The initial idea is, in brief, that any act of knowing involves an ontological commitment to separate the knower from the known, to detach the referrer from the referent.[18] But referential detachment also covers a basic ontological relation that human beings (and presumably other animals, *mutatis mutandis*) have with the world. With regard to desire and freedom, it points towards a position of existential singularity and independence in the process of primary polyadisation. We are each separated by it, and the ensuing singular desire is located in each separate individual. This generates a sense of referential detachment and independence, but one that is immediately experienced in terms of *dependence*, on the satisfaction of a need *and* on another to provide it. This starts with basic needs for food and care, and someone to produce it. An infant's 'primal scream', as Bhaskar calls it, is the first act of referential detachment, indicating the real, existentially singular need to absent an absence, and for another to do so on the infant's behalf. This is axiological – that is, intrinsically necessary and valuable – for human being, and such a necessity remains with human beings throughout their life cycle. Whether it is the first need to be fed, sheltered and cared for, the later production of knowledge to make the world livable, or the general requirements for living across a life span, being in the world imposes existential demands that we must meet, but cannot do so alone. Referential detachment requires recognition of both our individuality *and* our reliance on others, and this is a prime example of what Bhaskar calls the reality principle in action.

Returning to our question of whether there are discrete routes to eudaimonia, we can now see how self-oriented desire and other-oriented solidarity are combined. The absence in need and desire, initially discovered in primary poly-adisation, involves living in a world where solidarity and trust are necessary. Primary polyadisation involves both individuation and reliance on another, and is the existential ground of both desire and solidarity. Thus, we move from desire to freedom via solidarising relations necessary for desire's satisfaction so that desirous agency and social solidarity come together as 'reflexive agency [that] is capable of judgement and so is subject to the dialectical universalisability of the judgement form' (DPF: 285). Individual agency and social trust support each other in the judgement form, leading to commitments to action and emancipation for self and other. This conjunction of agency and solidarity leads to 'an orientation to the totalising depth praxis to universal human emancipation which will usher in the good society, oriented to concretely singularised universal human autonomy' (ibid.). This can be expressed as a 'dialectic of education of desire' (DPF: 286) in which the 'reality of the social bond' is revealed through 'the trustworthiness of the primary polyad which endows the infant with the existential security that at once silences its scream, nurtures its self-esteem and lays the basis for the amour de soi which underpins solidarity and altruism alike' (ibid.). This 'primary existential of trust' works, however, with individual agency so that it 'quenches desire and, in the process of development, transforms its object . . . to wants and only collectively attainable needs by the axiological necessities which comprise the reality principle, understood as the alethic truths of four-planar contemporary society' (ibid.). In this way, self-oriented desire and other-oriented solidarity are brought together, and shown to inform each other, leading to the potential trajectory to eudaimonia, in which the freedom of each is a condition for the freedom of all. This then leads to an understanding of the different levels of freedom, and the way these combine individual- and other-oriented modes of being, as we shall now see.

The forms of freedom

Primary polyadisation links desire to trust and freedom to solidarity in a series of universalising moves that lead from primal scream to eudaimonia. On the way, it generates a series of concepts of freedom which, as they proceed, deepen the concept. Speaking generally, freedom involves a lack of specific constraints, while liberation is their absenting. More specifically, it can be graded into seven different, cumulative levels or 'ratchets'. Freedom at its most rudimentary level involves (1) a minimal conception of *agentive freedom*. This is 'the capacity to do otherwise which is analytic to the concept of action' (DPF: 262) itself. With this, Bhaskar associates legal freedom, the bare freedom to act within the law, as a basic, abstract and formal kind of freedom.[19] From this, he moves up a level to identify (2) that simple form of freedom discussed by Isaiah Berlin as *negative freedom* from particular constraints. This carries as its dialectical implication Berlin's alternative *positive freedom* to do something, for to 'be free from constraints on x' implies that it is in principle also possible 'to be free to do x' (ibid.).[20]

A third level of freedom is (3) *emancipation* from specific constraints, where 'emancipation is defined as the transformation from unwanted, unneeded and oppressive to wanted, needed and liberating (including empowering) states of affairs, especially structures' (ibid.). Emancipation is the point at which freedom becomes intrinsically related to a world structured by $power_2$ – indeed, in its original meaning, classical master–slave relations. By this stage, the demands on the concept of freedom have become greater: once we start speaking about emancipation, it becomes significant to think about whether it is simply for an individual, or for a group, or if it is to be universal. Of course this is already implicit in an idea such as that of legal freedom, for it is an implication of law that it apply universally. But talk of emancipation raises the stakes, for we now become interested in the possibility of 'universal human emancipation from (unnecessary) constraints as such' (DPF: 283), and what this would entail. At this point, the possibility of thinking about the universal in relation to the individual, the group or the whole makes it clear that such a conception interests us 'in criteria for rational agency and . . . the logic of dialectical universalisability' (DPF: 282) with a specific focus on how to achieve human freedom and emancipation.

Emancipation carries in it an implication of both negative and positive freedom, for it is both a freedom from constraints and a freedom to do things that are wanted and enabling. However, it also contains in itself the seeds of a further concept of freedom, which is that of (4) freedom as *autonomy*, involving self-determination. Here it is important to note what autonomy does not, or cannot, mean as well as what it does. It cannot mean a complete absence of causes, for we live in a natural and social world replete with causation in its various forms. Autonomy presupposes freedom of choice, but does not imply no grounds for choice. Among causes are those which are 'prior and external' to us and operate to control us against our wills, which affect our autonomy, and from which we wish to be emancipated. In contrast, our 'values, projects and rationality in attempting to accomplish them' (DPF: 281) restrict what we will do, but are not a check on our autonomy. Rather, they are a reflection of it, especially in so far as they involve our rationality (rational autonomy). Part of the sense of autonomy is simply the degree of 'axiological underdetermination' that accompanies choice by virtue of the power to do otherwise, but autonomy otherwise involves the ability to apply our values and reason to our action. This sense of autonomy allows that we may get things wrong, rather than the more demanding sense that acting rationally involves acting correctly, according to our genuine substantive interests. We could say that the person who acts autonomously is the person who 'possesses the power, knowledge and disposition to act in [her] real interests, e.g. wanted needs, or development or flourishing, including one's wants *for* others' (ibid.). However, Bhaskar would prefer to see this as a criterion for rational agency rather than autonomy, so that one can say that such a person uses her autonomy most rationally when she acts in such a way. Uses of one's autonomy may reflect on one's rationality, and vice versa, but it is helpful not to identify the two states too closely as if they were one. One can seek to act rationally in exercise of one's autonomy, but get it wrong.

In moving from emancipation to autonomy, it is important to see why they are closely linked. Bhaskar stresses that the key connection is that true emancipation must involve a person acting for herself – that is, through deployment of her autonomy. Only a person who 'has emancipated [her]self can be said to have become self-determining, i.e. autonomous' (DPF: 282), so that autonomy prefigures emancipation and emancipation is a condition of autonomy. It is the possibility of autonomous action in connection with emancipation which entails that the imperatival aspect of the judgement form must be assertoric rather than categorical. The addressee of any judgement can only be given advice or discussion, not be told what to do, if they are to act in a way that promotes their autonomy. Finally, since autonomy is limited by natural necessity in the world, it follows that it 'must be conceptualised as in nature and, as such, subject to the rights of other species' (ibid.). In a four-planar world, our ability to act in freedom depends on sustaining our relations with nature. It is also limited through questions of universalisability by the autonomy of others, and this extends 'over time, so that it extends to the rights of future generations' (ibid.). Just as the infant cannot do without the adult, so the adult eventually cannot do without the child. Autonomy is a projection of desire and freedom, but it is exercised in a world in which trust and solidarity, with other (including future) persons and in nature, is existentially necessary.

At this stage, we move to a fifth form of freedom that is associated not just with acting and the freedom to act, but with the substantive values that are implicit in positive freedom and emancipation. In particular, it involves the satisfaction of one's absolute needs, for example for survival, and one's relative needs, in the sense of what is necessary in a given geo-historical context to realise one's possibilities. This is freedom as (5) *wellbeing*, 'with the emphasis on the absence of ills and the satisfaction of needs' (DPF: 283), and, by extension through solidarity, as universal wellbeing. But this is still only a limited conception of the kind of freedom that humans can enjoy. A sixth ratchet would take us to (6) *flourishing*, 'with the emphasis on the presence of goods (benefits) and the realisation of possibilities' (DPF: 284). This involves the 'realisation of concretely singularised possibilities for development' for the individual, which also entails 'developing, and . . . further developing, four-planar social being' (ibid.) in terms of rights, grounded freedoms and the capabilities that one possesses only latently. This is limited only by 'the requirement of totality' that such flourishing 'does not transgress the concretely singularised grounded freedoms of others' (ibid.). This finally brings us to a universalisation of flourishing at level (7), which is *universal human flourishing*, or the eudaimonistic society. Here the universal flourishing of each is a condition for the universal flourishing of all. At this point, we are in the realm of concrete universality as singularity, which is 'truly the key to the realm of freedom – of each and all, and of each as a condition of all' (DPF: 264). This is the final ground of 'absolute reason, autonomy and the absence of heterology' in which 'each agent is true of, to, in and for herself and every other' (ibid.), but it was there from the beginning since the 'goal of universal human autonomy can be regarded as implicit in an infant's primal scream' (ibid.).

Let me summarise the argument of this section. The picture of the principles of dialectical rationality is now complete, moving out of the initial duality of primary polyadisation (individuality and sociality) into the dialectics of trust and solidarity on the one hand and desire and freedom on the other, and on to the developing content of freedom leading to eudaimonia. We have seen how the conjunction of dialectics of judgement and agency with that of knowledge, critique and discovery (the dialectic in ethical naturalism) establishes a strong ethical sense of the possibilities of developing human society to a position of universal human flourishing. The dialectic of desire to freedom, which reflects upon the different levels of freedom in the context of a commitment to solidarity, adds the final piece to the jigsaw. It identifies the eudaimonic state as a final form of human freedom, in which the ethical demands on the concept are stated at the highest level. In the process, we move from formal, abstract freedoms based on a core universal for human being to a conception of flourishing appropriate to individual concrete singularity. The crucial bridging concepts here are those of emancipation and autonomy, and these are important because they link basic forms of freedom, analytic to action, to advanced forms of individual wellbeing and flourishing by stressing self-activation and (self-)emancipation from power$_2$ relations.

It is important to grasp what Bhaskar is doing here. In modern discussion of freedom, philosophers tend to split into different camps: Kantians, Hegelians,

Marxists, Aristotelians and utilitarians. Bhaskar's point in formulating the different levels of freedom is to note that if one submits the concept of freedom to investigation in terms of an immanent dialectical rationality, the different approaches must all be recognised to have their place in a syncretic understanding of the concept (and the state of being that it connotes) as a whole. When different approaches vie with each other, that is a consequence of the necessarily limited way in which ethical attitudes present themselves in a world based on power$_2$ relations. The conflict between ethical paradigms is accordingly an irreducible level in any modern ethical debate, but it is important to grasp the underlying continuity between forms of freedom, as seen in a dialectic of their development from simpler to more complex forms. Thus, the forms of freedom, viewed at a metatheoretical level, journey from those articulated by Kant and the Enlightenment to those richer forms originally formulated by Aristotle in a dialectical movement that also reflects the individual and communitarian aspects in Hegel's ethics.[21] And what of Marx? As Gideon Calder (2007: 185) has noted, Marxists have tended to read their ethics in the different terms of Hegel, Aristotle (cf. Meikle 1985; Dean 2006) and Kant depending on their different predilections. For Bhaskar, the specifically ethical insight of Marx in this context is that of the conditionality of the freedom of each on the freedom of all (Marx and Engels 1968: 53). There is, however, a deeper level at which Marx plays his part, and which is taken up in the final section of this chapter. That concerns the way in which ethics must be grasped not only in the terms of dialectical rationality, but also in relation to the competing logic of dialectic's materialist diffraction (explored in Chapters 3 and 4). Thus far, we have let universalising principles of dialectical rationality have their say, but there is a question still to be asked concerning how these principles, founded in transcendental arguments about the nature of humanity, are to be grasped in the actually existing world into which individuals are thrown.

Constellating ethics and world

In this section, I consider how Bhaskar theorises the relationship between the dialectical rationality of his ethics and the materialist diffraction of dialectic and totality considered in earlier chapters. Is Bhaskar only dealing, as critics suggest, with ideal states of ethics and freedom, and how do these connect up with the actual world of which they are a part? His account of the dialectical rationality driving ethics raises the question of the relationship between dialectic as a historical, materially diffracted phenomenon, and as a set of propositions concerning the human condition across different historical periods. While discussion of material diffraction takes us to the geo-historical processes that shape humankind, its ideas and its ethics as well as its practices, discussion of dialectical rationality takes us from knowledge to judgement to solidarity, and from desire to freedom. This is a very different route to ethics from that pursued by material diffraction. One might ask whether Bhaskar, having diagnosed the problems of split in modernity,[22] has not fallen prey to one himself.

The response to such a question ultimately draws on Bhaskar's theory of totality and the idea of a constellational relationship between the ethical and the historical, as outlined in Chapter 4. I begin by considering how this works. Thereafter, I examine two instances of ethical constellationality, where Bhaskar discusses the relationship between what I shall call 'the ideal' and 'the actual' in modern ethics, and develops his conception of concrete utopian thinking and its relation to practice. I then develop a third instance in response to critiques, both deconstructionist and critical theory based, in which it is claimed that 'the ideal' is subsumed by actuality under modern (or postmodern) conditions. In all three cases, it is the constellated co-presence of materialist diffraction and grounds of dialectical rationality that informs dialectical critical realist ethics, and gives it its specific form.

Constellating ethics

There is a crucial passage at the beginning of Bhaskar's account of the different forms of freedom in which he seeks to crystallise his philosophical method with regard to ethics. He wants to

> make it explicit at the outset that here I am, in a sense, engaging in an exercise of metacritical (metatheoretical) concrete utopianism; that this is not a historicist enterprise of anticipating the trajectory of a future which has yet to be caused, but rather depends in part upon us; instead I am attempting to articulate the tendential$_b$ . . . *rational directionality of geo-history*.
>
> (DPF: 279)

Two points can be made about this. First, the reference to 'metacritical' or 'metatheoretical' concrete utopianism signifies that the philosophical base for Bhaskar's ethics is not to be found in immediately graspable facts about the actually existing human world. 'Meta-' denotes 'beyond' or 'before'. One needs to operate at a meta-level on which the formulation of matters of judgement and solidarity, or desire and freedom, pertains to what it means to be human, but not in a way that necessarily reflects how humans actually or necessarily act in the world as it is. We know, for example, that practical solidarity between people is often very weak, that judgements may be insincere, and that people often desire things that work against their freedom, understood in a broad, deep or even strategic way. It is to reflect the gap between the different *levels* (see Chapter 4) in human being, between how humans actually are and what can be said at a deeper level about their being, that Bhaskar speaks of the metatheoretical or metacritical nature of his inquiry. This is also seen in his reference to its 'concretely utopian' character, for it is 'utopian' precisely in that it does not reflect how things actually are, but it is 'concrete' in the sense that it is developed out of a sense that there is nonetheless a seam in human being into which these meta-arguments tap. Principles of dialectical reality are immanent in human being, and have their effects on it, but not in terms of a straightforward or unmediated relationship between underlying principles and actual practice in the here and now. The starting point is a realist understanding of meta-ethical principles that reflect how human being *is* at a most basic level. Dialectical arguments for freedom and solidarity reflect a realist understanding of natural necessity as it operates on and in human existence.

Second, there is a point about the relationship between this metatheoretical exercise and history. Bhaskar wants to argue that history is important to ethical development, but without subscribing to a position that would reduce ethics to history or, equally importantly, vice versa. He speaks of the 'tendential$_b$ ... rational directionality of geo-history' (ibid.), by which he means a weak tendency indicating a possible direction in development rather than a direct causal relation either one way or the other between history and ethics, or one that would necessarily be realised under all normal circumstances (see DPF: 78). What he is getting at here is the sense not just that the tide of history may ebb and flow, or that it may exhibit regressive as well as progressive tendencies. Rather, it is the sense that how things go depends upon how humans themselves act in history, in a development that 'depends in part upon us' (DPF: 279). Here, I do not think he is simply invoking the need for people to be active in making their own history, though that is obviously a part of it. Rather, he is pointing to a sense of the autonomy that people have in relation to history, and this comes from the sense that there is more to people than their historical 'thrownness' into an historical world. What is that 'more than'? In Chapter 4, we saw it to be the significance of agency in the agency/structure dual. Here, it is the transcendental deduction of what human being is, and where it leads, by virtue of the meta-level of judgement and solidarity, and desire and freedom, that matters. It provides a sense that there is more to the human condition than history provides, even if that condition cannot be understood apart from history. Human being-in-society-in-nature is inseparable from history, but is not reducible to it, for it contains different, but co-related, levels.

I shall return to this, but let us follow the passage we have been discussing, which now pursues the idea of being thrown into a pre-existing historical world, and how this relates to ethics:

> Our 'vehicular thrownness' establishes the explanatory primacy (in the Extrinsic Aspect) of the political over the ethical, while the extended argument of this chapter from absence to referential detachment to the logic of . . . alethic truth, entailing . . . the conception of social science as emancipatory axiology, suggests the normative primacy (in the Intrinsic Aspect) of the ethical over the political. (This is the constellational unity [and fluidity] of the ethical and [into] the political within the political.)[23]

(DPF: 279)

Here Bhaskar pursues the relationship between history and the ethical by placing it in the context of two different perspectives, the 'extrinsic' and the 'intrinsic'. Referring to what I am calling 'the historical' as 'the political' in contrast to 'the ethical', he argues that from an extrinsic perspective the political (the historical) has explanatory primacy over the ethical. But if we switch perspective to look at matters from the intrinsic point of view of emancipatory axiology, the ethical has primacy over the political. Is this then simply a 'perspectivalist' theory of the relation between ethics and history, in which two different visions of human being vie with each other, and one opts for one perspective or another depending upon one's interests or purposes? No, because Bhaskar argues for a philosophy in which real ontology grounds the premises of thought and being, so he is arguing for a conception of the world in which the intrinsic and extrinsic are *both* realistically grounded ways of understanding ethics. Ethics are inherently related to, but *in that relation* separated from, politics or history, or our 'vehicular thrownness' in the world. This conception of conjunction and separation is expressed, most importantly, in the final sentence in the above passage as 'the constellational unity . . . of the ethical and . . . the political within the political'.

Totality-based ideas such as the level and the constellation are thus central to Bhaskar's account of how ethics and history co-relate, and they take us back to Chapter 4. We saw there the role the constellation plays in Bhaskar's account of totality as one of the ways of thinking how things that are separate are also inherently connected. By virtue of the real nature of entities in a dialectical totality, individual things enjoy relations of constellational connection, containment, embedding and unity with other things. These figures occur throughout Bhaskar's dialectical development of existing critical realist philosophy, for example in the relations between the duals of thought and being, the transitive and the intransitive, the identity of the self and the other, theory and practice, and so on. The constellation is a figure that sustains the real significance of its embedded terms while insisting on the intra-relation between them. It identifies an overall co-relation, which depends on the real relation of the individual terms, together with a relative autonomy between them. The latter is sustained by hiatus-in-duality and enables perspectival switch. Bhaskar's idea is that of constellational *unity* rather than *identity* (*pace* Hegel), for he wishes to stress co-constitution and mutual inter- or intra-action within constellational terms. Hence, his way of understanding ethics and history and their relation is expressed in terms of their co-embeddedness in a constellational unity, expressed here as that of 'the ethical and the political in the political'.

Note two things about this relationship. The first concerns the ways in which constellational terms relate. The idea of the ethical being constellated with the political (the historical) does not signify a clear line between two terms, but rather an intermixing and a fluidity, so that ethical impulses are mixed into and emergent from political and historical developments, while the development of history sediments and generates ethical forms. Thus, the forms of freedom we discussed above cannot be thought of in pure separation from historical development. At the same time as they can be formulated as different, developing levels or 'ratchets' in a meta-logic of freedom, it is plain that they can also be conceived in historical terms as developments brought about severally by the Greek world and in the world revolutions of the late eighteenth and early twentieth centuries. There is an interacting, fluid relation between ethics and politics or history, which does not stop us from theorising their ethical truth alongside their historical development

in a real, open, emergent and developing totality. Indeed, it is precisely our ability
to do both, without reducing either one to the other, that permits us to claim neither
that history determines ethics, nor vice versa, but rather the weak, possible but by
no means necessary 'tendential$_b$ . . . rational directionality of geo-history' (DPF:
279). It is thus from the overall position of totality that it becomes possible to think
of how things should be seen in separation, while being co-embedded with others.
The figures of the constellation and the dual, the idea of different, co-related levels
of being, of perspectival switch and hiatus-in-duality, which we have used to
express Bhaskar's conception of the relationship between ethics and history, are
all figures evolved in the context of thinking about totality.

The second thing to note about the constellational relationship is that relations
in a constellation differ from constellation to constellation, and within particular
constellations one term may exercise a certain dominance. The constellational unity
of ethics and politics (history) to which Bhaskar refers is one in which there is a
'constellational unity . . . of the ethical and . . . the political *within the political*'
(DPF: 279; emphasis added). Hence, the political (the historical) has a certain
position of dominance in this particular relationship. This takes us to the final part
of the passage we have been discussing, in which Bhaskar explores the result of
ascribing ultimate dominance to the political, and identifies the overall tension that
this provides between the political and the ethical in the constellational relationship:

> My project is normative. I shall be making much use of the logic of dialectical
> universalisability. But, because . . . we are inhabitants of a dialectical
> pluriverse, characterised by complex, plural, contradictory, differentiated,
> disjoint but also coalescing and condensing development and antagonistic
> struggles over discursively moralised power$_2$ relations, subject to regression,
> entropy and roll-back, we cannot expect the *dialectic of real geo-historical
> processes*, from which the logic of totality, i.e. of dialectical universalisability,
> starts and to which it always returns, to be anything but a messy affair. This
> logic is a spatio-temporally, multiply and unevenly distanciated developmental
> process, in which so long as dialectical universalisability is not seen as a
> *transfactual, processually oriented, concretised, transformatively directional
> norm, subject to the constraint of actionability* in a world in which agents act
> on their perceived interests (including their perceptions of the interests of
> others), it is often going to seem to be falsified.
>
> (DPF: 280)

The metatheoretical level is there in human being, but in a world of open totality
subject to detotalisation, alienation and heteronomy we need not expect it to be
acted upon, except to the extent that people do in fact act upon it. Slightly later,
Bhaskar concludes that it is 'a dialectic, not an analytic, of dialectical universalisability that I am about' (ibid.), and this is crucial in understanding the
relationship between the kind of materially diffracted, detotalised dialectic outlined
in Chapters 3 and 4, and the logics of dialectical rationality described in this
chapter. There are two kinds of dialectic here, and their relationship is itself

dialectical, generating a dialectic of material history and dialectical univers-alisability organised around the constellational dual of the (intrinsically) ethical and the (extrinsically) political, where the latter enjoys a certain predominance. The material diffraction of dialectic and its fracturing in open totality, without reducing models of dialectical rationality to epiphenomenal status, conditions and affects our ethical possibilities. It does not, however, rule out further possibilities for thinking in terms of the logics of judgement and solidarity, and desire and freedom. This is a non-reductive, historical account of the development of *human being*-in-society-in-nature as essentially ethical in character.[24]

The constellational unity of ethics and politics (history), like that for example between structure and agency, involves a two-way relationship. Just as agency is constellationally embedded within structure but can transform it, so are ethics embedded in history while containing their own power to affect it. Yet the constellational unity of the ethical and the political 'within the political' retains a sense of the fragility and contingency in *any* sense of rational or ethical direction-ality. Any development depends upon the weight of social, political and general structural (historical) conditions in the extrinsic *and* the force of agential practices, involving metacritical and metareflexive ethical conceptions in the intrinsic, and there is a recursive connection between the two. Despite their perfectionism, Bhaskar's ethics are realist in a double sense. First, they reflect the natural necessity at the core of human being in terms of its desire for freedom and need for solidarity. Second, the ensuing dialectically rational principles of judgment, solidarity and freedom are constellationally located in the spatio-temporal world of which they are a part, while capable of playing their part in changing it. To affirm these two sides is not to argue in a contradictory fashion, but to argue for a dialectical understanding of how human being, in its intrinsic and extrinsic aspects, within an open totality, *is*. Bhaskar's dialectic of constelled co-presence between the intrin-sic and the extrinsic, of the ethical and the historical, permits a non-reductionist, non-hypostatised account of the relative autonomy of ethics in the world.

The ideal in the actual

If constellationality grounds the (limited) autonomy of ethics, this leaves questions about how ethics actually operate in the modern world. This is plainly an enormous topic, and Bhaskar's ethics primarily operate, as we have seen, at the meta-theoretical level. His main aim is to understand the general ontological status of ethical inquiry. Nonetheless, I will discuss here three ethical modes that result from the relationship between a perfectionist, ideal,[25] ethics based on principles of dialectical rationality and an actual world where existing moral forms reflect power$_2$ relations. The first mode reflects the ways in which an ideal ethics are accommodated in practice in an actual, always-already moralised world (the ideal *in* the actual). The second reflects the ways in which an ideal ethics operates as a critique of that world by providing exercises in concrete utopianism pointing to the limits of the actual (the ideal *beyond and against* the actual). The third comments on the critical and postmodern view that ethical ideals are only means of articulating power under modern social and historical conditions (the ideal *under* the actual).

For those who see Bhaskar as an ethical idealist, rather than one who promotes a vision of the ethically whole, and in that sense ideal, it is important to note that he is aware of the need to reflect upon the relationship between his perfectionism and the actually existing world. There are two elements in his vision of modern ethical inquiry. First, there is identification of the actually existing ethics of the day, which, by virtue of his ethical naturalism, can be known and engaged with; and second, there is the morally realist and alethic transcendental deduction of a perfectionist ethics by the logic of dialectical universalisability. These two dimensions, however, give rise to a third, which is the dialectical relationship between them. A constellational view of ethics gives rise, as we have seen, to 'a dialectic, not an analytic, of dialectical universalisability' (DPF: 280). This is a dialectic of dialectical universalisation and actually existing morality, or a 'dialectic of dialectical universalisability and immanent critique'.[26] Ethics involves thinking through the relationship between the ideal logic of dialectic universalisation and the ways in which a society puts, or does not put, it into practice, giving rise to a 'developmental dialectic of the logic and practice of dialectical universalisability' (DPF: 280).

At the risk of repeating earlier themes, it should be recalled that we live in a world of 'transitional rhythmics or processes . . . characterised by complex, plural, contradictory, differentiated, disjoint but also coalescing and condensing development' (DPF: 280). Behind such rhythmics there exist 'antagonistic struggles over discursively moralised power$_2$ relations, subject to regression, entropy and rollback' (ibid.). The development of human nature-in-society-in-nature can be linked to a totalising logic of dialectical universalisability, but the dynamic of real geo-historical processes, with which it is constellationally united, can only be a 'messy affair' (ibid.). The tendential$_b$ rational directionality in history, in the limited way that it exists, operates as much 'underground' as through the established ethical forms of a given geo-historical period. We have a sense of an interlaced development in which ethical demands may be absent at one level, yet present at another. The coexistence of ideal and actual ethical forms gives rise to conflict as the different levels feed off and inform, reflect and contradict, each other. Dialectical universalisability operates in relation to 'a spatio-temporally, multiply and unevenly distanciated developmental process' (ibid.). It must be seen as a 'transfactual, processually oriented, concretised, transformatively directional norm' (ibid.), but this will nonetheless appear to be falsified to the extent that agents act on what they wrongly (or rightly *in situ*) perceive to be their interests, or according to the logic and forms of the actually existing world.

Does the possibility of historical falsification not tell against the validity of any such norm? In terms of its potential for actualisation in a given period, it does, but not in terms of its underlying validity, for 'norms, although they can be broached and discarded, cannot be falsified by the irrationality of actual geo-history' (DPF: 280). They can only be falsified 'by the provision of a better, nobler, norm more fitting to the needs and propensities of developing four-planar socialised humanity' (ibid.). What it *does* tell against is a purist or dogmatic application of morality to the world. Any ethics based upon the dialectical universalisability of the autonomy, emancipation and flourishing of concrete singularity will in any case be programmed to recognise pluralism and diversity. It needs, however, also to acknowledge fallibility and inconsistency, and this is especially the case where we are dealing with people seeking ethical ways to behave in a context of power$_2$ relations. Here, moral 'inconsistency . . . must be conceded a value in its own right' (ibid.).

What Bhaskar has in mind here is a sense of the possibility of moral failure, but also of progress even where the ideal is not attained. Incompleteness, fallibility and inconsistency are part of the messiness of morality, raising the question of how we measure positive moral developments. What is required is a sense of progress towards the desired end state by any specific action, or in any specific period (DPF: 220). In judging ethics in context, one requires 'only that the process be progressive (or minimally regressive)' (DPF: 285), and that one apply in any context 'a principle of fold-back', which specifies 'only optimal progress . . . in the direction to which the logic of dialectical universalisability flows' (DPF: 293). This may at times put 'a constraint on the constraining of constraints, which may on occasion be a necessary condition for any moral or social progress at all' (ibid.). Whether a development is progressive or not is, Bhaskar notes, 'obviously an issue for debate' (DPF: 285), but it is not an issue, in a world where the reality principle operates, where one cannot hope to apply judgemental rationality to the question at hand. Nonetheless, the (ideal) road to eudaimonia is not a straight one, and (actual) wrong turnings, not to mention regressions, are to be expected along the way.

To consider the ideal in the actual also leads to the issue of moral 'backsliding'. Dialectical universalisability rests upon an understanding of rational agency for the concretely singularised individual, and it can be argued that it is in a person's real interests to flourish, so that the deduction of morally right action from any situation may be achieved. But persons as concrete singulars are also submitted to a spatio-temporal context, and as such they are subject to their own diffracted, heteronomous conditions. In a world that is an open system in spatio-temporal process, and subject to detotalising tendencies, contingencies and effects arise which in the circumstances may lead to, and in a sense justify, 'backsliding' (DPF: 293). When they do, backsliding is more than just a failure to act morally. It is a sign of the limits of, or limited possibilities for, moral advance in a particular context. Consistency of development in an ethical process is therefore measured according to the potential in the overall processual context, and it would be a false criterion to measure moral development, individual or collective, simply by achievement or failure of the ethically desired end state.

This argument does, however, lead to a question. What of the person who backslides too easily, or gives too limited a commitment to another, or acts cynically or deceitfully? Dialectical rationality means that 'every speech act must be regarded as making an axiological commitment' so that 'not to assist or em-power [the other] when it is in one's capacity to do so is to be guilty of [theory/ practice] inconsistency *ceteris paribus*' (DPF: 222). For human beings in the here and now, the logic of dialectical universalisability applies. However, note the *ceteris paribus* rider in this passage, which moderates its effects in the light of what is possible in a given situation. One should act according to principles of truth and solidarity unless there are valid countervailing reasons not to. Accordingly, there may be morally good – or bad – reasons for limiting one's commitments. Bhaskar refers to this as the application of practical *phronesis* in moral matters (DPF: 179), using the Aristotelian conception of 'the mean' or practical wisdom as a way of handling the dialectic of ethics. In knowing what to do ethically, it is important to have in mind not just the desired ethical end state of human flourishing, but the particulars of a given situation, and the limits of the possible in the present. This requires the application of balanced judgement that can hold onto the ideal and apply it to the actual, but such judgement pertains only in that relation.

Phronesis is the meta-ethical virtue that demands skilful application case by case (DPF: 169), and is associated both with trying to do one's best in a morally bad world and with living the good life in the eudaimonic society,[27] where a balance between different kinds of action is also required. If we bear in mind both that *amour de soi* (in distinction from *amour propre*) is an appropriate and necessary condition of human life,[28] and that the object of solidarity is to support and not to substitute for another's autonomous action, any commitment, in both the ideal and the actual world, has its practical limits. This, however, must not be an easy 'escape clause', for dialectical universalisability entails that there is a presumption in favour of doing the best one can. As with acting on truth under ethical naturalism, the onus is on the backslider to justify how they limit their help or deploy *ceteris paribus*. Accordingly, there is a distinction between acting in moral balance in either an ideal or an ideal-in-the-actual situation, and acting cynically or deceitfully with regard to both.

The ideal beyond and against the actual

The constellational unity of ethics and geo-history asserts both the independence and the dependence of ethical thought, and this means that it must be attuned to the existing world and retain its metacritical vision of a world that could be different. Having considered how this operates in terms of the ideal working within the actual, we now consider the alternative possibility of its working beyond and against the actual through exercises in concrete utopianism. These operate by producing images of an ideal world, grounded in developments in the present but transcending them by virtue of deploying the logic of rational universalisation. In fact, any discussion of the principles of dialectical rationality, whether it be in terms of desire, trust relations, assertoric judgements or freedom, is already an exercise in concrete utopianism (DPF: 279). This is because it moves from what exists to what is logically implicated by it, but which is not, or not yet, in existence. So, in designating for example the seven levels of freedom, and particularly the higher forms, we are already thinking beyond the actual in favour of concrete utopianism.

But we can go further in indicating what a better world would look like. It would be one in which, economically, the 'totality of master–slave-type relations would be done away with, including the end of the generative separation of the immediate producer and the fivefold alienations which result from it' (DPF: 267).[29] To abolish alienation would be to bring about 'a massive change in four-planar human nature', and to place people in situations where a genuine exercise of autonomy would become possible, for 'to be alienated is to be separated from oneself or something essential to one's nature or being' (ibid.). We would be looking at a society where there was a 'massive and global redistribution of resources, tending to a core equality in virtue of our common humanity (i.e. our shared species being), with differences justified by particular mediations, specific rhythmics and individual singularities' (PE: 149). There would be a vast expansion of rights and of participation in democracy, with recognition of the underlying truth that 'it is only if I recognise the concrete singularity of each and every other individual that I am not guilty of theory/practice inconsistency and heterology in asserting my own' (ibid.).

Politically, it would push towards cosmopolitan forms of governance at the international level, recognizing the global nature of problems facing humankind. Nationally, Hegel's triad from the *Philosophy of Right* (Hegel 1952), of individual (abstract) right, moral obligation and individual self-realisation in ethical life, would be inverted so that what are the later terms in the Hegelian progression would become the earlier ones in Bhaskar's. The connection of desire and freedom to trust and solidarity indicates that the eudaimonic world is not rooted in abstract individual willing, from which social and ethical life is then derived. Social solidarity is the only context in which human agency can survive, develop and flourish. A domain of unquestioned personal choice is, however, retained, and this is entailed by Bhaskar's conception of agency and autonomy, but this is subject to the recognition of others' rights 'in a normative order based on care, solidarity and trust' (PE: 150). In this regard, the middle term of moral obligation and duty, suitably developed, is crucial for its role in promoting diversity within the social world. It provides the mediating middle ground for reflexive self-monitoring and learning in a morally, socially and technologically evolving world. It encourages 'initiative and enterprise, economies and ecologies' on the one hand, but also supports 'necessary but tedious or unpopular work' (ibid.) on the other. Democratically, the realm of social obligation would be the place where a multiplicity of independent public spheres (in a plural, open totality) would produce differing conceptions of the good for dialogue and debate.

On a personal level, the same realm would provide opportunities for the mediation of the agonistic and existential aspects of still developing four-planar social being, including for example the evolving relation between *amour de soi* (the basis for love of the other) and *amour propre* in human behaviour. It is important to stress such aspects, for to propose concrete utopian forms is not to suggest a world in which every conflict is resolved. To live freely on the condition that everyone lives freely suggests ongoing work in which autonomous persons engage with each other and debate and resolve their conflicts. Since, on the other hand, concrete utopianism points beyond totalising structures that deny autonomy, its negative critical function is crucial and points to the elimination of non-existential, non-intrinsic forms of conflict. Once these are cleared away, it would be possible to appreciate what the remaining agonistic grounds of conflict are and how they might be resolved, or at least mediated.

It should be recalled that in an open world based on concrete singularity and human agency, the future for human being remains open and underdetermined, so to some extent these ideas second-guess what we have still to find out about our species. Accordingly, concrete utopianism 'is not a prescription for the future' and dialectic 'is not in the business of telling people, in commandist (Stalinist) or elitist (Social Democratic) fashion what to do' (DPF: 297). It is better conceived 'as an inner urge that flows universally from the logic of elemental absence (lack, need, want or desire)' which 'manifests itself wherever power$_2$ relations hold sway' (ibid.). It is 'the heartbeat of a positively generalized concept of freedom as flourishing and as autonomy and as reason', and as such 'is irrepressible' (DPF: 297–8), but it cannot be dogmatic or categorical in its demands. As with the totality in which it operates, exercises in concrete utopianism must retain an open, questioning, adaptive attitude to their fields of action.

For some, exercises in concrete utopianism become ways of avoiding the terrible issues facing the world today, ideal dreams to assuage the waking realities. They can also be dangerous to the extent that elements from a concrete utopian vision are taken from the whole and implanted into a world where dominant power$_2$ relations remain in place. In such a situation, they can become shiny new ways of achieving control. Thus, invocations of 'community', and the expanded social freedom it promises, can be co-opted for domination under cover of an ethical reaching out. There is a clear line of argument, for example, which links the communitarian philosophy of the 1980s to the authoritarianism of the Anti-Social Behaviour Order (the 'ASBO'), the signature penal policy of British 'New Labour' (Ramsay 2010). Or, to take another example, the advance of universalising, cosmopolitan forms of justice in the name of human rights can be a way of legitimising 'victor's justice' in a world where ethically valid doctrines of freedom and justice in international law are constellated with the pursuit of national interest, strategic resources and global hegemony (Norrie 2008). In such contexts, the ideal becomes subsumed in the actual, and is in danger of being (wrongly) rejected outright on account of the way it has been actualised. Nonetheless, it has to be asked what kinds of visions of the future we have in mind when we express our unhappiness with the present, and a consistent rejection of the world and all its works takes one only so far. At some point, one has to act for the future, and one has to think what the future might be in order to do so. Recall from Chapter 2 the dialectical theorem of the presence of the future in the present and the past. Exercises in concrete utopianism, for all their fallibility, give us a sense in the here and now of possible futures and what they might hold, and are valid provided they are not actualised against their promise. We should also remember that they are not blueprints, but broad indicators to help us think and act beyond the present.[30]

The ideal under the actual

Finally, in the light of these strictures on the false actualisation of the ideal, it is worth reflecting on the popular critical theme that the ideal has under modern conditions been subsumed within the actual, and been turned decisively against its original emancipatory promise. Such an idea is seen for example in Theodor Adorno and Max Horkheimer's (1997) argument that reason has turned from a means of emancipating people into a means of their technocratic enslavement, or in Adorno's claim (1973) that Kantian freedom is a means of submitting humans to domination. Although Frankfurt School thinking and French poststructuralism are usually thought to be very different, a similar theme is to be found in the latter, where for example Jacques Derrida (1990) sees modern liberal law as immersed in the spirit of economic calculation and turned against a deeper sense of justice that is represented by deconstruction.[31] Taking a similar line, Roland Barthes once expressed the subsumption of universal law to power as follows:

> And this universal language (law) comes just at the right time to lend a new strength to the psychology of the masters: it allows it to take other men as objects, to describe and condemn at one stroke.
>
> (1973: 45)

Here, Barthes inverts the theme of Hegel's master–slave dialectic by seeing modernity as the place where the master finds a new mode of domination, in the rational universality of law. I use this passage because it seems to show a kindred quality to Bhaskar's nomination of modern power$_2$ relations as 'generalised master–slave-type relations'. Yet Bhaskar's account of the relation between the ideal and the actual is more nuanced because he identifies a real basis for both material diffraction of dialectic and, at the meta-level, dialectics of rationality and universality. The latter is not to be subsumed a priori within the former, but constellated with it. Bhaskar's criticism of deconstruction, accordingly, is that its philosophical techniques of inversion and erasure are too one-sided to be adequate to their task (DPF: 250). Put in terms of the ideal and the actual, to subsume the rational, the free, the universal as ideals under actually existing modes of domination so that they are taken to have no independent value and become the way in which the actual does its business in the world is to see only one side of the issue. Such an approach is not without its validity as an inversionary corrective to idealising and abstractive practices of liberal philosophy, but, for dialectical critical realism, the methods of inversion and erasure cannot explain how the ideal *may* be subsumed within the actual, but may also not be, or may be incompletely and messily so. There is no clear line on this, but an essential intermingling of the categories and modes in their constellational duality. Such a dialectical inter-relation, and the ensuing need for a posteriori realist investigations of the topography and choreography of the ideal and the actual in particular settings, not only protects the ideal against subsumption, but also provides a sense of the unquenchable, because real and omnipresent, hope that resides in the desire for – the pulse of – freedom.

There is much more to be said on this, but little space in which to say it. In recent work on law, I have sought to explore how law partially subsumes the ideal within the actual, but also how the ideal continues to inhere in difficult, occluded ways in it. The ethical complexity of 'in', 'beyond and against' and 'under' for law is caught, for example, in the changing relationship between the ideal and the actual in Hegel's account of the Beautiful Soul and its orientation to modern law as he moves from his early theological writings through the *Phenomenology* to the *Philosophy of Right* (Norrie 2005a: ch. 10). It is also seen in the ambivalence that Adorno ultimately reveals in his understanding of the enduring moral significance of legal freedom, despite his default tendency to reduce it to a subsumptive mode of 'identity thinking' (Norrie 2005a: ch. 9). Finally, it is also seen in Derrida's juxtaposition of 'the conditioned' (the actual) and the abiding 'unconditional' (the ideal) in his account of ethical issues such as forgiveness and their relation to law (Derrida 2002; Norrie 2008). In this work, I argue for an ethical understanding of modern law in terms of a difficult, occluded, partial sense of freedom that can neither be extolled in straightforward liberal terms nor damned by inversion in deconstructive or critical terms. What underlies the argument is a dialectical critical realist understanding of what, in the light of this chapter, can be described as a dialectic of the ideal and the actual or, and more precisely, a dialectic of dialectical rationality and the outcomes of materially diffracted dialectic, or, put differently, a dialectical constellation of the ethical and the political within the political, in the sphere of totality. Whichever, it is helpful to imagine law as a site, in different times and contexts, of relations between the ideal in, beyond, against and under the actual, and not to reach for a 'one size fits all' theory. Dialectical critical realism with its emphasis on the constellationally related ethical within the historical and political permits a posteriori investigations into concrete relations and institutions to take the place of a prioristically drawn conclusions. I return to this issue in Chapter 8.

Conclusion

The ethics of dialectical critical realism represent possibly the hardest element to grasp in Bhaskar's system. This chapter is itself an extended counter-argument to my own earlier effort, referred to in Chapter 1, to explain them in a very different way. With Nick Hostettler, I argued previously for a split between Bhaskar's ethics and his materialist diffraction of dialectic, taking what I then saw as his contradictory attitude to Habermas as indicative of a problem:

> If the core innovation of Bhaskar's critical realist dialectics is the reaffirmation of real ontological features of depth, space, time, absence, emergence and open totality, how can he develop his ethical theory on the basis of an extension of Habermas's irrealist, positivist, linguistified speech community? Bhaskar cannot extend Habermas on the basis of everything that he, Bhaskar, is most fundamentally against.
>
> (Hostettler and Norrie 2003: 46)

What I then failed to grasp was the role of Bhaskar's conception of totality and his concepts of constellation, duality, levels and perspectival shift in holding together the different levels of human being-in-society-in-nature, which permits both a logic of dialectical universalisation and the materialist diffraction of dialectic to co-relate in a complex, non-reductive manner. At first sight, it appears that the dialectical rationality of absenting, alethic truth and moral realism, of ethical naturalism and critical knowledge, of judgement and solidarity, and of desire and freedom represent a domain that is not anticipated by the development of a theory of materialist diffraction. It leads us, via Marx, into the fracturing of human life under conditions of generative separation and heterology (alienation). But diffraction also denotes the sheer 1M difference that is the basis for 3L concrete universality/ singularity, and, within that, the core universals of agency, desire and solidarity. What holds dialectical rationality and diffraction qua fracturing together is a dialectic of co-presence permitted by the constellational embedding of the intrinsic in the extrinsic, and, behind these, the duals of agency in structure and ethics in politics or history on the terrain of open totality. They permit us to see how it is possible to hold onto an emergent sense of what human being means within geo-history and nature, without either hypostatising the former or reducing it to the latter.

The result in practice is an understanding of the ways in which real, grounded ethics operate as ideals in actual worlds, in necessarily difficult ways. We end up with both a perfectionist account of the broad thrust of ethical possibility and a need to conceive dialectically of the interplay of the ideal and the actual in the world as is. Modern ethical forms, usually split and detotalised, tend to be essentially dilemmatic in their form. Accordingly, 'backsliding' and *phronesis* represent different responses to tension, while concrete utopianism represents a more progressive tack, though one to be treated with care. A third response to the tension is seen in the overstated and a prioristic account of the subsumption of ethical possibilities within the actualities of power associated with both poststructuralist and critical theory. Here, dialectical critical realism proposes an a posteriori investigation of the possibilities of subsumption in place of a prioristic necessities. When a 'utopian' or 'mystical' access to justice is maintained in the face of subsumption, this represents a possible common ground, for the ideal is reintroduced thereby. *Why* it should be reintroduced is, in my view, best explained by dialectical critical realist meta-ethics. The three relations between the ideal and the actual are the product of a theory that explains well the real problems of ethical agency in a fractured and crisis-ridden here and now, while holding keenly to the sense that ethics can overreach the present and offer a critique of it. Bhaskar's ideal ethics are far from the idealist, dehistoricised vision they are thought to represent. They are constituted by a thoughtful, potent, innovative way of conceiving the relationship between the ideal and the actual under modern social conditions.

6   Metacritique I

Philosophy's 'primordial failing'

We have now developed the four key elements in dialectical critical realism, which move from 1M real difference or non-identity in the world to the 2E role of real determinate absence informing change. From there, we observed the role of 3L open totality in locating absenting process and the relevance of context, and then 4D ethical agency. The last, it should be noted, is grounded in 3L constellated totality, 2E absenting absence and 1M difference as concrete universality so that the Bhaskarian dialectic works as a whole, backwards and forwards. The foregoing chapters accordingly complete the main work of *Dialectic* as I outlined it in Chapter 1 – that is, the dialecticisation of critical realism according to the MELD schema, and, at the same time, the 'critical realisation' of dialectic. This, however, still leaves us with the third main aim of *Dialectic*, which, it will be recalled, is to provide the elements of 'a totalising critique of western philosophy in its various . . . forms' (DPF: 2), and the aim of this chapter is to consider Bhaskar's argument here for what he calls metacritique.[1]

One of the most novel and exciting aspects of *Dialectic* and *Plato Etc.* is the analysis of the historical development of western philosophy from its beginnings with the ancient Greeks to its present condition of malaise and, in Bhaskar's appropriation of Hegel's term, Unhappy Consciousness.[2] As the title of his latter book suggests, Bhaskar follows Alfred North Whitehead's view that '[t]he safest general characterisation of the European philosophical tradition is that it consists of a series of footnotes to Plato' (Whitehead 1978: 39). In the relationships between Plato and the pre-Socratic philosopher Parmenides on the one hand, and Plato and Aristotle on the other, Bhaskar detects what he calls the 'primordial failing of western philosophy' (DPF: 74, 355, 406). This chapter's main aim is to elucidate what this is and its effect on the tradition. On its basis, Bhaskar develops a series of philosophical sketches that reveal how the subsequent trajectory of philosophy is informed by this fateful Platonic heritage. More specifically, it is the first steps established by Parmenides, Plato and Aristotle that establish that western philosophy is generally irrealist[3] in its forms. However, since living, and therefore thinking, in the world entails essentially realist premises, as seen for example in 'referential detachment' or the 'reality principle', the Platonic heritage means that western philosophy has struggled with an underlying conflict. Cast in mainly irrealist terms, its hidden 'other' is the realism that living in the world entails. It would not be wrong, Bhaskar suggests, to describe 'the history of philosophy as that of explicit idealism and implicit realism' (DPF: 308), and this combination is to be found among the earliest philosophers in the tradition. The claim that philosophy combines problematically idealist and realist elements is not new to Bhaskar's dialectical work. What is new is his tracing it back to the Greeks, and his identification there of an underlying problem, associated with what he calls ontological monovalence.[4]

To isolate this problem in its initial forms and to trace its evolution to the present is to provide a radical critique of western philosophy. In addition, it is to tell us something about the ways in which we live in the western world today. Thinking is in itself an active process, and philosophy, as the most general and would-be universal way of thinking about the world, both reflects and is implicated in the western world's structure and design. In thinking critically about the problems of philosophy and relating these to the non-philosophical, we are in the realm of metacritique, which, as we saw in Chapter 2, is linked with the various forms of critique (transcendental, immanent and explanatory) and is divided into meta-critique$_1$ and metacritique$_2$. Philosophical critique identifies a point of difficulty or inconsistency in a theory or a practice, and a metacritique$_1$ identifies the general absence or incompleteness underlying it. A metacritique$_2$ then explains the absence or incompleteness in terms of some more general problem or set of issues of a political or socio-historical kind. In so doing, the metacritique$_2$ operates as a bridge between the theory or practice under scrutiny and the wider world of structured power relations which the theory reflects on, participates in and embodies. Putting together systematic problems in philosophy (metacritique$_1$) with their underlying grounds of existence (metacritique$_2$) provides us with a basis for grasping the structured problematicity of philosophy. This can be formally recognised as a Tina formation, structurally located in a constellated totality, and substantively evaluated as a citadel of the Unhappy Consciousness.

The chapter has four main sections. In the first two, I shall analyse the two moves that have been fateful for western philosophy: the one, from Parmenides to Plato, abolishing absence in favour of the positive and the actual, the other establishing what Bhaskar calls 'the Platonic–Aristotelian fault-line' at the base of the tradition. In the first, the key element is Plato's correction of Parmenides's outright denial of non-being as change by finessing it in terms of difference. This sequesters absence and promotes ontological actualism, and will be explained in the first section. In the second, the key is provided by the extra work that mind or ideas have to do to provide foundations for knowledge in the presence of ontological actualism and the resulting absence of a grasp of natural necessity in the world. This implicates Aristotle through conceptions of form and *nous* in Plato's project of denying change and idealising the world, albeit in the context of a more 'materialist' philosophical project, which at one level was particularly concerned with change's possibility. Both Plato and Aristotle in their different, contrasting, yet linked ways develop the epistemic fallacy and what Bhaskar calls 'subject–object identity theory'. The shift is from denial of non-being (creating ontological monovalence) to a substitutive commitment to the constitutive significance of thought (through the epistemic fallacy). The mediating link between ontological monovalence and the epistemic fallacy is provided by the doctrine of ontological actualism, a conception of a world without depth. The main work of this chapter will be focused on this analysis, in effect a metacritique$_1$ of Greek philosophy.

In the third and fourth sections, I shall consider some of the effects of these moves on the subsequent development of western philosophy. In the third, I shall briefly relate Bhaskar's account of the development of modern philosophy after the Greeks from Descartes to Hume and beyond. This is much more sketched than the discussion of the Greeks, and the reader is referred to the fuller discussions (themselves by no means complete) in Bhaskar's own texts (DPF: ch. 4, PE: chs 9 and 10). In the fourth, I consider what a dialectical critical realist engagement with postmodern thinking would look like in the light of the arguments of this chapter, using Jacques Derrida's deconstruction as example. Here, I suggest that there is something Platonic 'in reverse' in Derrida's radicalised notion of difference, which limits deconstruction's critical potential. While deconstruction and dialectical critical realism have something in common, the former lacks the basis either to grasp philosophy's deepest problems (at the level of metacritique$_1$) or to develop a metacritique$_2$ of them. In consequence, it is itself subject to both a metacritique$_1$ and a metacritique$_2$.

Parmenides to Plato: absence as difference

In this section, I develop the argument stated briefly in Chapter 2 concerning the importance of non-being for our understanding of change in the world, and how this was suppressed, first by Parmenides and then, in a more sophisticated way, by Plato. In particular, I explore the philosophical argument as Plato engages with the more troubling consequences of the Parmenidean demand that one must not speak of non-being. What must be grasped is that Plato wants to deny absence, in the Bhaskarian sense of the real, determinate non-being that underpins change, but he finds a place for an emasculated version of it in the more superficial doctrine that non-being equals difference. This move sets the scene, as we shall see in the following section, for the debate between Plato and Aristotle. Bhaskar's argument is that the denial of non-being involves the denial of the possibility of real change in the world, and that both Parmenides and Plato, despite the latter's criticism of the former, are party to it. This crucial move sets the scene for the 'primordial failing' of western philosophy.

What is the 'primordial failing' of western philosophy?

There is, however, an initial puzzle in Bhaskar's account as to what the primordial failing is. It is traced back to the Parmenidean–Platonic–Aristotelian axis with which western philosophy commences, but what exactly is the failing? In different places, Bhaskar identifies two candidates. One is the epistemic fallacy, the reduction of statements about being to statements about our knowledge of being, a problem with which critical realism always concerned itself, even, indeed especially, in its original form (Bhaskar 1975, 2008a). Bhaskar now identifies the epistemic fallacy in all three of the ancients, and he links it to the development of modern philosophy in Descartes, Hume, Kant and Hegel. Thus, he writes that what 'Aristotle and Hegel share is the epistemic fallacy (the primordial failing of western philosophy)' (DPF: 74). This, then, is the first candidate for primordial failing, but has Bhaskar's dialectical turn not deepened his understanding of philosophy's problems? The second possible candidate emerges explicitly from dialectical critical realism. It is ontological monovalence, the elaboration of a purely positive account of reality, which, Bhaskar also states, 'must be regarded as the primordial failing of western philosophy' (DPF: 406). Thus, both the epistemic fallacy and ontological monovalence are canvassed as western philosophy's primordial failing. Which is it to be?

A third possibility is that the fundamental problem may be in some way a compound of the first two, and this Bhaskar also suggests. The primordial mistake 'can be looked at in two ways'. The first is as the epistemic fallacy, for it is this that leads to the 'primal squeeze' on natural necessity, and powers the drive to the dominant 'subject–object identity theory'[5] (DPF: 355) in western philosophy. Second, it can be looked at as involving ontological monovalence, barring the possibility of grasping absence in the world. This approach suggests that the basic problem combines both elements, but how are they connected? These formulations do not tell us. A clue is provided in another passage where Bhaskar comments that it is difficult to say which problem 'is the prime mover in the positivisation, reification and eternalisation of current knowledge and more generally the status quo', for they 'function to the same effect, buttressing each other' (DPF: 184). The idea of a relationship in which two errors buttress each other calls to mind the idea of the 'Tina compromise formation', discussed in Chapter 4, in which a group of errors constitute a mutually entailing problematic. But does one error entail the other for Bhaskar so that it has primacy? Apparently not, for he writes that either error can be taken as primary, just so long as we recognise that 'there are two mutually reinforcing category mistakes – ontological monovalence and the epistemic fallacy' (DPF: 357).

In this chapter, I will propose a closer, more intrinsic, link between ontological monovalence and the epistemic fallacy than this last comment suggests. I will argue that there is both a logical and an historical progression from ontological monovalence to the epistemic fallacy via the crucial mediating doctrine of onto-logical actualism, which is common to both. Moving from Parmenides to Plato, and then from Plato to Aristotle, ontological actualism is first generated by ontological monovalence and then becomes the surface ontology that invokes the epistemic fallacy as its necessary (but problematic) complement in the absence of absence, ontological depth and natural necessity. The context for a 'primal squeeze' on depth and necessity is prepared by the prior denial of absence in favour of a purely positive account of reality. If the move from Parmenides to Plato confirms the denial of absence in favour of positivity and the ontologically actual, the positions established by Plato and Aristotle both rest on this prior denial and take it forward into the territory now ruled by actualism, which then necessitates the epistemic fallacy. The result is subject–object identity theory, and its creation reveals the crucial role of Greek philosophy in creating the terms, *mutatis mutandis*, for the philosophical axis that would be constituted in modernity by Descartes and Hume on one side, and Kant and Hegel on the other. In effect, western philosophy represents, in the language of Chapter 4, one huge Tina compromise formation which (crucially and irreducibly) develops and changes historically, but which is ultimately stuck in an initial set of Tina moves. These are initiated by the denial of absence (ontological monovalence) and the constitution of actualist ontology, then Tina buttressed by the claimed primacy of knowledge over being (the epistemic fallacy) in subject–object identity theory. In this view, the *compound* nature of the two errors, one building on the other, is Tina necessitated, and the links in the chain of error proceed from the initial denial of absence to the subsequently entailed assertion of the primacy of knowledge. That, at least, will be the argument of this and the next section.

Change and difference: their mutual irreducibility

Before turning to the Greeks, we need to clarify what we mean by change and difference and to see why they should be distinguished. Plato will, as we have said, analyse change in terms of difference, so we need to appreciate why this should be a problem. Though the two may be connected, change cannot be analysed simply in terms of difference because it, unlike difference, 'presupposes the idea of a continuing thing in a tensed process' (DPF: 45). This claim stems from Bhaskar's analysis of the relationship between absence, causal determination and change, the triunity of space, time and causality, discussed in Chapter 2. To describe a situation of change as one simply of difference fails to capture significant elements of the situation. If I say, 'Sophie was dyeing her hair on Wednesday', I refer 'to a process of substantial change which cannot be captured by the formal difference between the statement that her hair was grey [on Tuesday], but brown [on Thursday]' (PE: 8). To speak of change is to invoke the absenting or determinate negation of a past state. A past state is absented by changes that occur in causally constituting the present,[6] and absenting and change are essential to our understanding of being over time. It is crucial to our ability to understand the way the world works that a statement concerning change is distinct from one concerning difference, for the latter can tell us something, but not all that we would want to know, about a situation of change. Change entails difference but is not reducible to it. For example, to return to the example from Sartre in Chapter 2, the *change* constituted by Pierre's absence from his chair in the café is not explained by noting the *difference* constituted by Genet having taken his place. It may be related to the additional, causally efficacious fact that Pierre has gone off to play football, rather than waiting to meet Sartre (DPF: 45). An account of Pierre's absence, which elaborates the tensed process leading to his not being in the café, cannot be exchanged for a simple statement of differentiating fact. That Genet sits where Pierre should have been may be of interest in itself, but it too invokes inquiry as to the causal processes explaining the change; why is he present while Pierre is absent?

Further, if change cannot be analysed in terms of difference, neither can difference be analysed in terms of change, because difference 'includes the idea of two or more non-identical tokens, which cannot be necessarily reduced to a unitary origin' (DPF: 45).[7] Change entails continuity (as well as disjunction) in a thing, a context or a situation. We can, however, have different things in the world, for example elephants and quartz, without having to contemplate a situation of connection and change. If the significance of change is underpinned by the reality of tensed process working on a product in the triunity, then the import of difference stems from the simple fact of alterity – irreducible real difference – in the world. This is an ontological requirement for life, including human life, to be possible. Without irreducible difference, there could not, for example, be referential detachment. We need to allow for two (and by extension, an indefinite number of) non-identicals in the world for any discourse to be possible, for an entity 'to be able to talk about something other than itself or even to talk about itself at all' (ibid.). It is only the existence of real difference that permits me to detach myself from other persons and things. Intransitivity, the ontological separation of the referrer from the referent, is transcendentally necessary for discourse, and it relies on difference. This, however, is a state of being that is different from, even if it is connected with, change. Thus, while we may speak of differentiating changes and changing differences, it is important to see that at their heart, there are two categories here that must be analysed separately, and respected for their distinction.

Why does this matter? Bhaskar argues for the irreducible significance of both change and difference. Implicated in both is a sense of negativity or absence, but they are not the same. If Sophie has changed her hair colour, then the grey hair is no longer grey but brown, the *difference* being statable in negative terms (grey/not grey – *differentiated* as brown). At the same time, Sophie has brought about a *change* in her hair colour that is absenting (negating) the grey in favour of the brown (grey/not grey – causally and processually *changed* to brown). Statements concerning differentiation and change can both be explained in terms of negation, but both are necessary, and necessarily distinct. Philosophers, however, have not always kept them apart. Historically, indeed, there has been a tendency to see these two categories, both entailing negativity, as one, and to analyse processes of change reductively, in terms of difference. This indeed is the legacy of Parmenides and Plato to western philosophy. Parmenides inaugurated a purely positive account of the world by denying non-being, and in the process denied the possibility of real change, and Plato supported him by analysing, more subtly, situations of change as non-being or negation in terms solely of difference. Fatefully for western philosophy, he elided the distinction between the two forms of negation found in change and difference. For Bhaskar, the process is then completed in modern times 'by the Kantian error of supposing that one can always replace statements about negativities or their derivatives by ones employing purely positive predicates' (DPF: 45).[8] So doing, Kant replicates Plato, and confirms his significance for western philosophy.

However, we are getting ahead of ourselves. For the moment, we should note two things from this preliminary analysis of change and difference and their relation to absence and negativity. First, it is important for an understanding of ontology that both change and difference, with their distinct approaches to non-being, be acknowledged in themselves and respected for the distinction between them. Second, there is an indication that western philosophy has not done this in a crucial inaugural moment. In the process, absence, in the critical realist sense of real, determinate non-being, 'out there', informing change and causal necessity in the world, is in danger of being ignored by virtue of an ancient confusion. With these points in mind, let us now analyse this early false step in western philosophy and consider why it might be the basis for its primordial failing.

Denying absence as change: Parmenides

For Bhaskar, the story of western philosophy 'must begin with great-grandfather Parmenides', though a story with 'firmer historiographical credentials can be told from Plato on' (DPF: 309). Parmenides sought 'an unhypothetical starting point, something unconditioned and one' (DPF: 354) as the incorrigible guarantee of an unchanging world. Negativity, or not-being, was banished for its connection with change, in terms both of the generation of the new and of the perishing of the old. Parmenides's contribution to philosophy was to write a poem that articulated a purely positive account of the world – that is, one based on a doctrine of onto-logical monovalence. As we saw in Chapter 2, he did this by insisting that the world was a monist whole, 'the One', and that of this whole, one could not speak of absence or negativity, of what 'is not', only of 'what is'. The Parmenidean bar bears repeating:

> Never will this prevail, that what is not is – bar your thought from this road of inquiry.
>
> (Barnes 1987: 82)

To establish secure foundations for being and to guard against change, Parmenides's poem begins by distinguishing two ways of knowledge, that of truth and that of opinion. The way of truth distinguishes two roads of inquiry, one of positive being 'that it is and that it cannot not be, is the path of persuasion (for truth accompanies it)' (Barnes 1987: 80). The other is that of non-being or absence, 'that it is not and that it must not be – this I say to you is a trail of utter ignorance' (ibid.). One cannot speak or think of what is not, only of what is: 'you could not recognise that which is not . . . nor could you mention it' (ibid.), for '[w]hat can be said and be thought of must be; for it can be, and nothing cannot' (Barnes 1987: 81). Being itself is as a result total and unchanging, 'ungenerated and indestructible, whole, of one kind and unwavering, and complete' (Barnes 1987: 82). Were it to have been generated at any point in the past, then it would have emerged out of what is not, and that Parmenides 'shall not allow' (ibid.). 'Thus generation is quenched and perishing unheard of. Nor is it divided, since it all alike is – . . . it is all full of what it is', 'whole and unmoving', so that 'generation and destruction have been banished far away' (Barnes 1987: 83). These are explicit ontological statements about the world, what it contains, what it can and cannot be. Non-being is clearly linked here to the rejection of change either as generation of the new or as perishing of the old, and it is denied.

For Bhaskar, we see here in rudimentary form the beginnings of the western philosophical tradition. First, at the level of metacritique$_2$, in the socio-political background, is the elite concern to protect against change. What exists was never generated from something else, but has always been there, and consequently can never perish. Parmenides was a lawgiver, and his position fundamentally shapes his philosophical endeavour. If the existing world had at some stage come into being, then it could also pass from being, so the denial of change is crucial, and the doctrine of ontological monovalence makes this possible. The socio-political background thus leads, second, to a philosophical foreground at the level of metacritique$_1$, where we have an ontology of pure presence, in the sense of an unmoving and full Parmenidean whole. Parmenides says it is 'completed on all sides, like the bulk of a well-rounded ball, equal in every way' (Barnes 1987: 84), undisruptible in its completeness, ensuring that no absence or change is possible or admissible to thought. All is what it is in already perfect symmetry and equilibrium. For Bhaskar, this is so stringent a doctrine that it cannot ultimately stand. It not only makes *change* as 'absence, change, becoming, finitude, error, voids and motion . . . impossible', it also makes *difference* as 'alterity, diversity and multiplicity' (PE: 177) unthinkable. Negativity as *both* change *and* difference are abolished, for everything is for Parmenides part of 'the One', complete, undifferentiated and unchanging. This is an untenable metaphysical doctrine, so, if the aim of denying *change* is to be maintained, a modified version of the Parmenidean doctrine is required, and it is here that we turn to Plato.

Just before doing so, however, we should note a significant connection emerging in Parmenides between ontological monovalence and an anticipatory over-reliance on, and substitution of, epistemology for ontology (a proleptic epistemic fallacy). Accompanying his ontology is a foundationalist, proto-rationalist epistemology, the 'way of truth' against the 'way of opinion', and this formulation buttresses the bar on speculation about what is not. Taken by itself, however, the way of truth introduces a potential to shift from saying that knowledge is *of* the whole, to saying that knowledge, in some sense, *constitutes* the whole. Knowledge begins the process of offering itself as an alternative, epistemological foundation for ontology, in place of the ontological grounding of knowledge provided by the world itself. In the claim for a way of truth, there emerges a first tentative potential for identity between subjective thought and objective being: for subject–object identity theory. The overall emphasis, however, rests with the object in Parmenides's poem: 'what is not', absence, non-being, the potential for change are all denied as *ontological* possibilities, which cannot therefore be known. This is the strange legacy Parmenides leaves to Plato, of which he must make sense.

Finessing absence as difference: Plato

In the face of so extreme a doctrine, Plato's contribution was to 'seek to defuse its more absurd conclusions while still working within a Parmenidean framework' (PE: 177). To this end, he did two things. First, in his late dialogues he analysed (absenting) change in terms of (positive) difference, thereby finessing the problem of non-being and securing a monovalent ontology. Second, he aligned this analysis with his already developed theory of the Forms as an ideal, epistemological grounding for being in place of Parmenides's ontological One, thereby developing the significance of epistemic fallacy and subject–object identity for philosophy. Let us deal with these separately.

As regards the analysis of absence and change in terms of difference, Plato's argument is to be found in *The Sophist*, one of those late works in which he begins the process of developing an analytical problematic for philosophy. This development of analytics is significant, as we shall see, but let us first look at how Plato substitutes absence as difference for absence as change. This involves a dialogue between Theaetetus and a wise 'Visitor' in which the latter apparently controverts Parmenides, but ultimately defends his underlying objective of protecting the world from absence as change. The Visitor begins by taking the bull by the horns: not-being is possible, and so is change. A being cannot have 'intelligence, life and soul' and be 'at rest and completely changeless even though it's alive' (Plato 1997a: 249a); change therefore is a part of being. Further, it is also clear that as part of a process of becoming, change really is or involves 'something that is not', though, the Visitor adds, it also 'partakes in *that which is*' (Plato 1997a: 256d). This seems anti-Parmenidean, and indeed the Visitor says as much. He reminds Theaetetus of Parmenides's injunction 'Never shall it force itself on us, that that which is not may be', but, against this, says 'we [have] shown that *those things which are not* are' (Plato 1997a: 258d). So, the Visitor disputes Parmenides, but the disagreement turns out to have a specific focus, and this is on the *form* in which 'that which is not' appears, which is the form of 'the different':

> VISITOR: So it has to be possible for *that which is not* to be, in the case of change and also as applied to all the kinds. That's because as applied to all of them the nature of *the different* makes each of them not be, by making it different from that which is.
>
> (Plato 1997a: 256e)

It becomes clear in consequence that the spirit of the Parmenidean standpoint is not offended, for to speak of 'that which is not' is only to speak of that which, as differentiated being, also *is* – that is, is identified in terms of its (positive) difference. It is in this sense that not-being, in the form of change, 'partakes in *that which is*' (Plato 1997a: 256d). Importantly, in this move, talk of not-being as the *contrary* of being – that is, as not-being per se – is rejected:

VISITOR: So we won't agree with somebody who says that negation signifies a contrary. We'll only admit this much: when 'not' and 'non-' are prefixed to names that follow them, they indicate something *other* than the . . . things to which the names following the negation are applied.

(Plato 1997a: 257c)

In this way, Plato is loyal to Parmenides's concern to sequester change as the real absence or non-being that brings about the generation and perishing of things. All that exists is not-being as difference, and change is a specific form of this. For Bhaskar, this is a crucial moment for the development of philosophy, for Plato does two things here. First, he sequesters and disarms the ontological possibility of real determinate non-being, thereby conflating 'the different and mutually irreducible categories of difference and change' (PE: 180), and supporting Parmenides while appearing to disagree with him. Second, he lays the basis for the argument that what is important in philosophy is a method that can aid the analytical differentiation of phenomena in the world, for:

VISITOR: . . . *that which is* has a share in *the different*, so, being different from all of the others, it is not each of them and it is not all of the others except itself.

(Plato 1997a: 259b)

Plato moves in this way to constitute philosophy as analytical in its tasks. He assumes that all statements involve reference between a subject and a predicate, so that what Bhaskar calls here 'the existential "is"' drops from the picture in favour of 'the predicative "is"'.[9] His account of predication in turn leads to an ontologically actualist theory of identity 'to the effect that everything is the same as itself and other than everything else', and he thereby lays down 'the lineaments of . . . the "analytical problematic"' (PE: 180). Knowledge becomes a matter of the naming and differentiation of things:

VISITOR: Knowledge is a single thing, too, I suppose. But each part of it that has to do with something is marked off and has a name peculiar to itself.

(Plato 1997a: 257d)

These two moves, finessing change and non-being as difference, and differentiating phenomena analytically, are linked. Having resolved Parmenidean worries about change in the form of non-being, analytical differentiation as an actualist ontological practice becomes possible. However – and this is a key point – this analytical differentiation of things into what they are and what they are not does not ultimately resolve the problem of change for Plato. Having evaded it at the level of Parmenidean non-being, it returns in Plato's own philosophy as the problem of how to fix or control kinds as the universals under which phenomena analytically fall. An analysis of the differentiae of things may ward off a discussion of real non-being as change, but it is exposed to the sort of challenge offered by the Sophists, in the (supposed) manner of Heraclitus,[10] that the universals under which things may be grouped lack fixity, permanence or genuine universality. Differentiae may escape analytical classification. In a world where change continues to exist and is now interpreted as difference, there is a danger that it will be radically and sceptically generalised as flux and impermanence. Having been denied 'upfront' as real, determinate change, a form of irreal 'hyperchange' – as constant flux – appears in its stead. In consequence, the predication of things under universal categories may prove impossible, for what could protect the universality of phenomena, in analytical categories, from the danger of constant flux? To this question, Plato's answer was the theory of the Forms, and it is to this that we now turn.

The Forms and the epistemic fallacy

In Parmenides, we saw that there is already the beginning of a claim that knowledge, cast properly as the 'way of truth', could offer a ground for securing the foundation of being, though his philosophy rests more obviously on a monist ontology of the One, rather than an epistemology of truth. Plato maintained the distinction between truth and opinion, in the form of *episteme* (knowledge) and *doxa* (belief), but he developed the theory of the Forms to operationalise knowledge as an epistemological foundation for being. The Forms establish a basis for asserting the ideal universality and fixity of worldly phenomena, despite their submission to processes of becoming and perishing in actuality. Plato maintained the goal of philosophy to be the rational elucidation of unchanging foundations for knowledge and being, establishing a two-world theory of ideal Forms and phenomenal flux. So doing, he seeks to achieve the goals of Parmenidean (onto-logical) monism by way of thought. Once the assertion of ontological completeness as the block on change was discounted, the resort was to idealist epistemology in its stead. The challenge of real change had not gone away just because Plato analysed it as positive difference; indeed, it had taken on the new form of radical difference or flux. The Forms represent Plato's own effort, on the terrain of idealist epistemology, to control change as difference. Bhaskar summarises the motivation behind the theory of the Forms as follows:

> Plato's theory of the forms attempted to specify what must be the case for knowledge (*episteme*) rather than mere opinion (*doxa*) to be possible. Already impressed by the certainty of mathematics, Plato assumed that knowledge must be real, unitary and unchanging; whereas ordinary things were patently subject to decay, multiplicity and conflicting characterisations. He was thus led to posit an autonomous realm of abstract ideas or Forms, existing outside space and time and independently of their particular manifestations.
>
> (PE: 179)

In the face of change, represented as the possibility of constant flux in worldly matters, Plato buttresses the ontological actualism (a world of difference) of his account of phenomena with a resort to rationalist criteria for knowledge. The permanence that things lack in the here and now is secured at the level of universal Ideas or Forms. Philosophical knowledge seeks to fix things that are otherwise in danger of running out of control, but in the absence of any understanding of why things actually change as they do. If the reality of absenting change as natural necessity, the real determinate operation of causal processes that generate the new and perish the old, is denied, then understanding such change is also impossible. In place of understanding, Plato establishes the Forms so that what had been a secondary element in Parmenides's philosophy becomes primary in his: the foundational guarantee of worldly stability by virtue of an epistemological 'way of truth'. Plato thus develops (metacritically$_1$) a form of the epistemic fallacy and subject–object identity theory in order to establish (metacritically$_2$) a sense of stability in a world of threatening change, where the road to understanding has been barred by Parmenides and his own ensuing analysis of absenting change as difference.

Plato to Aristotle: difference and universals

Why is Plato's correction of Parmenides relevant to us today? Bhaskar's argument is that it set the scene for western philosophy because it established a problematic that is governed by different forms of subject–object identity theory. In them, the epistemic fallacy and certain characteristic problems such as those of universals and particulars (among the ancients) and induction (among the moderns) consequently govern the field. This is only possible, Bhaskar argues, because a deeper set of issues concerning the nature of ontology, especially absence and causality in natural necessity, was excluded. The pre-Socratics had a better intuitive grasp of these ontological issues than did Plato. Yet it is Plato's reading of change and non-being as difference, together with his resulting argument that phenomenal flux be countered in eidetic terms, that has proved crucial. In this section, we move the story forward from Plato to Aristotle, and I set the scene for this encounter by describing the two great problems of Greek philosophy: that of 'the one and the other', and 'the one and the many'.

The two great problems of Greek philosophy

The first problem, of 'the one and the other', is especially associated with pre-Socratic philosophy. The second, of 'the one and the many', is linked with Plato and Aristotle. For Bhaskar, both problems, and the way they succeed each other in the Greek tradition, are related to the transition from ontological monovalence to the epistemic fallacy. The first problem is especially linked to the existence and denial of real absence, while the second involves the control of difference and the emerging import of the epistemic fallacy. The second has, accordingly, been particularly significant in setting the terms of the western tradition, but on the basis of the first having been finessed. Bhaskar describes the problems thus:

> (α) the problem of 'the one and the other', of diremption from an assumed original unity, of negation and of change – the dialectical problem par excellence; and its analytical counterpart, (β) the problem of 'the one and the many', of order and its opposition, the problem of chaos.
>
> (DPF: 309)

These problems are sometimes given different names. The *Cambridge Dictionary of Philosophy* (Audi 1999: 630) refers to the first as the 'one–many' problem, and the second as the 'one over many' problem. These terms seem too close and prone to confusion, and the two problems do need to be kept distinct. Sticking with Bhaskar's terms, the problem of 'the one and the other' was central to pre-Socratic philosophy because it essentially concerned the nature of being, what we now call ontology, and how it was possible to understand that many different things might (or might not) possess a single nature such as water, air or some other general substance. The problem of 'the one and the many' in contrast is a problem for Plato and post-Platonic philosophy, for it is the problem of how different things may be grouped together under a scheme of universal categories. There is, it will be noticed, a certain parallelism between the terms in which the two problems are described, but the difference is crucial, for the second emerges as the problem of how we *know* the universal within the particular, and therefore has an essentially epistemological cast in comparison to the ontological cast ('what is the nature of things?') of the one–other problem. Put in different terms, the first problem relates to the nature of change, the second to the nature of difference.

For Bhaskar, the main point is that the importance of the first problem as an essential issue in ontology is lost by focusing on the second as an issue in epistemology. His critique of ontological monovalence and the ensuing restoration of categories of determinate absence, holistic causality and natural necessity at the alethic core of being is an attempt to reinstate the ontological problematic latent, though quite undeveloped, in the problem of 'the one and the other'. But Greek philosophy did not follow such a direction, and here we turn to the relationship between Plato and Aristotle. With Plato, the problem of 'the one and the other' was effectively denied. It was 'dissolved' by Plato in his analysis, really mystification and repression, of negation and change in terms of difference, and, as we saw, this was done in favour of promoting the second problem, that of 'the one and the many'. But 'the one and the many' presented its own problems. Moving from Plato to Aristotle, these were addressed by the latter, and purportedly '"resolved" [in his] immanent theory of knowledge' (DPF: 355). Yet Aristotle was at the same time acutely aware of issues of change and development in the world – that is, of matters which relate to the terrain of 'the one and the other' – and his philosophy also attempted to deal with these. Ultimately, Bhaskar will argue he was not successful in so doing because he remained in thrall to Plato. Staying on the terrain of the epistemic fallacy and subject–object identity theory, he 'only sets the scene for the generation of a new transcendent' (ibid.). The Aristotelian categories of form and *nous* remain tied to Platonic idealism and cannot do the job of a realist ontology. They cannot address issues of material change on the terrain of 'the one and the other'. This is the argument to which we now turn.

The problem of 'the one and the many': from Plato to Aristotle

The above contention may raise some eyebrows. There is a temptation to take the evident differences between Plato and Aristotle as evidence of their essential opposition to each other. Plato is the philosopher of the Ideas and of two worlds, while Aristotle is the philosopher of science committed to investigation of how things work in this world. In our terms, one might say that if Plato is concerned to rationalise and finesse change as difference, then Aristotle is concerned to understand how change actually works in the world. Aristotelian conceptions such as *kinesis* (change, movement), *dunamis* (potentiality), *energeia* (actuality) and *genesis* (coming to be) point in the direction of a non-empiricist, realist understanding of the powers that inhere in things and that can emerge and be actualised in their development. Similarly, Aristotle's emphasis on the drive in things towards their completion and perfection ensures for him considerable support among Marxists and other left-leaning thinkers, including, to a degree, as we saw in the ethics of the previous chapter, Bhaskar himself (cf. Meikle 1985; Dean 2006). Such a view is hardly compatible with seeing Aristotle as in thrall to Plato. Now, Bhaskar acknowledges the import of Aristotle in these terms, but he also identifies a primary sense in which Aristotle, for all the advances he made, retained damaging Platonic commitments. Bhaskar recognises the 'vital' import of the Aristotelian critique of Platonic transcendence (DPF: 309), and that Aristotle 'did indeed seek (and sometimes find) good scientific explanations' (DPF: 138). His emphasis on investigating nature had the important result that knowledge was henceforth 'a form expressing the essence of a thing [which was] susceptible to non-equivocal statement in a real definition' (PE: 5), so he generated the possibility of a real, classificatory science (taxonomy). Yet for all his good scientific work, there are serious limits to what Aristotle achieves.

To get at these, Bhaskar focuses on what is perhaps the less appreciated side of Aristotle, the manner in which his thought *obstructs* the understanding of science. He failed, Bhaskar argues, to theorise ontological structure and stratification, or the natural necessity in things. Despite his appreciation of real change and difference in the world, there is an absence in his philosophy of 'the concept of transfactually efficacious tendencies . . . in a differentiated, . . . structured, and open, world' (DPF: 138). The signs of this absence are his reliance on *nous* (meaning intellectual intuition, but linked to a divine, constitutive knowledge of the world), his idea of form in nature (his fundamental, hylomorphic account of being), and the unresolved aporiai to which his system gives rise, of matter and form, and essence and accident. Here I focus in particular on *nous* and form, and their inability to establish a conception of natural necessity in the world, a story that can be introduced in terms of Aristotle's reaction to the problem of 'the one and the many' he inherits from Plato.

The problem of 'the one and the many', as we have seen, concerns the relationship between universals and particulars. Plato was concerned to acknowledge that difference existed in the world, and this would become the basis for the analytical developments seen in his late dialogues. But difference per se presents a danger to rational knowledge, for, if pushed to its limit, it leads to fragmentation and flux. It breaks down into further and further differences. Plato, it will be recalled, wanted to safeguard the possibility of knowledge (*episteme*) as distinct from opinion (*doxa*), and he did so in order to protect a sense of the universal in the face of the difference he acknowledged. To this end, he posited the theory of Ideas or Forms, which he held to exist alongside and in relation to 'the transient sensate material world of flux' (PE: 5). However, this two-world theory of Forms and flux generates the problem of the one and many. Plato himself acknowledged it in the dialogue known as *The Parmenides*, but Aristotle focused on it as a means of developing his own, apparently more materialistic, metaphysics via the problem of the 'third man'.

The 'third man' problem works as follows. Each ideal Form, such as that of 'the large', must be a universal 'one' if it is to cover all cases of largeness ('the many'). But if I compare 'the large' as the ideal of largeness with other large things, I posit another idea of largeness by which the comparison occurs. Thus, as Plato himself put it, 'another form of largeness will make its appearance . . . alongside largeness and the things that partake of it, and in turn another over all these. . . . Each of your forms will no longer be one, but unlimited in multitude' (Plato 1997b: 132b). Aristotle exemplified this with discussion of the 'third man'. The Forms provide a universal understanding of the particulars they represent and over which they stand, so the Form of man establishes the ideal in which actual men participate. But if we know actual men by what they share with the Form of man, then we recognise that both actual men and the Form of man have something in common. This recognition must entail reference to a further Form, under which both the actual and the ideal are collected. Hence, we need to posit a further form, a third man, alongside the ideal and the actual. This in turn gives rise to a fourth and a fifth, ultimately to an infinite regress of forms. In this, the claim to universality of the ideal is lost, for it cannot ultimately be known.

In place of such an ideal two-worlds metaphysic, Aristotle argued that knowledge had to be both universal and rooted in this world. It was to be established by observation of the empirical, and in the early formulation of the *Categories* the root idea is that of the universal as primary substance, involving particulars in the world such as individual men, animals, plants, and so on (Lear 1988: 269–70). However, Aristotle became particularly interested in ideas of movement and change among particulars, so he needed a theory that could explain how particulars do not remain just as they are. To do so, he developed his theory of how things are made up of two distinct elements, form and matter. Because entities are subject to growth and development, they change their particularity over time, and his new theory understands this in terms of the way in which things combine raw matter with form immanent in them. In understanding the relationship between form and matter, what is it that now establishes the primary substance, the essence, of a thing? Aristotle said it could not be matter because matter can only be defined negatively, as that which has neither quality nor quantity, nor anything else which determines a thing. Matter is, as R. G. Collingwood put it, no more than 'the unrealisedness of unrealised potentiality' (1945: 92), and as such is reliant on form to make it into any special thing. This was Aristotelian hylomorphism ('matter changing'), but it raised the question as to how things understood as in-formed matter were to be known. They could not be known just as matter, for this provided no means of differentiation, yet was subject to change. His answer was that they had to be known according to their form.

Forms were universals immanent in matter, but not matter per se, and this gives rise to a difficult question concerning the ontological status of form. It is in the world, but, in its independence from matter, not of it. It must have a separate ontological existence from that which it informs. The only way in which Aristotle was ultimately able to explain it independently from worldly matter was in its connection with, indeed ultimately in its very existence as, mind. What he required, says Bhaskar, was a 'procedure whereby an identity was achieved between the essence actualised in the object of knowledge and that actualised in the mind of the knower' (PE: 5). Jonathan Lear develops the point as follows. For Aristotle, form as universal and primary could not be matter, which was purely concrete, so it had to be related to what was immaterial, which was mind. It had 'to be con-templated by a mind', for only 'mind is immaterial, and when it is contemplating form it *is* the form it is contemplating' (Lear 1988: 292). Further, form cannot be a question of this or that mind: if substance is 'to be capable of independent existence, it must not depend on a mind to contemplate it; it must *be* a mind that is actively contemplating' (ibid.). The trajectory of Aristotle's thought from primary substance as particular (in his *Categories*) to the combination of form and matter in which form informs and changes matter is one which ultimately implicates mind as a universal phenomenon. If form is to be distinguished from the matter it informs, Aristotle 'needs a mind that is actively thinking primary substance. Such a mind would be the primary substance that is thinking' (Lear 1988: 293).

Aristotle's Platonism

We can now begin to address Aristotle's Platonism. If form is reflected on, and ultimately constituted, by mind, Bhaskar asks, 'in what sense do Aristotelian forms differ from Platonic forms? Are they not, as both universal and separable, liable to exactly the same objections that Aristotle [himself] advances' (PE: 182) against Plato? The Aristotelian conception of form, despite its author's rejection of Platonic two-worlds theory, and his insistence on looking for primary substance in a way that embraces phenomena of change and development, represents a back door to the ideal forms Aristotle had sought to avoid in the search for scientific knowledge of things. Accordingly, it is not surprising that Aristotle's own account of universals and their connections with things should be subject to aporiai of (ideal) form and (real, concrete) matter, or of essence and accident.[11] Further, grasping the universal as form independent of, though immanent in, matter also reveals the role of *nous* in Aristotle's philosophy. If form is essential to being, development and change, but has to be grasped as a universal in thought by mind, what is it that grounds the universality of mind? Aristotle needs a sense of mind beyond minds, and he finds this in the eternal mind, which is God. *Nous* is the thinking in and of a world which discerns form, and is something in which humans participate. When they do so, however, they insert themselves into a universal process that is essentially divine. Aristotle's world, as Lear puts it, 'manifests a rational order for which God is responsible [and is] the final cause', so that 'form or primary substance at its highest level actuality simply is God' (Lear 1988: 295). In Collingwood's succinct phrase, 'God and the forms are not two but one' (1945: 87–9).

In this light, we can now appreciate Bhaskar's criticism of Aristotle. The problem of universals, of 'the one and the many', is a problem for Plato, but also for Aristotle. He holds onto the idea of a universal *in* the world only by virtue of a theory that takes it *beyond* the world. Both philosophers reveal an unresolved problematic of the ideal (the universal) and the actual (phenomena, matter), and of (knowing) subject and (material) object. This is the Platonic–Aristotelian fault-line, as Bhaskar calls it, because both resort to mind's capacity to think, and thereby to ground, being. Both are proponents of a subject–object identity theory in which mind acts as constitutive in relation to things. Plato carries this out in a two-worlds manner, positing ideal forms separate from nature, while Aristotle holds that things in the natural world have essences (Lear 1988: 269), but essence in the real draws on form beyond it. Both are accordingly guilty of committing early forms of the epistemic fallacy, in which mind substitutes for the real grounds in things. For Bhaskar, it is the absence of natural necessity, providing the alethic truth of things in the world, that is the problem. In place of such necessity, Aristotle can only develop, in light of the theory of the forms, a conception of what Lear calls 'hypothetical necessity'. For all his scientific awareness of the changes that occur in things, this is not a necessity that is established philosophically in realistically grounded, differentiated and explained matter. Rather, hypothetical necessity 'flows backward from the achieved end to the process directed toward that end' (Lear 1988: 43), and the reliance on hypothetical necessity, through the ideal telos of the forms, is precisely the point where Aristotle reveals his debt to Plato. As F. M. Cornford put it, 'For all [his] reaction towards the standpoint of common sense and empirical fact, Aristotle could never cease to be a Platonist. His thought, no less than Plato's, is governed by the idea . . . that the true cause or explanation of things is to be sought, not in the beginning, but in the end' (quoted in Guthrie 1967: 126). His Platonism is seen precisely in the teleological point of view and his account of the forms (ibid.; cf. Lear 1988: 266–7, 269).[12]

Returning to the two great problems of ancient philosophy, what we get in both Plato and Aristotle is an understanding of knowledge as pertaining to universals and particulars ('the one and the many'), and this substitutes for *and blocks* the investigation of the structured grounds of things ('the one and the other').

What is needed to avoid the problems of particulars and their universality (of matter and its forms) in Aristotle, says Bhaskar, is a concept of the 'multi-tiered stratification of being, or ontological depth' – that is, 'grounds for the universal distinct from the universal concerned and other than its instances' (PE: 5). Aristotle lacks 'a non-homological[13] account of ontological stratification, [and] must [therefore] supplement induction by *nous* or intellectual intuition' (ibid.), and an account of formal cause. In his own time, he helps constitute, and is then stuck on, the Platonic–Aristotelian fault-line. Looking forward, he is caught in an 'epistemological squeeze or vice between Plato and Hume' (PE: 183). Why Plato and Hume? The Aristotelian problem of identifying universals later 'morphs' into the problem of induction, resting on the fact that the 'grounds for a universal principle are restricted to its instances' (PE: 4), and this may always be denied by a modern sceptic. In a different intellectual context, the problem of universals assumes a different form. For Hume, of course, the problem of induction and universal laws is central, hence the vice he constitutes with Plato.

In this way, Aristotle's account complements rather than replaces Plato's, so that the two establish a flawed basis for the western philosophical tradition:

> Early (and sometimes all) western philosophy is sometimes presented as if it were a case of Plato or Aristotle. Here I am suggesting we are dealing with a case of the tacit complicity of opposites (or dialectical counterparts) grounded in a common mistaken problematic (defined by Parmenidean monovalence, Parmenidean/Platonic epistemic fallacy and the Platonic/Aristotelian fault-line or primal squeeze) . . . that is, Platonism and Aristotelianism as necessary conditions of each other. . . . [It] is at best misleading to counterpose the two as idealist and materialist. Instead what one has . . . is the dialectical connection of opposites . . . which helps explain the aporeticity or . . . the constitutive problematicity, of philosophy.
>
> (PE: 185)

It is important to understand what this does not mean. Bhaskar is not saying that Plato and Aristotle are in any sense identical in their philosophies, but rather that, for all their difference, they share a common ground, and this structures the different, indeed conflicting, directions their thought takes. Aristotle's reaction against Platonism takes him into the material world, but he is unable to understand the things that he finds there (movement, change, inner potentiality, its realisation) in terms of a natural necessity in the materiality of material things. Against such an approach, he favours a formal, universal, mindful, and therefore hypothetical, necessity which reveals his debt to Plato. Accordingly, if Aristotle's most fruitful discoveries are to be maintained and defended, it is necessary to recast his metaphysics in terms that would theorise natural necessity. If we do not do so, these elements will not be properly located in the real materiality of things, and will flounder in the face of sceptical attack.

In this and the previous section, we have witnessed western philosophy's early turning away from an understanding of real change in the world. Understood (or at least 'place-marked') in early Greek thought as the ontological question of 'the one and the other', the Platonic finesse of real absence and change as difference was controlled by ideal universals (generating the problem of 'the one and the many'). This problematic then became the basis for Aristotle's half-cocked effort to understand change in a material world. Because he did not escape Plato, we have an initial basis for affirming Whitehead's claim that western philosophy represents a series of footnotes to his philosophy. In the following section, we will pursue the claim further. Before doing so, however, we should, in the light of the confusion outlined at the beginning of this chapter, return to Bhaskar's own argument and consider just what the primordial failing of western philosophy turns out to be.

The primordial failing revisited: a compound fracture

If we now return to the two underlying category errors that generate the problems of 'the one and the other' and 'the one and the many' in Greek philosophy, we can consider how they relate to each other. Which one, the epistemic fallacy or ontological monovalence, is 'the primordial mistake of philosophy' – or is it a matter of their combination? In his fullest consideration of the matter (DPF: 355–7), Bhaskar suggests that we can look at the matter in two ways. Either we can see the question in terms of how the epistemic fallacy structures things, or we can see ontological monovalence as the underlying driving force. The latter approach, he suggests, is the more 'elegant' (DPF: 357), but he outlines in greater detail the former. This, however, only makes clear the primary importance of ontological monovalence. Ontological monovalence is, after all, the key Parmenidean starting point, and though it can be said to entail, and to anticipate, the epistemic fallacy, this is the secondary aspect in his philosophy, where ontology prevails. Epistemic fallacy becomes the primary aspect only in the Platonic–Aristotelian philosophies of the Idea, form and *nous*, and only once ontological monovalence has been asserted, and absence and change finessed. At that point, the epistemic fallacy can play its full part in setting up the western philosophical problematic as constituted by a variety of subject–object identity theories.

Let us look at Bhaskar's argument favouring primacy of the epistemic fallacy. If we start with it, we can note that it underlies subject–object identity theory and that it stipulates that knowledge is a surrogate for being. This is 'the single defining characteristic of the irrealist tradition' (DPF: 355), and it stems, he says, from Parmenidean monism. In a monist world, knowledge is, as part of the whole, complete and self-sufficient unto itself. Identity between subject and object and their co-constitution is assured in a world that is One. This argument, linking the epistemic fallacy to Parmenides, has substance, but the core Parmenidean argument concerns not the oneness of knowledge and being, but more simply the oneness of being per se, and accordingly the lack of absence. The barring of absence can, of course, be backed up by the (wrong) epistemological argument that if we cannot know a thing, it cannot exist (a form of the epistemic fallacy), but the first Parmenidean claim is the ontological one that not-being cannot exist in a complete world. When Bhaskar argues that 'it is the epistemic fallacy that necessitates the doctrine of ontological monovalence, on this way of looking at things' (ibid.), this gets it round the wrong way in terms of the structuring of the problematic. In Parmenides, it is the ontology of being, not the epistemology of knowing, that drives the argument forward.

This leads us to the role of ontological actualism, which is linked to the denial of absence. Bhaskar notes that the 'absence of the concept of absence . . . necessitates actualism which . . . reduces the possible . . . and the necessary . . . to the actual and accounts for the 'primal squeeze' and the third great absence, of *alethic truth*, in the unholy trinity' (ibid.).[14] This focus on the link between absence and ontological actualism is just right, for what leads to the onset of actualism is not the epistemic fallacy per se, but the *prior denial of absence* in ontological monovalence. The denial of absence immediately entails actualism, because a world that is complete, self-sufficient and self-present, at one with itself, will be one that simply exists in its actuality. All that there is is there, so that 'what you see is what you get', that and no more. A world without absence is one of pure presence and completeness: ontological monovalence begets ontological actualism. At the same time, an actualist world is one in which the possibility of development through natural necessity in things does not arise, for there is no depth and no emergence or change out of depth. Actualism is thus initiated by a purely positive account of reality, and this leads to a vision of the world that excludes natural necessity. This then leads, in a world where change is to be explained, to the need for supporting epistemic criteria to provide a necessity that has otherwise been denied: enter Aristotle. The logical order is thus: (a) denying absence in ontological monovalence leads to (b) ontological actualism, which *then* leads to (c) the epistemic fallacy in a Tina buttressing movement.

Against this, Bhaskar suggests that, if we assume the explanatory primacy of the epistemic fallacy, this does not undermine his earlier argument for the conceptual primacy of absence.[15] Absence remains 'implicit in every act of referential detachment and explicit in any act at all, including the primordial Eleatic statement of monism (a tradition-creating act) just as it is implicit in the coming into being of the monist itself' (DPF: 356). Yet if the epistemic fallacy is the primordial failure of western philosophy, this does somewhat undermine the role of absence, for it focuses us on the Platonic–Aristotelian fault-line, and away from the Parmenidean–Platonic debate over absence. It detracts too from the sense that the dialectical turn in critical realism adds something radically new, for the epistemic fallacy has always been central to critical realism, while it is the argument about absence and ontological monovalence that provides the novelty of the Bhaskarian dialectic. Hence, seeing ontological monovalence as the primary, initiating move in the western philosophical tradition seems right and, from the point of view of dialectical critical realism, appropriate. A purely positive world of surface is one in which empirical difference in phenomena exists, but its actualism frustrates the search for both universals and explanations in the problematic constituted by Plato and Aristotle. It also leads, ultimately, to the problems of modern philosophy crystallised in the philosophy of Hume and beyond. Thus, it is ontological monovalence, the denial of absence, that induces a positive, actualist ontology, invokes the problem of universals and difference, and induces the co-constitutive role of epistemology in the initiation of subject–object identity theory.

This is not, however, an argument for the simple primacy of ontological monovalence as the primordial failing of western philosophy. The best under-standing of this formative period is one that sees the journey from Parmenides to Plato, and then from Plato to Aristotle, as one in which two problems overlie and compound each other. The problem of 'the one and the many' is given a special status in the tradition just because it arises on the basis of a partial interrogation and resulting marginalisation of the problem of 'the one and the other'. The problem of difference and universality becomes *the* problem precisely because it is given its special position by the previous effort to 'resolve' (really deny) the problem of absence and change. So, there is a double and serial knot here: the suppression of change (Parmenides), and its reinterpretation as difference (Plato), giving rise to the problems of universals as a two-worlds theory entraining subject–object identity theory through both Platonic idealism and Aristotelian hylomorphism. Something of this knotted quality is present in Bhaskar's account when he notes that the really important point is to see that there 'are two mutually reinforcing category mistakes' at play. What we have is a cumulative problem, a compound fracture, whose overlaid logic tracks the historical development from Parmenides to Plato, and then from Plato to Aristotle, and which establishes the 'primordial failing' of western philosophy.

Plato to Hume: the rationalist-empiricist vice

In this section, I sketch the argument that the Platonic–Aristotelian fault-line was indeed fateful for western philosophy, providing the basic driving force for its modern development. There is no space to consider the moderns in the same way as we have examined the ancients, so I will only indicate the overall argument here. Early in *Dialectic*, Bhaskar describes Aristotle as 'already caught in a vice between Plato and Hume – a vice that was to determine the subsequent trajectory of western philosophy' (DPF: 16). He describes the two sides of the vice as formed by (ancient) rationalist epistemology and (modern) empiricist ontology, with the ultimate predominance of the latter under modern social conditions. The result is that irrealism rules:

> [I]rrealism has been historically determined by rationalist epistemological criteria, which were subjectivised and inwardised by Descartes, to lay the way open for the structural domination of solipsistic empiricist ontology, essentially laid down by Hume, but involuted and modified by Kant.

> (DPF: 383)

The historical development *within irrealism* is from rationalist epistemology to empiricist ontology. How does this happen? We have already seen how ontological monovalence in the Parmenidean–Platonic analysis of not-being and difference generates ontological actualism, which, ignoring ontological depth and natural necessity, provides an inadequate basis for the establishment of universals in both Plato and the Aristotelian reversal of Platonic two-world theory. Aristotle's resulting theory of knowledge lacks a proper ontological basis for the grasp of things, and therefore invokes 'eidetic-kinetic' conceptions of form and *nous* to complete itself. This then 'sets the scene for the generation of a new transcendent', a move that will be repeated throughout subsequent philosophy, most usually in the form of 'God or social convention' (DPF: 355). Because irrealism lacks an adequate grasp of ontology, it compensates by resorting to epistemology. In the predominant form of subject–object identity theory (a generic approach to philosophy, open to many variations on its central theme), the knowing or rational subject is called upon to do work it cannot do. Truth lies in the objective world, which knowledge contingently accesses, not the subjective world, where knowing comes illicitly to ground the world it knows. This is the realm of the epistemic fallacy and the constitution of guaranteed knowledge foundations by a false fusion of knowledge and being.

While Aristotelian *nous* 'cannot do the job' that Bhaskar has 'tailored *alethia* to do' (DPF: 355), it marks the point in western philosophy at which philosophy becomes prone to various aporiai concerning taxonomic and explanatory knowledge. The 'best known of [these] are the problems of universals and induction, to which Aristotelian *nous*, Christian faith, Cartesian certainty, Humean custom, Kantian synthetic a priori, Fichtean intellectual intuition, Hegelian autogenetics . . . or Strawsonian dissolution cannot provide an answer' (DPF: 309–10). Once real determinate absence with its link to change has been sequestered, and subject–object identity theory ensconced on the throne, philosophy must 'inevitably lead to the generation of a new transcendent' (ibid.) in the absence of a concept of ontological stratification. Actualist ontology fails to grasp 'the transfactuality of relatively enduring causal structures and generative mechanisms in open systems' (ibid.). It is the consequent 'elimination of . . . natural necessity – if only as a place holder for an eventual alethic realism' that constitutes the 'original fault-line, around which the irrealist tradition has played' (DPF: 309).

Thus, 'the fault-line' and 'the vice' centre on irrealism's demand for knowledge as a foundation for being in compensation for the 'primal squeeze' on natural necessity, and it is fateful for the tradition. In terms of modern philosophy, can some meat be put on the bones of this claim? Bhaskar begins with Descartes, for modern philosophy 'starts with the Cartesian ego' (DPF: 329) and the rationalist demand to find grounds for the incorrigibility of the new mathematical science. Descartes's quest, as with the Greeks, was to find foundational criteria for knowledge, but his approach was to seek such foundations not in Forms or *nous* but in the human ego. This move decisively foregrounds epistemology, insisting that 'the question of our access to reality takes definitive precedence over – and indeed determines – the question of the nature of reality' (PE: 185). Descartes thereby 'sets the cast of the representationalist view of knowledge' (ibid.) and so establishes the paradigm subsequently taken up by other philosophers. He first asks the question 'how do I know?' and 'assumes that the only way to answer the question is to begin from the immediate data of consciousness' (ibid.), but in so doing he only manages to sow 'the seeds for the scepticism, subjective idealism, classical empiricism and solipsism to come' (ibid.). The irony of Descartes's philosophy is that a man dedicated to defending rationalist criteria for knowledge ends up exposing that knowledge to the radical scepticism of a Hume, for 'Cartesian premises lead to Humean conclusions' (PE: 190), with Hume drawing out 'the subjective idealist implications of the Cartesian turn' (PE: 191). Descartes's pivotal role in western philosophy is to take rationalist criteria for knowledge and, by inwardising and subjectivising them, to ensure the eventual triumph (the 'structural domination') of empiricism. Cartesian doubt 'opened the way for Lockian scepticism about essences, Berkeleian scepticism about matter and Humean scepticism about everything' (PE: 190).

Moving to Hume, we move to an extraordinary figure on the intellectual stage, one whose 'interpretive antinomies are at least as remarkable as Hegel's' (DPF: 360). Bhaskar depicts his thought as a revolving turntable on which those who seek 'will locate a multiplicity of philosophical options' (PE: 193). While Bhaskar identifies as many as seven potential options from Hume, three will concern us. These are, first, that Hume is the 'arch-positivist, providing the hard-core of most significant subsequent philosophy – from Kant, Hegel, Nietzsche to postmodernism, from Mill and Mach to Russell and both Wittgensteins, to Dummett, Davidson, Rorty and Quine' (DPF: 359). What grounds this tradition (or traditions) is the acceptance of empirical realism, ontological actualism and a reductionist analysis of laws as constant conjunctions of events. Second, Hume is the 'all purpose sceptic, inimitably exemplifying the aporetic-dogmatic character' of modern philosophy, and waking Kant from his 'dogmatic slumbers' (DPF: 360). Yet it should be noted that this arch-sceptic, on the basis of actualist ontology and empiricist epistemology, is also, third, a 'fideist' who stands by common sense and convention. This aporetic compensatory stance is necessitated by the ontology and epistemology that he both accepts and, in his scepticism, attacks.[16]

Hume sets the sceptical challenge to Kant, which Kant accepts while retaining terms that remain Hume's. Kant accepts Hume's empirical realism and ontological actualism in his account of causal laws as entailing the constant conjunction of events plus a subjective contribution of mind. But in order to sustain the concepts of the necessity and universality of laws, what should be understood as an *ontological* structure generating actual events becomes involuted into an *epistemological* form, the transcendental subjectivity of mind. Kant argues that 'an objective manifold is a condition of the possibility of the subjective transcendental unity of apperception which reciprocally allows us to synthesise the empirical manifold presented by a world unknowable-in-itself' (DPF: 335). But from this transcendental idealist position there then ensues 'a radical de-ontologisation of the world which is the price Kant pays for resurrecting structure within a fundamentally Cartesian model of man' (PE: 204). The synthetic a priori leaves the 'thing in itself' (the place marker, in Bhaskar's terms, for natural necessity as the alethic truth of the real) inaccessible. Kant's marriage of transcendental idealism and empirical realism de-ontologises reality and engenders the split between the noumenal and the phenomenal in Kantian philosophy. The noumenal, sponsoring the thing in itself, must both be posited and be unknowable as the effect of a radical subjectivisation of knowledge and de-ontologisation of being. This is the outcome on the terrain of German idealism of Cartesian doubt and Humean scepticism, both of which are founded on the prior denegation of ontology on the Platonic–Aristotelian fault-line.

As for morality, Kant's noumenal/phenomenal split is also significant, in that it establishes an unbridgeable gulf between a morality established by and for rational beings and that engaged in by actually existing human beings:

> Morality loses its agent-directing power. We are each, because of the systematic interconnection of the world . . . individually responsible for everything that has ever happened and will ever happen in virtue of a primordial choice made in the noumenal realm . . . prior to our birth and outside time. There is no ground here for the assignment of elected, legal responsibility (which depends upon the imputation of causal responsibility) for any particular act and hence no ground for sanction or punishment for, say, an individual act of theft.
>
> (PE: 205)

Indeed, as regards punishment, Kant ends up with his own two-worlds theory based around the noumenal and the phaenomenal spheres of life.[17] Such a position truly exemplifies the alienation of Unhappy Consciousness in modern philosophy. These are problems for Kant, but they result from his place in the trajectory of philosophy from Plato and Aristotle to the moderns. The ontological actualism and empirical realism he inherited from Hume necessitate the subjective idealism he deploys as a means of grounding and guaranteeing knowledge, even if it can only proceed by producing the antinomies that render it unsatisfactory. Nor do the problems of irrealism stop with Kant, though now I can only indicate the overall argument. While Kant involuted structure to produce the melancholic impotence that is transcendental subjectivity and the synthetic a priori, Hegel historicised the issue while still insisting on an idealist solution to the problems of actualist ontology. He produces in the process another version of subject–object identity theory that also generates its own splits and dualisms (PE: 206–9; see Chapter 3 above). And the problems continue as the tradition wends its way to the present:

> Nietzsche deconstructed knowledge but left Humean ontology intact. The late Wittgenstein could only duplicate the problem of induction but to the question of how we know the rules of the language game we are playing . . . , he could give only a fideist-conventionalist response. When the crises of twentieth-century thought and life struck home, philosophy could only follow the transmutation route from the absolute foundationalism of logical positivism through conventionalism, pragmatism and a variety of other positions to the overt irrationalism and judgemental relativism which is the inexorable outcome of its primordial quest.
>
> (DPF: 359)

That 'primordial quest', as we have seen, has its roots in how Plato corrected Parmenides, and Aristotle pursued the quest for an understanding of the possibility of scientific knowledge. Underlying the whole trajectory of philosophy is the problem of ontological actualism as the outcome of ontological monovalence. Actualism effaces the determinate non-being observed in change and causation. With that, it occludes the causal powers of natural kinds and the structure and depth that constitute the natural and social worlds. This leads it to generate the epistemic fallacy in a range of subject–object identity theories. It should be noted that this is not a reductionist thesis, for the resort to epistemology varies significantly from Parmenidean monism to Platonic eidism and Aristotelian hylomorphism among the ancients, and from Cartesian rationalism to Humean positivism, Kantian transcendental idealism and Hegelian phenomenology and absolute idealism among the moderns (DPF: 399). Similarly, actualism may take a variety of forms including the Humean theory of causal laws as constant conjunctions, the 'reduction of the real, necessary and possible' to 'the manifest, evident or apparent' in Hegel, and the maintenance of 'the eternal [as] universal-and-necessarily-certain' (DPF: 234) characteristic of Aristotle. More generally, it involves the 'reduction of structures and generative mechanisms to events or states of affairs, of change to difference, and difference to generality', and this indicates an overall line 'between the Parmenidean one, Platonic mind–body dualism and the analysis of negation in terms of difference . . . , the subsumption of difference under generality, Cartesian mind–body dualism and deductivism and the Kantian split between the noumenal and phenomenal realms' (PE: 205).

The fate of philosophy is *mutatis mutandis* linked generally to its failure to think real absence in the world. Reversing the damage done requires a double move. First, original critical (transcendental) realism is needed to make sense of ontological structure and depth and to accommodate epistemic relativity (in the transitive dimension) with ontological realism (in the intransitive dimension), while holding onto an overall judgemental rationality. Second, we need 'dialectical critical realism to place absence and absenting at the heart of a non-monovalent ontology, and so avoid the detotalisations and reifications that would otherwise result' (DPF: 310). One example of detotalisation and reification is the existence of the kinds of splits and antinomies in philosophy we have tracked in this section. In the final section, I consider how another critical philosophy, Derridean deconstruction, deals with such matters, and in the process consider how it relates to the analysis of this chapter.

Metacritique and poststructural philosophy

Postmodern or poststructural philosophy[18] presents an interesting challenge to critical realists. For some it is an unproductive diversion; for others, its contribution to philosophy must be recognised and understood. Andrew Sayer, for example, while generally negative about postmodern thinking, recognises that it reveals 'the ways in which binary distinctions or dualisms typically obscure connections, hierarchy and differences' (2000: 6). Binary distinctions and dualisms within connected hierarchies reflect the same kinds of concerns expressed by Bhaskar in his idea of detotalising splits, discussed here and in Chapter 4. That postmodern thinking should cover similar ground to dialectical critical realism, and produce such ambivalent reactions among critical realists, makes it an important object for study and engagement from a critical realist point of view. For me, it is the dialectical turn in critical realism that provides the most effective engagement with it. In this section, the example of such thinking is from Derrida, and here I compare and contrast Bhaskar's metacritique (involving both meta-critique$_1$ and metacritique$_2$) with deconstruction. I will show what they have in common and then indicate how Derrida's focus on radical difference locates him metacritically$_1$ in the western philosophical tradition as an anti-Platonist on the terrain of Plato and thereby limits his critical potential in terms of both a metacritique$_1$ and a metacritique$_2$.

Metacritiques$_1$ and $_2$

To set up the comparison between deconstruction and dialectical critical realism, I begin by recalling the relationship between the two forms of metacritique in Bhaskar's philosophy. Despite references to Tina thinking and the Unhappy Consciousness, our analysis in this chapter so far has focused on a philosophical critique of western philosophy, and has remained essentially at the level of metacritique$_1$. We have been primarily concerned with philosophical engagement with the truth of things, summarised in the formulation of philosophy's overall problematic as one of 'explicit idealism and implicit realism' (DPF: 308). We have not reflected especially on the relationship between philosophical problems and underlying social relations as in a metacritique$_2$. Yet we saw in Chapter 2 that Bhaskar is concerned with how structured power, or power$_2$, relations inform thought, and we saw in Chapter 4 how this relates to the idea of the Tina formation in the context of totality.[19] If we have looked mainly at the 'intrinsic', metacritical$_1$ problems in western, especially Greek, philosophy, it is important to acknowledge also the 'extrinsic' aspect provided by metacritique$_2$, which stems from the sense of philosophy being constellated in and with the emergence of social and historical relations. We can do this once we recall that the discovery of the importance of absence and its denial in the philosophical tradition takes us in two directions. Metacritically$_1$, it takes us into systematic error in the tradition, while, meta-critically$_2$, it takes us through the MELD schema (where 2E negativity leads to 3L totality with its concepts of the dual and the constellation) to a grasp of how thought is historically embedded in a social totality. Thus, the metacritical$_1$ problems of ontological actualism, the epistemic fallacy and subject–object identity theory resulting from ontological monovalence are metacritically$_2$ related to the role of philosophy in reflecting and informing power$_2$ relations. Philosophical problems must be related to how philosophy is historically embedded in a world where absence as the prospect of substantial social change is always present, yet denied. This is philosophy's hidden secret, its repressed other, which always returns, among other things, as the problems of philosophy itself.

For Bhaskar, something is fundamentally amiss with philosophy. There is something mysterious in the way that the problems it generates – for example, those grouped around Humean scepticism – seem to have nothing to say to a common-sense understanding of the world. Hume himself contrasted the sceptical products of his philosophical reflection with the experience of the world he enjoyed with his backgammon-playing friends. For all that we are said not to be able to prove that a law of gravity exists, we tend to leave the building by the ground-floor exit in preference to the second-floor window. There is something artificial and unserious in the sense that philosophical problems are ultimately unresolvable, rather than possessing 'real, multiple and possibly contradictory geo-historical grounds and conditions' (DPF: 315). There is also something unsatisfactory, and in Bhaskar's term detotalising, in seeing the problems of philosophy as matters for a distinct discipline sequestered within the walls of the academy, away from worldly activity. The idea of a 'professional philosopher' designates a lack. Bhaskar's broader point is that philosophy has entrapped itself metacritically$_1$ in unserious positions because it works, metacritically$_2$, against the backdrop of underlying exploitative social relations that it would wish to deny, evade or even overcome, and yet, despite itself, unconsciously expresses. The ivory towers of the academy enclose philosophy just because its scepticism and stoicism render it, in the Hegelian term, a citadel for the Unhappy Consciousness.[20] *Pace* Hegel, however, these are not stages in a quasi-historical rational process, but real, historical, power$_2$-inflected philosophical positions.

How did philosophy get here? While it seems the least power invested and the most abstract of disciplines, philosophy is nonetheless imbricated in power$_2$ relations that appear distinct from its operations, but are not. Just as the Parmenidean, Platonic and Aristotelian shifts in Greek philosophy articulate underlying contexts and structures of aristocratic domination, which dispose it to deny the real grounds of absence and change, so too does modern philosophy reflect changing structures of power. The ultimate success of a Hume-inspired scepticism, based on ontological actualism and empirical realism, reflects a world in which the exchange of commodities between seemingly free subjects results in the domination of commodification and its ensuing modes of alienation. It is these that are reflected in stoicism, scepticism and Unhappy Consciousness more generally. Such observations help us see metacritique as the constellational layering of philosophy in a social totality, so that the problems of the historical world are articulated in abstract thought. Philosophy is constellationally embedded in a particular geo-historical world, and this shapes it, just as it contributes to the ongoing relations of that world. Generalised master–slave-type, power$_2$, relations, expressed *mutatis mutandis* in specific historical forms, work through philosophical concepts to give them their shape and quality. They do so non-reductively, across specifically philosophical territory, in a language that is characteristically philosophy's own, and varying according to specific contexts.

Thus, the Greek 'solution' to ontological monovalence is not the same as that provided by the moderns, though both negotiate the same problem field. Both articulate a specifically philosophical problem in the context of the broad and specific socio-historical characteristics of a period. Accordingly, if 'it is as a problem of opposites – mind and body, reason and cause, the forms and the flux, universals and particulars, social [versus] natural science, hermeneutics [versus] positivism, analytic and synthetic – that the problems of philosophy are most typically posed' (DPF: 320), the detotalising problem of splits in and across different historical periods, then behind the back of these problems is the changing world that produces them. From Parmenides onwards, there is a 'preoccupation with the archetypal problem of opposites', and this 'is a natural symptom of a class and multiple power$_2$ relationally divided world' (ibid.). Once again, just how those opposites manifest themselves depends in one part on the specifics of geo-history, in another on how those specifics are mediated by the philosophical tradition of which they are a part. And, it must be recalled, this all takes place against the backdrop of the reality principle, philosophy's efforts to articulate, however inadequately, truths about the world. Why it proves inadequate is examined metacritically$_1$ as philosophy's failings and metacritically$_2$ in terms of the power$_2$ contexts that predispose it to fail. If that is how dialectical critical realism's metacritique handles split, how does deconstruction relate to it?

Dialectic, deconstruction and Platonism

Bhaskar's starting point is that there is common ground between deconstruction and dialectical critical realism in that deconstruction can be viewed, at first sight surprisingly, as a form of dialectical critique. However, it is limited in that it blocks the connection of philosophy to a world of real material change by screening discussion of absence and geo-history in favour of the philosophical practice of erasure. Because it lacks an understanding of absence as change, it has no meta-critique$_2$ and remains stuck at the level of absence as difference. It cannot align the critique of difference with the underlying level of absence as change. Its terrain, in terms of our 'two great problems of philosophy', is that of 'the one and the many', and it fails to see the real ontological problematic of 'the one and the other'. Its critique is insufficient to get to the deeper problem. On the terrain of 'the one and the many', to be sure, deconstruction has a novel role, essentially taking the side of 'the many' against 'the one'. Its championing of difference involves a reversal of Plato's dialectic (where the one governs the many), so it is anti-Platonic, but anti-Platonic *on the terrain of Plato*. There is no grasp of real absence, no understanding of change, and therefore no possibility of a metacritical$_2$ level to deconstruction. It does not reach down below difference to the layer of change and 'tensed rhythmic process' (DPF: 320) in the world, to that level marked as the terrain of 'the one and the other'. Without it, deconstruction must itself be subject to metacritique$_2$. In Derrida's engagement with Marx, he writes that Marx's critique of capital's spectrality is 'classical, traditional (dare I add 'Platonic'?)' (Derrida 1999: 258). Dialectical critical realism turns the question back on Derrida. Is there not an element of Platonism, albeit against Plato, in deconstruction's singular attention to difference as the basis for diagnosis of the aporias (splits) in philosophy?

Bhaskar nowhere develops a sustained discussion of deconstruction, yet we can build a picture from several comments scattered across his work. In deconstruction, 'philosophy . . . is seen as characterised by hierarchised pairs in which the privileged term is shown to be constituted by what it suppresses, marginalises or excludes, which will later return to haunt it. Inversion, chiasmus and erasure are the features of this method' (PE: 199). This relation of constitution and suppression gives rise to the claim that deconstruction can be linked to dialectical critique. Risking only the charge of 'anachronism', Bhaskar interprets Derrida as a 'dialectical commentator' (DPF: 146). Dialectical comments identify the 'common grounds . . . of apparently opposed but mutually complicit dialectical counterparts' (DPF: 11), and this process of analysing concepts for sameness and difference is consonant with deconstruction. Derrida's account, for example, of undecidability exhibits the basic form of a dialectical opposition ((e) and (-e)) without the prospect of an *Aufhebung* (DPF: 31; see also Norrie 2005a: 141–6). Similarly, his concept of 'supplementarity', in which an additional element is invoked to support a claim but then proceeds to undermine it, displays the kind of internal connection and contradiction typical of dialectical thought. Supplementarity can be invoked as one mode of dialectical argument that is possible after dialectic's materialist diffraction, when the dialectical armoury has been expanded beyond Hegel's rather limited selection of weapons.

To some, it may seem strange to align Derrida with Hegel, of whom Derrida is a critic. Yet Derrida's own position is ambivalent. While deconstruction targets 'the limit, the interruption, the destruction of the Hegelian *relève wherever* it operates' (Derrida, cited in Barnett 1998: 26), Hegel is also, for Derrida, 'the thinker of irreducible *différance*' (Derrida 1997: 26). As Gayatri Chakravorty Spivak notes, Derrida is 'at once inside and outside a certain Hegelian . . . tradition' (Derrida 1997: xviii).[21] For Bhaskar, with his expanded account of dialectic, there is ample room for a dialectical critique of Hegelian dialectic, and it is in that spirit that he sees Derrida's deconstruction of Hegel as dialectical, or at least quasi-dialectical (DPF: 96). He also compares his own account of the Tina formation, with its account of the buttressing of competing ideas in compromise formations, to deconstruction (DPF: 118).

However, this is only one side of the picture, for Bhaskar criticises the irrealism of deconstruction. The claim that 'there is nothing outside the text' is unsustainable and entails performative contradiction. After all, Derrida's own text 'is materially inscribed and causally conditioned writing (in the media of pen, computer and microcassette), replicated, published and discussed by jet-flying, video-watching, hamburger-eating, defecating human beings' (DPF: 15). Ontologically, Derrida has 'an unfortunate tendency to elide the [real] referent' (PE: 199), and his general lack of a concept of referential detachment means that he 'cannot maintain the coherence of textual deconstruction' (PE: 217). Derrida 'obviously intends to be read, and so communicate, which presupposes a necessary minimum quotient of logocentricity', so he is 'guilty of self-referential paradox' (DPF: 147). Recalling the Hegelian figures grouped around the master–slave dialectic, he suggests that there is a 'stoic indifference to reality' in social constructionist philosophy generally which gives rise 'to a post-structuralist collapse to scepticism' and the kind of duplicity seen in the 'unhappy consciousness of a pragmatist like Rorty, who considers that there is a reality . . . but forbids us to talk about it' (DPF: 213).[22] While Derrida's practice of inverting the priorities given to one element in a pair reveals a 'welcome disrespect for tradition' (DPF: 250), and alerts philosophy to the 'phenomenality of diversity and change', his practice of submitting inverted pairs to erasure is not a solution to philosophical problems (ibid.). He also has a tendency 'to neglect the material and cultural structures whence texts derive their meaning' (PE: 200), linked to his 'irrealist, unstratified, actualist . . . ontology – and in particular an insufficiently stratified and distanciated concept of the self and space-time' (DPF: 148).

Deconstruction and the two metacritiques

The question raised by these criticisms concerns how they relate to the Platonic prioritisation of the problem of 'the one and the many' over that of 'the one and the other'. To answer it, I will focus on the method of erasure, the tendency in Derrida to neglect material and cultural structures, and the consequence in terms of an understanding of justice. According to Spivak, erasure involves 'the mark of the absence of a presence, an always already absent present, of the lack at the origin that is the condition of thought and experience' (Derrida 1997: xvii). For Bhaskar, it 'begins with Nietzschean negligence, traverses Heideggerian being and can only end in writing itself out by erasure' (DPF: 147). The paradigm of writing under erasure is Nietzsche's 'theses of the necessity and impossibility of knowledge, requiring an active forgetting of the illusory character of truth' (DPF: 148) in a world of radical difference and flux. If truth's illusion must be forgotten so that it may be acted on, then any truth claim is always already subject to an accompanying negation, which erases it. Against this, Bhaskar argues for substance in truth in the form of 'non-arbitrary dialectical interconnection' (ibid.), for there is a sense in which 'what is necessary is not what is untenable' (ibid.). There is a level in science, experience, signification, in short in the forms through which humans live in the world, that cannot be erased in favour of radical difference, even if the world involves falsehood and the non-necessary. Not everything can be deconstructed by erasure. What *are* untenable are those metaphysical conceptions of science and being 'on which the Nietzschean tradition imposes a quite appropriate dialectical comment' (ibid.), but there is otherwise something exaggerated about the claims of deconstruction. Placed in the context of something like a realist understanding of human being in a power$_2$-structured world, deconstruction offers valid critical concepts to diagnose the hidden workings and pretensions of power, and the philosophical and other antinomies these generate. Left to itself, however, it overstates its case and misses a large part of the point, as concerns structured relations of power.

Deconstruction's reliance on erasure and radical difference is coupled with neglect of the material structures that give human being its particular historical forms, values and problems. Bhaskar suggests that Derrida's later work on Marx shows him attending more to the effect of structures on philosophy (PE: 200), but Derrida insists there on a mode of philosophical analysis that trumps Marx by virtue of radical difference. We have already seen his suggestion of a certain representational 'Platonism' in Marx. Deconstruction goes beyond this to

> a universal structure of experience . . . : it refers in every here-now, to the coming of an eminently real, concrete event, that is to the most irreducibly heterogeneous otherness. Nothing is more 'realistic' or 'immediate' than this messianic apprehension, straining forward toward the event of him who/that which is coming.
>
> (Derrida 1999: 249)

Now, Bhaskar himself supports the idea of irreducible difference (emerging from 1M critical realism) and he invokes Derrida's support for it. Alongside change, there is 'equally a case for a category of difference, . . . established by distinct emergent domains or by sheer alterity or otherness (that is real determinate other-being) . . . without . . . a unitary origin, a case', Bhaskar notes, 'forcibly prosecuted by Derrida' (DPF: 6). But Bhaskar is interested in negativity as both difference and change, whereas Derrida is interested only in the former. In contrast to Bhaskar's account, which would want to grapple with ontology[23] on the terrain of 'the one and the other', where the issue of absence as change is raised, Derrida offers only difference and erasure on the terrain of 'the one and the many'. In consequence, structured power relations are marginalised in his account. A good illustration of this is seen in Derrida's influential essay on law (Derrida 1990), where he describes two critiques of law. The first is 'possible and always useful', though it is marginal to his account. This is 'a critique of juridical ideology, a desedimentation of the superstructures of law that both hide and reflect the economic and political interests of the dominant forms of society' (Derrida 1990: 941). Useful it may be, but Derrida proceeds to put aside this socio-historical critique in favour of his deconstructive pursuit of a 'more intrinsic structure'. This involves the 'very emergence of justice and law' in a 'performative and therefore interpretive violence' (1990: 941). It consists in a '*coup de force*, . . . a performative and therefore interpretive violence'. Such violence is a foundational act and as such is 'neither just nor unjust', neither 'legal nor illegal', having a foundation that is 'mystical' (Derrida, 1990: 941–3). This fundamental *coup de force* gives rise to the problematic of 'Force of Law', which is founded on oppositions between legal justice as regular and calculable, and a deeper sense of justice that goes beyond law, that is singular and incalculable, and that ultimately evades description. At this deeper level, deconstruction of a present legal justice resorts to an 'infinite "idea of justice", infinite because it is irreducible, . . . owed to the other, . . . before any contract . . . , without calculation and without rules, without reason and . . . rationality' (Derrida, 1990: 965). Justice in this sense is the unconditional against, though within, the conditioned, and as such is elusive and ineffable.

   This notion of justice as infinite is important. I think it marks the place of a justice that in Bhaskar's terms would respond to the concrete universality/singularity of each human being in an open and unfinished moral world (cf. Norrie 2005a: 12–14). Yet the concern is that it is presented in a way that marginalises the social and historical dimension in any account of justice, and thereby desituates it. It thereby produces its own split notion of justice, between that which is conditioned and the unconditional. In consequence, it produces an Unhappy Consciousness with regard to justice, since it is impossible to establish any grounds for judgement. What Derrida calls 'the law of the responsible transaction' is, he says, 'the most difficult moment'. Indeed, it 'is more than difficult; it is infinitely distressing. It is night' (Derrida 2002: 56). This melancholic situation of judgemental impotence arises from the forced splitting of the unconditional and the conditioned. It occurs by virtue of Derrida's block on talking about the socio-historical context as the irreducible here-and-now of judgement in which a sense of the ethically universal has to be located.[24] And it results from his basic move to establish the grounds of justice on the Platonic terrain of 'the one and the many', in isolation from the underlying terrain of 'the one and the other'. The problem is that deconstruction does not possess a conception of absence as change, or of the tensed rhythmic process through which change operates, or of the natural and social totality in which change occurs. The problems of philosophy are not properly or fully addressed as those of free-floating, no matter how radical, difference, for the problematic of difference, even in the radicalised anti-Platonic-within-Platonism form provided by Derrida, is already a position established *within philosophy*. The problem of 'the one and the many', whether one takes the side of the one or the many, is a displacement of the underlying problem of 'the one and the other'. Plato's aim was to tame difference in the flux of phenomena through identity in the Forms, so Derrida's reliance on difference places him in opposition to Plato, but in an opposition located on the Parmenidean–Platonic baseline. This is the limit of deconstruction, and it renders it prone to both metacritical$_1$ and metacritical$_2$ comment. The metacritical$_1$ comment concerns the failure to get beyond radicalised Platonism, while the metacritical$_2$ comment concerns how deconstruction blocks or marginalises the question of power$_2$ relations, locating it in the citadel of the Unhappy Consciousness, and rendering it, no doubt against itself, a party to such relations.

Conclusion

The possibility of a metacritique of western philosophy arises only after the Bhaskarian dialectic has been developed to the third level of totality, for it involves 'a *totalising* critique of western philosophy in its various . . . forms' (DPF: 2). It is at the level of 3L totality, building on 2E negativity and 1M non-identity, that it becomes possible to see how a metacritique will contain both metacritical$_1$ and metacritical$_2$ elements, where the former focuses on the 'intrinsic' problems of philosophy elucidated by transcendental and immanent critiques, while the latter considers the 'extrinsic' contexts illuminated by depth-explanatory critique in which they emerge. Of course these two sides to metacritique are not separable 'in practice', for a process of mutual entailment and co-constitution is at work in shaping how philosophy emerges and interacts with its environment. As with our discussion of ethics in Chapter 5, we see here a dialectical relationship between thinking and its context, one that is caught by the idea of a constellational unity of the intrinsic (the philosophical) and the extrinsic (the political or historical) within the political/ historical.[25] At the same time, such a totalising standpoint is possible only on the basis of an understanding of how 2E absence works in relation to 1M real non-identity or difference, and how it grounds the triunity of space, time and causality. It is once we understand that human being is 'thrown' in a world of spatio-temporal causality that we grasp that geo-historical realities condition its forms, including its understanding of that world. The paradox that Bhaskar's account brings out is that the very thing that must lie at the core of an understanding of human being in the world is the very thing that the philosophical tradition denies: real determinate absence. Hence, the discovery of the significance of absence is at the same time a discovery of its denial in the philosophical tradition through the doctrine of ontological monovalence. The latter provides the key to a metacritique$_1$ of ontological monovalence, and, with it, ontological actualism, the epistemic fallacy and subject–object identity theory. At the same time, the spatio-temporality of human being in different geo-historical contexts provides the key to a metacritique$_2$ concerning why the western world has remained so obdurate in its monovalence, while indicating why its obduracy should take the forms it does. For example, rationalist epistemology in ancient Greece initiates the tradition by virtue of aristocratic elitism, while empiricist ontology animates the present under modern conditions of the domination of commodities and capital. Of course, there is nothing very new in making such claims, but what is new is a philosophical system that can organise these claims reflexively within its own terms, within the MELD schema. Meanwhile, holding both ancient and modern together, and explaining the underlying philosophical unities across the periods – ontological monovalence in Parmenides, Plato and Kant, subject–object identity theory in Aristotle, Hume and Hegel – is the totalising concept of generalised master–slave-type relations, which operate *mutatis mutandis* on philosophical analysis.

Bhaskar's account of the Parmenidean–Platonic–Aristotelian core of western philosophy is radical and innovative. His recognition of absence and its denial as the underlying category lost to the development of the tradition stands alongside his account of ontological actualism and epistemic fallacy to enrich our under-standing of the whole. The result is an account of western philosophy's fundamental starting point in a compounded set of problems that saw ontological monovalence generate ontological actualism, which was then fused with epistemic fallacy to produce ancient and modern forms of subject–object identity theory. In the process, the ontological problematic of 'the one and the other' which was central to pre-Socratic philosophy was passed over in favour of the Platonic–Aristotelian problem of 'the one and the many'. Yet it was the former that marked the place where an alternative understanding, under different social and historical conditions, might have emerged. The pre-Socratic interest in how things change into other things represented an early interest in processes of being and becoming blocked by the Parmenidean–Platonic–Aristotelian standpoint, which is resolutely not unblocked by subsequent philosophy. What was needed was a sense of the natural necessity in both natural and social entities, and, of course, human beings are both. Natural necessity points to the structured, deep, caused, spatio-temporal quality of being, and it is that that Bhaskar's own MELD scheme seeks to provide.

In the process, dialectical critical realism is able to shed new light on the alternative postmodern critique of identity by locating it as a radical inversion of Plato on Platonic terrain, and thereby to appreciate both its critical quality ('the many' brought to bear on 'the one') and the limits of its critique (how 'the one' changes into 'another'). A double focus on the problems of absence and change and absence and difference brings us, finally, to the point where we can relate our discussion back to our initial starting point in this book, to the relationship between being and becoming as the key to understanding being in the world. In the next chapter, we shall pursue this discussion by considering how being and becoming operate as a structured unity, as product-in-process and process-in-product, in the context of a deeper engagement with poststructural philosophy.

7 Metacritique II
Dialectic and difference

I have now set out the main elements informing Bhaskar's metacritique of philosophy. In this chapter, I pursue the theme of the final section of the previous chapter, and at the same time bring us back to our initial setting of dialectical critical realism in Chapters 1 and 2. I want to move, in other words, from a consideration of poststructuralist difference to our initial dialectical critical realist understanding of being and becoming.

Why pursue poststructuralism? Bhaskar's *Dialectic* was published in 1993, at a time when postmodern or poststructuralist themes were at their most influential in western philosophy. It has therefore spent the first fifteen years of its life alongside, perhaps in the shadow of, such philosophy. Yet it has always been my conviction that dialectical critical realism had more to offer than postmodernism or poststructuralism. Its opening up of dialectic (its diffraction), its pluralisation and partialisation of totality, its conception of a conflicted ethics (of the ideal and the actual) and its understanding of philosophy as split and aporetic all offer approaches that chime with postmodern concerns. Yet its insistence on the real significance of structure and historicity, its assertion of the possibility of ethical grounds of freedom and ethical development, its argument for the need and possibility for judgemental rationality, and its general grounding of thought and action with regard to 'the reality principle' all provide a way of avoiding the problems of de-historicisation, relativism and irrealism that dog postmodern and poststructuralist thinking. Dialectical critical realism, in short, gives us reasoned grounds for believing in the existence of a human 'pulse of freedom', even in a world in which structured power relations exist and are expressed *inter alia* in philosophy.

These seem to me to be the positive achievements of dialectical critical realism as against postmodern and poststructuralist philosophy, but I think it is possible for philosophical inquiry to go deeper, and, taking further the previous chapter's metacritique, to conduct an engagement between dialectical critical realism and poststructuralist thinking that brings out more fully the roots of both. That is the aim of this chapter, and it leads ultimately to a consideration of how both approaches deal with fundamental issues of ontology, caught in dialectical critical realism as the issue of structured being and becoming, and in poststructuralist thought as the issue of radical difference or non-being as pure becoming. Here my target is the seminal work by Gilles Deleuze, *Difference and Repetition* (1993), a work that, alongside Deleuze's account of Nietzschean philosophy, provides a good basis for grasping the underlying ontological concerns of poststructuralist philosophy. There is a certain intrigue and piquancy here, for a first reading of Deleuze's work picks up some striking similarities between his argument for non-being as difference and becoming, and Bhaskar's argument for non-being as non-identity and becoming in relation to being. Part of my aim accordingly is to clarify the difference between their two approaches. But the underlying point is to ask about the two approaches' basic ontologies, and which one can claim to be the more profound. To bring this issue out, the chapter focuses ultimately on their two readings of the pre-Socratic philosopher Heraclitus, whom both invoke as a Greek precursor of their thought. This operates as a way of elucidating the deepest moves in both philosophies, and comparing and contrasting them.

The chapter has two main sections, one on Deleuze and one on Bhaskar. In the first, I introduce Deleuze's philosophy through elaboration of the opposition he draws between difference and dialectic in his critique of Hegelian negation. I also compare Deleuze's critique of Hegel with that provided by Bhaskar in order to orient a discussion of the two approaches. Thereafter, I elaborate Deleuze's account of difference and trace it back to Nietzsche's account of the Dionysian, identifying the role that flux or radical becoming plays in Nietzsche's, and therefore Deleuze's, ontology. I then show how this account draws on Heraclitus, who becomes the first philosopher of radical difference, what is called 'eternal return' in Nietzsche, a view that is carried forward in Deleuze's philosophy. In the following section, I then compare Deleuze's and Nietzsche's Heraclitus with Bhaskar's in order to bring out a more rounded account of Heraclitan philosophy, in which elements of becoming and flux coexist with accounts of structure and being. In this way, I reinvoke the two questions of Greek philosophy discussed in Chapter 6, that of 'the one and the many' and of 'the one and the other' at the core of the western tradition. This is the route to an ontology of real determinate being in its connection to absence, change and structure, and this takes us back to the early chapters of this book.

Non-being and difference: Deleuze, Nietzsche and Heraclitus

Comparing Bhaskar and Deleuze

One reason for choosing Deleuze's *Difference and Repetition* is that it positively invites comparison and contrast with Bhaskar's dialectical critical realism, and this is where I begin this section. Both share a conviction that the problem at the core of western philosophical thought is one bequeathed to modernity by the ancient Greeks, and by Plato in particular. Both advance critiques of Hegelian dialectic in terms of its reinstatement of positivity through dialectical negation. Both share an understanding that a central issue to be addressed is that of non-being in its relation to being. Both see philosophy as requiring an in-depth analysis of its hitherto existing discontents, and both offer a critique of its development in which critique of identity thinking and of representation are crucial. At the same time, there are important differences between the two on all these issues. Why and how Plato is to be addressed in order to understand the roots of the western tradition differs for Bhaskar and Deleuze. Their critiques of Hegel are similar only at a certain level. The ways they understand ideas of non-being and depth diverge significantly, and this means that they offer different ways of grasping the critique of representation and identity in their philosophies. At heart, there is a large difference between founding critique on difference and founding it on dialectical critical realism, and this chapter's main aim is to explore that difference.

In modern philosophical terms, the difference can be expressed as follows. Bhaskar's philosophy operates by way of a materialist and realist dialectic in which Marx is used for leverage against Hegel, in the context of critical realism's existing ontological commitments. For Bhaskar, Hegelian dialectic must be overcome, but something is retained and, set in a new context, a dialectical critical realist critique of Hegel becomes possible. Marx plays an important role as intellectual midwife in this process. For Deleuze, Hegelian thought also represents a fundamental problem, but the aim is to go beyond *all* dialectic to what appears a more radical philosophical position, one based upon difference. Deleuzean difference derives from a Nietzschean position on radical multiplicity, giving rise to concepts of 'eternal return' and 'will to power'. The stage is set for an encounter between two philosophies, one of which sees a radical reworking of the Hegel–Marx heritage as the way forward, while the other proposes what appears a deeper mode of critique of that heritage on a different, more radical ground. The aim of this chapter is to inquire into the nature of that further ground, and to ask in what its radicalism consists.

These, however, are modern philosophical reference points, and though they are central to Bhaskar and Deleuze, there is a deeper historic layer to both as concerns their relationship to the ancient Greeks. For Deleuze, through Nietzsche, the key philosophical move is a critical inversion of Plato, which reflects the thought of Heraclitus. For Bhaskar, as we saw in Chapter 6, the key move is a critique of Heraclitus's opponent Parmenides and Plato, but there is also space in Bhaskar's account, as we shall see, for a brief positive reference to Heraclitus. For both Bhaskar and Deleuze the key to subsequent developments lies with the Greeks, with Plato as a central figure. That is why Bhaskar entitles one of his books on dialectic after Whitehead's dictum that philosophy represents a series of footnotes to Plato, and perhaps also why Deleuze describes Whitehead's *Process and Reality* (1978), in which the Plato dictum appears, as 'one of the greatest works of modern philosophy' (Deleuze 1993: 284–5). The scene is set, then, for a double, contrasting engagement with Plato and Heraclitus.

While making comparative references to Bhaskar, my aim in this section is to trace the links between Deleuze, Nietzsche and the Greeks. I begin by outlining Deleuze's philosophy, and I do so by taking up his critique of Hegel's account of negation and Plato's account of non-being. The first of these provides a point of contact with dialectical critical realism, for Deleuze, like Bhaskar, critiques Hegel for using the negative in philosophy to reinstate the positive. This then takes us to Plato's account of differentiation in *The Sophist* (1997a), for it is here that Deleuze finds an original position on the negative in philosophy, which he opposes, like

Bhaskar, to an account of non-being. In their joint resort to this text, there is a fascinating parallel between the two philosophers, but only at one level, for I then show how Deleuze's account of non-being is embedded in an analysis of difference and repetition, which brings out the connection to Nietzsche in his thought. Beyond that – and here I distinguish Bhaskar and Deleuze – I argue that Deleuze's anti-Platonism in fact reveals a Platonism in reverse. This involves examining the role of the doctrine of Heraclitan flux in his, in Nietzsche's and also in Plato's philosophy. The discussion thus moves from Deleuze's critique of negation in Hegel to his overturning of negation in Plato in favour of 'simulacra', and then to how his philosophy is grounded in Nietzsche and Platonism in reverse, both under the aegis of Heraclitus as a philosopher of radical flux.

Deleuze's critique of negation: Hegel, Plato and difference

For Deleuze, a central target of his philosophy of difference is Hegel's dialectic and its will to affirm identity via the philosophical practice of negation. Hegelian dialectic understands itself as a radical mode of thinking, but through it, difference, the truly radical element in thought and being, is tamed. We will see what difference means in a moment, but Deleuze's point is that Hegel suppresses it by virtue of what seems the radical element in his thought, the process of dialectical negation. Its role is to control difference in a process whereby it (i.e. difference) 'finds its own concept'. It becomes 'qualitative, synthetic and productive' (Deleuze 1993: 45) as it is domesticated, for identifying contradictions in phenomena is part of the process that transforms them into, on the one hand, the 'effectively real', and, on the other, 'passing or contingent phenomen[a]' (ibid.). Hegelian dialectic marginalises radical difference by differentiating and imposing identity in the process of negation. Radical difference is thereby sanitised by the play of identity, and identity is established through the play of contradiction. Negativity, at the heart of contradiction, *appears* to be a way of opening up the world to difference, but is in fact a form of closure:

> Hegelian contradiction does not deny identity or non-contradiction: on the contrary, it consists in inscribing the double negation of *non*-contradiction within the existent in such a way that identity, under that condition or on that basis, is sufficient to think the existent as such. [Dialectical negations] are logical monsters . . . in the service of identity. . . . Difference is the ground, but only the ground for the demonstration of the identical. Hegel's circle is. . . . only the infinite circulation of the identical by means of negativity.
> (Deleuze 1993: 49–50)

We may pause briefly to note the parallel between Deleuze's account and Bhaskar's, which, it will be recalled from Chapter 3, also identifies in Hegel the affirmation of identity through the dialectical sublation of reason, and the restoration of self-identity and positivity by means of analytic reinstatement. There is common ground here, and Deleuze's critique of Hegelian negation also takes him back to the beginnings of dialectic, to Plato's account of non-being as different, meaning analytically distinct or differentiated,[1] being in *The Sophist*. There, Deleuze argues that Plato presents us with two unacceptable alternatives. Either we accept that there is no non-being, and negation is illusory and ungrounded (the Parmenidean position), or we accept that there is non-being, and this commits us to an acceptance of the negative and negation in being. This, however, establishes the differentiation of things only in terms of what they are and are not, difference in the circle of identity. However, for Deleuze there is a third possibility, and that is to say '*both* that there is non-being *and* that the negative is illusory' (1993: 63). What is he getting at here? For Plato, dialectic proceeds by way of engagement with questions and problems, from which principles emerge, and the principle 'measures the problems as such and distributes the corresponding solutions' (ibid.). For Deleuze, however, problems are not to be understood as mistaken or incomplete forms of knowledge which discovery of a principled ground can resolve. Rather, a problematic structure is part of every object and this relates to the profound nature of 'Being',[2] which through an 'opening', a 'gap' or an ontological 'fold' relates being as *radical difference* to any questions and problems that are superficially manifest. Being ultimately *is* this kind of difference, and what it generates is a sense of non-being in which '*non-being is not the being of the negative*; rather it is the being of the problematic, the being of problem and question' (1993: 64). Difference is not, *pace* Plato (and later Hegel), the negative, but, at a deeper level, that which the negative (alongside the positive) excludes, a more radical sense of non-being.

Pursuing this point, and reflecting the fundamental nature of his claim for radical difference as a deeper sense of non-being beyond negation, Deleuze suggests that 'non-being should rather be written (non)-being or, better still, ?-being' (1993: 64) to denote the fact that the claim of Being (qua radical difference or (non-)being) is 'less a proposition than the interrogation to which the proposition' (ibid.) should respond. Non-being in Deleuze's sense (i.e. (non)-being or ?-being) is the 'differential element in which affirmation, as multiple affirmation, finds the principle of its genesis' (ibid.), while the negative is the superficial 'shadow of the difference' produced alongside the affirmative by the force of multiple affirmation:

> Once we confuse (non)-being with the negative, contradiction is inevitably carried into being; but contradiction is only the appearance or the epiphenomenon, the illusion projected by the problem, the shadow of a question which remains open and of a being which corresponds as such to that question (before it has been given a response). . . . Beyond contradiction, difference – beyond *non*-being, (non)-being; beyond the negative, problems and questions.
>
> (ibid.)

Deleuze's critique of negation in favour of non-being (radical difference qua (non-) or ?-being) thus indicates a deeper ontological level which opposes, yet is connected to, the terrain constituted by negation, identification, differentiation and representation. Deleuze writes of what he calls matters of 'extensity', or quantity, and quality, which he juxtaposes to matters of 'intensity'. Matters of extensity or quantity and quality are tied to identity or representational thinking, the first as giving rise to differences of degree, the second to differences of kind, but differences of degree and kind *both* constitute only surface qualities of difference. Beneath them, and inhabiting them, but habitually unobserved, is the 'entire nature of difference', meaning difference that is intensive, which accesses the radical sense described above. Such difference lies underneath quantity and quality, and it is *only* in its relation to quantity and quality that it appears, more superficially, as 'the negative' in the process of differentiation:

> Difference is not negation. On the contrary, the negative is difference inverted. . . . Difference is inverted, first, by the requirements of representation which subordinate it to identity. Then, by the shadow of 'problems' which give rise to the illusion of the negative. Finally by extensity and quality which cover or explicate intensity. *It is underneath quality and within extensity that Intensity appears upside down*, and that its characteristic difference takes the form of the negative (either of limitation or opposition). The fate of difference is tied to the negative only within extensity and quality, which precisely tend to cancel difference.
>
> (Deleuze 1993: 235)

Finally, driving home the point against Hegelian or Platonic negation and dialectic, where matters of extensity and quality are central, Deleuze argues that wherever we find ourselves 'confronted with qualified oppositions and in an extensity in which these are distributed, we must not count on an *extensive synthesis* which would overcome and resolve them' (ibid.; emphasis added). For Deleuze, Hegelian dialectic is a philosophy of 'extensive synthesis', and his critique of the negative and the synthetic and the falsely restorative possibilities to which they give rise constitutes an argument against Hegel in favour of radical difference. As I have pointed out, there is some similarity here with Bhaskar's account of Hegel as the rationaliser of positivity and the restorer of the analytic moment in thought. Note also the similarity, but also the difference, with Bhaskar's account of Plato. Both Bhaskar and Deleuze note the untenability of the Parmenidean denial of non-being, and both contest Plato's solution in terms of non-being as difference (in the sense of the differentiated in the circle of identity). Deleuze, however, *radicalises difference* on the Platonic terrain of the one and the many to derive a further sense of non-being in terms of radical difference or multiple affirmation. By contrast, Bhaskar argues (see Chapter 7) that the one–many terrain of Plato, which *can* be subjected to a critique by radical difference, is nonetheless only the problematic surface rendition of a deeper problem and denial. This is the problem of the one and the other, and the denial of the real determinate absence it implies. To pursue the differences between the philosophers, however, we need to delve further into Deleuze's thought, its critique of Plato, its relationship to Nietzsche, and through both its reliance on the doctrine of Heraclitan flux. A key idea here is that of simulacra as the expression of radical difference.

Overturning Plato: revenge of the simulacra

In *Difference and Repetition*, Deleuze writes that the task of modern philosophy is 'to overturn Platonism', but, he adds, it is desirable that this should conserve many Platonic characteristics (1993: 59). At the core of his argument is the critical relationship between radical difference and what he calls repetition on the one hand, and philosophies of identity and representation on the other. The latter philosophies are generic to the western tradition, and they are ways of excluding ideas based on the former. They establish a realm of logic, identity and representation, and Plato plays a crucial role in bringing about the transition to representational thinking, the orderly, analytic mode of thought which represses difference. Platonism subordinates difference 'to the powers of the One, the Analogous, the Similar and even the Negative' (ibid.). To overturn Platonism is to challenge this order of the same and the different, the distinguished and the negated, and to do so through the use of a philosophy of radical difference. One must subject 'the Same to a conversion which relates it to the different', and in so doing,

> [t]he things and beings which are distinguished in the different suffer a corresponding radical destruction of their *identity*. Only on this condition is difference thought in itself, neither represented nor mediated. The whole of Platonism, by contrast, is dominated by the idea of drawing a distinction between 'the thing itself' and the simulacra. Difference is not thought in itself but related to a ground, subordinated to the same. . . . Overturning Platonism, then, means denying the primacy of original over copy, of model over image; glorifying the reign of simulacra and reflections.
>
> (Deleuze 1993: 66)

Simulacra represent 'the many', discarded in Platonic philosophy in favour of 'the one'. To glorify them is to turn Plato upside down, and here we see the link not just to Platonic inversion, but also to Nietzsche. Deleuze associates difference with what he calls repetition, and this he grounds in Nietzsche's doctrine of 'eternal return'. This 'means that each thing exists only in returning, copy of an infinity of copies which allows neither original nor origin to subsist' (Deleuze 1993: 67). That which returns is 'the power of (formless) Being', which sees the simulacrum not as the failed copy of the original but as 'the true character or form – the "being" – of that which is' (ibid.). When the identity of things dissolves, and their being returns, being becomes 'univocal' and 'begins to revolve around the different' (ibid.). The doctrine of repetition or return is, in other words, another way of stating the constant fluidity of multiply particular things from the perspective of formless being or radical difference. 'That which is or returns has no prior constituted identity: things are reduced to the difference which fragments them, and to all the differences which are implicated in it and through which they pass' (ibid.). Nor does it have foundations:

> For eternal return . . . allows no installation of a foundation-ground. On the contrary, it swallows up or destroys every ground which would function as an

instance responsible for the difference between the original and the derived, between things and simulacra. It makes us party to a universal *ungrounding*. By 'ungrounding' we should understand the freedom of the non-mediated ground, the discovery of a ground behind every other ground, the relation between the groundless and the ungrounded, the immediate reflection of the formless and the superior form which constitutes the eternal return.

(ibid.)

Here lies the overturn of Plato, for Plato gave the establishment of identity and differentiation (i.e. the grouping of things under Ideas) as the goal of his own dialectic, but real difference does not lie between the model, the copy and that which is then established as the discard, the simulacrum. The eternal recurrence of difference collapses this ordering of things and releases simulacra from the margins of identity. Things are indeed 'simulacra themselves, simulacra are the superior forms, and the difficulty facing everything is to become its own simulacrum' (Deleuze 1993: 67). If we compare this with Plato, is this triumph of simulacra not the chaos against which Plato sought to establish eternal principles, an ideal order of things? It is. Was not Plato's argument against the Heraclitans, who now make their entry, and the Sophists that they were the harbingers of just such a chaos through their refusal to distinguish between things? It was, but for Deleuze this is their *positive* contribution. The Sophist is the one who 'raises everything to the level of simulacra and maintains them in that state', and, in so doing, represents, in the manner of Nietzsche, the connection between chaos and eternal return, which 'are not two different things' (Deleuze 1993: 68). Platonism 'is erected on the basis of this wish to hunt down the phantasms or simulacra which are identified with the Sophist himself, that devil, that insinuator or simulator, that always disguised and displaced false pretender' (Deleuze 1993: 127). The aim of Platonism was thus to subordinate difference to the 'supposedly initial powers of the Same and the similar, that of declaring difference unthinkable in itself and sending it, along with the simulacra, back to the bottomless ocean' (ibid.). The Deleuzean challenge to Plato is that what has been repressed, the simulacra, will return. They will resist their control by the Ideal forms, and maintain their right to be themselves:

> The different, the dissimilar, the unequal – in short, becoming – may well be not merely defects which affect copies like a ransom paid for their secondary character or a counterpart to their resemblance. But rather models themselves, terrifying models of the *pseudos* in which appears the power of the false.
>
> (Deleuze 1993: 128)

What is a threat for Plato is an opportunity for Deleuze, for simulacra 'provide the means of challenging *both* the notion of the copy *and* that of the model' (ibid.). Under pressure of simulacra, the model 'collapses into difference, while the copies disperse into the dissimilitude of the series which they interiorise' (ibid.), so that one can no longer say what is copy, what is model. Against the Platonic cosmos, where transcendent Ideas control the possibility of chaos, Deleuze affirms 'the immanent identity of chaos and cosmos, being in the eternal return, a thoroughly tortuous circle' (ibid.), a point at which 'everything changes nature, at which copies themselves flip over into simulacra and at which, finally, resemblance or spiritual imitation gives way to repetition' (ibid.).

From Deleuze to Nietzsche . . .

In considering Deleuze, we have referred to Nietzsche's doctrine of eternal return. Nietzsche is central to Deleuze, for it is his Zarathustra, like his earlier Dionysus,[3] that links eternal return to the possibility of complete change and the irreducibly unequal and incommensurable difference in things. Eternal return, as we saw, is 'the power of (formless) Being' which 'has no prior constituted identity'. It involves in consequence a 'cruelty' which seems monstrous, and a 'groundlessness in which original Nature resides in its chaos, beyond the jurisdictions and laws which constitute only second nature' (Deleuze 1993: 242). Eternal return generating sheer difference is 'purely intensive' rather than qualitative or extensive. Its being (qua (non-) or ?-being) represents a 'will to power' beyond all attempts at closure or identity. For Nietzsche,

> the eternal return . . . is said of difference. [It] does not hold without [the will to power]. The will to power is the flashing world of metamorphoses, of communicating intensities, difference of differences, of *breaths*, insinuations and exhalations: a world of intensive intentionalities, a world of simulacra and 'mysteries'. Eternal return is the being of this world, the only Same which is said of this world and excludes any prior identity therein. . . . Nietzsche . . . sought . . . to make chaos an object of affirmation.
>
> (Deleuze 1993: 243)

In this regard, Zarathustra betokens the Deleuzean philosophy, for he

> is the dark precursor of eternal return. The eternal return eliminates precisely all those instances which strangle difference and prevent its transport by subjecting it to the . . . yoke of representation. Difference is recovered, liberated, only at the limit of its power – in other words, by repetition in the eternal return. The eternal return . . . eliminates the presuppositions of representation, namely the Same and the Similar, the Analogue and the Negative.
>
> (Deleuze 1993: 300)

We have now followed Deleuze from his critique of Hegelian negation to his challenge to negation as differentiation in Plato, carried out in terms of radical (non-)being as difference. Difference exposes Plato to the revenge of simulacra, and this involves repetition, recurrence and will to power, concepts that draw heavily on Nietzsche and the figures of Dionysus and Zarathustra. Underlying it all is the affirmative possibility of radical difference, meaning unformed multiplicities in flux, a world of formless being forever forcing itself against forms and representations, established via negations. Finally, this leads us to the primordial in philosophy itself, and here we encounter Heraclitus and the doctrine of flux.

... to Heraclitan flux

Heraclitus makes only a limited appearance in *Difference and Repetition*, but his role in Nietzsche's thought, and for Deleuze through Nietzsche, is well brought out in Deleuze's earlier work *Nietzsche and Philosophy* (Deleuze 1983). Here, I refer to passages in both works, and to Nietzsche's own account of the ancient. My aim is to draw out the particular role Heraclitus plays in the Deleuzean–Nietzschean scheme, and this requires reference to Nietzsche's own, more detailed comments. Thus, while my focus is on *Difference and Repetition*, this requires a broader treatment in order to bring out how the text works.

In *Nietzsche and Philosophy*, Deleuze's Nietzsche sees Heraclitus as the 'tragic thinker', the thinker of eternal return. His thought is of radical innocence, understanding existence as based on the instinct of play, on aesthetics rather than morality or religion. Heraclitus had 'taken a deep look, he had seen no chastisement of multiplicity, no expiation of becoming, no culpability of existence' (Deleuze 1983: 22). He is the philosopher who affirms that there is no being, only becoming, so that being can only be understood as the being of becoming. Becoming in turn is understood in relation to multiplicity as the sole unity, as the thing that returns eternally. He is known as 'obscure' in Greek thought, but this is precisely because he leads us 'to the threshold of the obscure' (Deleuze 1983: 23) – that is, the question of the being of becoming. Being as becoming is understood as the basis of eternal return: 'Return is the being of that which becomes. Return is the being of becoming itself, the being which is affirmed in becoming. The eternal return as law of becoming' (ibid.) In this conception, there is no justice beyond eternal return, so that 'the aeon (time), says Heraclitus, is a child who plays, plays at draughts' (ibid.).[4] It is the instinct of the game, played in eternity, that lies at the base of being and life, in the form of endless becoming, difference, return.[5]

With this passage in mind, the significance of briefer references in *Difference and Repetition* to Heraclitus becomes clear. There, Heraclitus is the philosopher who opposes Plato and the move to representation in Greek thought. Platonism is the Apollinian in philosophy, emphasising reason and identity, and the suppression of the Dionysian, the violent and transgressive, but matters remain at an early stage. Platonism is accordingly 'like an animal in the process of being tamed, whose final resistant moves bear witness . . . to a nature soon to be lost' (Deleuze 1993: 59). The 'Heraclitan world still growls in Platonism' (ibid.), for it was only with Aristotle that the categories of representation were developed fully. Plato had to base his position on a theory of Ideas and a further moral vision of the world rather than on the representation of things themselves. Because the victory was not yet complete, the threat posed by simulacra rumbles on in his theory:

> Insinuated throughout the Platonic cosmos, difference resists its yoke. Heraclitus and the Sophists make an infernal racket. It is as though there were a strange *double* which dogs Socrates' footsteps and haunts even Plato's style, inserting itself into the repetitions and variations of that style.
>
> (Deleuze 1993: 127)

Heraclitus for Deleuze is the enemy within the Platonic gate, and in this he follows Nietzsche, who addressed the philosophy of ancient Greece in two early works, *The Birth of Tragedy* (1872) (Nietzsche 2000a) and the incomplete and posthumously published *Philosophy in the Tragic Age of the Greeks* (1873) (Nietzsche 1962). He then returned to comment on his early discussion in a section of the late work *Ecce Homo* (1888) (Nietzsche 2000b). Here, he affirmed his early support for a Heraclitan view of philosophy against the Socratic–Platonic tradition at the core of Greek thought. While the subsequent development of Nietzsche's thought involved criticism of this early work, as smelling 'offensively Hegelian' (Nietzsche 2000b: 726), this does not appear to have affected his view of the importance of Heraclitus, or his associated early discovery of the Dionysian element in the pre-Socratic lifeworld.

In *The Birth of Tragedy*, the contrast is drawn between the Dionysian and Apollinian tendencies in ancient Greece. Dionysian 'charm' works against Apollinian separation to renew 'the union between man and man', and under its spell nature is reconciled with her lost son. This early reconciliative vision, which does indeed bear a Hegelian resonance, generates an image of the Dionysian as follows:

> Freely, earth proffers her gifts, and peacefully the beasts of prey of the rocks and deserts approach. The chariot of Dionysus is covered with flowers and garlands; panthers and tigers walk under its yoke. . . . Now, with the gospel of universal harmony, each one feels himself not only united, reconciled and fused with his neighbour, but as one with him . . . before the mysterious primordial unity.
>
> (Nietzsche 2000a: 37)

While this sounds rather beautiful, it is plain that what Deleuze calls 'original Nature' (1993: 242) was also a site of horror, of the 'most savage natural instincts' (Nietzsche 2000a: 39) and a 'horrible "witches' brew" of sensuality and cruelty' (Nietzsche 2000a: 40) – a nature red in tooth and claw, without restraint. In this regard, the human world is understood as a combination of the Dionysian and the Apollinian so that, for example, the onset of Socratic–Platonic philosophy, which is Apollinian in its search for knowledge, truth and form, operates 'as a remedy and a prevention for this breath of pestilence' (Nietzsche 2000a: 97). Nonetheless, there is also a sense of the irremediable conflict between the Dionysian and the

Apollinian ways of being, and it is the role of the philosopher to grasp the basic split in modern life initiated by the Greeks.

As for Heraclitus, in both the *Birth of Tragedy* and *Philosophy in the Tragic Age of the Greeks*, he is the philosopher associated with Dionysus. In the former, he is the representative of the 'purifying fire spirit', which represents the power to judge what 'we now call culture, education, civilisation' (Nietzsche 2000a: 120) in the name of a 'playful construction and destruction of the individual world as the overflow of a primordial delight' (Nietzsche 2000a: 142). In the latter, Nietzsche elaborates more fully the Heraclitan world of amoralism and flow (coming-into-being, becoming, in place of being). In this account, Heraclitus 'altogether denied being' in favour of a world 'supported by eternal unwritten laws, flowing upward and downward in brazen rhythmic beat' (Nietzsche 1962: 54). Here, the 'everlasting and exclusive coming-to-be, the impermanence of everything actual, which constantly acts and comes-to-be but never is . . . is a terrible paralysing thought' (ibid.). Controversially, we shall see, Nietzsche has Heraclitus say the following about 'stepping into the same river twice':

> I see nothing other than becoming. Be not deceived. It is the fault of your myopia . . . if you believe you see land somewhere in the ocean of coming-to-be and passing away. You use names for things as though they . . . endured; yet even the stream into which you step a second time is not the one you stepped into before.
>
> (Nietzsche 1962: 52)

This is a famous, though not uncontroversial, argument associated with Heraclitus, and, as we shall see, the radical Heraclitan Cratylus sought to better it. For the moment, however, all we need note is its emphasis on perpetual flow, fluidity, flux. Underlying flux is the 'strife', or 'war', of opposites, a 'contest [that] endures in all eternity' (Nietzsche 1962: 55), and which reveals eternal justice. Heraclitus is the inspiration here. Already in Nietzsche's early account, we see the idea of eternal recurrence take form in a conception of a world of constant flow and becoming, and 'eternal substantive multiplicities' (Nietzsche 1962: 57). Here, there are no foundational values, only the play of fire through becoming and change, structuring and destroying 'without any moral additive, in forever equal innocence' (Nietzsche 1962: 62).

This is the early Nietzsche, but his vision does not substantially change with regard to Heraclitus, even when he criticises his own earlier work. In the late work *Ecce Homo*, Nietzsche writes of

> Heraclitus, in whose proximity I feel altogether warmer and better than anywhere else. The affirmation of passing away *and destroying*, which is the decisive feature of a Dionysian philosophy; saying Yes to opposition and war; *becoming*, along with a radical repudiation of *being* – all this is clearly more closely related to me than anything else thought to date. The doctrine of the 'eternal recurrence', that is, of the unconditional and infinitely repeated circular

course of all things – this doctrine of Zarathustra *might* in the end have been taught already by Heraclitus.

(Nietzsche 2000b: 729–30)

Heraclitus may not have got as far as eternal return in Nietzsche's view, but most of the steps towards it are present in his thought, especially the doctrine of becoming in repudiation of being – that is, of flux. To summarise, we have now traced Deleuze's ideas of non-being as difference and repetition in so far as they inform a critique of Hegel and Plato, and draw Deleuze to Nietzsche, and both to Heraclitus. My aim in identifying these links is to establish a line of critical thought concerning non-being that takes us back to the Greeks in general and Heraclitus in particular. Bhaskar also traces philosophy to this terrain, as we already know, so now we turn to dialectical critical realism and its position on non-being, the Greeks in general, and Heraclitus in particular.

Non-being as real absence: Bhaskar and Heraclitus

In this section, I begin with some comments comparing poststructuralist difference and dialectical critical realist absence. I then move to consider Bhaskar's view of Heraclitus as philosopher of being *and* becoming, a view that I test interpretively against Heraclitus's surviving writings. In the light of this, I then consider how both poststructuralism and dialectical critical realism sit in relation to the early development of western philosophy, and consider just how radical a philosophical move radical difference permits.

Bhaskar and Deleuze

Despite striking parallels in terms of the same critical references to Hegel and Plato, and a similar language of negativity and non-being, Bhaskar and Deleuze move in very different directions. Like Deleuze, Bhaskar sees Hegel as restoring identity through negation. He sees too the Platonic analysis of non-being as leading to a false step for philosophy by restoring absence to positivity as what is differentiated. However, Deleuze's move is to a more radical sense of difference as '(non-)' or '?-being', whereas Bhaskar's is to an underlying, hidden problematic of being as real determinate absence, becoming and the possibility of change. These are two very different paths to follow. Which should we take? Deleuze might say that Bhaskar's focus on the determinacy of non-being leaves his philosophy entangled in identity and blocks the more radical possibilities of untamed multiplicity and difference. Bhaskar in turn would say that real absence is always this-worldly, and in a developing, determinate world the possibilities for absence and change must always be grounded in what already exists. This is the case even for the radically new, which may emerge *de novo*, but not without ground, *ex nihilo*. A notion of radical multiplicity or difference represents an abstract and undifferentiated ontology, which tells us nothing about the nature or conditions of actual change. Radical difference reflects the sense that the new may emerge in an open totality, but if the possibility of change remains at the level of the purely undifferentiated, it tells us nothing about how change could have occurred. Where radical difference is brought to bear, which is everywhere, we must be constantly surprised. This would be true a priori, but also, where dialectical critical realism locates the possibility of explanation, in terms of the a posteriori too.

On the other hand, the 'everywhere-everywhen' nature of change under multiple affirmation is a refreshing reminder to take nothing for granted, shows a welcome disrespect for philosophical tradition, and alerts us in general to the 'phenomenality of diversity and change' (DPF: 250), as Bhaskar says of Derrida. But its generic, non-specific quality makes it a place-marker for a fuller ontology that could put flesh on the bones of change in terms of human and social potentials and geo-historical circumstances. Such an ontology would not close down the range of possibilities for change, for in an open totality the genuinely new and the unanticipated are real possibilities, even if they are always emergent from what is, as their underlying grounds of possibility. Without a sense of how change is actu-alised, Deleuze produces a radical ontology of difference and becoming that is also radically flat and unstructured in its form, and which therefore bears the charge of ontological actualism. A conception of change qua difference that is ubiquitous in time and space is so over-inclusive and under-determining as to be unserious about its real possibility. It abstracts and hypostatises to the extent that it becomes ultimately unserious about the category of change itself, rendering it irreal.

In making these comments, I have recapitulated some of the criticisms Bhaskar makes of Derrida that we considered in the previous chapter. Derrida and Deleuze can be treated as similar in their two philosophies of difference, and so the immanent critique of one is also relevant to the other. My aim in this chapter, however, is to pursue the critique of poststructuralism in terms of tracking its historical sources through the links between Deleuze and Nietzsche and Plato and Heraclitus. Deleuze, as we saw, wants to overturn Plato, but I want to press home the question as to how radical this overturning is, and whether it does not remain on the terrain of Platonism. In this section, I pursue this dialectical critical realist argument by considering Bhaskar's view of Heraclitus, and then relate this to extant fragments of Heraclitus's thought.

Bhaskar on Heraclitus

It must be said that Bhaskar's sketch of Heraclitus is brief, a few lines only. Nonetheless, there is a valuable counter to Nietzsche and Deleuze in what he has to say:

> Heraclitus argued that the unity of things was to be found in their underlying, not superficially apparent, essential structure or *Logos* rather than in material. In this sense Heraclitus was a Pythagorean or vice versa. But although the structure underlying and accounting for change was for Heraclitus of paramount significance, he believed that the structure not only accounted for but depended on the ubiquity of change, analysed in terms of the essential

connection (i.e. the dialectical contradiction) of and reaction between opposites, which he poetically termed strife or war. Knowledge of *Logos* was wisdom, which he distinguished from the perception of change. It is worth pondering what the subsequent trajectory of western philosophy might have been like if Plato had not come across Heraclitus's ideas in their absurdly one-sided Cratylan form.

(PE: 176–7)

In this account, Heraclitus is not a philosopher of flux, but one who combines in a complex way matters of structure and change (flow), of becoming and being, of process and product. There is an account in his philosophy of the way in which the unity of opposites, thought of as strife or war, operates as an underlying structuring element that makes possible the appearance of things. Nietzsche and Deleuze in contrast stress only one side of this, the phenomenality and changeability of all things at all times. Whereas their Heraclitus is the philosopher of flux, multiplicity, formlessness, becoming and perpetual change, Bhaskar emphasises the importance of questions of structure and being in complex conjunction with questions of flow. For Nietzsche and Deleuze, 'strife and war' as constant change represent the central significant element in Heraclitus's thought; for Bhaskar it has to be placed in a broader context.

In this regard, Bhaskar's reference to Cratylus is relevant, for it was he who pursued the doctrine of flux to its conclusion. Against the supposed Heraclitan argument that one cannot step into the same river twice, Cratylus contended that one could not step into it once, where all was flux or flow.[6] The negative consequences of this argument for reference and for the relationship between the world of phenomena (where all is forever in flux) and the possibility of a stable reality were brought out and opposed by Plato in his Socratic dialogues,[7] and hence it can be said that Plato came across Heraclitus in an 'absurdly one-sided Cratylan form'.[8] The significance of that for us is that it is precisely the Platonic–Cratylan account of Heraclitus that lies at the heart of Nietzsche's and Deleuze's version, in which structure and being-in-relation-to-becoming are missed. For Plato, as for Nietzsche and Deleuze, Heraclitus is the philosopher of perpetual change or simple becoming who *denies* being, and who therefore de-structures it as permanent flow. On the Bhaskarian account, Heraclitan flux must be seen in the context of his thought as a whole, which includes ideas of structure and process, of being as well as becoming, of being in relation to becoming.

Heraclitus, structure and flow

It is helpful to pursue Bhaskar's claim a little in order to consider the validity of these different interpretations. Of course, the pre-Socratic philosophers will always remain obscure because so little is known of their philosophies as a whole, and Heraclitus is in any case often enigmatic in his pronouncements. Nonetheless, a brief examination reveals the validity of Bhaskar's account. Let us begin with the famous vexed question of stepping into the same river twice. Here is how Plato recounts Heraclitus's view (note the similarity with Nietzsche's version mentioned above):

> Heraclitus says somewhere that 'everything gives way and nothing stands fast,' and, likening the things that are flowing of a river, he says that 'you cannot step into the same river twice'.
>
> (Plato 1997d: 402a)

This, however, is what the two fragments most clearly attributable to Heraclitus actually say:

> In the same rivers ever different waters flow . . .
> We step and do not step into the same rivers . . .
>
> (Barnes 1987: 70)

The first fragment reflects a realist understanding of how entities are composed of elements that make the whole different from the parts. The concept of a river requires a holistic or structured understanding of how the flow of water must be grasped at two different levels: as, first, a constant flow of water molecules in, second, the naturally structured whole that is the river. The paradox in the statement (same . . . different . . .) reflects such an understanding, and its consequence is that, once you understand what a river is, you *can* properly be said to step into it twice. It would involve a reductionist understanding of a river to deny this, and this is precisely illustrated by the second fragment. Regarding the river as ever-flowing water, you cannot, it is true, step into the same one twice (or once?), but regarding it as a holistically constituted, structured *river*, you can. Hence, we step *and* do not step into the same river, depending on how we understand what a river is. The Platonic (and Nietzschean) account, apparently influenced by extreme Heraclitanism, is a one-sided reduction of Heraclitus's point. On Heraclitus's own words, Heraclitan flux is a partial account of his argument.[9]

We can pursue the matter a little further. The importance of structure is also seen in a second fragment, that concerning the bow and the lyre, where Heraclitus states that

> the diverging agrees with itself: a structure turning back on itself, such as that of the bow and the lyre.
>
> (Hussey 1999: 96)

What we have here is the sense of a thing that is constituted not by its passing into something else, its becoming, but by the active tension, the becoming, in the elements in its structured being. A bow is wood and string held together by the tension in its forms, and similarly with the lyre. In this regard, Edward Hussey argues that a key term for Heraclitus, alongside strife, war and fire, is *harmonie*, which in Greek usage meant 'a purposive mutual adjustment of components to produce a unity' (Hussey 1999: 110) through a process.[10] From this point of view,

Heraclitus can state that 'Latent structure is master of visible structure' (Hussey 1999: 91), pointing to a view of knowledge in which the discovery of underlying hidden structure is its goal, for 'Nature likes to conceal itself' (ibid.). The vision of a structured whole creating the appearance of things is clearly seen in the following:

> Combinations – wholes and not wholes, concurring differing, concordant discordant, from all things one and from one all things.
>
> (Barnes 1987: 71)

Of course, such a view is not in keeping with an emphasis on perpetual change or flux in isolation from being, and nor are other fragments that reflect a world understood in terms of being as well as becoming. The following two paradoxes are hard to represent at all in terms of simple becoming:

> The sea is most pure and most polluted water: for fish, drinkable and life-preserving; for men, undrinkable and death-dealing.
>
> (Barnes 1987: 52)

As with the flowing river, the paradox here draws on a realist understanding of the nature and properties of things and the active parts they play, here the specific properties of sea water, fish and men. Or consider the following, which reveals the tricks of words in the face of underlying truths about the world:

> People are deceived in the knowledge of what is manifest, much as Homer was . . . ; he too was deceived by boys who were killing lice [about their persons], when they said 'those we took we left behind, those we did not take we carry with us'.
>
> (Hussey 1999: 91)

The homely joke reveals a philosopher who is much less coldly melodramatic than Nietzsche has him. There is worldly humour in this paradox, and in virtue of it, an underlying demonstration of how everyday being *is*, rather than a denial of being in favour of pure becoming. Nietzsche describes Heraclitus as a 'star devoid of atmosphere' with a 'dead and icy' eye (Nietzsche 1962: 67). This seems an overstatement for a philosopher who is as concerned with boys picking lice off themselves and, to put it grandly, the different spatio-temporal realities of being or not being lice-infested.

To be sure, the Heraclitan vision is a complex and conflicted one, and it is not my intention to argue for Heraclitus as a critical realist *avant la lettre*. No doubt his understanding of structure was limited by what was understood of the natural and social world in his time. Nor would I want to suggest an easy transplantation of a pre-Socratic worldview onto modern concerns. The critical realist position on reading Heraclitus would be that there are nonetheless important proto-realist themes in his philosophy, and that he began to grasp the need to think change and structure in process – that is, the interrelation of becoming and being, and their irreducibility the one to the other. It is therefore essential to take up the several aspects of his thought in order to grasp the different aspects of philosophical truth he can manifest. Nietzsche for his part, and Deleuze in his train, see only the philosopher of flux and change that Plato described via Cratylus. In the process, questions of flow, becoming and change in the philosophy of being are hypostatised, wrenched out of their relation to structuring elements. In Heraclitus, there is the beginning of an understanding of these different yet necessarily combined elements. As Hussey notes, Heraclitus 'is committed to the recognition that there is a system, though a concealed one, in things, and a systematic way of thinking about them, once the clue, the "latent structure", has been found'. This, he adds, is 'the structural pattern that may conveniently be called "unity-in-opposites"' (Hussey 1999: 93). These are thought-provoking claims not only for an understanding of Heraclitus, but also in terms of a modern understanding of how change occurs in structured ways. Heraclitus's examples point to the relationship between real, structured being and becoming in a way that the doctrine of Heraclitan flux cannot grasp. One conclusion from this might be that 'we moderns' would see things better if we sought to understand the complex combination of being and becoming in pre-Socratic philosophy, not taking one side apart from the overall context. All such interpretations are fraught with difficulty for a variety of reasons, but some are more fraught than others.

Metacritique versus difference

Thus far, we have considered Bhaskar's account of Heraclitus and shown how it is grounded in a closer reading of the philosopher than informs the Nietzschean understanding. The latter may, however, suggest that this hardly matters. There are different interpretations of any philosopher, and what matters is the validity of each interpretation in terms of the philosophy it produces, not its loyalty to an origin. Early philosophy is sufficiently malleable to invite different readings, and to be claimed by different philosophers. We have just considered Heraclitus as the prototype for what becomes in Deleuze's work an anti-Hegelian position. Yet we could contrast this with Hegel's own view that Heraclitus was a 'deep' and dialectical philosopher, in whose thought 'we see land; there is no proposition of Heraclitus which I have not adopted in my Logic' (Hegel 1892: 279).[11] Origins don't matter. This, however, misses the point. All philosophies make some claim to truth, even if it is to the truth of being as becoming, or the impossibility of truth, as is the case with Nietzsche and Deleuze. No doubt this leads to the kind of self-referential paradox described in the previous chapter, but that is a problem for Nietzsche and Deleuze, not for the claim to truth. Equally, all philosophers have an interest in building arguments to make their case, and that includes arguments concerning the tradition of which they are a part. Both Nietzsche and Deleuze want Heraclitus on their side in an historical reading of the foundational problems of western philosophy. To denote a primordial turning point is to make a real claim about the nature of ancient and modern philosophy, and to ground the latter in the former.

Nietzscheanism involves a claim to a radical position on the edge of the western philosophical tradition. It makes claims about what that tradition and its limits are, and it sees Heraclitus both as pointing to those limits and, in his historical positioning, as evidence of how the tradition developed. Heraclitus also grounds the radical position in ontology based on multiple affirmation and becoming, which Nietzsche wishes to see as the excluded other of the western canon. As philosopher, historical figure and ontological proponent, Heraclitus matters: 'So this has existed – once, at least – and is therefore a possibility, this way of life, this way of looking at the human scene' (Nietzsche 1962: 23–4). In this early essay, Nietzsche wants the 'polyphony of Greek nature at long last [to] resound once more' (ibid.). Heraclitus, prototype for the Dionysian and Zarathustra, is the philosopher in whom this scene echoes. For Deleuze, the ancients 'only approximately and partially believed' in eternal return, so that Nietzsche's discovery was 'his own invention' (Deleuze 1993: 242). Yet as Nietzsche said, there was enough in Heraclitus that he *might* have articulated the doctrine. The unrepresentable exists for Deleuze, and lies at the core of philosophical history as that which was excluded, or his anti-Platonist philosophy of difference could not exist. If Platonism is his enemy, Heraclitanism (as he understands it) is, 'approximately and partially', his friend. One can take irrealism only so far, and Deleuze certainly wants to promote a Heraclitan/Sophist vision of the simulacra against a Platonic espousal of the image and its copy. Ontological claims are at stake here for both philosophers, and Heraclitus grounds the historical diagnosis of radical difference; how one reads him matters.

The comparison with Bhaskar, however, brings out the limits of these ontological claims with regard to Heraclitus. His analysis also identifies Deleuze's and Nietzsche's own intrinsic connection to Platonism, which they purport to oppose. Nietzscheanism presents itself as at the edge of the philosophical tradition, but it turns out to be complicit in it. Eternal return is based upon ideas of formless being, multiplicity and perpetual flux, but these are at the core of the Platonic problematic. They emerge from Plato's engagement with the Sophists and the Cratylan version of Heraclitus. The terms of engagement between the forms and the flux, taken up by Nietzsche and Deleuze, were set by Plato in his own context. The Deleuzean revenge of the simulacra is possible only because Plato has established simulacra as the complicit dialectical pair of images and their copies. Multiplicities and flux oppose Ideas or Forms, but assume their own possibility and position in relation to them. In fact, Deleuze pursues the inversion of Platonism even further in that 'Ideas' founded on radical difference ('erewhons')[12] are opposed to the ideal Platonic Forms promoting identity. The inversion, however, simply leaves the original terms of the Platonic terrain in place, and Platonism, across the *whole* problematic it draws for philosophy, is no innocent first step. Deleuze and Nietzsche of course know this in terms of what Plato positively set out to do (posit the Forms), but not in terms of what he sought to marginalise (the simulacra in the flux). They see 'the one' as the problem, but not its dialectical counterpart, 'the many' in the radicalised form they give it. The flux is as much a creation of the Platonic problematic, shaped by the Cratylan version of Heraclitus, as the Forms. Had it not already existed as a fashionable and troubling way of talking in contemporary Athens, one might say that Plato would have had to invent it. If Platonism represents an idealised account of the Forms in counterposition to the unaccountable flux of worldly phenomena, then Deleuzean difference as simulacra or erewhons represents an idealised account of phenomenal flux. As with Derrida, it is a counter-Platonic move on the terrain of Platonism, substituting an idealisation of the flux for Plato's idealism of the Forms.

What is missed out in this reversal on the terrain of Platonism? Bhaskar's account of Heraclitan being and structure alongside becoming, in the context of an understanding of the sequestration of real absence in the Parmenidean–Platonic axis, gives a deeper analysis of what was lost in the occlusion of pre-Socratic themes than inverting Plato permits. For Bhaskar, as for Deleuze and Nietzsche, there is a profound closure in the development of pre-Socratic philosophy to Plato, but its terms are more complex. What Deleuze and Nietzsche see as the basic conflict between Forms and flux, Bhaskar sees as the site of a deeper denial masked by the tacit complicity of dialectical opposites. This takes us back to the relationship between Parmenides and Plato on the one hand, and those developers of Greek philosophy in more subversive directions such as the real Heraclitus, and others,[13] on the other. For Bhaskar, Heraclitus's early efforts to understand being in its relation to becoming was blocked by an axis of Parmenidean and Platonic thought which denied the possibility of change, of the generation and perishing of being. For Parmenides, being had to be stripped of its relation to becoming in favour of a static conception of the whole. It was the possibility of not-being – that is, of change, of generation and destruction, of becoming and begoing – that was troubling. Parmenides's ultimate success was not the achievement of his doctrine of the One, but the split he instigated between being and becoming. After him, the (Cratylan) argument for becoming became predominantly one that denied being, just as Parmenides's argument for being had denied becoming. Heraclitan flux is the distorted mirror image of the Parmenidean One.[14] Platonic idealism is an attempt to mediate these dialectically complicit opposites in favour of oneness or identity, the Forms over the flux, the one over the many. Parmenides and Plato both, the latter drawing on the superficial other of Heraclitan flux, worked together to deny, and then to finesse, real absence and the possibility of change. In sporting parlance, they sold philosophy a dummy, and Nietzsche and Deleuze[15] bought it.

Conclusion

From the point of view of dialectical critical realism, poststructuralism's irrealist ontology is deeply problematic, and this chapter seeks to establish what its ontology, with its roots in Nietzsche and a certain, limited, kind of anti-Platonism, is. From the point of view of poststructuralism, however, dialectical critical realism would be problematic because of its realism and allegiance to dialectics, and its failure, as poststructuralism sees it, to make an additional move beyond dialectics to the deeper level of difference. Is the poststructuralist right? The nub of the issue concerns the validity of what poststructuralism sees as the further move to difference in its philosophy. The key question is whether this represents the deepest level of critique available to philosophy, as poststructuralism maintains, or whether, as dialectical critical realism claims, it is itself a limited level in thought, which limits the potential of critique. For dialectical critical realism, in line with the metacritique developed in the previous chapter, the move to radical difference, while valid at one level, avoids the most radical move in philosophical critique, that from difference to change, under the sign of real absence.

To Nietzscheanism, the Platonic battle against radical difference looks like the inaugural moment in the western philosophical tradition, a moment when wild Dionysian energy is challenged by Apollinian reason, and Heraclitus alone stands as a Dionysian thinker, the Greek proponent of 'eternal return'. But is this a genuine inaugural moment of the tradition? Recall from Chapter 6 the overlay of two problems, 'the one and the other' and 'the one and the many', with the latter dialectically emergent from, and coming to sequester and occlude, the former. In the light of this, Nietzscheanism, for all its endorsement of radical difference, looks like a participant on the side of Plato in the suppression of those root ontological questions expressed, in rudimentary fashion, by the pre-Socratics. And this includes a more rounded version of Heraclitus, whose philosophy the doctrine of Heraclitan flux misrepresents. The problem of 'the one and the other' marks the place where the ontological issues foregrounded by dialectical critical realism at least begin to be discussed. It raises the problem of real change (how some determinate thing becomes something else) and therefore indicates the necessity of thinking the relationship between structured being and becoming. Parmenides had seen as much, and that is why he argued against non-being as a means of opposing the possibility of generation or perishing – that is, real change. Dialectical critical realism seeks against Parmenides and Plato, and, given its anti-Platonism on the terrain of Plato, against a poststructuralist ontology of radical difference, to retrieve this hidden chapter at the start of western philosophy as the initiating site for its own broader concerns.

In Bhaskar's account, Heraclitus is a subversive philosopher, as Nietzsche and Deleuze agree, but his subversiveness does not reside in the hypostatisation of becoming in separation from the structuring of being. Heraclitus's radicalism rests rather upon the prototypical meshing of ideas of becoming and the structuring of being, and here Heraclitus foreshadows the critical realist emphasis on the significance of real determinate absence alongside the stratification of reality, the ways in which being and becoming exist in structured relations. For Bhaskar, the denial of absence in favour of the positive sequesters not only the possibility of thinking real absence and change, but also the possibility of thinking the grounds of change, and these are located in underlying structures, relations, mechanisms, and the like. Hence, retrieving the philosophy of Heraclitus takes us in two directions, first, via the Cratylan–Platonic–Nietzschean–Deleuzean reading, to the flow of things, becoming, and second to their stratification, to being and becoming in an overall context. The first of these, wrenching Heraclitus out of context, misses the true radical potential which dialectical critical realism is positioned to develop. This second direction is pursued by virtue of its understanding of absence, being and becoming (see Chapter 2), of material change and its effects (Chapter 3), of the resulting conception of open totality (Chapter 4), and of agency and ethics (Chapter 5). It takes us to the structuring of flow (becoming) in a complex totality of being, in which the becoming represented as radical flux is a core element, but one that can and should never stand alone. This, it should be said, is not a denial of what is important in the Nietzschean emphasis on radical difference, which is the sense of restless life as the force within becoming. That force, it might be said, is also present in Bhaskar's account of becoming, and especially in his idea of the pulse of freedom that underlies his dialectic. But if we are to understand and nourish that pulse, we need to see that it never comes alone. It should be neither hypostatised nor reduced, and it both informs, and is in-formed in, structured being as the heart of life.

8   Conclusion

Natural necessity and the grounds of justice

We have now considered the three main aims Bhaskar set himself in *Dialectic*. These were, first, a qualitative development of original critical realism as its dialecticisation; second, a renovation of dialectic on critical realist ground; and third, a metacritique of the general trajectory of western philosophy on the basis of the first and second. In this concluding chapter, I will summarise the overall argument, and focus in particular on the ethical dimension in Bhaskar's work. I do so because it brings out most clearly the unity of his thought, and highlights its significance for today. In particular, it draws together the fruits of his ethics, explored in Chapter 5, though on the basis of developments explored in previous chapters, and the results of his metacritique, developed in Chapters 6 and 7. The chapter has three main sections, in the first of which I review the account of natural necessity developed in Chapters 1 to 4, and then, in the second, consider the role natural necessity plays in his ethics. In the third section, I consider the effect of thinking about natural necessity in relation to other modern critical ethical theories, and in particular draw on Bhaskar's metacritique of poststructuralist theory to consider deconstructive ethics. If the first section develops the conception of natural necessity, the second and the third treat this as it relates to establishing the grounds of justice. The second section accordingly picks up the idea from Chapter 5 of the constellated nature of ethics within the historical and political. The argument is that modern ethics involve historically generated and grounded variations on the theme of a relation between 'the ideal' and 'the actual', where these terms are extruded and limited expressions of an underlying moral truth about the ethical powers and potentials of human being.

The third section is concerned with the grounds of ethics and justice in the light of Bhaskar's metacritique. That the metacritique might be brought together with his ethics may seem surprising, for the former focuses on the denial of natural necessity (presaged as the problem of 'the one and the other' in Greek philosophy) in favour of a trajectory in western philosophy emphasising matters epistemological. The denial of natural necessity leads to ontological monovalence, ontological actualism, subject–object identity theory and the epistemic fallacy. These are not obviously ethical matters, but an understanding of ethics is at stake here, for the denial of natural necessity promotes the problem of 'the one and the many' as *the* problematic of western philosophy. As such, it focuses attention on problems of the universal (the one) and the particular (the many), and here ethical issues are brought to the fore, for two of the main critical approaches to ethics today involve pursuit of either a universalising or a particularising strategy. The former is especially observed in Kant, Kantianism and in Hegel, and in ethics Bhaskar's focus is the engagement with Habermas that orients his position as set out at the beginning of Chapter 5. Ethically particularising strategies are especially noticed in poststructural, post-Nietzschean philosophy, and these were examined in Chapters 6 and 7, in pursuit of Bhaskar's metacritique. Thus, in so far as a modern metatheory of ethics investigates either a universalising or a particularising strategy, it is valid to consider both moves as rooted, *mutatis mutandis*, in the grounding problematic of 'the one and the many', which western philosophy inherits from Plato. And in so far as this is the case, it is helpful to pursue Bhaskar's interest in the deeper problematic of natural necessity, linked historically to the problem of 'the one and the other' that Plato finessed. In this way, we see how discussion of primary moves in modern ethics pulls together our discussion of Bhaskar's ethics and his metacritique, and do so in the general context of his understanding of natural necessity. In this way, we see how dialectical critical realism provides the basis for a modern *metaphysics* of 'the grounds of justice', in the broad Aristotelian sense of fundamental or 'First Philosophy', rather than, say, Kant's more specific idealist meaning.

Natural necessity as 'material meshwork'

Here I consider the nature of natural necessity as it emerges from Bhaskar's dialectic, and in the way that he explains the thrownness of human being in the 'material meshwork' of things. His initial arguments in favour of absence and spatio-temporal causality lead to his account of materialist diffraction, and thence to the development of a concept of totality. In this section, I consider the 1M to 3L evolution of his argument, and in the next we bring this together with the 4D emphasis on moral agency in order to identify the grounds of justice.

The material meshwork of things

We began this study of Bhaskar's *Dialectic* in Chapter 1 with an account of original critical realism and a key move to develop it. That involved taking existing critical realist ontology, with its existing grasp of natural necessity, and developing it in relation to absence and becoming through spatio-temporal causality. Natural necessity operates in the social sphere just as in the natural, but with the difference that society and social structures operate only by virtue of intentional human agency. Explanation of events in the social sciences is concept- and activity-dependent, and a crucial role is played by actors' reasons operating as causes. These link agency to social structure as an irreducible condition of its possibility. Human agency in original critical realism is made possible by the special nature of human being, which possesses mental and agential powers emergent from the physio-logical structures that ground them (in the doctrine of 'Synchronic Emergent

Powers Materialism', SEPM). Agency is the effective condition for the re-production and transformation of social structures, but just as agency is irreducible to structure, so is structure irreducible to agency (the 'Transformational Model of Social Action', TMSA).

To this original (1M) understanding of natural necessity in the natural and social worlds, with the latter entailing the agency of human beings through reasons acting as causes, Bhaskar's first innovative development in *Dialectic* is the introduction of the (2E) second edge of absence or negativity (see Chapter 2). This adds to the sense of real materiality, depth and difference (i.e. non-identity) in the world an additional understanding of the dynamic and always changing nature of things. Nothing stays still, but rather everything is involved in movement or process, and that involves the real negation of what exists as it changes into something else. The original emphasis in critical realism on structured being as the sheer, real alterity in things is thus enhanced by the significance of 'becoming' or change, where every becoming is also a 'begoing', an absenting of what was previously there. Change is linked to causality, and it is also linked in the social world to agency, for agency under original critical realism is causal. Hence, agency, originally understood as one element in a structure/agency dual, is now also understood in relation to becoming and begoing, as a form of causal absenting in space and time.

The consequence of this new (2E) analysis is that we now think of causation in its processual aspect. All causal change is transformative negation or absenting, and all such change is rooted in specific contours of space and time. Negativity or absenting lie at the core of a dynamic, caused world in which nothing stands still, and everything is in process. This gives rise to the 'tri-unity of causality, space and time', and stresses the role of absenting in the world through a variety of processual terms such as negation, contradiction, development, becoming, emergence and finitude. On this basis, natural necessity entails both structured being (or product) and becoming (or process), and gives rise to a fourfold 'polysemy' of product, process, product-in-process and process-in-product which constitutes the material meshwork of things. Natural necessity insists on the real materiality of spatio-temporal things as dynamic, established by their past, containing their future, and as existentially constituted by what lies 'outside' them as well as that which provides them with their specific (and changing) identity. It insists on the spatio-temporality of being and the geo-historically rhythmic quality of living, and therefore generally on the material thrownness of human being in the world.

This second edge insistence on real negativity, spatio-temporal causality and material thrownness provides the initial dialecticisation of original critical realism. It pushes Bhaskar's argument towards a confrontation between Hegel and Marx (Chapter 3), and what I called there the 'critical realisation' of dialectic. Here Marx's materialism, which is epistemologically and ontologically realist, and practical and agential in its character ('men make history'), forms the basis for an understanding of dialectic on the side of 'the (material) object' rather than 'the (idealist) subject'. In particular, it leads to an understanding of contradictions as materially grounded unities of opposites, and the general idea of the diffraction of dialectic. The latter concept reflects both the fractured, contradictory nature of the social world and also its diffuse, plural and complex character. Here Bhaskar's engagement with Marx and Hegel pushes forward the sense, already present in original critical realism but brought out in its dialecticised version, of a connected and contradictory world in process, in which the separate, diffracted parts are also unified or grounded. Note two things, however. First, identifying the plurality of phenomena in the world that are worthy of explanation does not entail a pluralist theory. Dialecticising critical realism and the critical realisation of dialectic rather leads to an understanding of how complex and plural things hang together as a whole – that is, to an understanding of the world as a totality. Second – and this point has not been made previously – Bhaskar's reading of Marx at this point in the progression of his argument is incomplete. Marx is a materialist for Bhaskar on epistemological, ontological and *practical* grounds, but this idea of Marx as a practical materialist means that Marx must be read in the light of Bhaskar's account of agency and its link to ethics, in the context of his dialectic as a whole. In that sense, to call Marx a practical materialist is to point to the discussion of Chapters 4 and 5 on the nature of agency, and the underlying humanist implications of Bhaskar's ethics for Marx himself. To be a materialist is not necessarily to be a determinist, as Bhaskar's account of agency, SEPM and the TMSA makes clear, and as did the young Marx.[1]

The need for totality

Moving to the third-level (3L) understanding of the whole presaged by material diffraction (in Chapter 4), we saw how Bhaskar's conception of totality is in line with the understanding of a dynamic material world responding to natural necessity, in which the material meshwork of being is constituted by the tri-unity of causality, space and time. In the causal inter- and intra-relationships between material entities lies the need to understand how things work as a whole. But in an emerging, changing, dynamic world, totality is never finished, so Bhaskar's account must balance a whole governed by the material causation of product-in-process with a sense of openness and incompleteness, of process-in-product, and the possibility of emergence and the new. He does so by focusing on the idea of partial totality and noting the plurality of forms it may take. Within this conception, he argues for holistic causality involving a complex co-relation of the whole and the parts, and for a series of figures that constitute the architecture of totality. The purpose of these figures is to identify the various ways in which the parts and the whole are related, and these include the idea of entities operating at different levels, mediating each other, and working in overall relations. A specific figure of the whole is that of the constellation, a concept which identifies the co-relatedness of different elements such as, for example, epistemology and ontology, analytics and dialectics, or structure and agency. These are held together as a unity in a constellational relationship, and this both safeguards against the reduction of one element to another and insists on the complex co-relation of the constellated terms. The constellation is a place in which duals, which otherwise appear as one-sided anti-nomies, can be articulated in their connection and real difference. It will be recalled from Chapter 5 that a constellated understanding of the ethical and the spatio-temporal or geo-historical was central to Bhaskar's ethics, and this point will be taken up shortly.

As regards this architecture of the totality, further concepts pertain to the specific dual of structure and agency, and these are particularly significant for thinking about the possibility of moral agency. This dual is rooted in original critical realism as the basis for differentiating the subject matter of the natural and social sciences. It operates on the basis of emergent human mind and action (the theory of SEPM), and how mind provides reasons that operate as causes in the social world (under the TMSA). Mind and agency as specific ontological features of human being work in and through structures and are irreducible to them. This understanding of structure and agency is brought forward into Bhaskar's dialectical theory, where the person is now conceived in four-planar being as a partial totality working in relation to further (partial) totalities of which s/he is a part. In this context, Bhaskar introduces new concepts to develop the structure/agency dual, beginning with the moment of hiatus-in-duality affirming the separation and connection of minded agency and structure. This leads in turn to perspectival switch, as the agent shifts from thinking about her personal lived experience to her objective position in the whole, and then to the possibility of generalised reflexivity in relation to the whole. This is the meta-reflexive situation as the in-principle possibility of reflecting globally on the different aspects of one's existence.

This development of original critical realism's insights into the irreducible ontological powers of minded agents is further deepened at the level of totality by concepts that bring out the special particularity and difference of each singular partial totality that is a person. Here we encounter Bhaskar's idea of the concrete universal-singular, in which the weight is placed on the specific, and for each person different, spatio-temporal placing they have in the world. Our material throwness and diffraction provides each individual with a different place and being (our concrete singularity) without, at the same time, denying a basic under-standing of each of us as members of the human species (our continuing, basic sameness). This idea of the agent as a concrete universal-singular is further ela-borated in the idea of four-planar being, involving an understanding of how people are formed in relations with nature, with other persons, in social relations, and, finally, with themselves as evolving psychic entities.

Two things must be noted here. First, if we go back to the dynamic nature of a world governed by spatio-temporal causality, each person in their concrete universality-singularity under four-planar conditions is subject to change over time so that identity changes and assumes a dispositional form. Second, and held in balance against the radical geo-historical reading of the self this implies, this does not mean that earlier irreducible possibilities for mind and agency canvassed in the original SEPM or TMSA models are lost, or that understanding of hiatus, perspectival switch, reflexivity and the meta-reflexive situation is abandoned. Four-planar being, for example, pushes the idea of structure in the structure/agency dual to a much more sophisticated understanding of human being in a structured world, but it does not in the process disable the agential qualities within the original dual.

Further, the idea of the concrete universal-singular not only stresses the spatio-temporal thrownness of each person, but also provides the basis for an ethical understanding of the uniqueness of each individual as a concrete singular being. This in turn is balanced against a basic equity stemming from the universality of persons, but only as one moment in the partial totality that is the concretely universal-singular person. These real bases for both equality of treatment and respect for concrete singularity (difference) might already be present in the original critical realist understanding of the agent, but they are developed and made clearer through concepts of concrete universal-singular and four-planar being. They lead us to Bhaskar's discussion of ethics.

Finally, in considering totality, we must not forget the possibility of sub-totality, the splitting, detotalising tendencies that may exist in a given totality. These are associated with different kinds of exploitative social relations, which Bhaskar summarises as power$_2$, or generalised master–slave-type, relations. Under modern conditions, Bhaskar draws on Marx to identify a geo-historical generative separation entailing the alienation of immediate producers from their conditions of production, which in turn leads to alienation across the four planes of human being: in people's relations with nature, with each other, in their social relations and ultimately with themselves. Sub-totality can operate at many different levels in a totality. One level is that of the (partial totality that is) individual human being, giving rise to the splits across four-planar being just described. At another level, it may work its way into the core philosophical debates by which a society seeks fundamentally to understand itself. We considered sub-totality in this regard when we examined the claim that western philosophy could be seen as one huge, though highly differentiated and periodised, Tina syndrome, in which philosophical thinking as a whole is 'a veritable citadel of the Unhappy Consciousness' (DPF: 406).

Whichever level one takes it at, however, the existence of alienating social forms, penetrating social thought or individual lives, cannot be seen as necessarily *determining* either philosophical thought or the living of one's life. At the individual level, we have to see people as complexly formed, singularised, multiply thrown, spatio-temporal creatures, and this includes living under and internalising master–slave-type standpoints. But even if we decentre our subject at one level, this does not rule out SEPM or agency in the TMSA, or 'the possession of well-grounded and causally efficacious reasons, ordinate in a hierarchy of projects' (DPF: 276) at another, in line with the in-principle possibility of a meta-reflexively totalising situation. In this regard, the ability to recognise our decentred or multiply thrown nature is already an example of meta-reflexivity. Of course, in practice such a possibility may not be at all easy to achieve, but it is not impossible even in historical periods that make it more difficult (ibid.). And what is true at the individual level for persons is also true at the philosophical level for thought: to say that philosophy is generally structured around a Tina problematic, which affirms ontological monovalence and denies real determinate absence, and supplements both by ontological actualism, subject–object identity theory and the epistemic fallacy, is not to deny the possibility of meta-reflexively grasping that this is the case. That, after all, would have to be Bhaskar's own self-reflexive explanation of what he is about. Nor is it to belittle those who struggle with the problems of the tradition without overcoming them, for theirs is a pursuit of meta-reflexivity too.

In any case, what these comments point to is a sense of the totality involving constellated relations between agency and its context, and involving the enduring possibility of agency in a materially thrown world. Thus, the moves from original critical realism and 1M real non-identity to 2E real negation in a dynamic world, and to the 3L sense of the whole in which spatio-temporality operates, lead us finally to the need to understand how moral agency is possible.

Natural necessity as 'reality principle': the real, ideal and actual

In this section, I begin with 4D moral agency and its relation to a metaphysical grounding of ethics, and then proceed to Bhaskar's metacritique. From these two sources, we identify as a critical target the universalising and particularising strategies that underlie much modern ethical argument, and move to consider in a brief and illustrative way the grounds of justice.

Natural necessity as moral reality

We have followed Bhaskar's dialectic from natural necessity, structure and agency and the grounding of real difference at the initial (1M) level of original critical realism to real negativity and the tri-unity of causality, space and time as the initiating (2E) dialectical move. Thence we turned to the materialisation, diffraction and 'critical realisation' of dialectic, and to the (3L) nature of totality. In all this, we have a strong sense of the 'material thrownness' of human being in Bhaskar's dialectic. This, however, is coupled with the continued assertion of its special character as minded and agential in line with SEPM and the TMSA, and as combining elements of the universal and the singular in every concrete, materially developed, four-planar individual agent. Human being possesses, by virtue of what it is, powers or qualities pertaining to reason and action, but these need to be developed. Human powers also include the cognitive, affective, conative, expressive and performative, and, as I suggested in Chapter 5, the normative too. This SEPM-derived and extended empowerment of the individual and her agency is maintained through natural necessity as the material meshwork of causality, space and time in order to ground Bhaskar's ethics. Indeed, at another level, that of the evolution of the species, the SEPM possibility to act is a part of it, for where acting is possible, it is also in one sense always necessary.

In this, accordingly, there is natural necessity too. Human agents act as practical, material causal agents in their own right and are able to reproduce and transform structural contexts. Generalising the capacities we possess by virtue of SEPM to include their cognitive, affective, conative, expressive, performative and normative aspects, and switching perspectives from the 'extrinsic', descriptive and explanatory, viewpoint to the intrinsic, first-person, standpoint, we can see that moral sentiment is a first-order capacity relating to what it means to be human.

This lies at the core of human agency, even if it necessarily operates in, and is mediated by, structure. Thus, it is the case that our capacities to be cognitive, affective, and so on could not exist save in social relations that bring them out. There is an irreducibly 'learned' quality to our abilities, but in the sense that we are 'educated' – that is, 'led out' (from the Latin) to them, as potentials ingredient in the species. Accordingly, our capacities are human powers developed for and by each human being within social relations. It is this dual quality of human being-in-society-in-nature that forms the ground state for the possibility of ethics and justice, and it works at both an individual and an historical level. The basis for ethics consists in understanding a kind of animal that emerges as mindful and active (under SEPM), acts to reproduce or transform structures (under the TMSA), and possesses a full range of powers that we know to be human. The human animal is a creature whose ethical possibilities are at the same time naturally endowed and socially enabled. Even as we are thrown into a structured, spatio-temporal social world that pre-exists us, we are creatures whose powers, activities and ethical capacities recursively generate that world.

If this is the core ontological ground for human being, how is it elaborated into a specifically ethical framework? At the core of Bhaskar's account (Chapter 5) is the final (4D) dimension of his dialectic concerning the emergence of processes of dialectical reason which are rooted in what it means to be human. If the dialectics of trust, solidarity and judgement, or desire and freedom, are explicated there as principles of dialectical reason, they are as much processes of natural, real necessity if human beings are to survive, live and flourish in the world. Natural necessity operates at different levels in the Bhaskarian totality, and is seen in both the judgement form and the desire for freedom as different aspects of what he calls 'the reality principle'. Judgement involves placing oneself in the position of the other and committing to advice relating to their concrete singularity. Judgement is assertoric rather than categorical or hypothetical. It is grounded in the reality principle for the concrete individual, and generalisable to all others similarly placed. The desire for freedom is based on absenting absences or ills, in which the experience of unfree necessity is negated. Both are initially conjoined in the process of primary polyadisation, which occurs with the birth of every infant. This is at once the establishment of the reality principle for her, the emergence of a new position of referential detachment in and on the world, and a place of natural need that must be absented if the infant is to survive. It is the starting point for a process of moving from the desire to absent need to freedom from it. At the same time, primary polyadisation sets up a social relation of trust and solidarity between the infant and a parenting figure without which the infant could not survive. This is the fundamental starting point of human being as both natural and social, and it continues throughout the life cycle. Wherever we are in our lives, we experience needs that we desire to meet or overcome, which we must do in order to survive, and which we cannot do without the support and solidarity of others. Desire operates as the point of mediation between necessity and freedom, and its satisfaction relies on the solidarity of others in whom we must place our trust. The desire for freedom, achieved in solidarity, represents the real basis of ethics.

Putting desire and solidarity together, then, we find dialectical logics that are embedded (according to Bhaskar's moral realism) in the human natural-social condition, and which lead to the pursuit of freedom at seven different levels. These are buttressed by the solidarising commitment to find out the truth in things that enable or block such a pursuit (his ethical naturalism). The desire to freedom starts with primary polyadisation and the need to absent an absence of care, but it proceeds through agentive freedom to negative and positive freedom. From there, it goes to the higher forms of emancipation, autonomy, wellbeing, individual flourishing and the universal human condition of flourishing, which is the eudaimonic state of freedom for each and all, and for each as a condition of all. Meta-ethically, these are both real *and* necessarily ideal states under present conditions. They are given in what it means to be human as a natural and social being, and to have human capabilities, and their truth is not undermined by their lack of actualisation in the here and now. Under an expanded SEPM, human beings are agents with certain kinds of powers who develop under conditions of trust and solidarity and are at once natural and social beings. Under concrete universality-singularity, they contain a core common humanity and a specific particularity. The dialectic of freedom reflects both, pursuing a path to eudaimonia that both treats everyone the same (reflecting universal humanity) and treats everyone as different (reflecting particular singularity). Thus, the end state is one in which the full freedom of each, reflecting singularity, is a condition of the full freedom of all, reflecting equality.

Extruding the real: the ideal and the actual

Nonetheless, to say that these are real possibilities given the nature of human being as being-in-society-in-nature is to point up the contrast between the real and the actual, for it is clear that modern societies do not get very far down the road to universal human flourishing. They are not without their conceptions of freedom, and in the lower levels of freedom (e.g. legal freedom) we can perhaps glimpse the higher levels (Norrie 2005a). It is because of this tension between the real and the actual that what in the Bhaskarian sense is referred to as 'the real' in all its ethical depth becomes extruded under modern conditions as 'the ideal', meaning a vision of freedom that is perceived as idealistic or utopian in its quality. This points to an understanding of the relationship between the fullest possibilities in ethics on the one hand and politics or history on the other in which the two constitute a constellated unity, and in which the ethical demands emergent from a sense of what human natural and social being is are intermingled with the political and historical contexts that either enable or suppress particular ethical possibilities. Modern capitalism, at least in its originating, first world contexts, permits a certain level of agential, negative and legal freedom supplemented by limited commitments to positive freedom under welfarist or social provisioning. The latter, as Habermas (1987: 361–3) points out, is limited in itself by virtue of the way in which it is administered to individuals. Capitalism's conceptions of emancipation and autonomy and its commitments to human flourishing are also limited, to the extent they exist, and often self-seeking or hypocritical. Yet the limited forms of freedom that are available point to the possibility of higher forms, which are otherwise marginalised or suppressed under modern conditions. There is therefore a constellated unity of the ethical and the political (or historical) within the political, for ethics retain their sense of a real autonomy from the political (or historical) within the constellational relationship, but the political (or historical) is ultimately what determines how far the ethical can come out in a particular society. This is not, however, a deterministic conclusion because the political is at once the place where politics and history have got to, and at the same time the place where change brought about by human agents, acting meta-reflexively, is possible.

What we have here is an understanding of ethics and ethical possibilities that both validates their reality and moral truth and locates their being on a structured historical terrain. The problems of ethics are situated in a world where natural necessity as the material meshwork of process and product is itself enmeshed with the natural necessity and truth of human being and its drives to freedom and solidarity. This overall relationship points to a 'dialectic, not an analytic, of dialectical universalisability' (DPF: 280), and it means that the terrain of modern ethics is at once historically limited, and latent with fuller ethical possibilities. This suggests a series of dialectical relations between 'the ideal' (the extruded, real ethical possibilities for human flourishing) and 'the actual' (actually existing ethical forms with the limited, often contradictory, possibilities for freedom they offer). In Chapter 5, I suggested that among these one could identify relations of the ideal *in*, *beyond and against*, and *under* the actual. In the first, the focus is on the possibility of acting morally in an immoral world, where one knows that what one does may not effect any real change, yet there is still an obligation to act. In the second, conceptions of 'the ideal', drawn from reflection on developed, as yet unactualised, ideas of freedom become the basis for exercises in concretely utopian ethical thinking and practice, though it is necessary to guard against the 'false actualisation' of such thinking in the present. In the third, there is the possibility that accounts of freedom may themselves become partially or wholly subsumed under structured power relations, though it is stressed that whether or not this is the case is a matter not of a priori theoretical deduction, but of a posteriori investigation as to the dialectical development of the constellational relation between the ethical and the historical.

The point is that all three ethical moves can be identified in modern ethical thinking as it comes to terms with the extrusion of the morally real under power$_2$ conditions, which forces it into formulae of the ideal and the actual. These provide a dialectical critical realist phenomenology of the materially diffracted nature of modern ethical forms At different times and in different places, and also for different people in different social locations, it will seem more or less appropriate to cast ethical inquiry in one of these modes or another. Different critical realists, for example, have adopted different ethical strategies, which reflect a focus on the ideal in, beyond and against, and under the actual. It is not, or not just, that one is right and the other wrong, but that under modern conditions all three ethical positions are available as limited 'takes' on moral reality. A recent example of viewing 'the ideal in the actual' is Alex Callinicos's espousal of the values of egalitarian liberalism in providing an immanent critique of capitalism, while coupling this with an 'ideal beyond the actual' move to Aristotelian eudaimonia (Callinicos 2006: 220–2, 227). The power of Bhaskar's system in contrast to such an approach, however, is that, while endorsing the (limited) validity of different ethical standpoints, it *theorises* the connections between them, and locates them historically and philosophically in a syncretic system that avoids eclecticism.[2]

For an example of an 'ideal under the actual' position, my earlier work on criminal responsibility and justice (Norrie 2001) flirts with such an approach, while my later work insists that alongside a repressive element in the idea of individual criminal justice (the ideal *under* the actual), there is also a need both to recognise a Kantian element in criminal justice thinking (the ideal *in* the actual), and to see how it invokes Aristotelian character elements (the ideal *beyond* and *against* the actual) (Norrie 2000). Criminal responsibility and justice in liberal society embodies *all three* moments of the ideal in, beyond and under the actual. Why it should do so is explained by the peculiar structure of modern ethics with their underlying, unrealised, relationship between a full sense of human ethical possibilities and their limitations and blocking under modern social conditions. The pulse of freedom contained in an ethics that is repressed and controlled in modernity results in the different, limited, conflicted, diffracted ethical standpoints that are actually available in a sphere such as law.

In the light of these comments, one could perhaps identify three different ethical moments in modern ethical thinking as the Kantian (the ideal in the actual), the Aristotelian (the ideal beyond and against the actual), and the critical (in both an early Frankfurt and poststructuralist sense, emphasising the ideal under the actual). This in itself is not particularly interesting, but it is the underlying relation between the ethically ideal and the actual as a modern extrusion or displacement of the morally real or alethic that gives a sense of the modern moral-historical totality and the limited, fragmented and contradictory ethical shapes it assumes. This underlines the import of the constellational relationship between a dialectical ethics of real needs and possibilities for human beings as natural and social animals and as a species that has evolved through particular historical and political conditions, including structured power relations, as the metaphysical basis for understanding ethics and justice under modern conditions.

Natural necessity, the universal and the particular

In this section, I reflect on Bhaskar's approach by comparing his position to examples drawn from two modern protagonists and tendencies in meta-ethics. The first is poststructuralist, which, as we saw in Chapters 6 and 7, invokes a radical, indeterminate heterogeneity that stands opposed to any attempt at universalisation.[3] Radical alterity or difference in the work of Derrida and Deleuze, drawing on a Nietzschean ontology, denies the possibility to universalise normative experience, and promotes a sense that ethics are subsumed under power or discourse. This essentially 'ideal under the actual' strategy is tempered by the possibility of a destabilising, undercover, 'ideal beyond the actual' move based on the possibility of radical difference. A critical understanding of what is happening here involves a brief revisiting of the central themes of Chapters 6 and 7, after which I will briefly illustrate the argument with Derrida's thoughts on justice, and what I see them as lacking. The second tendency is the kind of universalising ethical strategy developed by Habermas, which, we saw in Chapter 5, Bhaskar both builds on and critiques. Habermas develops his ethical philosophy on the nature of speech acts and the possibility of universal agreement in an ideal speech situation. In its pursuit of universal foundations for ethics, this is essentially a Kantian 'ideal in the actual' strategy, though one that seeks a different, 'postmetaphysical' terrain from Kant's on which to deliver it. Here, I argue that the universalisation strategy suffers from the same problem as the particularising strategy: a failure to relate it to natural necessity in the world.

Denying natural necessity: metacritique of the tradition

In Bhaskar's metacritique, it is not affirming natural necessity, the material meshwork of being, the tri-unity of causality, space and time and the fourfold polysemy of product and process or being and becoming that matters. It is rather the denial of these things that provides the key to an understanding of the development of western philosophy. Bhaskar's metacritique identifies the primordial failings of the philosophical tradition metacritically$_1$ in the denial of absence as determinate non-being and becoming, and metacritically$_2$ in elite interest in denying change. The analysis here is of how the Parmenidean bar on talk of non-being becomes the Platonic analysis of non-being in terms of difference, a position that is essentially maintained as late as Kant, where negative predicates are analysed in terms of positive ones. The pre-Socratic talk of non-being leads to ontological questions about the nature of being and how one thing becomes another ('the problem of the one and the other'), while the problem of non-being as difference takes us to the analytical distinction between entities, and how something is itself and not something else (this is the problem of what is a universal, or 'the problem of the one and the many'). The transition between the two problematics implicates the understanding of change itself, as in Platonic difference or Aristotelian hylomorphism, with the latter understanding formal change as immaterial, universal, mindful and ultimately God-like, thereby yielding an account of teleological and hypothetical, not natural, necessity in the world.

From dialectical critical realism's standpoint, the scene is set for ontological monovalence, leading to ontological actualism, the epistemic fallacy and subject–object identity theory in a compounded pair of blocking moves against non-being that establishes the contours of subsequent development for western philosophy as a whole. We have the faultline established by Plato and Aristotle, with the latter caught in a vice between Plato and Hume. What is squeezed in the vice is natural necessity and its correlative terms (the material meshwork, the tri-unity, the fourfold polysemy), and, as a result, what the pre-Socratic philosopher Heraclitus could sense, the (in effect) constellated relationship between structured being and becoming, gets lost to philosophy. Evading these issues, Plato launched a campaign against a convenient fool in Cratylus, who emphasised a shallow, though admittedly thoroughgoing, account of change as everywhere-everywhen becoming, or phenomenal flux. Against these, the Platonic forms are meant to constitute ideal, universal bulwarks, and Aristotle takes this up, albeit with a more scientific purpose, and on the level of empirical world immanence. Such ideas were reintroduced into western philosophy in the early nineteenth century by Hegel in the form of dialectical reason disclosing the Idea. This, however, followed the tradition in promoting an ontological actualism that lacked depth, and was rescued only by a triumphantly rationalist and historical form of the epistemic fallacy. In consequence, its absolute idealism only provided a stimulus for an anti-rational move later in the century by Nietzsche on similarly actualist terrain. The latter quite rightly smelled a rat in the tradition, and equally rightly traced it back to Heraclitus and Plato. For Nietzsche, however, Heraclitus was the Cratylan–Platonic philosopher of repetition and flux, of becoming as the radical, but simplistic, repudiation of being, rather than of the relationship between structured being and becoming. He was the Dionysian philosopher in opposition to Apollinian reason, the Zarathustran teacher. So, Nietzsche plays Plato's game, pressing on the other side of his problematic, on the many against the one, the flux against the Forms. He thereby lays the basis for the crucial move at the core of poststructuralist philosophy with its account of radical difference.

Ethically, this provides a stimulating way of challenging orthodoxy and bringing out the oppositional, aporetic quality of modern ethical debate. Understood as a radical other to identity, and ethically validated as the place of the unconditioned against all identity and conditioning, poststructural difference emphasises the life-affirming quality of becoming. In the process, it operates as a place-marker for Bhaskar's idea of the concrete universal-singular, emphasising singularity. Radical difference affirms, without properly understanding, what it is that makes the partial totality that is each individual life important. What it lacks is an understanding of how becoming inheres in structured human being, how the moment of concrete universality as singularity must be grasped with regard to its real and universal as well as its particular aspects, and how it must be seen in its reality as structured, spatio-temporally thrown, and four-planar. Drawing on the problematic of 'the one and the many' and ethically radicalising that problematic by validating the many against the one, poststructuralism fails to notice the hidden problematic of 'the one and the other' that underlies it. Its critique accordingly rests on an ontologically actualist basis, its particularism lacks depth, and it denies ethics full purchase on human being in the world. Poststructuralism denies, in short, natural necessity, and with it the possibility of determining the real grounds of justice.

The problem of radical particularisation illustrated

Poststructural radical particularism challenges any claim to universality in favour of a heterogeneous difference at the core of being. It accordingly focuses our attention on the irreducible ethical value in concrete singularity. In consequence, it loses sight of both those things that human beings have in common and the social context in which any singular life is lived. Ethically, this is problematic because ethical judgements concerning justice typically have to be contextualised to make sense. As an illustration, take Derrida's thoughts on the justice in acts of historical forgiveness and what he calls 'the law of the responsible transaction' (Derrida 2002: 56). This concerns an obligation to acknowledge wrongs and, where appropriate, to forgive them. This, Derrida notes, involves an awareness of the social and historical context in which forgiveness occurs. Thus, for Algeria to engage in a process of forgiveness today is different from a similar process in France in 1945, 1968 or 2000. Sometimes it is necessary to bring past wrongdoing to light, sometimes necessary to let it be. How does one decide on what is the right time, the right place, and to do what? It is impossible to know, because one is 'never sure of making the just choice; one never knows. . . . The future will give us no more knowledge, because it itself will have been determined by that choice' (ibid.). The right response on the justice of forgiveness accordingly 'is more than difficult; it is infinitely distressing. It is night' (ibid.).

In these comments, Derrida identifies important issues about justice and its relation to history and context. We can agree with him, first of all, that there is an ethical issue of justice to be addressed. He would explain this as responding, appropriately but impossibly, to the unconditioned wrong contained in any actual, conditioned act of wrongdoing. Dialectical critical realism would explain it by relating wrongdoing to the alethic truth of (the natural necessity in) human being as intrinsically and potentially free, worthy of respect, and in need of freeing from oppressive social structures and contexts. We can also agree that acts of forgiveness have real-world geo-historical effects which, in an open future, are unclear, and that there is therefore a real and open decision to be made as to the why, where and when of forgiveness. What is lacking in Derrida's account, however, is a philosophical understanding of how any act of forgiveness is contextually structured – that is, an understanding of how its structured historicity informs the ethical judgement. The historical structuring of forgiveness involves understanding how acts of forgiveness are intrinsically located in specific moral and political contexts that either negate, limit or validate the forgiveness that occurs. Taking the example that led to Derrida's own reflections, the Truth and Reconciliation Commission in South Africa, the ethical validity of forgiveness depended on whether it was part of a genuine process of change involving social structural concerns such as land reform and other social policies concerning the majority, or whether it was simply a convenient way of handing power from one elite to another (Asmal 2000). To say this is to note that a social, political and economic analysis of the South African transition, and of the structural qualities that it entailed, is crucial to our understanding of the ethical quality of the forgiveness on offer. This surely diminishes the sense of distress involved in justice and helps illuminate the 'night' in which it occurs.

Derrida in fact recognises this to the extent that he notes the importance of context, and maintains that to see 'these "contextual" differences is an entirely different thing from an empiricist, relativist, or pragmatist resignation' (ibid.) to events. But the question is, on what *philosophical* basis would he understand that these contextual issues are intrinsic to the work of ethical judgement?[4] To this he has no answer, for the relationship between the present as a conditioned world and the ethical as the unconditional inhering in it takes the form of an abstract, mysterious, ungrounded, antinomial connection to the messianic 'other'. There is an ethical abstraction in Derrida's radical particularism which requires, alongside its quite proper respect for the particular and the other, a sense of how our ethical decision-making is socially and politically structured. Ethical action does not occur alone, but in real history – that is, in a world governed by natural necessity and its correlatives – and this casts a sharp light on questions of justice in the here and now. To judge an act is also to judge the context in which it occurs, and this requires a philosophy that *thinks* this relationship. On the dialectical critical realist view, this is not a reductionist position in ethics, for an ethical judgement must consider both agential and structural elements under the irreducible terms set by SEPM and the TMSA. Dialectical critical realism proposes an understanding of ethics as involving the intra-relation between the different levels of the social and historical and the individual and agential, and is fundamentally relational (Norrie 2000). Justice involves judging individuals in context in a way that refuses to reduce responsibility either one way (simply to individuals) or the other (simply to contexts), and this standpoint is grounded in the dialectical relationship between individual agents and the social and historical relations and structures of which they are a part.

The problem of abstract universalisation illustrated

Turning now to Habermas, here too we find an ethical abstraction, though this time on the side of the universal. A brief illustration is provided by some recent observations on the possibility of communicative action and procedural justice in modern western societies occasioned by the destruction of the Twin Towers in New York in 2001. Habermas notes that western societies are peaceful and well-to-do, but that they 'contain a *structural* violence that [involves] unconscionable social inequality, degrading discrimination, pauperisation, and marginalisation', and that they are 'permeated by violence, strategic action and manipulation' (Borradori 2003: 35). Despite this, such societies offer a 'praxis of our daily living together [which] rests on a solid base of common background convictions, self-evident cultural truths and reciprocal expectations' (ibid.). These provide for 'the coordination of action through . . . ordinary language games, [and] mutually raised and at least implicitly recognised validity claims *in the public space of more or less good reasons*' (ibid.). At the same time, however, there is a structural violence that induces conflicts arising 'from *distortion in communication*, from misunderstanding and incomprehension, from insincerity and deception' (ibid.), leading to the possibility of a spiral of violence and communication breakdown.

What is unclear from this argument is how a society based on ('permeated by') structural violence also manages to contain a sphere of action based on 'ordinary language games' and 'mutually raised and . . . recognised validity claims', providing for a 'public space of more or less good reasons'. Why does structural violence, which permeates modern societies, not *structure* this public space and irredeemably colour these otherwise 'good reasons'? Why does it only lead to the *possibility* of distorted communication, suggesting the continuing possibility of its undistorted form? If, on the other hand, as Habermas puts it slightly later, '*systematically* distorted communication' (ibid.; emphasis added) does exist, where does that leave these same 'good reasons', and those lifeworld things that ground them? The prospect is that 'the public space of more or less good reasons' cannot be maintained, as it is swallowed up by the structural violence permeating such societies. In which case, the philosophical basis for a procedural justice in western societies is undermined.

If we think with Habermas of modern western societies as legitimate because they provide conditions of possibility for undistorted communication in a public space of more or less good reasons, we have to ask what are the consequences for legitimation of also acknowledging that such societies are based on a structural violence which systematically distorts communication. In making a point about structural violence, Habermas is in essence accepting the existence of an historical terrain of power$_2$ relations, but he refuses to see that this must profoundly limit the validity of what public procedures deliver. This is not an argument against the existence of a public sphere or public deliberation, but it is one that poses different questions about how public discourse is structured (constellated) under power$_2$ conditions, how the dialectic of rational debate and political power is orchestrated, and how valid claims to legitimation according to supposedly special conditions of the European lifeworld are to be handled. There is, again, a need to evaluate justice forms in terms of the structured whole of which they are a part.

This brief description of Habermas's thinking draws on his account of communicative action and the relationship between the giving of reasons in discourse and the possibility of ethical commitments under modern social conditions. The problem is how the two spheres, broadly of what Habermas calls 'system' and 'lifeworld', are kept apart, as they must be if lifeworld potentials are to ground an ethical standpoint in relation to the world of systems. For Bhaskar, as we saw, the criticism of this approach is that it becomes abstract and antinomial.[5] It becomes abstract because the emphasis on communication and discourse as the basis for universality tends too easily to separate Habermas off from real-world actions and agents, and antinomial because it results in a false separation between the place in which undistorted communication occurs (the lifeworld) and the place where it does not (the system). Habermas's Kantianism may not resort to an overall 'philosophy of consciousness', but it nonetheless repeats a Kantian antinomy, 'that between phenomenal system and noumenal lifeworld' (Bhaskar 1989: 189). From the point of view of dialectical critical realism, universalisation needs to be relocated away from a reliance on discourse and communication and a resulting consensus theory of truth, and in an understanding of the alethic or moral truth in things. In that way, it can be extended into an understanding of the real nature of human being and in particular the possibilities for freedom and solidarity inhering therein. A 'perfectionist' ethical basis becomes thereby available from which to judge imperfect, actually existing ethical forms. At the same time, however, it involves the historical constellating of transcendentally naturalistic dialectics with the material meshwork of things. This leads to a political and historical structuring relative to ethical demands, understood in terms of the figure of the constellation, a structuring that provides for 'a dialectic, not an analytic, of dialectical universalisability' (DPF: 280). This in turn provides a sense of the structuring and limiting of real ethical possibilities on the historical terrain from which they emerged.

For Bhaskar, there are positive sides to both Habermas and Derrida. Habermas represents an appropriate attempt to pursue a universalisation strategy, but one that needs both to be extended beyond discourse into other aspects of human (natural and social) being, and to be constellated with an understanding of the historical structuring, and limiting, of universality. Grounding ethics in the possibility of a discursive community represents a partial move into ontology by a philosopher who otherwise denies it. In consequence, Habermasian ethics establish an onto-logically inadequate, irreal, basis for thinking ethics.[6] Derrida on the other hand represents a welcome challenge to, indeed a dialectical remark on, the identitarian assumptions of orthodox philosophy, though his programmatic reliance on methods of inversion, chiasmus and erasure is too limited and a prioristic. It is unconnected to the historical structuring of aporia or antinomy, and as a result itself falls back into them. It is too hard on the possibility of universalising strategies properly grounded in human natural and social ontology. In one way, Habermas and Derrida can be seen as philosophers in fundamental opposition to each other, but in another way they appear as dialectically complicit antagonists, obscuring a common failure. Their shared lack is of a conception of natural necessity as structured being and becoming and its relation to philosophical ideas. Habermas fails to read universality in conjunction with both the real demands on human being and its place in history, while Derrida fails to see that aporiai are historically generated for human-being-in-nature-in-society. Both abstract philosophically from natural necessity, so that while their philosophical moves look significantly different (universalising versus particularising), they share a common absence. Neither philosophy thinks the nature or value of its central strategy in the light of natural necessity as structured being and becoming. In consequence, both philosophies have an essentially abstract quality, and this can be seen in the ethical positions they assume on different matters. Bhaskar's meta-ethics, on the other hand, represent a way between these two poles of abstract universalisation and (equally abstract) radical particularisation on the basis of an analysis of natural necessity.

Conclusion

In this chapter, we have considered a dialectical critical realist metaphysics of the grounds of ethics and justice, drawing on arguments established in Chapters 5–7. This is based on natural necessity, which is first seen as the material meshwork of being, developed in the first four chapters of this book. It is then explored as 'the reality principle' at the core of what it means to be human. The ethical principles that derive from this standpoint must be constellated with the material meshwork of things via the theory of totality to produce the dialectic of history and ethics with its broad tendential$_b$ development described in Chapter 5. This generates out of the constellated relation between the ethically real and the historical a modern set of ethical relations of 'the ideal' and 'the actual', where the ideal is a placeholder and representative of the alethic as the morally true and real, which can only be represented in ideal terms under modern conditions. This gives rise to a historical phenomenology of ethical forms (the ideal in, beyond and against, and under the actual), and a key point is the structured terrain out of which actually existing ethics (expressing in a limited way real potentials) are emergent. It is the embedding of ethics, reflecting but limiting real ethical possibilities for human being, in the structural, material meshwork of things, including power$_2$ relations, that constitutes the constellational grounding of ethics and of justice. Modern ethical values are real, but limited in their scope, and at the same time socially and historically emergent.

Against this ethico-historical dialectical phenomenology of actually existing ethical forms, other currents in critical philosophy draw upon either abstractly universalising or particularising strategies. But these, grounded ultimately in the old problematic of 'the one and the many', ignore questions of natural necessity scouted by the pre-Socratics in the problem of 'the one and the other'. Thus, if we think of justice with Derrida in terms of an account of what is owed to people by virtue of a wrong that has been done to them, this must be understood both in terms of what the specific wrong was, and in terms of the context that produced that wrong. The wrong will not be requited fully unless its conditions of possibility are addressed at the individual level, but also at the structural level that made it possible. To judge an act of wrongdoing is to judge its conditions of possibility, which means to judge the structural relations in which it occurred. Similarly, if we think of procedural justice with Habermas, there is a false separation and hypostatisation of the forms of ethics and justice from the material grounds that generate and limit them, and this is *necessary* if they are to play their ideal in the actual role. The consequence of hypostatisation, however, is the legitimation of the illegitimate.

What is important, against both abstract universalising and particularising strategies, is a grasp of the co-embedded relation between the spatio-temporal and the ethically real. This provides us with an understanding of the historical structuring of modern ethical possibilities in ideal/actual formulae, and makes that historical structuring a crucial element in ethical judgement. At the same time, it affirms the underlying ethical reality of which these formulae are partial extrusions, and retains the real promise of a possible eudaimonic future. The underlying alethic truth is what Bhaskar calls 'the pulse of freedom', and we live it, in a process called dialectic.

Notes

1 Introduction: natural necessity, being and becoming

1 Hereafter referred to as *Dialectic*. Since I quote frequently from it and *Plato Etc.*, I refer to them as DPF and PE in citation, rather than using the standard reference style for other works in the text.

2 Starting with Bhaskar (2000). A full list of Bhaskar's work up to 2006 is included in Hartwig (2007: 504–6).

3 Sketching the movement in his thinking, Bhaskar refers to these four elements in his dialectic as involving a 'first moment' (non-identity), a 'second edge' (negativity), a 'third level' (totality) and a 'fourth dimension' (ethical agency). He then abbreviates these elements as 1M, 2E, 3L and 4D, giving rise to the shorthand of the 'MELD' schema. I will introduce these shorthand terms in the text below, and also in the following chapter at pp. 28–9.

4 These comments are all taken from the back cover of the original edition of *Dialectic*.

5 Meaning an ontology that only permits one mode or 'value' – that is, what is positively present: see p. 14, and Chapter 2 at pp. 42–4.

6 I offer this only as an illustration at this point. I sketch the question of ethics in the final section of this chapter, and of course in the body of the book (in Chapter 5).

7 See Norrie (2005b) for the argument that poststructuralist philosophy is ontologically committed, and see Chapter 7.

8 Creaven's wide-ranging review of *Dialectic* combines a favourable overall assessment with a swingeing critique of several of its aspects. See also Creaven (2007: ch. 1).

9 'Critical realism' is a composite term eliding and combining the general philosophy of transcendental *realism* and the specific social scientific philosophy of *critical* naturalism in one phrase. 'Critical', like 'transcendental', retains the reference to Kant's philosophy, while 'realism' indicates the difference from it. Realism is also close to 'naturalism' in its import, so 'critical realism' combines what was essential in the original terms (Bhaskar 1998b: ix).

10 We may, for example, have knowledge 'not just of actions but of characters; not just of historical events but of social systems' (Collier 1994: 6). The seemingly noble actor may act for bad reasons, while the historical event may be cast in an heroic and principled light while disclosing underlying ignoble purposes. Marx's account of the relationship between exchange and production relations is an example of the contradiction between appearance and underlying reality.

11 Note that the emphasis in *Dialectic* is on the study of social dialectics, so that the question of a 'dialectics of nature' is not central to its argument. The same is accordingly true here, though presumably what Bhaskar has to say generally about becoming and process would be as relevant to natural as social processes. Becoming in causal process involves absenting, and this occurs in both the natural and the social worlds *mutatis mutandis* according to the different accounts of causation operative in both. Compare Callinicos (1994: 12) and Creaven (2002: 133).

12 I return to the MELD schema in Chapter 2. The progression of this book broadly follows the terms of Bhaskar's dialectic from the nature of being as irreducibly distinct (original critical realism's 1M starting point described in this chapter as the existence of real, irreducible natural necessity) to the significance of real negativity (2E absence in Chapter 2), and from there to 3L matters of totality in Chapters 3 and 4 and 4D questions of agency in Chapter 5. Chapters 6 and 7 on metacritique will return to the importance of 2E negativity by virtue of the critique of ontological monovalence (the absence of absence) in the western philosophical tradition. They will also draw on the 3L account of totality to provide a double critique of philosophy, one that is 'intrinsic' ('metacritique$_1$'), the other 'extrinsic' ('metacritique$_2$').

13 This section is more schematic than the two previous ones.

14 See Chapter 4, pp. 99–101.

2 Accentuate the negative

1 See DPF: chs 1.3, 2.1, 3.5.

2 As will be seen almost immediately, my own usage of terms involves a fair degree of interchangeability.

3 See Chapter 4, pp. 99–101.

4 DPF: ch. 1.3.

5 DPF: ch. 2.1.

6 Thus, absence is present in both being and becoming, for being entails absence and is always in process of becoming. The two cannot be kept separate, though they can be distinguished.

7 As we shall see in Chapter 3, real negation is the most general form of absence or absenting for Bhaskar, and it includes as sub-types transformative and radical negation.

8 An example of process-in-product is the way in which our geo-historical location influences what we are, while an example of product-in-process is the way in which any entity has effects in the world. Recursive embedding means that one can also talk of a process-in-product-in-process to denote the constant interaction between entities and their environment.

9 Bhaskar notes that even where he uses the same terms as Hegel, he gives them a different meaning. Thus, by negativity he means real determinate non-being, and by totality he means open rather than closed totality. On the former, see Chapter 3; on the latter, Chapter 4.

10 Defined as 'the truth of, or real reason(s) for, or dialectical ground of, *things*, as distinct from *propositions*, possible in virtue of the ontological stratification of the world and attainable in virtue of the dynamic character of science' (DPF: 394).

11 See pp. 88–93.

12 For example, the missing collar stud and other simple examples referred to in Chapter 1, p. 14.

13 In DPF: ch. 3.5.

14 See Chapter 4, pp. 99–101.

15 I pursue this theme in the next section and also in Chapter 6.

16 Compare the broadly similar argument in Creaven (2002: 129–33), though Creaven's complaint (at 130) that absence is trivialised unless tied to real determinate negation is met on this reading of *Dialectic*.

17 Callinicos presents his own book in terms of a transcendental question (2006: 10), and, despite arguing that ontology is inescapable for knowledge, concludes that any ontology claim is a priori and 'enormously open to arbitrariness and the extravagances of the imagination' (ibid.: 245).

18 'So we won't agree with somebody who says that negation signifies a contrary. We'll only admit this much: when "not" and "non-" are prefixed to names that follow them,

they indicate something *other* than the . . . things to which the names following the negation are applied' (Plato 1997a: 257c). Thus, non-being was allowed as differently constituted being, but what Bhaskar calls real non-being – that is, absence – was still denied by Plato. I shall develop the argument in Chapter 6.

19 'There is an infinite number of realities which are not only objects of judgment, but which are experienced, opposed, feared, etc., by the human being and which in their inner structure are inhabited by negation, as by a necessary condition of their existence . . . [I]t is impossible to throw these negations back into an extra-mundane nothingness since they are dispersed in being, are supported by being, and are conditions of reality' (Sartre 1956: 55–6). One can see the similarities with Bhaskar's account of determinate negation, but Sartre places *négatités* within a phenomenology of human experience as part of a unity that 'the Germans call a *Gestalt*' (ibid.). Bhaskar's discussion of Pierre copies Sartre's work, where a figure with that name makes a brief appearance (1956: 53). On Bhaskar's view of Heidegger, see Chapter 5 at note 3, p. 238.

20 Here, Bhaskar has in mind in particular transitional moments or 'nodes', where it is unclear whether an event or situation should be classed as absent or present (see further Hartwig (2007: 497–98)). For our purposes, it is the idea of the positive and the negative, ontological bivalence, brought into focus by the reality of absence in the world, that is relevant.

21 The argument is most developed in PE: ch. 9, and in Chapter 6 of the present book. This account of the core moves in western philosophy is also discussed in the context of the 'Tina formation', a figure of totality, in Chapter 4.

22 Thus, the brief account above of the problem of ontological monovalence and its effects on western philosophy is an account of Bhaskar's metacritique$_1$ of the western philosophical tradition. It moves by philosophical method to identify the absence of absence within it.

23 See Chapter 4, pp. 112–13. Generalising the idea of master–slave-type relations has been criticised for its failure to be specific about different forms of exploitation. There is some validity in this critique, but I argue below that Bhaskar's usage is legitimate in terms of the overall philosophical perspective and purpose he brings to bear, in the context of the long history of western philosophy from the Greeks to the present.

24 The existence of metacritiques $_1$ and $_2$ is made possible, we shall see, because of the way dialectical critical realism views philosophy both as a mode of intellectual activity in its own right (the terrain of metacritique$_1$) and as a moment in a socio-historical totality (the terrain of metacritique$_2$). There is a constellation, to use that term again, of philosophical thinking and historical practice at the level of totality. See Chapter 6 at pp. 183–5.

3 Diffracting dialectic

1 Heraclitus, that other Greek dialectician, will be given special consideration in Chapter 7.

2 Hereafter, I will capitalise the letters U, D and R where I refer to these three moments in full, to indicate the link to the abbreviated form: for example, 'negative Dialectical critique'.

3 Compare the Nietzschean, poststructuralist critique of this view, to be discussed in Chapter 7.

4 See especially Chapter 6.

5 See e.g. Hegel's account of the judge applying the law in Hegel (1975: 114) discussed in Norrie (2005a: 140).

6 Dialectical connection and contradiction will be compared in the next section.

7 See Chapter 1, p. 12.

8 Hegel was challenged by a Professor Krug to deduce by reason the existence of his pen, a challenge Hegel declined: see Inwood (1983: 360).

9 A point he develops later: 'Of course Hegel does not believe that the geo-historical process has totally stopped. Hence he refers to Russia and America as lands of the future. But these belong to what I will call the *"demi-actual"*. The future is *demi-present: constellationally closed*' (64).

10 One should really speak here of 'partial totalities' since, in the logic of totality, there could be only one. In Bhaskar's account this would necessarily be open and incomplete. See Chapter 4, pp. 91–2.

11 Thus, outcomes may retain and repeat a contradiction; an outcome may resolve a problem but in an irrational way. Resolutions may be achieved which do not lead to a higher ordering of conflicts, and higher orderings of conflicts may not reconcile the two sides to them. All such outcomes are possible in the world, but must conform to Hegel's U-D-R movement, which must *eventually* assert itself.

12 I provide more detailed treatment of the splits in Hegel's *Philosophy of Right* around issues of crime and punishment and the relationship between the 'ideal' and the 'actual' in his thought in Norrie (1991: ch. 4) and Norrie (2005a: ch. 9). For a different view of Hegel's philosophy in light of social contradictions, see Fine (2001).

13 Hegel Mark I would not offer a significantly different philosophical route for dialectical theory, for what is at stake is more a different political and ethical inflection in the early Hegel than a fundamentally different philosophical standpoint. Hegel was always an ontological actualist and, in consequence, an idealist practitioner of the epistemic fallacy. Bhaskar also sketches the limits of a more radical Hegel, whom he calls 'Xegel' (DPF: 75–8).

14 As they do with regard to 'negativity'. See p. 83.

15 It should be said that Bhaskar finds many Hegelian residues in Marx, in an oeuvre that is uneven, developing and focused largely on one particular science (political economy).

16 The TMSA (see Chapter 1) is perhaps well represented in Marx's comment in the '18th Brumaire' that '[m]en make their own history, but they do not make it just as they please; they do not make it under circumstances chosen by themselves, but under circumstances directly encountered, given and transmitted from the past' (Marx and Engels 1968: 96).

17 Picking up the language of generative mechanisms associated with 1M critical realism.

18 These four planes across which alienation is spread constitute what Bhaskar calls 'four-planar being': see Chapter 4, pp. 115–16.

19 At pp. 112–13.

20 See Callinicos (2006: 190–208) for further discussion of this issue.

21 Square brackets are mine. See Chapter 2, p. 38 and Chapter 4, pp. 99–101 on the idea of the constellation.

22 We can accordingly speak of 'the idea of the constellational unity of analytical and dialectical reason within dialectical reason' (DPF: 99) where we understand dialectical reason in this broader way.

23 Dialectical thought is superior but depends upon analytical thinking for the concepts it will rework to generate its raw materials. Any dialectical logic must work with and against analytical logic, and what dialectic takes to be analytics's secret value is precisely what the latter finds problematic. Dialectical fertility in the form of oppositions or contradictions reveals the failures of an analytical approach by itself. Here, Bhaskar and Hegel agree. As J. M. Findlay says in the foreword to Hegel's *Phenomenology*, dialectic is 'a richer and more supple form of thought advance than mathematical inference' (Hegel 1977: vi). Bhaskar's materially diffracted dialectic brings out the overreaching significance of the material field of play of dialectics, here through the concept of the constellation, in a way that rationally resolutory dialectic cannot.

24 See p. 32.

25 The quotations in this passage are from a letter to Engels of 14 January 1858, where Marx expressed the thought to outline his relation to Hegel in a few pages.

26 Creaven would also refuse Bhaskar the underlabouring role on the basis that there is insufficient that is new in *Dialectic* with regard to Marxian dialectic to justify it (Creaven

2002: 110–13). This suggests that the range of positive philosophical advances Creaven finds in Bhaskar's dialectic (2002: 135–6) is somehow disconnected from Marxist social science, when his comments indicate that it is not.

27 That is, a belief in the end of history under socialism.

28 See p. 57.

29 Hartwig (2007: 141) comments that with diffraction, 'we are dealing with a unity-in-diversity, not a fragmentation or splitting'. This comment is accurate in that it denies a simplistic idea of fragmentation or differentiation, but I am unsure that 'unity-in-diversity' conveys Bhaskar's sense, given its Hegelian implication. The sense of the whole that grounds what is diffracted, and gives it its 'unity', will be addressed in the next chapter. If the term is used, it should be made clear that the distinction is between a thought-expressive (Hegel) and a materially grounded (Bhaskar, Marx) unity-in-diversity.

4 Opening totality

1 See pp. 16–17, 38, 74–5.

2 Sub-totalities are linked to the idea of detotalisation, to be discussed in the third section.

3 In Popper's critique of holism, he distinguishes (a) totality as 'all the properties or aspects of a thing, and . . . all the relations holding between its constituent parts' from (b) 'certain special properties or aspects of a thing, namely those which make it appear an organised structure rather than a "mere heap"' (2002: 70). Popper accepts (b) as a valid usage, and notes that even a 'heap' has a holistic aspect, while he rejects (a). We cannot 'observe or . . . describe a whole piece of the world, or a whole piece of nature', or 'a whole, concrete social situation' (2002: 71–2). Bhaskar agrees: see the lines from DPF: 126 quoted in the next paragraph. Bhaskar is in any case interested in Popper's (b) rather than his (a) position, in totalities *in* things established a posteriori rather than the totality *of* things, and his insistence on open, unfinished, partial totality would anyway block the way to (a). Further, he agrees with Popper that even heaps have to be understood according to their holistic properties. I discuss this below, with regard to 'levels'. On the poststructuralist critique of totality, see Callinicos (2006: 202–3).

4 This is repositioned from original critical realism, where it first emerged as crucial to social life in the TMSA.

5 He also notes a limited semantic sense of heterology to describe something that is not true of itself (where the contrast is 'autology'). A word or concept may have the property it designates, as in 'short' is a short word. This is an autological word, and its opposite would be heterological – 'long' is not a long word. Autology is significant for semantic or self-referential paradoxes, which interest Bhaskar from the point of view of the way they thrive on the failure to grasp ontology holistically (DPF: ch. 4.2). The example of the 'heap paradox' will be discussed later.

6 See pp. 68–9.

7 Another example is of the river, which must be understood as both a continuous flow and a structured entity. Thus, it would be wrong to say simply that one cannot step into the same river twice, but correct to say with Heraclitus that one can and cannot step into the same river twice; see Chapter 7, p. 207.

8 It should be noted that 'containment' has both a negative and a more neutral meaning in this context. To contain can mean to 'control', or simply 'to hold within'. When Bhaskar criticises Hegel for constellational containment, he means the former, whereas he himself uses the idea of containment in the more neutral sense.

9 Though he depicts Hegel as deploying constellational thinking, and notes that Adorno (1973) uses the term, the constellation here is Bhaskar's own 'term of art' (DPF: 114). On Adorno's usage in relation to critical realism, see Norrie 2005a: 169–70. On Adorno's debt to Walter Benjamin, see Coole 2000: 173–9. Interestingly, Popper talks of constellations as mere sums of parts in contrast to wholes (2002: 16).

10 See pp. 60–1.

11 Bhaskar elaborates as follows: 'I . . . want to insist on the practical nature of all theory and the quasi-propositionality of all practice, insofar as it is dependent upon, but not exhausted by, its conceptual, and thus belief-expressive aspects ("actions speak louder than words"). This immediately generates the theorem of *the duality of theory and practice*, in that by means of a transcendental perspectival switch, each can be seen under the aspect of the other' (DPF: 66), though, crucially, 'this does not annul their distinction (DPF: 69).

12 Bhaskar terms the moment of stasis the 'negative generalisation of the transformational model of social activity' (DPF: 158–60). That the hiatus should move from theoretical concept into historical form reflects the nature of critical realist philosophy where terms express real-world elements or possibilities.

13 See Chapter 2, pp. 45–6.

14 This argument recapitulates what was said in Chapter 2 at pp. 42–5. A much fuller statement of the argument will be found in Chapter 6.

15 There is a pun in 'Unholy': a trinity that lacks holes (absences).

16 On Derrida and Hegel, see Barnett (1998), and on both in relation to Bhaskar, see Norrie (2005a: ch. 8; 2005b). I now disagree with the latter essay's position on Bhaskar's ethics.

17 See pp. 33–4.

18 'Ideologies . . . necessarily constitute Tina formations and, as such, are liable to explanatory critique. But insofar as they are causally efficacious, the social relations and interests underpinning them (and thus also the ideologies themselves) will not bend to explanatory critique alone' (DPF: 117).

19 The Beautiful Soul has a radical and critical dimension in the young Hegel as its sense of alienation turns it into an Unhappy Consciousness. It is given a more negative turn in the *Phenomenology*, where the virtue in being a Beautiful Soul/Unhappy Consciousness is denied. From this period in Hegel's writing, it is seen as an irrational failure to engage with modern social relations: see Norrie (2005a: ch. 10). Bhaskar draws on the young Hegel for his vision of alienation, and sees the figures of the *Phenomenology* as expressions of the alienation his (Hegel's) younger self had directly challenged.

20 The position also lacks seriousness since the sceptic's 'deeds belie his words. He leaves his study by the entrance to the building rather than the second floor window' (ibid.). It is this kind of ontological scepticism that Bhaskar attacks rather than the more limited scepticism that is to be found, for example, in issuing a negative, critical dialectical remark. It would be necessary to develop the comment about the selling of labour power to include other historical forms of exploitation, for scepticism, like the exploitation it shadows, is not only a modern phenomenon.

21 See Chapter 3 at p. 69.

22 For other purposes, for example the study of particular forms of power in a concrete, historical setting, it would be inappropriate to generalise about power relations. Sean Creaven (2002: 117) also detects a tendency in Bhaskar towards a neo-Weberian, pluralised vision of power relations since he argues that modern master–slave-type relations include 'nationality, ethnicity, gender, religious affiliation, sexual orientation, age, health and bodily disabilities more generally' (DPF: 333). Such a view could lead to a pluralised vision, but it depends how plurality is theorised. My argument is that Bhaskar's commitment is to consider how plurality is structured, either in diffraction or in holistic causality, and always in the light of inquiry into real social relations established a posteriori by concrete social sciences.

23 This paragraph draws on Inwood (1992: 302–5).

24 The social cube is a metaphor that conveys both the plurality of conditions and dimensions which compose any concrete singular. Where the social cube refers to, say, a particular social formation, it can be said to have a number of sub-dimensions, of power, communicative, normative and ideological relations. The social cube is also a 'space-time cubic stretch or flow' (DPF: 13) that 'highlights the differentiation and

dislocation within four planar being' (DPF: 403). To the objection that the social cube ought to have four rather than six planes to be an accurate metaphor, Hartwig helpfully suggests that the fifth and sixth planes in the cube are the 'negative' ones of the 'not yet', the future, and the 'intransitive determined' (2007: 421), reflecting its spatial and temporal dimensions as a stretch-flow.

25 Four-planar being and concrete universality provide the response to Kathryn Dean's charge (2006: 124–5) that Bhaskar deploys an apolitical, de-politicised and de-socialised account of human nature in his dialectical as well as in his pre-dialectical philosophy.

5 Constellating ethics

1 This is the space for a constellational framing of ethics, developed in the final section below.

2 Symbol in original text omitted. Here, Bhaskar is reflecting upon Marx's theory of the mysterious, fetishising quality of the value and commodity forms recalling the idea of D_3 ideology critique discussed in Chapter 3.

3 For a fuller discussion, see Hartwig (2007: 24–30). It should be noted that, despite the similar terms, there is no special link between Bhaskar's alethia and Heidegger's 'aletheia'. The latter is bound up with the distinction between the 'ontical' and the 'ontological' in Heidegger, with ontology being essential to philosophy and the concept of *Dasein*, the 'being of beings' (Inwood 1999: 147). Since *Dasein* is linked to human being, what Heidegger presents as fundamental ontology is from Bhaskar's point of view anthropocentric and lacks the understanding of natural necessity provided by critical realist ontology. For Heidegger, 'being was always mediated by *Dasein*, human being, and ontology was unstratified, so that he did not break with the anthropism and actualism characteristic of the western philosophical tradition' (PE: 199; DPF: 229–30). This was also seen in his account of non-being, which, like Hegel's and Sartre's, fails to account for real, determinate non-being (DPF: 239).

4 Hence, a minimal definition of dialectic would be the absenting of absence, and its maximal definition would be 'the progressive, though contingent and non-linear, development of freedom' (DPF: 208).

5 These last comments are based upon the argument of *Plato Etc.* at p. 151, where Bhaskar explains how his discussion of moral realism in *Dialectic* as essentially transitive must be more fully understood.

6 For Bhaskar, traditional theories of truth (performative, correspondence, coherence and pragmatist) attach to one aspect of these (DPF: 214), where a more complete picture can afford to be syncretic. A similar approach is seen in what follows, in his account of the different levels of freedom, incorporating Kantian, Hegelian and Aristotelian moments, among others.

7 Axiology is 'a branch of philosophy concerned with the study of the nature of value (worth) and what kinds of things have it' (Hartwig 2007: 47). For Bhaskar, it is connected to morally committed agency tending towards the absenting of ills or emancipation from them, hence 'emancipatory axiology'.

8 The value of truth-finding, and change in its name, is subject to the condition 'all other things being equal'. The clause extends to ethical decision-making in non-ideal contexts, generating for example the problem of moral 'backsliding' (DPF: 284, 293). See the final section of this chapter.

9 Bhaskar writes of action that it should be understood as a 'cognitive-affective-conative-expressive-performative vector' (DPF: 164). It should also be conceived as having the essential facet of being normative. Cf. Sayer (2005: 214): 'making normative judgements is a condition of being able to live'.

10 For 'agency has discursive presuppositions and judgement practical ones' (PE: 141).

11 In what follows, I shall question this, suggesting that Bhaskar's use of the dialectics of judgement and solidarity and desire and freedom is cumulative.

12 There is significant overlap between the 'judgement form' we are about to examine and the truth tetrapolity outlined in the previous section.

13 Bhaskar associates this with 'personalism', a falsely abstractive and hypostatising account of the moral responsibility of individuals (DPF: 179).

14 In Kantian terms, the assertoric is a form of imperative that lacks the certainty of universal, apodeictic (categorical) judgement, but is subjectively sufficient for belief. Hypothetical imperatives involve general rules of skill and prudence (Caygill 1995: 78, 300).

15 '[T]he judgement form through its fiduciary-imperatival and descriptive-plus-evidential aspects has a theoretico-practical duality built into it. Theoretical reason, which merely says the world is so-and-so, still implies a commitment to act on it. And so by a perspectival switch it informs practice' (DPF: 221).

16 My term, not Bhaskar's.

17 This is the point of the two-way arrow between (2) and (3) in the following passage.

18 Referential detachment is 'necessary for our discourse' if it is 'to be able to talk about something other than itself or even to talk about itself at all' (DPF: 45).

19 In *Plato Etc.*, Bhaskar describes nine levels of freedom by dividing the first two into four (PE: 145). There, he states that formal, legal freedom neither implies nor is implied by negative freedom. Since legal freedom is institutionally designated, its form is in principle not tied to any particular, even minimal, conception of human agency. Yet in practice, legal theorists do argue for such a minimalist conception, often with problematic consequences. Compare, for example, Moore (1993) and Norrie (2000).

20 *Plato Etc.* gives negative and positive freedom as separate ratchets on freedom.

21 'In fact the three great philosophical systems – those founded by Aristotle, Kant and Hegel – all find a niche in the dialectic of freedom' (DPF: 374). Utilitarianism finds its place not as an overriding philosophical system, but as the need to identify ergonic efficiency in processes that are genuinely designated as technical.

22 See Chapter 4, pp. 105–13.

23 The passage in fact refers to the 'EA' and the 'IA'. I have expanded the abbreviations in conformity with the text.

24 The following passage from the early Marx captures something of the same vision: 'For not only the five senses but also the so-called mental senses, the practical senses (will, love, etc.), in a word, *human* sense, the human nature of the senses, comes to be by virtue of *its* object, by virtue of *humanised* nature. The *forming* of the five senses is a labour of the entire history of the world down to the present' (Marx 1975: 353). When Marx says that the forming of the five senses, or the practical capacities such as will and love, 'is a labour of the entire history of the world', he does not mean that that is *all* it is. Will and love represent historically evolved, non-reductive, capacities in human being.

25 Note I say 'ideal', not 'idealist'. The ideal ethical expression of an ultimately eudaimonic state is realistically grounded as alethically true for human beings at a meta-level of their being, but because it is not fully actualised in the world, this realistically grounded possibility appears as an ideal, and to speak of a real possibility appears idealistic.

26 There are two conjoined, yet distinct, sides to the dialectic of modern ethical life. On one side, there is 'the alignment of dialectical reason, alethia, [theory/practice] consistency, dialectical universalisability, non-heterology in an expanded sense of being true to for and of oneself and each other and autonomy'. This is the side of dialectical rationality. On the other side, there is 'susceptibility to dialectical comment, [theory/practice] inconsistency, immanent critique, Tina formation, heterology and non-autonomy, absence, detotalisation and split' (DPF: 222).

27 Phronesis is necessary in eudaimonia as the state of universal human autonomy because it is 'subject to the constraints imposed by (i) the needs and rights of future generations and other species (ii) and ecological limits and (iii) the principle of balance or the dialectical mean' (DPF: 286). It is associated with 'the criteria of mean, balance, totality,

health and wholeness' (DPF: 281), and this is true both with regard to eudaimonia and with regard to what it is sensible to seek to achieve in a given here and now context (ibid.).

28 *Amour de soi* is 'the basis of altruism' and the condition of empowerment for 'only the empowered can empower' (DPF: 222), and we cannot care for another unless we care for ourselves. There is an existential limit to our commitments.

29 See Chapter 3.

30 In Bhaskar's terms, this critical reflection on concrete utopianism between the ideal and the actual reflects the two-way process in the ethical tetrapolity between ethical commitments and practice and explanatory critical theory.

31 Though deconstruction works 'madly' and 'mysteriously' in law, and in Adorno there remains a utopian element of freedom, despite subsumption of the ideal. This continuing moment of ideal justice in both approaches constitutes common ground between dialectical critical realist ethics, negative dialectics and deconstruction.

6 Metacritique I: philosophy's 'primordial failing'

1 This was introduced in Chapter 2 at pp. 45–6.

2 See Chapter 4, pp. 110–13.

3 Why 'irrealist' rather than 'non-realist' or 'idealist'? 'Irrealist' denotes philosophies that possess inadequate ontologies but still have a claim to some realism. Kant's philosophy is idealist but combines transcendental idealism with empirical realism. In one sense he is, then, a realist, though his (ontologically actualist) realism is maintained by virtue of his idealism in a subject–object identity theory. 'Irrealism' captures this fusion of forms present in 'any incomplete, inexplicit or ineffable realism . . . such as empirical, conceptual, intuitional and/or transcendent realism' (Bhaskar 1986: 9).

4 This was briefly canvassed in Chapter 1 at pp. 18–19 and in Chapter 2 at pp. 42–5.

5 This is a term developed by Bhaskar in his pre-dialectical work to indicate how philosophies of science illicitly fuse subjective and objective elements in the knowledge process to the detriment of an understanding of both. Thus, where the epistemic fallacy operates, being is epistemologised through the illicit role given to knowledge in its constitution. At the same time, knowledge may be naturalised and de-socialised, as its social conditions of production are denied (Bhaskar 1991: 32). There are many possible variants on these themes, depending on the particular stress in different versions of subject–object identity theory. See DPF: 399 for the gamut of classical forms, and this comment: 'Without a transcendental realist ontology, philosophy is driven to identity theory, and in particular by its generalised form, actualism.' This comment summarises the argument of this chapter.

6 While the past, according to the theorem of the past in the present discussed in Chapter 2, retains a continued presence within the present.

7 As we will see in the final section, it is this that provides the common ground with Derrida's account of deconstruction.

8 In his *Critique of Pure Reason*, Kant analyses nothing as an empty concept, object or intuition [A289/ B345] (1993: 231–3). At [A574/ B602], he writes that '[w]hen we consider all possible predicates . . . , we shall find that some indicate a being, others merely a non-being. The logical negation expressed in the word *not*, does not properly belong to a concept but only to the relation of one concept to another . . . , and is consequently quite insufficient to present to the mind the content of a concept'. An 'affirmation indicates a reality', while a negation 'indicates a mere privation' and nothing 'corresponding to [a] representation' (Kant 1993: 398).

9 This ensures the containment of existential questions about being within the frame of linguistic references to being, whereas, Bhaskar argues, 'the generalised notions of reference, referent and existence, deny such an easy distinction' (PE: 180).

10 See the discussion in Chapter 7.

11 Leading to unresolved disputes between scholars: see Cohen (2008) and Lear 1988: 273–93 for discussions.

12 Compare G. E. R. Lloyd's account, which stresses the difference between the two philosophers in terms of Aristotle's immanence theory of form (Lloyd 1968: 302), and the way this provides a better solution than Plato's to the problem of change in Parmenides (ibid. 64–5). Lloyd nonetheless notes that the 'active' account of reason, which underlies his theory of intelligible form, leads Aristotle to posit the immortality of the soul and divinity of reason as the source of intelligibility in the world. In this regard, he remained a Platonist (ibid. 195–201).

13 By this, Bhaskar means an account that does no more than reflect the nature of a world of particulars and universals and adds nothing new to it. The account is therefore homological with the problem, ignoring as it does the nature of absence as change, of ontological depth and the stratification of being, and the way these ground particulars and give them their concrete universality in the world.

14 The Unholy Trinity, it will be recalled from Chapter 2, is constituted by the epistemic fallacy, ontological monovalence and the primal squeeze on natural necessity. In this comment, Bhaskar equates natural necessity with the 'truth of things', their alethic truth.

15 See generally Chapter 2, pp. 34–40.

16 Here is a composite list of other aspects of Hume drawn from *Dialectic* and *Plato Etc.* He is, fourth, 'the first great modern irrationalist who accepts the unhappy consciousness of a deductivist analysis of inductively unknowable causal laws' (DPF: 359). Fifth, he is an ironist whose quest for literary fame was achieved not by his ahistorical philosophy but by a history, which, on his philosophical premises, should not have been written (PE: 193). Sixth, he is the 'conventionalist conformist who upholds law, order, private property and the prevailing order of things, epistemic and social alike' (ibid.). Finally, seventh, he is the amoralist who refuses to deduce an 'ought' from an 'is', supports emotivism, thus paving the way for the cynicism and nihilism that was to come, yet dies content in his humanist atheism (PE: 193).

17 'When . . . I enact a penal law against myself as a criminal it is the pure juridical reason (*homo noumenon*) in me that submits myself to the penal law as a person capable of committing a crime, that is, as another person (*homo phaenomenon*) along with all the others in the civil union' (Kant 1965: 105; cf. Norrie 1991: ch. 3).

18 'Postmodernism' is the broader term, covering movements in the arts and architecture as well as philosophy, and seeking (controversially) to explain a period of social and historical change in modern western societies (Callinicos 1989: 2–3). 'Poststructuralism' is the approach to philosophy associated with postmodernism, and including the work of Foucault, Deleuze and Derrida among others. The terms are, however, often used interchangeably with regard to philosophy.

19 See pp. 45–6, 105–13.

20 See Chapter 4, pp. 110–12.

21 In her translator's preface to *Of Grammatology*, Spivak helpfully elucidates the various philosophical influences on deconstruction, including Heidegger, Nietzsche and Freud. To pursue these here is beyond the scope of this work, though I shall explore the influence of Nietzschean ontology on a second poststructuralist, Gilles Deleuze, in the following chapter.

22 For Bhaskar's critique of Rorty, see Bhaskar (1991).

23 Derrida refuses the term 'ontology' as part of the metaphysical tradition he deconstructs (1999: 258), but he substitutes for it an account of being including difference which he calls 'hauntology' (1994: 10). What stops this being an expression of what ontology *is* for deconstruction? See Norrie (2005b: 96–100) for discussion.

24 Bhaskar's own approach to 'the unconditioned' and 'the conditional' in ethics is seen in Chapter 5, in the constellational relationship between dialectical universalisation and historical contextualisation. This generates a variety of relations between the ideal and

the actual mediated by a notion of judgemental rationality. Of course, judgement as a human act always retains an irreducible element of choice, but it is nonetheless grounded in a naturally and socially developed conception of freedom, which operates alongside a socio-historical critique of how freedom is actualised under different sets of social relations.

25   See pp. 144–56.

7 Metacritique II: dialectic and difference

1   In what follows, it is important to bear in mind these two senses of difference. One is that of the *distinction* between concepts or entities identified according to philosophical protocols of an analytic or representational kind. A philosopher like Plato is interested in difference in this sense, as the basis for rationalising the possibility of non-being, on the terrain of 'the one and the many'. It is also the basis, Deleuze argues, for distinguishing the identity of the model and the copy from the 'simulacra', things that in the flux of phenomena falsely appear to be the same. A second is radical difference as the underlying flux of phenomena, which renders all differences in the first sense provisional. This is the irreducible *difference* that is opposed to distinct or differentiated identities, and which lies at the heart of Nietzsche-inspired poststructural thought, and which is represented there as 'the many' working against 'the one'.

2   Capitalised in the original (Deleuze 1993: 64).

3   On the relationship between Dionysus and Zarathustra, see Deleuze (1983: 179–83).

4   The full passage reads: 'Eternity is a child at play, playing draughts: the kingdom is a child's' (Barnes 1987: 50). In the passages from Heraclitus cited below, I use two translations as appropriate and give the source, either Barnes (1987) or Edward Hussey's essay on Heraclitus in *The Cambridge Companion to Early Greek Philosophy* (Hussey 1999).

5   Deleuze notes that Nietzsche nuances his interpretation, and that Heraclitus 'had only a foreboding of eternal return' (Deleuze 1983: 190). See also Deleuze (1993: 242). This does not gainsay both philosophers' view of core common ground between Nietzsche and Heraclitus.

6   This gives rise to Aristotle's famous story about Cratylus's refusal to speak. Where all is flux, reference becomes impossible. For Aristotle, 'It was this belief that blossomed into the most extreme of the views . . . , that of the professed Heraclitans, such as Cratylus, who finally did not think it right to say anything but only moved his finger, and criticised Heraclitus for saying that it is impossible to step twice into the same river; for *he* thought one could not do it even once' (Aristotle 1984: 1010a10). As Bhaskar notes, it is unclear how saying nothing and pointing one's finger gets around the problem, for silence is 'saying something; just as in pointing he was indicating a relative persistent' (PE: 53, note).

7   For the wry use of a *reductio* argument against extreme Heraclitanism, see Plato (1997c: 179e–180c).

8   The claim is traced back to Aristotle: Plato 'having in his youth first become familiar with Cratylus and with the Heraclitan doctrines' (Aristotle 1984: 987a30).

9   Cf. Hussey (1999: 99) and Graham (2007). For the claim that Heraclitus did espouse the flux theory, see Barnes (1982: 65–9).

10 Barnes (1987: 50) translates *harmonie* as 'harmony' and not 'structure', but Hussey argues this is misleading.

11 Hegel, interestingly, also views Heraclitus as a philosopher of process, becoming and flux, in the manner of Platonism. He too failed to see the structuring of becoming in Heraclitus's philosophy, as, indeed, he fails, in virtue of his actualism, in his own.

12 'Ideas are multiplicities: every idea is a multiplicity or a variety' (Deleuze 1993: 182).

13 Bhaskar also sketches the potential of the atomism argued for by Leucippus and

Democritus to open up an argument for natural necessity in Ancient Greece. Against Sophist relativism and Heraclitan flux, the 'brilliant' atomists offered a 'far more cogent explanation of the physical world . . . which challenged the Eleatic implication that voids cannot exist, postulated constant atomic motion and interaction, and explained the differences in appearances (theoretically) in terms of posited differential constitutions' (PE: 177).

14 In his lectures, Nietzsche makes this point, though without seeing the dialectical complicity it suggests between Heraclitus and Parmenides: 'Heraclitus thus sees only the One, but in the sense opposite to Parmenides' (Nietzsche 2006: 63). It is in this sense that Alain Badiou is correct to describe Deleuze as 'the most radical thinker of the One since Bergson' (quoted in Hallward 2003: 176). Badiou's philosophy is itself an innovative reconfiguring of the problematic of the one and the many with its argument for a 'counting-as-one' in place of the one, which is then the basis for a 'presentation' of 'plurality' as 'consistent multiplicity'. This is contrasted with the flux of 'inconsistent multiplicity' as 'the void' of pure, limitless, unpresentable otherness (Badiou 2005: 23–37). Badiou's philosophy emphasises the structured presentation of situations on the terrain of the one and the many as a means of overcoming the void, so his is not a philosophy that simply affirms difference. (Peter Hallward (2003: 176) correctly describes Badiou as the Plato to Deleuze's Presocratic.) However, his account of structured presentation is a prioristic and irrealist, and it sets up a split between his thought and natural necessity in the world. Accordingly, his 'characterisation of all human situations . . . as *immeasurably* infinite multiplicities . . . dramatically *simplifies* these situations, leaving no space for . . . effectively universal structuring principles (biological, cognitive, linguistic . . .) . . . , or of certain "specifying" attributes (based on culture, religion, class, gender . . .)' (Hallward in Badiou 2001: xxxii). See Callinicos (2006: ch. 3) for an excellent critique.

15 In his later work with Félix Guattari, Deleuze's idealisation of flux becomes the basis for an irrealist and a prioristic account of flows which are 'coded' and 'decoded' socially under different historical conditions. This generates an antinomial account of the relationship between primordial becoming and socially structured being such that it becomes unclear whether capitalism, for example, is the problem or the solution for mankind – since it decodes flows (Deleuze and Guattari 1984: 260). For analysis of the problems arising from the abstraction in Deleuze-inspired thought, see Callinicos (2006: 140–51).

8 Conclusion: natural necessity and the grounds of justice

1 See Marx's first, third and eight theses on Feuerbach (Marx and Engels 1968: 28–31), and the comments from the early Economic and Philosophical Manuscripts, which reflect the same emphasis on human agency and ethics in history as one finds in Bhaskar (Marx 1975: 389–91).

2 Similarly, Andrew Sayer produces a critical-realist-based ethical naturalism which finds a place for the eudaimonistic ideal of a 'society in which the flourishing of all is the condition of the flourishing of each' (2005: 222), but he accepts that capitalism and therefore class structure is the only mode of social organisation available to humanity. Since structured class relations must be at odds with the core values of eudaimonia, its positing must be a case of the ideal beyond and against the actual as at best a 'regulatory ideal', or at worst a severe case of impotent Unhappy Consciousness. It is noteworthy that both Callinicos and Sayer, despite their criticism of Bhaskar's dialectic (see Chapter 1, pp. 3–4), have followed him in drawing on an account of eudaimonia.

3 It may be said that it too in its own way involves a universalising strategy, but I will not engage the point here.

4 The political context is noted by Derrida, but in a general way, so that it provides no means of distinguishing one political situation from another: '*All* Nation-States are born and found themselves in violence' (ibid.: 57).

5 See Chapter 5, pp. 123–4.

6 The failure is on two levels: to comprehend fully natural necessity as the reality principle for human beings, and as the material meshwork of spatio-temporal causality.

References

Adorno, T. (1973) *Negative Dialectics*. Routledge & Kegan Paul: London.

Adorno, T. and M. Horkheimer (1997) *Dialectic of Enlightenment*. Verso: London.

Althusser, L. (2005) *For Marx*. Verso: London.

Archer, M. (1995) *Realist Social Theory: The Morphogenetic Approach*. Cambridge University Press: Cambridge.

Aristotle (1984) *Metaphysics* in *The Complete Works of Aristotle* (ed. J. Barnes), vol. 2. Princeton University Press: Princeton, NJ.

Asmal, K. (2000) 'Truth, Reconciliation and Justice: The South African Experience in Perspective' 63 *Modern Law Review* 1.

Audi, R. (1999) *The Cambridge Dictionary of Philosophy*. Cambridge University Press: Cambridge.

Badiou, A. (2001) *Being and Event*. Continuum: London.

—— (2005) *Ethics: An Essay on the Understanding of Evil*. Verso: London.

Barnes, J. (1982) *The Presocratic Philosophers*. Routledge: London.

—— (1987) *Early Greek Philosophy*. Penguin: London.

Barnett, S. (1998) *Hegel after Derrida*. Routledge: London.

Barthes, R. (1973) *Mythologies*. Paladin: St Albans.

Bhaskar, R. (1975) *A Realist Theory of Science*. Leeds Books: Leeds.

—— (1979) *The Possibility of Naturalism*. Wheatsheaf: Brighton.

—— (1986) *Scientific Realism and Human Emancipation*. Verso: London.

—— (1989) *Reclaiming Reality*. Verso: London.

—— (1991) *Philosophy and the Idea of Freedom*. Blackwell: Oxford.

—— (1993) *Dialectic: The Pulse of Freedom*. Verso: London.

—— (1994) *Plato Etc*. Verso: London.

—— (1998a) *The Possibility of Naturalism*. 3rd edn. Routledge: London.

—— (1998b) 'General Introduction', in M. Archer, R. Bhaskar, A. Collier, T. Lawson, and A. Norrie, *Critical Realism: Essential Readings*. Routledge: London.

—— (2000) *From East to West*. Routledge: London.

Bhaskar, R. (2008a) *A Realist Theory of Science*. 3rd edn. Routledge: Abingdon.

Bhaskar, R. (2008b) *Dialectic: The Pulse of Freedom*. 2nd edn. Routledge: Abingdon.

Bhaskar, R. (2009) *Plato Etc*. 2nd edn. Routledge: Abingdon.

Bhaskar, R. and A. Callinicos (2003) 'Marxism and Critical Realism'. *Journal of Critical Realism* 1 (2), 91–116.

Borradori, G. (2003) *Philosophy in a Time of Terror*. University of Chicago Press: Chicago.

Calder, G. (2007) 'Ethics', in *Dictionary of Critical Realism* (ed. M. Hartwig). Routledge: Abingdon.

Callinicos, A. (1989) *Against Postmodernism: A Marxist Critique*. Polity: Cambridge.
—— (1994) 'Critical Realism and Beyond: Roy Bhaskar's Dialectic'. Working Paper 7, Department of Politics, University of York.
—— (2006) *The Resources of Critique*. Polity: Cambridge.
Caygill, H. (1995) *A Kant Dictionary*. Blackwell: Oxford.
Cohen, S. M. (2008) 'Aristotle's Metaphysics', in *Stanford Encyclopedia of Philosophy*. http://plato.stanford.edu/entries/aristotle-metaphysics/.
Collier, A. (1994) *Critical Realism: An Introduction to Roy Bhaskar's Philosophy*. Verso: London.
—— (1998) 'Realism and Formalism in Ethics', in M. Archer, R. Bhaskar, A. Collier, T. Lawson, and A. Norrie, *Critical Realism: Essential Readings*. Routledge: London.
Collingwood, R. (1945) *The Idea of Nature*. Oxford University Press: Oxford.
Coole, D. (2000) *Negativity and Politics*. Routledge: London.
Creaven, S. (2002) 'The Pulse of Freedom? Bhaskar's *Dialectic* and Marxism'. *Historical Materialism* 10, 77–141.
—— (2007) *Emergentist Marxism*. Routledge: Abingdon.
Dean, K. (2006) 'Agency and Dialectics: What Critical Realism Can Learn from Althusser's Marxism', in K. Dean, J. Joseph, J. M. Roberts, and C. Wight, *Realism, Philosophy and Social Science*. Palgrave: Basingstoke.
Deleuze, G. (1983) *Deleuze: Nietzsche and Philosophy*. Continuum: London.
—— (1993) *Difference and Repetition*. Columbia University Press: New York.
Deleuze, G. and F. Guattari (1984) *Anti-Oedipus: Capitalism and Schizophrenia*. Continuum: London.
—— (1988) *A Thousand Plateaus*. Continuum: London.
Derrida, J. (1990) 'Force of the Law: The "Mystical Foundation of Authority"' 11 *Cardozo Law Review* 11 (5–6), 919–1045. Also published in D. Cornell, M. Rosenfeld, and D. G. Carlson (1992) *Deconstruction and the Possibility of Justice*. Routledge: London.
—— (1994) *Specters of Marx*. Routledge: London.
—— (1997) *Of Grammatology*. Johns Hopkins University Press: Baltimore.
—— (1999) 'Marx & Sons', in M. Sprinker (ed.), *Ghostly Demarcations*. Verso: London.
—— (2002) *On Cosmopolitanism and Forgiveness*. Routledge: London.
Fine, R. (2001) *Political Investigations: Hegel, Marx, Arendt*. Routledge: London.
Graham, D. (2007) 'Heraclitus', in *Stanford Encyclopedia of Philosophy*. http://plato.stanford.edu/entries/heraclitus/.
Guthrie, W. K. C. (1967) *The Greek Philosophers*. Routledge & Kegan Paul: London.
Habermas, J. (1984) *The Theory of Communicative Action*, vol. 1. Polity: Cambridge.
—— (1987) *The Theory of Communicative Action*, vol. 2. Polity: Cambridge.
—— (1990) *Moral Consciousness and Communicative Action*. Polity: Cambridge.
Hallward, P. (2003) *Badiou: A Subject of Truth*. University of Minnesota Press: Minneapolis and London.
Hartwig, M. (2007) *Dictionary of Critical Realism*. Routledge: Abingdon.
Hegel, G. (1892) *Lectures on the History of Philosophy* (trans. E. Haldane). London.
—— (1952) *Hegel's Philosophy of Right*. Oxford University Press: Oxford.
—— (1975) *Hegel's Logic*. Clarendon Press: Oxford.
—— (1977) *Hegel's Phenomenology of Spirit*. Oxford University Press: Oxford.
—— http://www.marxists.org/reference/archive/hegel/index.htm.
Hostettler, N. and A. Norrie (2003) 'Are Critical Realist Ethics Foundationalist?', in J. Cruickshank (ed.), *Critical Realism: The Difference It Makes*. Routledge: London.

Hussey, E. (1999) 'Heraclitus', in A. A. Long (ed.), *The Cambridge Companion to Early Greek Philosophy*. Cambridge University Press: Cambridge.

Inwood, M. (1983) *Hegel*. Routledge: London.

—— (1992) *A Hegel Dictionary*. Blackwell: Oxford.

—— (1999) *A Heidegger Dictionary*. Blackwell: Oxford.

Joseph, J. (2006) 'Marxism, the Dialectic of Freedom and Emancipation', in K. Dean, J. Joseph, J. M. Roberts, and C. Wight, *Realism, Philosophy and Social Science*. Palgrave: Basingstoke.

Kant, I. (1965) *The Metaphysical Elements of Justice*. Bobbs-Merrill: Indianapolis.

—— (1993) *Critique of Pure Reason*. J. M. Dent: London.

Kaufmann, W. (1974) *Nietzsche: Philosopher, Psychologist, Antichrist*. Princeton University Press: Princeton, NJ.

Lear, J. (1988) *Aristotle: The Desire to Understand*. Cambridge University Press: Cambridge.

Lloyd, G. E. R. (1968) *Aristotle: The Growth and Structure of His Thought*. Cambridge University Press: Cambridge.

Marx, K. (1954) *Capital*, vol. 1. Lawrence & Wishart: London.

—— (1975) *Karl Marx: Early Writings*. Pelican: London.

Marx, K. and F. Engels (1968a) *Selected Works in One Volume*. Lawrence & Wishart: London.

—— (1968b) 'The 18th Brumaire of Louis Bonaparte', in *Selected Works in One Volume*. Lawrence & Wishart: London.

—— (1968c) *Manifesto of the Communist Party*, in *Selected Works in One Volume*. Lawrence & Wishart: London.

Meikle, S. (1985) *Essentialism in the Thought of Karl Marx*. Duckworth: London.

Moore, M. (1993) *Act and Crime*. Oxford University Press: Oxford.

Nietzsche, F. (1962) *Philosophy in the Tragic Age of the Greeks*. Gateway: Chicago.

—— (2000a) *The Birth of Tragedy*, in *Basic Writings of Nietzsche* (transl. W. Kaufmann). Modern Library: New York.

—— (2000b) *Ecce Homo*, in *Basic Writings of Nietzsche* (transl. W. Kaufmann). Modern Library: New York.

—— (2006) *The Pre-Platonic Philosophers*. University of Illinois: Chicago.

Norrie, A. (1991) *Law, Ideology and Punishment*. Kluwer: Dordrecht.

—— (2000) *Punishment, Responsibility and Justice*. Oxford University Press: Oxford.

—— (2001) *Crime, Reason and History*. 2nd edn. Cambridge University Press: Cambridge.

—— (2005a) *Law and the Beautiful Soul*. GlassHouse and Routledge: London.

—— (2005b) 'Theorising "Spectrality": Ontology and Ethics in Derrida and Bhaskar', in K. Dean, J. Joseph and A. Norrie, *Critical Realism Today*, special issue of *New Formations* 56.

—— (2008) 'Justice on the Slaughter-Bench: The Problem of War Guilt in Arendt and Jaspers'. *New Criminal Law Review* 11 (2), 187–231.

Norris, C. (1991) *Deconstruction: Theory and Practice*. Routledge: London.

Ollman, B. (2003) *Dance of the Dialectic*. University of Illinois Press: Urbana and Chicago.

Outhwaite, W. (1994) *Habermas: A Critical Introduction*. Polity: Oxford.

Plato (1997a) *The Sophist*, in *Plato: Complete Works* (ed. J. Cooper). Hackett: Indianapolis.

—— (1997b) *Parmenides*, in *Plato: Complete Works* (ed. J. Cooper). Hackett: Indianapolis.

—— (1997c) *Theaetetus*, in *Plato: Complete Works* (ed. J. Cooper). Hackett: Indianapolis.

—— (1997d) *Cratylus*, in *Plato: Complete Works* (ed. J. Cooper). Hackett: Indianapolis.

Popper, K. (2002) *The Poverty of Historicism*. Routledge: London.

Ramsay, P. (2010) *The Insecurity State: Criminal Law After the ASBO*. Oxford University Press: Oxford.

Safranski, R. (2002) *Nietzsche: A Philosophical Biography*. Granta: London.

Sartre, J.-P. (1956) *Being and Nothingness*. Washington Square Press: New York.

Sayer, A. (2000) *Realism and Social Science*. Sage: London.

—— (2005) *The Moral Significance of Class*. Cambridge University Press: Cambridge.

Schacht, R. (1983) *Nietzsche*. Routledge: London.

Taylor, C. (1975) *Hegel*. Cambridge University Press: Cambridge.

Whitehead, A. N. (1978) *Process and Reality*. Free Press: New York.

Index

absence 5, 15, 19, 22, 23–8, 35–8, 47,
   124–5
   and becoming 13–16
   and change 43, 49, 160–9
   and ethical agency 124–5
   as difference 43, 49, 160–9
   as ill 138
   as noun 15, 23–4, 47
   as product and process 26–8
   criticisms of Bhaskar's account 40–2
   denial of absence 19, 20, 46, 177, 212
   determinate absence 7
      negation 56, 57
      negativity 216
      non-being 48
      transformative negation 37
   fourfold meaning (polysemy) 27
   in Kant 163, 240
   meaning of terms 24–6
   negatively charged asymmetry 37, 48
   (non-being) in relation to change 36
   Parmenides and 164–5
   primacy 34–42, 48
   simple 26
   see negativity; non-being; process;
      product; tri-unity
absence of absence 48, 160–9
   see ontological monovalence;
      Parmenides
absent (verb) 24, 25
absenting 25, 30, 26, 41
   absenting of error 15
   as 'process' 27
   as verb 15, 23–4, 47
   complementing 'absence' 25
abstract universalisation 20, 230
'actual', the 20, 149–56, 222–4, 231
actualism 8, 61, 179, 181
   see ontological actualism
Adorno, Theodor 17, 155, 156

affective capacity of human beings 220,
   238
agency 10, 12, 15, 51, 116–17, 119
   see synchronic emergent powers
      materialism (SEPM);
      transformational model of social
      activity (TMSA)
aletheia 126, 238
alethia 121, 123, 126, 134, 238
alethic truth 29, 177, 231
   see moral realism
alienation 69, 97, 105, 106, 110, 118, 119,
   126
   and master–slave dialectic 110–13
alterity 29, 96, 99, 224
alterology 96, 97
Althusser, Louis: 'ideological problematic'
   109
amour de soi 152, 153, 240
amour propre 152, 153
analytical philosophy 74–5
antecedence 31
antinomialism 101, 103, 124, 182
   in Derrida 188–9
   in Habermas 124
   in Hegel 60
   in Kant 53–4, 181
antinomy 105, 230
aporia 230
Archer, Margaret 115
Aristotle 17, 19, 44–5, 53, 144, 158,
   169–78
   and dialectic 53, 78
   Categories 173
   'eidetic-kinetic' form 179
   hylomorphism 173, 181, 225
   hypothetical necessity 175
   nous 174, 179
   Platonism 173–6
   subject–object identity theory in 191